CREATED TO LEARN

A Christian Teacher's Introduction to Educational Psychology

CREATED TO LEARN

William R.
YOUNT

BROADMAN
& HOLMAN
PUBLISHERS

Nashville, Tennessee

978-0-8054-1206-2

Dewey Decimal Classification: 370.15
Subject Heading: EDUCATIONAL PSYCHOLOGY \ RELIGIOUS EDUCATION—PSYCHOLOGY
Library of Congress Card Catalog Number: 95–19109

Unless otherwise stated all Scripture citations are from the Holy Bible,
New International Version, copyright © 1973, 1978, 1984 by International Bible Society.

Typography by TF Designs

Library of Congress Cataloging-in-Publication Data
Yount, William R.
    Created to learn: a Christian teacher's introduction to educational psychology / William R.
Yount.
        p. cm.
    Includes bibliographical references.
    ISBN 0-8054-1206–9 (HB)
    1. Educational psychology. 2. Education—Religious aspects—Christianity. I. Title.
LB1051.Y59 1996
370.15—dc20   95–19109
                                                                          CIP

20 21 22 23 24 25   12 11 10 09

Contents

UNIT 1

Educational Psychology and the Christian Teacher

On the first day of class, several semesters ago, a student raised his hand and asked, "Why is this course offered in a seminary? What can we, as Christians, learn from secular theorists?" We spent several minutes in a conversation which revolved around faith and science, and the difference between "believing in" and understanding principles of learning proposed by the theorists. What can we learn from these who have given their lives studying specific aspects of human learning? What principles can we transfer into a Christian context?

The truth is that many ministerial students experience anxiety when confronted by a study of secular theorists and their ideas. "How will these ideas influence my thinking? My values? My faith? How far can I go in embracing secular theories before compromising my beliefs?" Unit 1 is intended to build the bridges.

The Disciplers' Model developed out of my burning desire to find a way to teach so that my learners would grow in the Lord. The seven elements of the Model provide a philosophical and theological framework for effective Christian teaching. The chapter ends with the linking of the Model with areas of study in educational psychology.

CHAPTER 1:
THE DISCIPLERS'
MODEL

Educational psychology is based primarily on a scientific foundation. How do we know what we know? Six ways of knowing are investigated. Scientific knowing is specifically defined.

CHAPTER 2:
INTRODUCTION TO
SCIENTIFIC KNOWING

Chapter

1

THE
DISCIPLERS' MODEL

HOW TO TEACH SO
THAT LEARNERS GROW IN THE LORD

This chapter establishes a seven-fold approach—the Disciplers' Model—to Christian teaching. The Model was developed in response to a question that would not let me go—"How should I teach so that my learners will grow in the Lord?" I wanted to move beyond lesson transmission to life transformation with God's Word. The chapter is more devotional than academic, yet it provides a theological and philosophical base for the remainder of the text. The final section links the model to subject areas in the field of educational psychology.

CHAPTER RATIONALE

Learners will demonstrate knowledge of the Disciplers' Model by drawing the model and labeling its components.

Learners will demonstrate knowledge of the relationship between the Disciplers' Model and educational psychology by matching model components to issues in the field.

Learners will demonstrate understanding of the components of the Disciplers' Model by properly categorizing educational issues by component.

Learners will demonstrate appreciation for the discipling approach by recounting their best and worst learning experiences.

CHAPTER OBJECTIVES

INTRODUCTION

Christian students often experience anxiety when confronted by a study of secular theorists and their ideas. "How will these ideas influence my thinking? My values? My faith? How far can I go in embracing secular theories before compromising my beliefs?" Remember this as you study: there is a difference between *believing in* a theorist's ideas and *understanding* those ideas. The purpose of this text is to suggest ways we as Christian teachers can profit from the discoveries of educational psychology to improve our teaching ministry—in the church, or in the classroom. There is no better place to begin building bridges between educational theory and church practice than the Disciplers' Model.

The Disciplers' Model[1] grew out of my struggles as a Sunday school teacher of adults and as a minister of education—struggles with "dry bones" in the education ministry of local churches. The Model was molded by studies in educational psychology and principles of teaching in seminary and the application of those principles in teaching youth and adults, both deaf and hearing, in Sunday school. The Model has been reinforced through nearly twenty years of serving churches, teaching seminary students, and leading teaching conferences across the nation.

The Model consists of seven elements that exist, ideally, in balanced tension. The remainder of the chapter defines these seven elements and explains how they work together. The Disciplers' Model provides a useful framework for the study of educational psychology.

THE LEFT
FOUNDATION
STONE: THE BIBLE

The left stone of the Model represents the Bible, the Word of God. Unless our teaching produces a clearer understanding of the Bible, with its call to personal commitment to Christ and His Church, all our efforts may produce "wood, hay, and stubble" (1 Cor. 3:12). For education to be rightly called "Christian," it must be built upon the sure foundation of God's Word.

Theories of inspiration thrive, conflicting interpretations abound, but God's Word still speaks across the ages to people today. How does Scripture define itself?

How Does the Bible Define Itself?

The Bible is divinely inspired. Scripture emphasizes that the Lord, not man, speaks through the Word. "Take a scroll and write on it all the words I [the Lord] have spoken to you" (Jer. 36:2). "The word of the Lord came to Ezekiel" (Ezek. 1:3). "The Scripture had to be fulfilled which the Holy Spirit spoke long ago through the mouth of David" (Acts 1:16). "All Scripture is God-breathed and is useful for teaching, rebuking, correcting and training in righteousness" (2 Tim. 3:16). "For prophecy never had its origin in the will of man, but men spoke from God as they were carried along by the Holy Spirit" (2 Pet. 1:21). The Lord spoke, and man recorded the message. The Lord revealed Himself, and man recorded the experiences.

The Bible is sacred. Scripture warns its readers and teachers not to alter it by adding to it or taking away from it. "Do not add to what I command you and do not subtract from it, but keep the commands of the LORD your God that I give you" (Deut. 4:2). "Every word of God is flawless; he is a shield to those who take refuge in him. Do not add to his words, or he will rebuke you and prove you a liar" (Prov. 30:5–6). See also Revelation 22:19.

The Bible is powerful in its influence. Scripture is more than words and symbols. It is an extension of God's power. "The gospel . . . is the power of God for the salvation of everyone who believes" (Rom. 1:16). "Take . . . the sword of the Spirit, which is the word of God" (Eph. 6:17). "It judges the thoughts and attitudes of the heart" (Heb. 4:12).

The Bible was written for a purpose. John wrote, "But these are written that you may believe that Jesus is the Christ, the Son of God, and that by believing you may have life in his name" (John 20:31). Paul wrote, "For everything that was written in the past was written to teach us, so that through endurance and the encouragement of the Scriptures we might have hope" (Rom. 15:4). And again, "These things happened to them as examples and were written down as warnings for us" (1 Cor. 10:11). "All Scripture is God-breathed and is useful for teaching, rebuking, correcting, and training in righteousness, so that the man of God may be thoroughly equipped for every good work" (2 Tim. 3:16–17).

Later in life, John wrote again, "I write these things to you . . . so that you may know that you have eternal life" (1 John 5:13).

The Bible reveals Eternal Truth. Scripture moves us upward from our daily experiences to eternal principles. "Your Word, O Lord, is eternal; it stands firm in the heavens" (Ps. 119:89). "The word of our God stands forever (Isa. 40:8). "My words will never pass away" (Matt. 24:35). "But the word of the Lord stands forever" (1 Pet. 1:25).

How Do Teachers Use the Bible?

God's Word is Eternal Truth. Few would argue about the nature of Scripture. But how do we handle Scripture as we teach? Whether or not we are effective in helping learners grow spiritually depends directly on *how we handle Scripture*. Even with the highest regard for Scripture, we may not help your learners grow in the Lord. What makes the difference?

"Ask thoughtful questions and lead learners into God's Word for the answers"

Talk about it. A popular way to handle Scripture is merely to talk about it. I remember spending hours each week preparing to "teach the lesson" on Sunday. I read the assigned passage, studied the accompanying teaching helps, and wrote out several pages of notes: my "lesson." On Sunday morning I stood behind a podium or at a desk and "taught my lesson." I can remember Sundays when I taught so hard (using sign language with deaf college students) that I would sweat through my suits! Yet several days later, members of my class remembered little of what I had worked so hard to teach. How could they become "doers of the Word" if they couldn't remember what the Bible said? Telling people about the Bible is a good first step, but there is a better way to help people grow as they learn.

"Let the Bible speak!" The better way to handle Scripture in the classroom—and the approach I've found to be helpful in really changing learners— is to let the Bible speak! When I ask thoughtful questions and lead my learners into God's Word for the Answers, I find that they remember what we've studied far better than when I simply

Needs

give them my own ready-made answers. The Bible, God's Eternal Truth, is the sure foundation of discipling Bible study. Let us unsheath our swords! Let the Word speak, that it may convict and comfort, warn and console, revive and refresh us—so we might become all He intends and do all He commands.

The companion foundation stone in the Model represents the needs of learners. Jesus taught people the meaning of Scripture by focusing it at their point of personal need. Zacchaeus was lonely. Jesus asked to have dinner with him (Luke 19:10). Jairus grieved at the death of his daughter. Jesus raised her to life (Mark 5:21ff). Nicodemus the Pharisee sought Jesus' words on the kingdom of God. Jesus gave him specific instructions (John 3). Jesus did not dine with everyone, nor raise all dead people, nor give special instructions to all. He met needs in the lives of people—the leper, the lame, the deaf, the blind, the lonely and the religious—and in doing so, taught us the essence of the Father. Jesus pointed to soils and light and salt and sheep. He illustrated eternal truths with basic things that were familiar to those who pressed close to hear Him teach. He had no need of attendance prizes or candy or free trips to manipulate interest or enthusiasm. He spoke the Words of Life we all hunger for! He shared with His learners a caring Father Who wants only the best for them. The "Eternal Truth of Scripture" became real to the persons He touched. It became "Truth that matters to me!"

THE RIGHT FOUNDATION STONE: THE NEEDS OF PEOPLE

People today share the same basic needs as people in Jesus' day. Many have rejected the Answers to their needs because Truth is often cloaked in religious jargon—"church talk"—or dark moralistic tones. We have made our lessons more important than our learners. We need to follow the Master's example. Love your learners and teach so they can apply Scripture in the nitty-gritty concerns of living. What the Bible says is unchanging (left stone), but how we explain it varies with those we teach (right stone). Why? Because our learners have different needs. These differing needs are both general and specific.

General learner needs are characteristic factors which people have in common. One such general factor is the learner's age. Preschoolers learn differently from children, and children differently from youth. The adult age range spans sixty or more years and involves major life changes. Learners within given age categories experience similar situations in life: growing, school, adolescence, marriage, family, home, career, retirement. Similarity of life experiences helps the group focus on the relevancy of Bible teachings.

Specific learner needs include individual differences, such as personal failures or successes, past tragedies, present struggles, and areas of spiritual drought. There are an amazing number of aches, pains, and scars in a church family or classroom. Make a point to know your learners as individuals, as persons. Rejoice with them when they celebrate and empathize with them when they hurt.

When learners discover you care for them, that you want them to succeed and grow and share with you, they not only listen better, but they take it in, absorb it, treasure it. They learn with their hearts as well as their heads.

Both foundation stones are required for the model to be stable. If either crumbles, the structure falls. Too much emphasis on Bible content, without consideration for learner needs, results in "unrelated history:" Bible study that never touches learners where they live. Too much emphasis on learner needs, without commitment to letting God's Word speak, results in group therapy: sharing our opinions and experiences but never hearing what God has said.

And so our road has a ditch on either side: unrelated history lessons on the left and shallow socializing on the right. Taken together, however, Eternal Truth and present needs provide a super highway for discipling Bible study. As you provide a place where the Word of God speaks directly to the real needs of your learners, you establish a personal ministry that is both relevant and eternal.

THE LEFT PILLAR: HELPING PEOPLE THINK

If you want to disciple those you teach, then you must help them to think clearly: not merely to parrot your answers, but to weigh evidence, to ask questions, to analyze the answers of others, to confront the status quo with God's Word. The "Thinking Pillar" represents the disciplers' objective focus in teaching. That focus is to help learners translate the familiar stories and passages of the Bible into principles and standards by which they will make decisions in everyday situations. How do we teach so that thinking skills are improved?

Three Stages of Thinking

Paul gives us a keen insight into the role of thinking in Christian growth in his letter to the Colossian believers:

"We have not stopped praying for you and asking God to fill you with the knowledge of his will through all spiritual wisdom and understanding" (Col. 1:9).

Here Paul presents us with three components of spiritual growth through using the mind. These are knowledge, understanding, and spiritual wisdom.

Knowledge. Knowledge commonly refers to facts that the learner commits to memory. "To know" something means to be aware of or to be able to recall or identify that something. It is more than giving learners information. When you teach for knowledge, learners remember what was taught. Teachers may focus more on Bible information than Bible knowledge. But Paul goes beyond the idea of "head knowledge" in the passage just quoted. He does not use the more common word for knowledge, *gnosis.* He was writing against the forerunners of the Gnostics who taught that, without special knowledge, Christians would not get to heaven.

The word Paul uses here is *epignosis.* The word means a knowledge that reaches out and grasps its object and is in turn grasped by its object. When I began to learn about football—to grasp the essentials of the game—football took hold of me. As I studied the game of chess, chess took hold of me. As I've worked to learn the game of racquetball, not only with my head but with my whole body, racquetball has taken hold of me. Epignosis moves beyond mere head knowledge to what we might call "heart" knowledge: a knowledge that affects the way we live. To be filled with the *epignosis* of His will means to take hold of God's Word, and allow God's Word to take hold of us.

The beginning point for effective Bible teaching is to convey what the Bible says. Clear interpretation of Bible teachings requires knowledge of Bible persons, terms, places, and events. Without an adequate background in the setting of a given Bible passage, the learner will naturally interpret Bible words in light of his own culture and experience. This leads to *eisegesis,* reading into the Bible what we believe or think, rather than *exegesis*, reading out of the Bible what He has said.

What does the Bible say?

Too much emphasis on background facts can limit the teaching time given to understanding and application. "I wish we could discuss that idea more, but I have three more verses to cover." If you only present facts, you will not help learners become better Bible thinkers. Lead learners beyond Bible information to a closer walk with Christ. Help learners think about the implications of God's Word for daily living. Doing this requires emphasis on understanding.

Overemphasis on facts inhibits thinking.

Understanding is the process of organizing knowledge into concepts and principles that can be used. When learners understand a passage, they can explain it to others in their own words. They can give examples of what words do and do not mean, and create examples and illustrations to clarify the idea.

Paul knew the Old Testament well. He had studied under the great Jewish philosopher Gamaliel. He was trained in the best Pharisaical schools. He was zealous in his persecution of "liberal" Jews who were following a dead Nazarene carpenter. He demanded that they return to the "Old Time Religion." But when he met the Risen Lord on his way to Damascus, he saw things in a completely new way. During three years in an Arabian desert, he studied the Old Testament all over. The Book of Romans gives us the result of his rethinking. Before, he knew what the Old Testament said; now he understood what it meant, in light of the Resurrected Lord.

What Does the Bible mean?

Is there a difference between what the Bible says and what the Bible means? Or do you believe that "the Bible says what it means, and it means what it says!"? There is a difference between "words" and "concepts." Knowing words and understanding concepts are two different things. Let's take "Love your enemies" as an example. Anyone who has been in Sunday school or church for even a short time *knows* that Jesus said "Love your enemies." But how many *understand* what He *meant* when he said this?

What do I do when I love enemies? And who are my enemies? Must I like my enemies? How will "loving enemies" change the way I live day by day? Jesus defined His own words in the passage as He said, "Love your enemies, bless them that curse you, do good to them that hate you, and pray for them which despitefully use you, and persecute you" (Matt. 5:44, KJV). *Agape* means blessing and doing good and praying for. Nothing here about how I feel about them. "My enemy" means those who curse me, and hate me, and use and hurt me. My enemy can be my best friend, my colleague, my wife, or a fellow church member. When people close to me hurt me, I do not feel like loving them. But I am commanded to love. Not to feel, but to act.

It is far easier to know the words "Love your enemies" than it is to understand their meaning. But until learners clearly understand what Jesus meant, they will not be able to "love their enemies" in the way He intended. Unless Bible teaching can move learners from isolated words to biblical concepts, we will see little spiritual growth in our learners. Without clear biblical understanding, learners tend to read their own meanings into Bible words. This is eisegesis again!

But even proper understanding isn't sufficient for life-changing learning. We have one step yet to take: growing in wisdom.

*Wisdom.*Wisdom is biblical understanding put into action. At least, this is my understanding of Jesus' definition in Matthew 7:24–26:

> everyone who hears these words of mine and puts them into practice is like a wise man who built his house on the rock . . . everyone who hears these words of mine and does not put them into practice is like a foolish man who built his house on sand.

The clear distinction between "wise" and "foolish" in Jesus' definition is the term *put into practice.* Wisdom is not related to schooling or position or diplomas. As we learn what the Bible says, understand what the Bible means, and then strive, labor, battle to live in its light, then the result is wisdom. Every Christian is called to this journey. But the Christian discipler is called to help others move from words to concepts to Christian action—doing the Word, not hearing only! Educational psychologist George Mouly writes, "Transfer of training is the cornerstone on which education must ultimately rest; unless the [student's] learnings help him to meet more effectively situations . . . later in life, he is essentially wasting his time."[2]

Do what the Bible commands. The emphasis in our teaching should be on "putting into practice." Using the example of "love your enemies" again, I can know the words. I can understand the concepts. Now the question is: *Do I actually go out and love those who are my enemies?* If I don't, then Bible study is nothing more than an academic exercise. The foolish man hears but does not put into practice.

It is in the living of Scripture that the Lord Himself becomes our Teacher. As we attempt to put the Bible into action, in our own personal, individual worlds, the Lord teaches us. As I live from day to day, I will suffer hurt and disappointment and frustration from those around me. How will I respond? If I respond in their best interest, I am loving them. If my actions follow this biblical pattern, I demonstrate wisdom. I am a "lover of my enemies" and I am living in line with the teachings of Jesus.

The process of growth is continuous. We gain knowledge. This increased knowledge allows us to clarify Bible concepts. As we apply these clarified concepts to situations in our lives, we grow in wisdom. As we grow in wisdom, we gain more knowledge, which in

Growth Is an Upward Spiral

turn allows us to clarify concepts, and so on throughout life. As we spiral through knowledge, understanding, and wisdom, we spiral upward in Christ. Paul writes to believers, "Do not conform any longer to the pattern of this world, but be transformed by the renewing of your mind" (Rom. 12:2). We have just seen the process for accomplishing this here in his letter to the Colossians: Know what the Bible says, understand what it means, and live it out at home, at work, and at church.

What happens as a result of this upward spiral? The purpose of this growth, says Paul, is not just to know a lot about the Bible, but to live biblically.

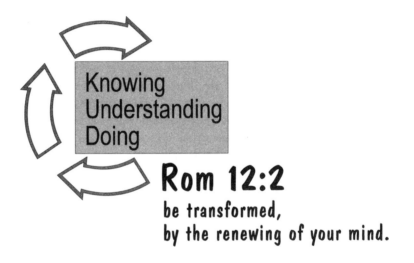

"We pray this in order that you may live a life worthy of the Lord and may please him in every way: bearing fruit in every good work, growing in the knowledge [epignosis] of God, being strengthened with all power according to his glorious might" (Col. 1:10–11). This is the left pillar of the Model. Teach in a way that helps people think biblically, in and out of class. The result for them is a worthy life, a life pleasing to God, fruitful and strong. Why? Because they know what the Bible says, understand what it means, and do as it commands.

THE RIGHT PILLAR: HELPING PEOPLE UNMASK

The subjective focus, represented by the right pillar, addresses the emotional aspects of Christian growth and maturity. Spiritual growth involves an emotional life that is balanced and controlled.

Proper Christian teaching helps learners use their emotions appropriately as they "rejoice with those who rejoice; mourn with those who mourn" (Rom. 12:15).

Jesus was real in the way He reacted emotionally to life. He wore no smiley-face mask. He dealt with the world realistically. He was not a dark-hearted prophet of doom, nor a light-hearted Pollyanna. He met life as it was and responded appropriately to the events of His life. When His good friend Lazarus died, Jesus didn't grin and shout "Praise the Lord anyway!" [sometimes shortened to

"P.T.L.A."]. He wept (John 11:35). When His disciples were exhausted by the press of the crowds and their ministry, Jesus didn't try to pump them up with false enthusiasm. He led them to a place of rest and recuperation (Mark 6:31). Even when dying on the cross, He arranged for His mother to be cared for (John 19:26). Jesus wore no pious mask to hide His inner feelings. Nor did He gush frothy feelings for all to see. He was not controlled by His emotions, nor did He repress them. He owned them and used them to manage life's circumstances. He directed them into tangible expressions of love and concern for others.

Classrooms where masks can be removed and the real is discovered have qualities distinct from classrooms where learners play it safe and silent. These qualities are class openness and a personal willingness to share.

Emotional Freedom

Openness. Students learn more in a safe, caring atmosphere than they do in a cool and indifferent one. They learn more, and they learn better, in a group that is open to one another. Masks cannot be removed unless there is an atmosphere of openness in the classroom. The teacher has the most control over how open learners can be. I have heard of a professor who would begin classes each semester by informing his students: "I am not here to entertain your ignorance. You are here to learn from me. So, please do not interrupt my lectures with your questions." What level of openness do you think exists in his classrooms? Is this teaching? Is it Christian?

Jesus changed the life of the woman at the well. He was able to teach her only after building a bridge between them. He did this by talking first about her immediate interest: water. He was open to her, a Samaritan woman. Remember, respectable Jewish men simply did not talk with women or Samaritans, and especially not Samaritan women! But He bridged the gap, with her interest, so that He could teach her. She became open to His words. He then told her of the Messiah, the Thirst Quencher, the Water of Life. She opened herself to His teaching, learned from Him, and finally followed Him.

Willingness to share. A willingness to share with others is a strong indication of trust—subjective strength—in the class. What do teachers do to weaken or inhibit the trust level of the class? Embarrass learners. Allow a few to dominate the class. Lecture too much. Treat learners' questions as "interruptions." Stand behind a podium or desk. Seat learners in rows. Respond harshly to questions or comments. Effective teachers strengthen trust in the class, which enhances learner willingness to share.

Removing Emotional Barriers

Folks who sit in our classes have hang-ups which keep them from trusting, growing, giving, serving, receiving. It is the subjective side of the Model that will touch them. Not doctrine, not logic, not words. But the gentle touch of caring, of listening, of loving. There are some in your classes who have personal hurts, secret burdens, heavy hang-ups that keep them from coming to the Lord or growing in the Lord. It is the subjective side of teaching that will make the difference in these situations.

Emotional Growth

What causes the majority of problems in a church? Is it doctrine? Is it worship style? No. Most conflicts and disputes within a fellowship come from some symptom of emotional immaturity: rash comments, fickle conduct, irritability, fear, anxiety, short temper, ambition, self-interest. The subjective focus of the Model reduces the effects of these destructive traits as learners develop love for and trust in one another.

Further, subjective teaching strengthens positive emotional traits as learners accept themselves and others more honestly. These positive traits include such things as working well with other learners, managing temperamental impulses, expressing good feelings without embarrassment, refraining from worry, and accepting constructive criticism.

Jesus brought unity to the fragmented personality of the Gadarene demoniac (Mark 5:1–20). He can also bring emotional coherence out of the chaos of uncontrolled feelings. Oh, how we need a strong dose of emotional growth in our churches!

The left and right pillars work together to support the structure. Both are necessary. But keeping a proper balance between the two is not easy. We tend to drift toward one side of the Model or the other.

Cold Dogmatism?

When the teacher places too much emphasis on the objective side of the model and neglects the subjective, Bible study becomes a means to a dogmatic end. The result of this is a cold, callous religious dogma that has little sympathy or concern for the feelings of others. Jesus warned against this error. His followers are to be "like little children" (Matt. 18:3). That is, they are to hold the Father in awe and wonder, and completely trust and depend on Him. Calling fire down from heaven on those who disagree with us is not Jesus' solution to problems (Luke 9:54–56).

Tepid Fluff?

When the teacher places too much emphasis on the subjective side of the Model and neglects the objective, Bible study becomes a means to an emotional end. The best term I know to describe it is "fluff." When experiential faith is not anchored by God's revealed Truth, the result is unstable, emotional "fluff." Immature believers throughout history, like the Ephesian Christians, have been tossed back and forth by changing doctrines of smooth-talking teachers who use deceitful methods to entrap them in their schemes (Eph. 4:14). Jesus warned us of these wolves in sheep's clothing. How do we escape from them? They sound so sincere! They sing so well! They make me feel good! They use the same words I do! Be very careful. Freedom comes by knowing the Truth (John 8:32), becoming "wise as serpents" (Matt. 10:16, KJV).

It is not a matter of being childlike or wise, but *childlike and wise*. Not cynically wise, nor callously wise, but lovingly wise. Not childishly trusting, nor naively trusting, but realistically trusting. Paul captures this objective-subjective tension when he writes, "speaking the truth" (left pillar) "in love" (right pillar), we will in all things grow up into . . . Christ" (Eph. 4:15).

We are not to speak the truth so harshly that it "breaks the reeds" or "quenches the flax" of faith. Nor are we to "love" others so sentimentally that we lose our integrity, in the name of graciousness, by winking at sin. We are to speak the truth in a loving manner. We are to love others with integrity. The writer of Proverbs said the same thing using this imagery: bind truth and mercy as an ornament around your neck (Prov. 3:3, KJV). Not truth or mercy, but truth-mercy. In this tension, we find favor with both God and mankind (Prov. 3:4).

THE CENTER PILLAR: HELPING PEOPLE RELATE

When Jesus was challenged to name the greatest commandment, He condensed all of the Law and the Prophets into two statements of relationship: "Love the Lord your God with all your heart, soul, and mind," and (the second is similarly important) "Love your neighbor as you love yourself." (Matt. 22:37, 39).

Our relationship with the Father ("Love the Lord your God") begins with faith in Christ and empowers all we do. Spiritual power for worship and service, praise and thanksgiving, repentance and renewal come through this vital link with the Lord.

The relationships with others ("Love your neighbor") involve missions, evangelism, equipping, ministering, and befriending. The central focus of "church" is to establish and strengthen relationships. And this is the central pillar of the Disciplers' Model.

People with People with Jesus in the Middle

The relative focus emphasizes the growth of relationships among believers as we worship God through Bible study, share our joys and concerns with fellow members, and reach out to the unchurched. Our lives become joined together. "People with people with Jesus in the middle" as a friend of mine once said. We build "community," the "Body of Christ," the "Church Family."

Masks on the Fringe. How sad to see people live on the fringes of the church. They come to services from time to time but never plunge into the family life. They keep up appearances, but never build bridges. They have no group where masks can be laid aside and the real discussed.

Then some tragedy strikes: a death, an illness, a divorce. Now they search in vain for "the church" and for "God" and wonder why neither can be flipped on like their "CableVision." The *koinonia* of Scripture and of the church grows over time. There are no shortcuts. Jesus established the church to reach the world. But an integral part of the mission of the church is to help change the world, to change the way people treat each other. The church is a living laboratory of human relationships.

Raw materials of growth. I used to wonder why churches suffered so much turmoil. If we are commanded to love one another, why do we find so much contention and fighting?

But the irritations, conflicts and confrontations that occur to some degree in every congregation of believers are a normal part of Christian growth—the social dimension! They are an essential part of the growth of koinonia, of relationship, of Family. We are called into the Family because of a mutual love for Jesus. But we are people with varying backgrounds, cultures, languages, and interests. Our conflicts are part of the process of becoming "one Family in Him." These social dilemmas and people problems are the raw materials of Christian character and community. God works in and through these human situations to grow us into the image of His Son, for "in all things God works for the good of those who love him, who have been called according to his purpose" (Rom. 8:28).

It reminds me of the day my wife and I walked down a beach in Florida. The rocks were polished and smooth—just beautiful. As we walked around the beach into a small bay, we noticed that the rocks were rough and dull. They were the same rocks. But they lacked the crucial ingredients that would make them all they could be: the pounding of the surf and the grinding of the sand.

Church members forfeit their opportunity to experience God's presence and care when they choose to remain aloof, neglect their gifts, refuse to join brothers and sisters in ministry. They are like the stones in the bay, undisturbed and unchanging. They stagnate in the status quo. Christians experience deep satisfaction and fulfillment as they learn to share with others, to serve with gladness, to use the gifts God gave them for the good of the Family, to pull with Jesus in the comfortable yoke He offers (Matt. 11:28–30). As they trust Him for strength and guidance, they are able to tackle larger tasks with confidence. The work brings frustration, as well as joy, but it is this bittersweet mix that matures us. Those who tackle new tasks, face new challenges, and elect the greatness of service become as polished stones—a prized possession in the Kingdom. Spiritual unity develops in believers as they gather in small groups to study the Bible, to share with each other, to affirm each other, to minister to one another.

So we have three pillars: the left pillar, helping learners think objectively; the right pillar, helping learners unmask appropriately; and the center pillar, helping learners build relationships. These are erected upon the left foundation stone, God's Word, the Bible, and the right foundation stone, the needs of learners, and support the capstone of discipling Bible study, "growing up" in the Lord.

THE CAPSTONE: HELPING PEOPLE GROW

There are four basic ways of talking about church growth. The most popular type of church growth is *numerical* growth, the rate of increase in membership. Numerical growth refers to church *size*. A second kind of church growth is *organic* growth, which refers to the strengthening of the internal structure—leadership, organization, vision—of the church. Organic growth refers to church *efficiency*. A third kind of church growth is *incarnational* growth, which refers to the church growing in Christlikeness. Incarnational growth enables the Church to *influence its culture*, to make a difference in its community in Jesus' name. The fourth kind of growth is *maturational* growth, which concentrates on the believer's *personal growth in Christ*. The capstone of the model represents this fourth type of growth, the process of growing individual believers in the Lord, of helping them become like Christ.

Paul's Treatise on Growth

Paul's treatise on church growth in Ephesians 4:11–16 fastens on this maturational theme. Christ gifts the church with four kinds of leaders. Pastor-teachers (the phrase "pastors and teachers" is thought to refer to one office) are given to the local church in order to "prepare God's people for works of service" (v. 12a).

Why? "So that the body of Christ may be built up" (v. 12b). This term "built up" does not refer to church size, but to church maturity ("and become mature," v. 13b).

What is the nature of this maturity? Unity in our faith and an intimate relationship with the Lord (v. 13a).

How mature does the Church have to be? Basically, Paul says, our task is done when everyone in the Church is as mature as Jesus: "attaining to the whole measure of the fullness of Christ" (v. 13b).

What is the result of this growing maturity? We will no longer be childish—fickle or gullible—tricked by religious con artists (v. 14) who mouth spiritual words but lust after worldly power. Instead, we will know and understand the Truth (left pillar), and we'll speak it in a loving way (right pillar), and by doing so we will grow up into Christ (capstone). Further, Christ, the Head, draws us together into oneness, a *koinonia*, a network of relationships (center pillar) "as each part does its work" (v. 16).

But how can I know if my class is maturing? How do I measure that? Perhaps the popularity of numerical growth is due to its ease of measurement. Churches with the most heads win. If this is what God intended, how is the church different from television ratings, or football ticket sales? Such a philosophy leads churches into all sorts of demeaning activities, all for "ten more next Sunday." A youth minister shaves his legs and wears jams to church, because the youth group reached an attendance goal. A pastor jumps into a vat of grits after Sunday morning worship, because their Sunday school goal was reached. This is circus, not New Testament churchmanship.

How Do I Measure This Growth?

Paul gives us a "spiritual yardstick" in his letter to the Galatians. This passage gives two lists of traits. One contains traits that should decrease in Christians over time. These "works of the flesh" include "immorality, impurity and debauchery; idolatry and witchcraft; hatred, discord, jealousy, fits of rage, selfish ambition, dissensions, factions and envy; drunkenness, orgies, and the like" (5:19–20). The second list contains traits that should increase in Christians over time. Called "fruit of the Spirit," these include "love, joy, peace, patience, kindness, goodness, faithfulness, gentleness and self-control" (5:22–23).

Disciplers measure spiritual growth by evidences of decreases in fleshly behaviors and increases in godly behaviors. The pillars of thinking, feeling, and relating—anchored on the Bible and the particular needs of learners in the class—culminate in a discipling process which reduces the fleshly and increases the heavenly. This is, admittedly, subjective. But focusing on the spiritual changes in the lives of learners is far more productive than simply drawing a crowd.

Make no mistake about what I am saying here. I want the church to grow numerically. I work to improve reaching and teaching. I keep and study attendance records. But the abuse of God's flock through guilt and manipulation for the sake of reaching strangers is also unscriptural. Jesus' command was clear: "Feed My sheep." We tend the flock, care for the lambs, provide nourishment, and God brings the increase.

The final element in the model is the circle, which represents the surrounding and indwelling Presence of the Holy Spirit of God. We have spoken of the "dry bones" of Sunday schools that have become mired down in routine. It is the Holy Spirit Who breathes life into

THE CIRCLE: HOLY SPIRIT AS DISCIPLER

dry bones. How do I allow the Holy Spirit to teach my class? What do I do to open up the spiritual communication lines? How can I become a "channel of His blessing" to my class? The three essential attitudes which determine how I answer these questions focus on prayer, priority, and position.

Holy Spirit

Prayer

If I want the Lord to have a part in my teaching, I must ask Him to take part. Remember the Lord's words to the Laodicean church? "I stand at the door and knock. If anyone hears my voice and opens the door, I will come in and eat with him, and he with me" (Rev. 3:20). Here the Lord has been shut out of the church, but He beckons to individuals in the church who desire fellowship with Him. The presence of the Lord is not automatic, even though He is omnipresent. We must ask Him, invite Him, welcome Him into our classes if we want Him to teach us.

Pray for the members of your class by name. As you think of each one, pray for his or her life situations, problems, needs. Pray that each might have experiences during the week that will point them to the Scripture passage to be studied Sunday. Pray that they will be ready to study Sunday morning. Pray for insights into the assigned Bible passage. Pray that you will be open to personal experiences that relate to scriptural truths. Pray that the Lord Himself will teach you as you prepare during the week. Pray for guidance in selecting learning activities as you develop the lesson plan. This prayerful preparation insures that Sunday morning Bible study is a joint effort between you and the Holy Spirit.

Priority

The proper priority for Christians is to "seek first the Kingdom of God." Still, a major problem in Sunday school work is the notion of "turf." By "turf," I mean the personal kingdoms that are built in classes or departments "in the name of the Lord." Somewhere along the line, the class becomes "mine." The "turf" teacher fights to hold on to "his" members. This is a misplaced priority.

Discipling teachers work in support of church goals. They see their work as part of the larger work of God. If a request is made that will help the overall Sunday school, disciplers do all they can to support that decision. They "model the role" of cooperation for their members. They are positive in their support for the "big picture." If some of their members are sought for teaching positions, they see this as a confirmation of their role as disciplers. Disciplers are mature enough to forgo "turf" as they maintain the proper priority of: "Seek ye first the Kingdom."

From the world's view, the most powerful position is at the top. R.H.I.P.—Rank Hath Its Privilege—is standard operating procedure. It is the position that permits us to control others. We talk about servanthood and sacrifice. We would like to think that these ideas function in our churches, but the truth is that this desire for power pervades any group that is not consciously surrendering to the Lord. Jesus came to give up His life as a ransom. He came as Servant, but He occupied the most powerful position in history.

Position

As a teacher, or a director, or minister of education, or pastor, or professor, am I a controller or a servant? If the Spirit is leading me, I am first a servant. The power of leadership comes from my ability to serve effectively. Jesus said it this way: "Whoever wants to be great among you must be your servant, and whoever wants to be first must be slave of all" (Mark 10:43–44).

These aspects of spiritual teaching—prayer, priority, and position—rise directly out of our dependence on and submission to the Holy Spirit. Programs come and go, plans succeed and fail, gimmicks for "ten more next Sunday" thrive and fade, but through all of this runs the Golden Thread of God's work: the drawing, winning, and maturing of people in Christ. This holy work proceeds only with surrendered disciplers. Fasten your eyes on this Golden Thread and find true success.

Spiritual Triad

Ours is a higher calling than transmitting religious facts. We are called to make disciples (Matt. 28:19) and to "prepare God's people for works of service . . . until we all reach unity in the faith and in the knowledge of the Son of God and become mature, attaining to the whole measure of the fullness of Christ" (Eph. 4:12–13). This is an awesome task! And we need all the help we can get!

If the Disciplers' Model appeals to you, then educational psychology will enhance your skills as a Christian teacher, a discipler. Educational psychology speaks to six of the seven elements of the Model directly. We introduce the links between the Model and educational psychology here. The rest of the text is devoted to establishing the place of educational psychology in Christian teaching.

THE RELATIONSHIP BETWEEN THE MODEL AND EDUCATIONAL PSYCHOLOGY

Left Foundation Stone: Content Mastery. The left foundation stone of the Model represents the Bible. The focus is on letting the Bible speak. Educational psychology concerns itself with educational content. Particularly important is the structure of the material. If one is to teach a subject effectively, he or she must be fluent in that subject. Vocabulary, concepts, principles, hierarchies, categories, relationships: these elements are essential building blocks for effective teaching, and educational psychology addresses how to master the content. Of particular importance are Jerome Bruner's ideas of structure and transfer.

Right Foundation Stone: Learner Needs. The right foundation stone of the Model represents the needs of learners. Educational psychology gives attention to individual differences and individual development. We will focus on Erikson's stages of personality development. We will analyze the emphasis on learner needs and values from humanistic learning theory. We will discuss the issues of learner motivation, as well as targeting learner needs through instructional objectives.

Left Pillar: Thinking. The left pillar represents the process of helping learners think. Critical thinking is an important issue in education circles today. We will focus on the cognitive development theories of Jean Piaget and Jerome Bruner. We'll analyze both behavioral and cognitive theories of learning and motivation, as well as Lawrence Kohlberg's theory of moral reasoning.

Right Pillar: Feeling. The right pillar represents the process of helping learners unmask and share themselves with others. We will study humanistic theories of learning and motivation, which emphasize emotions, values, and personal experiences. We will differentiate between classical humanism, secular humanism, and educational humanism, and we will discuss the strengths and weaknesses of the theories of Abraham Maslow and Carl Rogers for Christian teaching.

Center Pillar: Relating. The central pillar represents the building of relationships among learners. We will study the group dynamics issues of Kurt Lewin and Carl Rogers, as well as the impact of relationships in Erikson's psychosocial theory.

Capstone: Growth. The capstone of the Model is growth in Christ. Educational psychology emphasizes maturation through learning. We'll study implications of selected theorists—behavioral, cognitive, and humanistic—for human growth through learning.

Circle: Holy Spirit. The Circle of the Model represents the infilling and surrounding power of the Holy Spirit in the teaching process. As a secular discipline, educational psychology does not address the issue of spiritual growth. We cannot put God in a test tube. The Holy Spirit is like the wind, blowing where He will (John 3:8), which means He is not subject to research design. Even so, educational psychology opens up the human learning process in a way that helps us become better teachers—whether we teach a Bible study class of ten or a graduate seminary class of one hundred. May God bless you on the journey.

CHAPTER CONCEPTS

Cognitive development

Cold Dogmatism

Content mastery

Emotional freedom and growth

Fellowship vs. koinonia

General and Specific Learner Needs

Group Therapy

Growth as Upward Spiral

Holy Spirit as Discipler

Incarnational growth

Individual differences

Knowledge: Gnosis vs. Epignosis

Maturational growth

Numerical growth

Organic growth

Psychosocial development

Spiritual triad

Talk About the Bible

Tepid Fluff

The Disciplers' Model

Understanding

Unrelated History

Wisdom

DISCUSSION QUESTIONS

1. Consider your own teaching style. Where are you on the continuum of "Bible and Needs"? Do you emphasize content too much? Do you emphasize learner feelings and attitudes too much? Are you balanced?

2. Are you more a thinker or a feeler? Do you prefer to deal with biblical concepts or learner experiences?

3. How do you encourage bridge building between yourself and your students? How do you encourage interaction among students?

4. Consider teachers who have helped you grow spiritually through Bible study. How have they reflected the Disciplers' Model?

5. Consider for a moment that you are a professor in a Christian college teaching a nonbiblical subject. How would the Disciplers' Model help you as a teacher?

FOR FURTHER READING

If you would like more information on the Discipler's Model, write me at Southwestern Baptist Theological Seminary, Box 22428, Fort Worth, Texas 76122. The *Disciplers' Handbook* and two video series are available which detail the Disciplers' Model, the Disciplers' Method, and the Disciplers' Manner.

2

INTRODUCTION TO SCIENTIFIC KNOWING

HOW WE KNOW WHAT WE KNOW

Educational psychology is a scientific discipline. What does this mean? How does knowledge discovered by science differ from knowledge we gain in other ways? This chapter serves as an introduction to scientific investigation. Further, faith-knowing and science-knowing are compared and contrasted. Finally, the dichotomy between pagan thinking and biblical thinking is analyzed, providing a unique definition of the function of Christian teaching.

CHAPTER RATIONALE

Learners will demonstrate understanding of ways of knowing by:

CHAPTER OBJECTIVES

- explaining any of the six ways of knowing;

- comparing and contrasting pagan and biblical mindsets;

- explaining the dilemma of the Western Christian.

Learners will demonstrate knowledge of scientific knowing by defining the five ideals of science.

Learners will demonstrate understanding of scientific knowing by identifying situations which violate scientific controls.

INTRODUCTION

On an unexpectedly cool day in September, six seminary students discuss the issue of "modern Bible translations" as they eat lunch under the trees.

Student 1: "I use the King James Version because that's the translation I grew up using. Everybody in our church back home uses it."

Student 2: "I use the New King James because my pastor says it offers the best of beauty and modern scholarship."

Student 3: "I've prayed about what version to use. I like the New American Standard because it is so clear in its language. I know it's right for me."

Student 4: "I've tried five or six different translations for devotional reading and for preparation for teaching in Sunday school. After evaluating each one, I've come back again and again to the New International Version. It's the best translation for me."

Student 5: "The essence of Bible study is understanding the message, whatever translation we may use. Therefore, I use different translations depending on my study goals."

Student 6: "I use the New International Version because most of my congregation is familiar with it. In a recent survey, I found that 84 percent of our members use the NIV in their Bible study classes."

Each of these students reflects a different basis for knowing which translation to use. Which student most closely reflects your view? Let's investigate the most common ways we gain knowledge.

WAYS OF KNOWING

Each of the students' views represents a basic way people gain knowledge about the world in which we live. These are common sense, authority, intuition/revelation, experience, deductive reasoning, and inductive reasoning. Inductive reasoning is the basis for scientific knowing, which provides the foundation for educational psychology. Let's look at each of these ways we come to know what we know.

Common Sense

People learn by naturally absorbing the customs and traditions that surround them—from family, church, community and nation. We assume this knowledge is correct because it is familiar to us. It's just the way things are. People seldom question, or even think to question, the correctness of common sense because it just is.

"Naturally absorbing customs and traditions from others"

Unless there is an intentional effort to study the views of others, there is little or nothing to challenge our way of thinking. It's just common sense! Student 1's response reflects a commonsense kind of knowing: "that's the translation I grew up using."

But there are obvious problems with this kind of knowing. Common sense held that "the earth is flat" until Columbus discovered otherwise. Common sense said that "dunce caps and caning are effective student motivators" until educational research discovered the negative aspects of punishment. Common sense proclaimed that "if God had intended man to fly, He'd have given us wings." But millions fly all over the world. Common sense may well be wrong.

Authoritative knowledge is an uncritical acceptance of another's knowledge. When we are sick, we go to the doctor to find out what to do. When we need legal help, we go to a lawyer and follow his advice. Since we cannot verify the knowledge on our own, we must simply choose to accept or reject the expert's advice. It would be foolish to argue with a doctor's diagnosis or a lawyer's perception of a case. This is the meaning of "uncritical acceptance" in the definition above. The only recourse to accepting the expert's knowledge is to get a second opinion from another expert. Student 2's response reflects authoritative knowing: "My pastor says it offers the best of beauty and modern scholarship."

Authority

As Christians, we believe that God's Word is the authority for our life and work. The Living Word—the Lord Himself Who lives within us—confirms the Truth of the Written Word. The Written Word confirms our experiences with the Living Word. Scripture is a valid source of authoritative knowledge.

"Uncritical acceptance of another's knowledge"

However, we spend a lot of time discussing scriptural interpretations. Our discussions may deteriorate into defending "my pastor's" interpretations. We may use our pastors' interpretations as authoritative because of their influence in our lives. (Substitute any authoritative person here, such as a father or mother, Sunday school teacher, or respected colleague.)

The real question is whether the authority is correct. Authoritative knowing does not question the source of knowledge. Still, differing authorities cannot be correct simultaneously. How do we test the validity of an authority's testimony?

Intuitive knowledge refers to truths which the mind can grasp immediately. There is no need for proof or testing or experimentation. The properly trained mind, proponents say, "intuits" the truth naturally. The field of geometry provides a good example of this kind of knowing. Let's say that line segment A is the same length as line segment B. Also, line segment B is the same length as line segment

Intuition/Revelation

C. From these two truths, we can see that line segments A and C are equal. Or, in shorthand,

IF A=B and B=C, THEN A=C.

We do not need to draw the three lines and measure them. The mind immediately grasps the truth of the statement.

"Logical truths the mind grasps naturally"

Revelation reflects knowledge that God reveals about Himself. We need not test this knowledge or subject it to experimentation. When Christ reveals Himself to us, we know Him in a personal way. We did not achieve this knowledge by our own efforts; we received the revelation of the Lord (see Matt. 16:16–17). We cannot prove this knowledge to others, but it is Truth to those who have received it. Student 3's response reflects intuitive knowing: "I just know it's right for me."

Problems arise, however, when we apply intuitive knowing to ministry programs. "Well, it's obvious that regular attendance in Sunday school helps people grow in the Lord." Is it? We work hard at promoting Sunday school attendance. Does it actually change the lives of the attendees? Is it enough for people to think it does, whether or not real change takes place? Answers to these questions come from clear-headed analysis, not from intuition.

Experience

Experiential knowledge is "trial and error" learning. It is the result of trying to do something new and analyzing the consequences. You've probably heard comments like: "We've already tried that and it failed." Or: "We've found that holding Vacation Bible School during the third week of August, in the evening, is best for our church." The first is negative. The speaker is saying there's no need to try a ministry or program again because it was already tried. The second is positive. This church has tried several approaches to offering Vacation Bible School and found, at least for their particular needs, the best time. Their "truth" may not apply to any other church in the area, but it is true for them. They've tried it and it worked . . . or it didn't. Student 4's response reflects experiential knowing: "I've tried five or six different translations . . . [the NIV's] the best translation for me."

"Trial and error learning"

Much of the promotion of new church programs comes out of this way of knowing. We say, "This program is being used in other churches with great success." This usually means the church can have the same experience if they use the program. But how do we evaluate program effectiveness? What is success? How do we measure it? Sadly, the answer often reduces ministry to how many were present, not what happened to them. Such merchandising of people short-circuits true ministry.

Deductive reasoning begins with general principles and moves to specific applications. One develops general overarching statements of intent and purpose and then deduces from these principles specific actions. Such a reasoner determines a "world view" first and then makes specific decisions which logically derive from this perspective. Student 5's response reflects deductive reasoning: "The essence of Bible study is understanding the message [general principle] . . . I use different translations depending on my study goals [specific applications]." *Deductive Reasoning*

When a church makes the Great Commission their primary purpose, they have framed a world view for ministry. That is, whatever they do, they will reach people and teach them all things—around the world. Now, how do they do it? They deduce specific programs, plans, and procedures for carrying out the mandate. They eliminate programs that conflict with the mandate.

How do we arrive at this "world view?" Are our overarching principles correct? Have we interpreted them correctly? Have we deduced our programs correctly?

Inductive reasoning flows from specifics to general principles. Inductive Bible study analyzes several passages and then synthesizes key concepts into a central truth. Care must be taken to include all relevant passages; otherwise, the synthesis will be faulty. Science is inductive in its study of a number of specifics and in its use of these results to formulate a theory. The truths derived in this way are temporary and open to adjustment. Student 6's response reflects inductive reasoning: "84 percent of our members use the NIV." Apparently, when a large percentage of the congregation begins using another translation, Student 6 will change his preference to match. *Inductive Reasoning*

Knowledge gained in this way is usually related to probabilities of happenings. Common statements from inductive reasoning include the following phrases: "the data tends to indicate," "research suggests," "recent studies add weight to the argument that." **"From particulars to generalizations"**

By definition, science does not deal with absolute Truth. Science seeks knowledge about processes in our world. Researchers gather information through observation. Then they mold this information into theories. The scientific community tests these theories under differing conditions to establish the degree to which they can be generalized. The result is temporary, open-ended truth (I call it "little-t" truth to distinguish it from absolute Truth). This kind of truth is open for inquiry, further testing, and probable modification. While this kind of knowing can add nothing to our faith, it is very helpful in objectively solving ministry problems.

SCIENCE AS A WAY
OF KNOWING

Honest scientific knowing is based on precise data gathered from the natural world. It builds a knowledge base in a neutral, unbiased manner. It seeks to measure the world precisely. It reports findings clearly so that others can duplicate the studies. It forms its conclusions from empirical data. I qualify these definitions by the term "honest" because scientists, being human, are subject to the same problems of perception and bias as any one else. Let's look at the five ideals of honest scientific knowing.

Objectivity—
the Reduction of Bias

Human beings are complex. Personal experiences, values, backgrounds, and beliefs make objective analysis difficult unless effort is made to remain neutral. Optimists tend to see the positive in situations ("the glass is half-full"). Pessimists see the negative ("half-empty"). True scientists look for objective reality—the world as it is—uncolored by personal opinion or feelings.

Scientific knowing attempts to *eliminate personal bias* in data collection and analysis. Honest researchers take a neutral position in their studies. That is, they do not try to prove their own beliefs. They are willing to accept results contrary to their own opinions or values.

Precision

Reliable scientific knowing requires precise measurement. Researchers carry out experiments under controlled, narrow conditions. They carefully design instruments to be as accurate as possible. They evaluate tests for reliability and validity. They use pilot projects (trial runs of procedures) to identify sources of extraneous error in measurements. Why? Because inaccurate measurement, undefined conditions, unreliable instruments, and extraneous errors produce data that is worthless.

Think of two students who are equally prepared for an exam. When they arrive in class, one is healthy and the other has a temperature of 102°. They will likely score differently on the exam. In this case, illness introduces an error term into the second student's score.

When we gather data in a haphazard, disorderly way, error interferes with the true measure of the variable. Like static on a television screen, the error masks the true picture of the data. When this happens, the analysis of data will provide a numerical answer which is suspect. *Accurate measurement is a vital ingredient in the research process.*

Much of the evaluation of church programs is based on affective factors such as personal feelings and how many people attended. Christian teachers will help students with real growth only as they can accurately analyze life situations and make specific applications of Bible truths.

Science analyzes world processes which are systematic and recurring. Researchers report their findings in a way that *allows others to replicate their studies*—to check the facts in the real world.

Replication

These replications either confirm or refute the original findings. When researchers confirm earlier results, they verify the earlier findings. Research reports provide readers the background, specific problems and hypotheses of studies. Also included are the populations, definitions, limitations, assumptions, and procedures for collecting and analyzing data. Writers do this intentionally so that others can evaluate the degree to which findings can be generalized—applied to persons beyond their study—and perhaps replicate the study.

Empiricism is the view that "experience, especially of the senses, is the only source of knowledge."[1] Science bases its findings on empirical data—data which is "derived from . . . [or] verifiable or provable by means of observation or experiment."[2] That is, science bases its knowledge on *observations of specific events*, not on abstract philosophizing. Therefore, science deals with testable problems of recurring phenomena in the world.

Empiricism

Basic observations can be done with the naked eye. But observations are also made with instruments such as questionnaires, tests, attitude scales, or controlled experiments. Scientific knowing cares less about philosophical reasoning than it does about the rational collection and analysis of factual data relevant to the problem to be solved.

The goal of scientific research is not merely to catalog empirical data. Its goal is theory construction: the development of theories which explain the phenomena under study. The inductive process of scientific knowing begins with the specifics (data) and leads to the general (theories). What causes cancer? What makes it rain? How do we learn? What is the best way to relieve anxiety? What factors influence marital satisfaction?

Goal: Theory Construction

HINDRANCES TO
SCIENTIFIC KNOWING

*Selective Observation
and Recall*

The five ideals of science help establish empirically sound theories concerning our world. However, there are hindrances to gaining this kind of knowledge. Let's discuss four of these, and how science works to overcome their effect.

We live in a world of information overload. So much information surrounds us that we cannot adequately process all of it. Therefore we screen the information for the essentials. Selective observation screens information as it comes in. Selective recall screens information as it is remembered.

Selective observation hinders scientific knowing by gathering data that is biased by personal expectations. For example you stand at the airport waiting for a friend to deplane. One by one, passengers file out the door. You glance from face to face, looking for your friend. You focus on each face just long enough to eliminate it from consideration. Finally, your friend exits and you lock on. Recognition! Now, how much do you remember of those you eliminated from consideration? Very little. Their faces did not fit what you were looking for. Undercover agents escape detection because they dress and act like those around them. Magicians master sleight-of-hand skills which permit them to distract us in one direction while they do their tricks in another.

Selective recall hinders scientific knowing by gathering data that is biased by personal feelings. One of my great aunts was married to a man who treated her shamefully for years. As a very young child, I remember attending his funeral—my first. I remember hearing relatives quietly comment about how much better my aunt's life would be. But in a matter of months, she began "recalling" life with her husband—remembering what a good man he had been. She repressed the bad and emphasized the good. Some veterans recall their experiences in the military with horror; others with nostalgia.

The problem researchers face is the tendency to focus on their own expectations and miss important information they weren't looking for. Science combats selective observation and recall by taking random samples of data and analyzing them objectively. Researchers make a conscious effort to observe every event that relates to their study. They record data mechanically—checklists, inventories, video tape, tests—during the data gathering process to prevent selective recall.

Take a moment to look at the figures below. Label them before reading on.

Closure

Did you label the three dots a "triangle"? The 355° arc a "circle"? If you did, you experienced closure. You mentally drew lines between the dots to make them a triangle, and filled in the arc to make it a circle. Selective observation overlooks something that exists; closure fills in what is missing.

Science combats closure by collecting all the evidence that it can. It does not make decisions too soon, but laboriously collects data to provide an empirical foundation for hypotheses and theories.

"Scottish terrier" is a breed of dog. This is a fact. "Great Dane" is a breed of dog. This is also a fact. The class of animals called "dogs" includes hundreds of breeds which reflect a wide variety of color, size, and temperament. Breeds are specifics. "Dog" is a generalization. "Ford" and "Chevrolet" are specific makes of automobiles. But "automobile" is a generalization. The class of machines called "automobiles" includes hundreds of makes and models. To generalize is to move from specific objects to a class of related objects.

Overgeneralization

Overgeneralization occurs when we judge a class of people or events by a few examples. Our tendency is to project limited experiences with a few individuals or events to the whole class. This is a hindrance to scientific knowing because the projection is based on personal attitudes and has little to do with the reality of the whole.

Science combats overgeneralization by conducting research with randomly chosen samples. Large samples are used when possible. Sufficient data is collected in an objective manner to prevent the tendency to overgeneralize findings to the whole. Replication of experiments allows for cross validation of research findings.

Personal Involvement

As human beings we have, as a result of prior experiences and study, a personal set of values, beliefs, and prejudices. These form a subjective filter through which we see the world around us. Events and experiences are filtered—often distorted—by our subjective view of reality. Researchers are, obviously, human beings. Their studies are important to them. They have hunches about what they want to find. Their speculative hypotheses can be filters through which research data must pass. This distorts the data and renders the analysis invalid.

Science combats personal involvement by emphasizing objectivity. Two eyewitness accounts are considered objective if they report the same thing. A test is objective if subjects receive the same scores regardless of who grades them. An observation checklist is objective if two observers report the same data in an experiment. Objectivity provides neutral data regarding the study—data that is unrelated in any way to the researchers' personal biases.

FAITH AND SCIENCE

What is the relationship between faith and science? Are faith and science enemies? Can ministers use scientific methodology to study the creation and retain a fervent faith in the Creator? I believe we can—and should. But care must be taken to mark out the boundaries of each. There is a difference between faith knowing and scientific knowing, and that difference sometimes explodes into conflict—a conflict fueled by both sides. First we'll look at the suspicion of science by the faithful. Then we'll consider the suspicion of religion by scientists.

Suspicion of Science

Anselm wrote in the tenth century, "I believe so that I may understand." In other words, commitment and faith are essential elements in gaining spiritual understanding. His words reflect Jesus' teaching that He gives understanding to those who follow Him (Matt. 11:29; 16:24). Blaise Pascal in the seventeenth century wrote, "The heart has reasons which are unknown to reason. . . . It is the heart which is aware of God and not reason. That is what faith is: God perceived intuitively by the heart, not by reason." The truth of Christ comes by living it out, by risking our lives on Him, by doing the Word. We grow in our knowledge of God through personal experience as we follow Him and work with Him. We believe in order to understand spiritual realities. This approach to knowing is private and subjective. Such belief knowing resents an antisupernatural skepticism of open-minded inquiry.

Worse yet, for believers, is that some scientists consider the scientific method to be their religion. Their "belief in evolution" may be a justification for their unbelief in God. Science is helpful in learning about our world, but it makes a poor religion. So the faithful view science and its adherents with suspicion.

Sometimes, however, the suspicion of science by the religious has less to do with faith than with political power. In the Middle

Ages, the accepted view of the universe was geocentric ("earth-center"). The moon, the planets, the sun (located between Venus and Mars), and the stars all rotated about the earth in perfect circles. This view had three foundations. First, the church taught that the geocentric view was scriptural, based on Joshua 10:12–13. "Joshua said to the LORD in the presence of Israel: 'O sun, stand still over Gibeon, O moon, over the Valley of Aijalon.' So the sun stood still, and the moon stopped, till the nation avenged itself on its enemies, as it is written in the Book of Jashar. The sun stopped in the middle of the sky and delayed going down about a full day."

For the sun and moon to stand still, the church fathers reasoned, they would have to be circling the earth. Further, both Greek science (Ptolemy) and Greek philosophy (Aristotle) supported a geocentric view of the universe. The logic was rock solid for centuries: humankind is the pinnacle of creation. Therefore, the earth must be the center of the universe.

Then several scientists began their skeptical work of actually observing the movements of the planets and stars. Copernicus, a Polish astronomer, created a fifteenth century revolution in astronomy when he published his heliocentric ("sun-center") theory of the solar system. He theorized, on the basis of his observations and calculations, that the earth and its sister planets revolved around the sun in perfect (Aristotelian) circles. Keplar later demonstrated that the solar system was indeed heliocentric, but that the planets, including earth, orbited the sun in elliptical, not circular, paths. The Roman Catholic Church attacked their views because they displaced earth from its position of privilege and opened the door to doubt in other areas. But Poland is a long way from Rome (particularly so in the fifteenth century!), and so Copernicus and Keplar remained outside the church's reach.

Galileo was the father of modern physics and did his work in Italy in the sixteenth and seventeenth centuries. He studied the work of Copernicus and Keplar, and built a telescope to observe the planets more closely. In 1632, he published the book *Dialogue Concerning the Two Chief World Systems: Ptolemaic and Copernican*, in which he supported a heliocentric view of the solar system. He was immediately attacked by church authorities who continued to espouse a geocentric world view. Professors at the University of Florence refused to look through Galileo's telescope: they did not believe his theory, so they refused to observe. Very unscientific! Galileo, under threat of being burned at the stake, recanted his findings. It was not until October 1992 (yes, that's right) that the Roman Catholic Church officially overturned the decision against Galileo's book and agreed that he had indeed been right. Science questions, observes, and seeks to learn how the world works. Sometimes this process collides with the vested interests of dogmatic religious leaders.

Suspicion of Religion

Science is meticulous in its focus on the rational structure of the universe. Scientists look with suspicion at the simple faith of believers who glibly say "I don't know how, but I just know God did it." Such a statement reflects mental laziness. How does the world work? What can we learn of the processes? Many of the men and women who pioneered science were motivated by the Reformation and their newfound faith to discover all they could about God's creation.

But the skeptical neutrality of science often collides with the perspective of faith, acceptance, and obedience. When I was in the sixth grade, our science class began a unit on the water cycle. I had always believed that "God sent the rain to water the flowers and trees," because that's what my mom told me when I asked her why it rained. Now, before my very eyes was a chart showing a mountain and a river, and an ocean and a cloud. Carefully the teacher explained the cycle. "Water evaporates from the ocean and forms a cloud. The wind blows the cloud to the mountain, where water condenses in the form of rain. The rain collects and forms a river which flows back into the ocean. This is the water cycle." I can still vividly remember my confusion and fear—where was God in the water cycle? My dad helped when he got home that night. "Well, the water cycle certainly explains the mechanical process of evaporation and condensation, but Who do you think designed the water cycle?" My confusion was gone. My faith was strengthened—though less simplistic and naive than it had been before. ("If God sends rain to water the plants, why doesn't He send some to areas of drought where people are starving to death?") And, I had learned something about how the world works that I hadn't even thought about before. The faithful should not use "faith" as a cop out for mental laziness.

In Summary

And so, faith focuses on the supernatural and subjectively sees with the heart's eye the Creator Who made us. Scripture, the objective anchor of our subjective experiences, is a record of personal experiences with God through the ages. Science focuses on the natural and objectively gathers data on repeatable phenomena, the machinery, so that we may better understand how the world works. There is no conflict between giving our hearts to the Lord and giving our minds to the logical pursuit of natural truth. All truth is God's truth. Therefore the objective pursuit of truth does not conflict with faith.

Educational psychology is a scientific discipline which focuses on the nature of the teaching-learning process. It does not—it cannot, by definition—speak to faith issues. But it can, and does, provide wonderful insight for those who wish to excel in helping others learn.

There is one other dichotomy which needs some attention before we move into the actual study of educational psychology. This is the dichotomy of Greek versus Hebrew thinking.

The Greek mind-set is clearly reflected in Paul's encounter with the Epicurean and Stoic philosophers in Athens (Acts 17). Dr. Luke writes that these philosophers, as well as many Athenians, "spent their time doing nothing but talking about and listening to the latest ideas" (v. 21). There is no indication that these ideas had any impact on how they lived, how they treated their families, or how they related to others. It was as if they kept their lives in various compartments: a compartment for this philosophy, another for that religion, another for home, another for business, still another for their recreation. It is no wonder that the Greeks gave us the word hypocrisy: "the practice of professing beliefs, feelings, or virtues that one does not hold or possess; falseness."[3]

Western Civilization was birthed out of Greece and clearly reflects this compartmentalization. We have home lives and church lives and school lives and entertainment lives. Churchgoers proclaim commitment to strong family values at church, yet divorce rates differ little from society at large. Boy Scouts vow to be honest, yet research shows little distinction between the honesty of Boy Scouts and other boys. Teenagers have multiple sets of friends—one at church, another at school, and a third on Friday night. These groups may have widely divergent values and beliefs. At its worst, this compartmentalization can break people into pieces as each "life" demands more energy. Such compartmentalization explains how a prominent evangelist can preach against immorality and then rendezvous with a prostitute. Or how a Christian businessman can study about patient love on Sunday and abuse his employees on Monday. Or how a Christian woman can sing "I Surrender All" in a

GREEK AND HEBREW MIND-SETS

The Greek Mind-set: Compartmentalized Thinking

worship service and then slander the pastor because he didn't do exactly what she wanted.

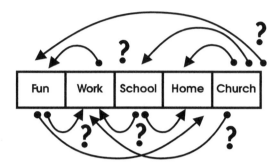

This compartmentalization causes us problems both as learners and as teachers. As learners, we tend to keep what we learn in school in our "school box," and what we learn in church in our "church box." Our learnings, then, have no impact or influence on each other. Our growth as believers is in reverse proportion to the extent we compartmentalize our lives; therefore, we must break down the walls between the compartments if we wish to grow.

As teachers, we are frustrated in our teaching as learners "box" our stuff and keep it neatly tucked away from their other compartments. As pastors, we are frustrated as our members "box" our sermons and keep them in their church compartment. Further, when we urge members to increase their commitment to the Lord, some consider it an invasion of their other boxes. To make the church box bigger, other boxes must be made smaller. "To give more time to the church means less time for family, or work, or recreation. I need to spend quality time with my family. I need to make a living. I need time for rest and relaxation." So the result is stiff resistance toward commitment, toward involvement, toward developing gifts. So, what's the alternative? How do we help people grow as Christians? We must move them toward a Hebrew mind-set.

The Hebrew Mind-set: Whole Living

All of the writers of the Bible, with the exception of Dr. Luke, were Hebrews. As we have noted, Greeks compartmentalize their lives. What they think may have little to do with how they live. But biblical writers, under the inspiration of God, focused on life behaviors—transgressions and sins on one hand and righteousness on the other. Ezekiel captures the thought when he writes, "Our offenses and sins weigh us down, and we are wasting away because of them. How can we then live?" (Ezek. 33:10). Just six verses later he answers, "He has done what is just and right; he will surely live" (v. 16).

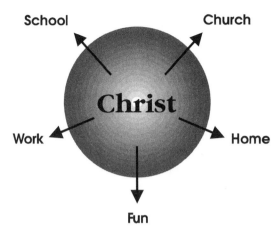

School   Church

Christ

Work   Home

Fun

Jesus emphasized behavior: "Everyone who hears these words of mine and puts them into practice is like a wise man who built his house on a rock" (Matt. 7:24). Paul wrote he was praying for the Colossians to be filled with the knowledge of God's will, with all spiritual wisdom and understanding. Why? "In order that you may live a life worthy of the Lord and may please him in every way. " (Col. 1:10). Peter wrote that Jesus died on the cross "so that we might die to sins and live for righteousness" (1 Pet. 2:24). The result of this, writes Peter, is that the believer "does not live the rest of his earthly life for evil human desires, but rather for the will of God" (1 Pet. 4:2). The Hebrew focus is on how to live. For New Testament believers, the focus is on living in union with Christ (John 15:5).

This new life of the believer is centered in the Lord: "the mystery that has been kept hidden for ages . . . which is, Christ in you, the hope of glory" (Col. 1:26–27). The diagram above illustrates this truth. The Lord is at the center of life, with various areas around Him. As we give Him freedom, He teaches us how to set proper priorities. What kind of husband would He have me be? What kind of father? What kind of seminary professor? What kind of churchman? I learn from Him as I study the Bible, and I learn from Him as I ask Him for guidance in daily struggles. Faith is not tucked away in a "church box" but is allowed to flow throughout all of our life's compartments.

Jesus said, "Take my yoke upon you and learn from me, for I am gentle and humble in heart, and you will find rest for your souls. For my yoke is easy and my burden is light" (Matt. 11:29–30). Jesus had carved many yokes in His carpenter days, carved them to fit a team of oxen just so. The yoke allowed the two to share the load. The yoke was fitted to each ox so that it would not irritate or chafe—it rode easy on their backs. The essence of the Christian life is accepting the yoke of the Lord. He is in one side, and He invites us to join Him in the other. As we pull together, He teaches us ("learn from me"). Just as a young stallion is broken to the traces by a seasoned plow horse, so the Lord teaches us how to excel in every area of life: home, business, school, church—and even recreation!

This is the Hebrew, biblical, Christian mind-set—obedience to the Lord of life, who wants nothing less than the best for us.

The compartmentalization of the Greek mind-set leads to personal anarchy. Each compartment takes on a life of its own. Various compartments compete for attention, compete for the limited amount of available energy. Live this way very long, and you begin to experience burnout and depression. Extreme cases can even lead to mental illness, where several compartments exist in separate spheres of consciousness, unknown to other compartments or to the one who is fragmented. This is not how God intended for life to be. Family and worship and work and rest are all to be components of a single whole, guided by the Lord—"learn from me."

The Hebrew mind-set provides a basis whereby the components of our lives exist in harmony, centered in a whole personality, guided by the Lord. This "united kingdom" produces emotional and psychological health, energy for facing life's problems, and a positive direction for living.

From Greeks to Hebrews in Perspective

The role of Christian teaching is to intersect the Greek mind-set of our learners and lead them toward biblical living. Educational psychology cannot speak to our faith, but educational psychology can inform our approach to teaching and learning.

We still find teachers in our churches who read the printed lesson materials to their adult classes. That adults continue to attend such classes is for me a strong apologetic for the resurrection power of the Lord! Adults need to confront the compartments of their lives. They need help in dismantling the walls which separate their lives into boxes—to move from pew-sitting spectator to ministering participant in the Lord's work.

We find teachers who do little more than baby-sit preschoolers. These children can learn Bible truths if they are taught appropriately for their age.

We find teachers who make young children sit in rows and memorize Bible verses. The abstract concepts of the verses and the lack of concrete application to the real life experiences of children hinder their growth.

We find teachers who lecture youth, telling them stories most of them have heard for years. Teenagers need to be challenged by biblical principles, involved in heart-felt discussions which tie Bible teachings to real life problems.

The bottom line is this: educational psychology offers objective, empirical, scientific insight into the dynamics of the process of learning. We can gain insight from educational psychology without exposing ourselves to any danger of losing our faith.

In this chapter we looked at six ways of knowing. We discussed specifically how scientific knowing differs from the other five. We made a comparison of faith knowing and scientific knowing. Finally, we differentiated Greek and Hebrew mind-sets, and described the problem this causes in Christian teaching.

SUMMARY

CHAPTER CONCEPTS

Authority	Heliocentric
Christian teaching	Inductive reasoning
Closure	Intuition/Revelation
Common sense	Objectivity
Deductive reasoning	Overgeneralization
Empiricism	Personal involvement
Experience	Precision
Geocentric	Replication
Greek mind-set	Selective observation and recall
Hebrew mind-set	Theory construction

DISCUSSION QUESTIONS

1. Describe at least two ways you have gained knowledge.
2. With which side of the "faith" versus "science" debate do you feel most comfortable? Take the other side and prepare a defense.
3. Define in your own words five characteristics of the scientific method.
4. What thoughts or experiences came to mind as you read the material on Greek and Hebrew mind-sets? Which description best describes your lifestyle now?

UNIT 2

The Learner

The learner is central in the teaching-learning process. The importance of the learner outweighs the content to be learned, the teacher who facilitates learning, or the process by which content is communicated. Jesus emphatically underscored the importance of learners in His teaching ministry (see Matt. 20:28; Matt. 16:26). John reinforced the importance of individual learners when he declared that the purpose of his writing was to insure that individuals could learn of Jesus, the Christ, the Son of God, and believe—and that by believing, they would have "life in his name" (John 20:31).

As we begin our journey into the principles and processes of educational psychology, we anchor our efforts in this central truth: the role of Christian teachers is to give themselves away for the good of their learners. Jesus stated this premise quite clearly:

> You know that the rulers of the Gentiles lord it over them, and their high officials exercise authority over them. Not so with you. Instead, whoever wants to become great among you must be your servant, and whoever wants to be first must be your slave—just as the Son of Man did not come to be served, but to serve, and to give his life a ransom for many (Matt. 20:25–28).

First the principle: "To become great, serve." Second, the example of His own life: "the Son of Man, as a ransom for many." My students do not exist to provide me a place to serve. My place to serve exists because of my students. They are not in the classroom for me. I am in the classroom for them. The congregation does not exist to edify the pastor; the pastor exists to edify the congregation. This is the example Jesus left us—the road to greatness as a Kingdom

The role of Christian teachers is to give themselves away for the good of their learners

citizen. So the fine-tuned focus of Christian teachers must be their students.

Who are these individuals who sit before us in classrooms and sanctuaries? How did they come to be who they are? What experiences do they carry with them? In what ways have they been shaped by life's forces? What prejudices do they carry? How open are they to learning?

These questions point to realities in the teaching-learning process overlooked by many teachers. An adult teacher once said, "The church didn't elect me to be a social worker or counselor. I'm to teach the Word of God, 9:45 on Sunday morning. So, don't expect me to visit or call my members. My job is to teach. That's it." Teachers like this may present lessons. They may fill Bible study or preaching time. But they will do little in the way of ministering to classes or congregations, of intersecting lives and helping believers grow in the Lord. The next four chapters focus on key issues regarding the nature of our learners.

Chapter 3

How We Develop as Social Beings

Erik Erikson's Theory of Personality Development

Chapter 4

How We Develop as Thinkers

Jean Piaget's Theory of Cognitive Development

Chapter 5

How We Develop as Moral Thinkers

Lawrence Kohlberg's Theory of

Moral Reasoning Development

James Fowler's Theory of

Faith Development

Chapter 6

Instructional Objectives

Setting Up Targets for Teaching

3

HOW WE DEVELOP
AS SOCIAL BEINGS

ERIK ERIKSON'S PSYCHOSOCIAL THEORY
OF PERSONALITY DEVELOPMENT

Teaching is a highly personal, social process. The ability of teacher and learner to relate to each other, to dialogue, to participate together in learning experiences determines the outcome. Erik Erikson's theory of Psychosocial development provides fundamental insights into the development of human personality and how that development can facilitate or hinder learning. Christians live in a real world and are not immune to the effects of abuse or neglect on their own personalities.

CHAPTER RATIONALE

Learners will demonstrate knowledge of Erikson's theory by matching stages of development with their respective definitions.

CHAPTER OBJECTIVES

Learners will demonstrate understanding of Erikson's theory by explaining selected terms in their own words.

Learners will demonstrate understanding of Erikson's theory by creating church-related case studies reflecting a given stage.

Learners will demonstrate an appreciation for spiritual growth by sharing how Christ has replaced a specific "fractured stage" with wholeness in their own lives.

HISTORICAL ROOTS

"Stop treating children in ways that mangle them" —Freud

Before Sigmund Freud's work in personality theory, circa 1900, children six years of age and younger were thought to be mindless creatures. They were thought to be too young to know or experience anything of substance.[1]

Through the clinical research of adults suffering from personality disorders, Freud discovered that much of personality development seemed to occur in the first six years of life. This is the basis for his famous saying, "The child is the father of the man."[2] Freud's ideas were shocking. Partly due to his radical ideas of child psychology, and partly for his emphasis on sexual drives and fantasies, he was feared and hated. His message? Parents must stop treating their children in ways that mangle them. In spite of popular opposition to his ideas, Freud demonstrated that significant parts of our emotional and personal development are formed during the first six years of life. His work gave clear support to the old adage, "As the twig is bent, so grows the oak."

Freud divided the first six years of life into three stages, each containing two years. The first he called the "oral stage," which extends from birth through age two. "Oral" refers specifically to breastfeeding, but generally to the quality of care received by the child. Proper care leads to trust and dependence on a stable, caring world. The second stage he called the "anal stage," which extends from two to four years of age. "Anal" refers specifically to toilet training, but generally to issues of self-control, which leads to independence. The third stage he called the "phallic stage," which extends from five to seven years of age. "Phallic" refers specifically to the discovery of sexual identity. Freud hypothesized a latency period until adolescence, at which time the adult character is formed from a synthesis of the previous stages.[3]

Erikson was a student of Freud, but believed his theory's focus was too narrow. Psychoanalytic theory, which fixes adult personality parameters at age six, was too deterministic for Erikson. He preferred a broader, more balanced, framework including stages through childhood and adolescence to adulthood. Further, Freud emphasized the negative aspects of personality. Erikson preferred balance between positive and negative aspects of each stage. Finally, Freud emphasized the sexual aspect of human nature in driving personality development, a psychosexual theory. Erikson included cultural and social factors in the developmental process, a psychosocial theory.

Erik Erikson was born in Frankfurt, Germany, on June 12, 1902. Shortly after his birth, his parents separated. About three years later, Erikson's mother married his pediatrician, Dr. Theodore Homburger. Through his childhood, he carried the name Erik Homburger.

ERIK ERIKSON

When eventually told of his real father, his own struggle with role confusion and identity problems began. These early experiences became the driving force behind his later thinking.

His role confusion was demonstrated in the years after he left high school before graduating. He traveled around Europe, enrolling in art schools. After three years in two art schools he moved to Florence and joined a group of young artists. He soon gained a reputation as a portrait artist, particularly for his portraits of children. A major turning point in his life occurred in 1933 when he was invited to a villa in Vienna, Austria, to paint a child's portrait. When he arrived, he met the child's father, Sigmund Freud.

A few weeks later, Erikson received an invitation from Freud to enroll in the Psychoanalytic Institute in Vienna. There he found his vocational identity as a child psychoanalyst. He did such outstanding work that he was given full status upon graduation, rather than the usual associate status. In 1936, as Hitler gained power in Germany, Erikson and his family emigrated to the United States.

He took a teaching and research position at Yale University. In 1939, he moved to the University of California at Berkeley and worked with a research team involved in a longitudinal study of child development. He studied American Indian tribes, normal and abnormal children, and soldiers returning from World War II. These experiences convinced Erikson of the importance of social and cultural factors in personality development.

In 1950, he wrote his first book, *Childhood and Society,* in which he introduced the Eight Ages of Man. His theory was adopted this same year by a White House Conference on Children. Other books include *Identity and the Life Cycle* (1959, 1980), *Insight and Responsibility* (1964), *Identity: Youth and Crisis* (1968), and *Vital Involvement in Old Age* (1986).

Erikson died on May 12, 1994, at the age of 91. The *New York Times* (May 12, 1994) noted in its obituary that Erikson's theory "represented a quantum leap in Freudian thought, suggesting that the ego and the sense of identity are shaped over the entire lifespan and that experiences later in life might help heal the hurts of early childhood."[A]

Erikson likened the development of personality to that of a baby in the womb. All the major subsystems of a human child are present in the first weeks of the pregnancy. But there are critical periods, or stages, in which the various subsystems develop best. Erikson held that the personality developed in the same way. Not randomly, but by design. Not automatically, but by a built-in drive toward a more complex system. This potential for personality growth he referred to as the *epigenetic principle*.[4] If there exists healthy interaction with others, and if the basic crisis is resolved appropriately, then the child is ready for the next stage. If the crisis is not resolved, it will become increasingly difficult to resolve it in the future.[5]

THE PRENATAL
FOUNDATION
FOR DEVELOPMENT

A key term for Erikson is "vital involvement."[6] By this he refers to the central truth of his theory: the development of personality as a result of interaction between the individual (psyche-) and the environment (-social). The basis for all development occurs before birth, as the individual (baby) pushes against the environment (the womb), and is limited by the environment. Listen to Erikson:

> But nothing could better clarify [vital involvement's] "original" meaning than a built-in linguisitic alliteration, for involvement is related to the prenatal containment in our mother's vulva, where, modern research suggests, *we were not just passively wrapped up but already had to prove our truly "inborn" capacity for involvement, which means our being alive,* by stimulating the "environment" as it stimulates us; for as we become vitally involved, we are also challenging the "environment" to involve us in convincing ways. *It is this psychological and social e-volve-ment that is newly extended in each stage of life,*

at first in close relations to the psychobiological growth that dictates the basic sequence of step-by-step development.[7] [italics mine]

Here Erikson clearly declares that the development of human personality, over the entire life cycle, is based on the individual pushing ever outward into the environment. This interaction, the very heart of personality development, begins before birth. This fundamental truth, this essential beginning, this central maxim, is nowhere to be found in contemporary educational psychology texts. Watch the pattern through the stages as the ever-growing individual interacts with an ever-growing environment. The various subsystems of the personality develop in eight specific stages.

Personality development can move in a positive, healthy direction or a negative, unhealthy direction. The desired outcome of each stage is to develop positive characteristics: trust, autonomy, initiative, industry, identity, intimacy, generativity, and integrity. Abusive influences can produce negative characteristics: mistrust, shame and doubt, guilt, inferiority, role confusion, isolation, stagnation, and despair. These eight positive/negative characteristics form the eight stages of personality growth.

Erikson's first stage begins at birth and extends to age two.[9] During this time children are totally dependent on adults for their care. The kind of care they receive determines their fundamental dispositions toward others.[10] The positive resolution of this stage is trust, a result of consistent, regular care for the child's basic needs. Infants who are touched, held, loved, fed and kept dry develop feelings of contentment and trust in those who care for them. In general, people who trust others are happier, better adjusted, and better liked than those who lack trust in others.[11]

The negative resolution of this stage is mistrust, the result of inadequate care, neglect, or abuse. Children who are not cared for adequately during the first two years of life develop deep-seated feelings of fear, suspicion, and hurt concerning the world around them. These feelings follow such children into adulthood as paranoia and insecurity.[12]

Ages two and three form Erikson's second stage. During this time, children begin doing things on their own, such as feeding and dressing themselves.[14] They crawl, walk, run and climb. In general, they change from helpless infants to self-controlled children.[15]

The positive resolution of this stage is autonomy, a sense of independence from Mom and Dad, of being able to do things "my own

THE EIGHT STAGES OF DEVELOPMENT

Stage 1: Trust/Mistrust Goal: Optimism, Security, Trust in Others Based on Satisfaction of Basic Needs[8]

"I can *depend* on you"

Stage 2: Autonomy/ Shame and Doubt Goal: Self-Reliance, Dealing with Setbacks Based on Setting Limits Without Blame or Rejection[13]

way" within limits.[16] Of course, toilet training is the best known example of this, but a larger issue is that adults begin imposing rules and expectations which call for self-control and self-denial.[17] If parents handle these situations appropriately, children can adjust without losing their sense of personal autonomy.[18] Emphasis should be placed on advice, reassurance, and confidence.[19]

"I can do it *myself*"

The negative resolution of this stage is shame and doubt, the result of parents who make too many demands or who force issues too early. When parents are overly restrictive or punish minor accidents, when they emphasize threats and punishments, when they smother their children with help,[20] children can develop a sense of shame at their own failures and begin to doubt their capabilities.[21] They do not develop a sense of personal autonomy and self-control, but feel completely dependent on the parents who control them. They lack confidence in their own power to deal with the world.[22] As adults they may experience difficulties in self-concept and impulse control.[23] They may exhibit frequent procrastination, the need for direction and structure, embarrassment when complimented, and a tendency to be easily influenced by others.[24]

Stage 3:
Initiative/Guilt
Goal: Initiative in Exploring the Environment Based on Tolerance, Encouragement, and Reinforcement[25]

Ages four and five form Erikson's third stage. During this time, children want to expand their world of experience. With a proper sense of autonomy, children push to explore and investigate their own capabilities. They want to "help" their parents, and need assurance that their help is welcome. They are curious and "into everything."[26]

The positive resolution of this stage is initiative, producing children who attack a task, who use their freedom to appropriately explore their expanding world and ask questions. Fours and fives like to show off and try new things. If they are supported and treated warmly during this time, and given guidance from parents concerning appropriate and inappropriate exploration,[27] they are likely to develop confidence in undertaking new challenges.[28]

"Into *everything*"

Stage 4:
Industry/Inferiority
Goal: Mastering the Developmental Tasks of Childhood Based on Success and Recognition of Progress[32]

The negative resolution of this stage is guilt, the result of parents who reject or punish the self-initiated activities of their children.[29] Guilt leaves children inhibited and afraid to try new things on their own.[30] Adults who fail to resolve this stage are easily depressed, self-abasive, and tend to have a low energy level.[31]

The elementary years, ages six to eleven, form Erikson's fourth stage.[33] Children turn outward from home base to the neighborhood and school, expanding their social environment from family to

Erikson's Eight Stages of Personality Development

Infancy	Trust	Mistrust
Early Childhood	Autonomy	Shame & Doubt
Play Age	Initiative	Guilt
School Age	Industry	Inferiority
Adolescence	Identity	Role Confusion
Young Adulthood	Intimacy	Isolation
Adulthood	Generativity	Stagnation
Old Age	Integrity	Despair

Adapted from Erikson, Vital Involvement, p. 36

friends. The key focus of the child is developing physical, emotional, and academic skills.

The positive resolution of stage four is industry, which garners recognition for successful doing, producing a general "can-do" attitude. Teachers help children negotiate this stage by engaging them in learning activities appropriate for their age and abilities, by helping them successfully complete the activities, and by praising them for their effort. Success leads to success in an upward spiral.[34] Skill-development is an enjoyable adventure.[35]

The negative resolution of this stage is inferiority, which develops as a result of unsuccessful experiences.[36] Children who are unable to produce, perhaps due to fractures in their earlier stages, fall farther behind in development because they do not have the emotional fortitude to attack a task, nor stay with a task, that they've been assigned. Failure to perform often brings derision from teachers or other children. Repeated requests for special help can make them more a bother than a blessing to harmonious classroom activities. Children easily pick up on teacher frustrations, and can move deeper into self-doubt and inferiority. Adults who fail to resolve this stage tend to be timid and overly obedient. They tend to be observers more than producers and frequently question their own abilities.[37]

The years of adolescence, approximately ages twelve to eighteen, form the fifth stage in Erikson's theory.[39] During this time, adolescents undergo major physical, emotional, social, and psychological

Stage 5:
Identity/Role Confusion
Goal: A Satisfying Sense of Personal Identity and Direction Based on Social Acceptance and Recognition[38]

changes. In fact, "change" is the key word of this stage, the most radical of the eight.[40] Adolescents are caught in the turbulent no-man's-land between the dependency of childhood and the interdependence of adulthood. The major questions they seek to answer are "Who am I?" and "Where am I going?"[41] During this time they begin to question the value system, beliefs, and attitudes they received from their parents, because they discover, to their shock, that adults are not always right.[42] The resolution of this stage determines to a great extent the basis for adult personality.[43]

"Who am I?
Where am I going?"

The positive resolution of this stage is identity, which produces a sense of being at home with oneself, a feeling of stability, of knowing who one is and what one will do with life. Fads, clothes, music, hairstyles, and special code words form part of the experimentation of this stage. Identity comes from reactions from significant others—parents, friends, respected teachers—as well as the choices adolescents make in role models. Adolescents need firm, caring adults who understand them and listen to them while providing security by enforcing limits of acceptable behavior.[44]

The negative resolution of this stage is role confusion, which is reflected in teenagers' sense of confusion about the future, worries about what they will become, what they'll do, who they'll marry: it is a basic uncertainty about who they are.[45] Sprinthall contends that Western culture has complicated the resolution of this stage because we have overextended dependency through the college years.[46]

The confusing mix of internal changes (glands, feelings, and perceptions) and external inconsistencies (rules and expectations) makes this stage the most difficult of the eight. James Marcia has suggested four basic outcomes of this stage, which he calls identity statuses.[47]

Research findings of James Marcia identify two major components of identity resolution. The first is whether or not the adolescent has experienced an identity crisis. The second is whether or not a commitment has been made. These two components combine to form four possible identity statuses. The chart on the next page summarizes the four.

The first status is called identity *achievement*. Adolescents who reach identity achievement have experienced a crisis of identity, explored options, and chosen, for themselves, who they are and what they'll do.[48] Adolescents in identity achievement tend to be less self-

conscious, more open to others, enjoy better communication with their parents, and
are more assertive.

The second status is called identity *moratorium*. Adolescents in moratorium are in
crisis, but have yet to make firm commitments concerning their personal identity.

The third status is called identity *foreclosure*. Adolescents in foreclosure have
not experienced an identity crisis. The
commitments they have are based on the
expectations of others: parents, teachers,
significant friends.

The fourth status is called identity *diffusion*. Adolescents in identity diffusion
have not experienced an identity crisis, nor
have they any firm commitment or direction for their lives.[49]

Adults who do not resolve this stage
lack confidence and tend to reject authority. They doubt their own sex role.[50] Establishing a "whole" identity is crucial for
developing healthy relationships with others.

Based on Dembo, p. 442

The years of young adulthood, beginning about age eighteen and
extending to thirty, form the sixth stage in Erikson's theory. During
this stage adults resolve the issue of giving themselves to others.
Having resolved personal identity issues, the young adult confronts
the crisis of intimate relationships with others.

The positive resolution of this stage is intimacy, which results in
the ability of one individual to form an intimate relationship with another. Our society has redefined "intimacy" in a sexual context—indeed, newer educational psychology texts emphasize multiple
sexual relationships. Dembo identifies this stage as "sexual union
and close friendship"[52] and Good defines intimacy as "long-term
sexual relationships.[53] Erikson had marriage foremost in mind—an
individual finding one significant other to give self to, giving for the
sake of giving, expecting nothing.[54] But we can also see in this stage
the hunger of young adults for social interaction as part of this

*Stage 6:
Intimacy/Isolation
Goal: The Ability to
Maintain Intimate
Personal Relationships
Based on Personal
Openness and Confi-
dence Plus Rewarding
Experiences with
Intimate Others*[51]

developmental process. Intimacy basically refers to personal relationships based on openness and mutual confidence.

"Two *I*'s become one *us*"

The negative resolution of this stage is isolation. Those who failed to resolve previous stages positively—becoming trusting, autonomous, confident individuals—have difficulty relating to others, sharing with others, or giving themselves to others. They move away from social intercourse and toward personal segregation, seclusion, and loneliness. Young adults become emotionally isolated, unable to give or receive love freely.[55]

A common criticism of Erikson's work is its male orientation. His theory is based on his own (male) experiences in development—particularly his difficulty in resolving what he later called the identity/role confusion crisis. More recent research indicates that males and females achieve identity differently. Males tend to be intrapersonal in forming their identity. That is, they look within themselves, to their own skills and competencies, to define who they are. Females tend to be interpersonal in forming their identity. They find themselves in the context of others. This means men tend to form their identity before moving into the intimacy/isolation stage; women tend to form deep personal relationships, out of which they form their personal identity.[56]

Stage 7: Generativity/Stagnation Goal: Developing Interest in Others: Family, Community, the World Based on a Rewarding Personal Life[57]

The middle adult years, ranging roughly between thirty and sixty-five, form the seventh stage in Erikson's theory. This stage, by far the longest, involves the crises of caring for aging parents, parenting and teaching children, and giving oneself to community concerns.[58]

The positive resolution of this stage is generativity, which results in adults who give themselves in guiding the next generation. Erikson emphasized the family context, "the interest in establishing and guiding the next generation"[59] where parents lovingly pass on their values and priorities to their children.[60] Beyond the family, however, generative adults care about their communities[61] and want to work toward bettering their society.[62] Generative adults are creative, productive, and engaged in teaching children.[63]

"Sharing self with others

The negative resolution of this stage is stagnation, or self-absorption. Rather than giving themselves to others, self-absorbed adults tend to hoard their possessions and gifts. They become self-centered.[64] They possess little interest in improving themselves or making a contribution to others.[65] Stagnation sets in and produces boredom and apathy.[66] Self-absorbed adults cannot find any meaning or purpose in life,[67] outside of self-indulgence.[68]

The resolution of this longest stage is crucial to the healthy approach of life's end.

The years of senior adulthood, beginning at retirement, form the final stage in Erikson's theory. During this stage, adults reflect on their lives and accomplishments as they move toward death.[70]

The positive resolution of this stage is integrity, which produces a general feeling of well-being, a satisfaction with life,[71] an acceptance of what they have done and who they are, failures and limitations included.[72] There is a sense of dignity and wholeness in one's life.

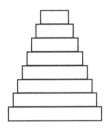

How different is despair, the negative resolution of this stage. Those who cannot resolve this stage appropriately look back at life in self-contempt and desperation.[73] They regret the things still undone and worry that time is running out.[74] They harbor bitterness at the shortness of life and the fact that they cannot start over. "If only I'd . . . " might best illustrate the despair of senior adulthood.

These eight bipolar stages form Erikson's original theory and reflect what you'll find in many educational psychology texts. Few writers move into Erikson's later work, which he formalized in *Vital Involvement in Old Age* (1986). These later insights are fascinating.

Erikson's early work left the impression that the positive resolution of each stage leads to healthy personalities. That is, parents and teachers should strive to build trust in infants (trust/mistrust) in order to avoid mistrust.

Erikson later wrote, however, that an unhealthy imbalance can occur on either pole of a stage. The positive pole ("trust" in trust/mistrust) he called a *syntonic* disposition. The negative pole ("mistrust") he called a *dystonic* disposition. Too much emphasis on the syntonic disposition can produce as much an unhealthy resolution of a developmental crisis as too much on the dystonic disposition.[75] That is, one can be too trusting, or too autonomous. Each stage possesses unhealthy extremes and a healthy balance. Erikson called imbalance toward the positive pole maladaptive, and imbalance toward the negative pole malignant. Clinicians would suggest that the first

Stage 8:
Integrity/Despair
Goal: Satisfaction with the Past and Readiness for the Future
Based on Resolving the First Seven Stages[69]

ERIKSON'S LATER WORK: MALADAPTIONS, MALIGNANCIES, AND STRENGTHS

would more likely cause a neurotic disturbance and the latter a psychotic disturbance,
requiring more radical intervention.[76]

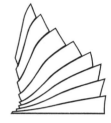

The balance between the syntonic and
dystonic dispositions produces the healthy
resolution to each developmental crisis.
Erikson calls this healthy resolution an adap-
tive strength.[77] The words used to describe the eight strengths refer,
Erikson admits, to adult characteristics which are eventually produced by healthy resolutions of each stage. But this is simply because the original experiences cannot be described in words.[78]

Let's look briefly at the extremes and the balance of each stage.

Stage 1:
Sensory Maladjustment
vs. Withdrawal: Hope

Trust taken to the extreme leads to sensory maladjustment. Parents may overdevelop trust in an attempt to avoid mistrust. "Over-
care" may produce "overcompliance" in older infants.[79] That is,
overprotective parents can produce an unhealthy dependency in
their children. These children may grow into adults who exhibit
characteristics of naivete and gullibility, who seek others whom they
can depend on to care for them.

"Hope: realistic trust"

Mistrust taken to the extreme leads to withdrawal. Long term neglect and outright abuse can produce a "pathological impact"[80]
which moves the infant beyond mistrust into withdrawal—a malignant avoidance of involvement with others.[81] These children may
grow into adults who exhibit characteristics of suspicion and paranoia of others. They enjoy provoking conflict because it both bol-
sters their own sense of power and drives others away.

The healthy resolution of trust/mistrust is hope, which Erikson
defines as "the enduring belief in the benevolence of fate, in spite of
dark urges and rages that also mark the beginning of existence." As
such, hope is the "basis of faith," brought about by the initial patterns of maternal care.[82] This sense of hope might be described as realistic trust in others.

Stage 2:
Shamelessness vs.
Compulsion: Will

Autonomy taken to an extreme leads to shamelessness and will-
fulness. Parents may overdevelop the sense of autonomy in an attempt to avoid shaming their children with rules and restrictions.
Such children may assert their own wants in a willful manner, without an appropriate sense of propriety. There is little or no self-
restraint.

"Will: Self-regulated
free choice"

Shame and doubt taken to an extreme lead to compulsive self-
doubt. When parents consistently and severely punish children for

minor infractions, when they personally shame and belittle them, they move children beyond mere shame and doubt to the place of malignant and compulsive self-doubt.[83] Such children lack any sense of determination to assert themselves.

The healthy resolution of autonomy/shame and doubt is will, which Erikson defines as "the unbroken determination to exercise free choice as well as self-restraint." A maturing will forms the basis for the "eventual acceptance of law and necessity."[84] This sense of will might be described as self-regulated free choice, the "beginnings of a sense of identity."[85]

Initiative taken to an extreme leads to ruthlessness. The initiative of children must be balanced by a capacity for guilt; otherwise they will extend themselves beyond the bounds of acceptable social behavior. Not all guilt is bad. True guilt warns of excessive or offending behavior, much as an automotive engine light might warn of engine problems. Without appropriate guilt feelings, children can become ruthless in their actions toward authority and other children.

Stage 3: Ruthlessness vs. Inhibition: Purpose

Too much guilt—and, in particular, false guilt—can lead children to develop a malignant sense of self-inhibition. The fear of punishment or false guilt imposed by adults can cause children to seek the shadows within their own internal world.

"Purpose: Constrained pursuit"

The healthy resolution of initiative-guilt is purpose, which Erikson defines as "the courage to envisage and pursue valued goals uninhibited by the defeat of infantile phantasies, by an imposed sense of guilt, and by the fear of punishment." Purpose is the basis for later ideals of action.[86]

Industry taken to an extreme leads to narrow virtuosity. Narrow virtuosity results when "the whole child" is channeled into an almost obsessive practice of a limited set of skills. [87] These skills can focus on a favorite subject in school, or dreams of Olympic Gold. The maladaption grows as balanced industry gives way to obsession.

Stage 4: Narrow Virtuosity vs. Inertia: Competence

Inferiority taken to an extreme leads to inertia. Repeated failure to complete tasks, the perceived inability to develop required skills over time, may lead to the malignant state of inertia, the "habitual inclination toward a sense of inferiority."[88]

"Competence: Wholesome mastery"

The healthy resolution of industry/inferiority is competence, which Erikson defines as "the free exercise of dexterity and intelligence in the completion of tasks, unimpaired by a forever threatening sense of inferiority." Competence becomes the basis for "cooperative participation in technologies and relies, in turn, on the logic of tools and skills."[89] This sense of competence might be described as mastering new skills with confidence.

Stage 5:
Fanaticism vs.
Repudiation: Fidelity

Identity taken to an extreme leads to fanaticism. In the search for self, the central crisis for Erikson, adolescents are influenced by adult role models, "whether present and active among the young person's mentors or apparent on the horizon as heroes and leaders."[90] If adolescents fixate on a role model, or an ideology, they may be unable to separate their own identity from the ideology. This is fanaticism, a state of being "possessed with or motivated by excessive, irrational zeal."[91]

"Fidelity:
True to self
True to others"

Role confusion taken to an extreme leads to repudiation. Too much confusion and contradiction between role models and ideologies can lead to a malignant "repudiation [rejecting, disowning] of otherness."[92]

The healthy resolution of identity/role confusion is fidelity, which Erikson defines as "the ability to sustain loyalties freely pledged in spite of the inevitable contradictions of value systems." Fidelity is the "cornerstone of identity."[93] This sense of fidelity might be described as becoming true to oneself and to one's own belief system within the context of others.

Stage 6:
Promiscuity vs.
Exclusivity: Love

Intimacy taken to an extreme leads to promiscuity. Young adults may experiment with others in their ever-widening environment. These experiments may include trial friendships and short-term sexual relationships. The self-serving nature of these alliances, coupled with a lack of long-term commitment, leads to the maladaption of promiscuity.

"Love:
Committed intimacy"

Isolation taken to an extreme leads to exclusivity. Young adults may fail to establish meaningful relationships. Perhaps imbalances in earlier stages—inability to trust, lack of initiative, incompetence, self-doubt—sabotage these efforts. Whatever the cause, young adults may move beyond isolation into the malignancy of "hate-filled exclusivity."[94]

The healthy resolution of intimacy/isolation is love, which Erikson defines as "the mutuality of devotion forever subduing the antagonisms inherent in divided function." Love is the "capacity for eventual commitment to lasting friendships and companionship in general, and [a long-term sexual relationship in particular]. Love is the basis for ethical concern."[95] This sense of love might be described as a personal commitment to another, as in marriage, and to others, as in devoted friendships.

Generativity taken to an extreme leads to overextension. The desire to "take care of what one truly cares for"[96] can become maladaptive when caring exceeds the capacity for including others. Simply stated, overextension results from being overly involved with one's environment: family, community, and society needs. A more familiar term for this condition is "burnout."

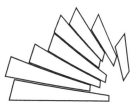

Stagnation taken to an extreme leads to rejectivity. Adults who habitually choose not to give to others, who consistently choose to care for their personal needs and desires alone, can move beyond stagnation into the malignant rejectivity—a condition in which adults "do not care to care—for anybody."[97]

The healthy resolution of generativity/stagnation is care, which Erikson defines as "the widening concern for what has been generated by love, necessity, or accident; it overcomes the ambivalence arising with irreversible obligation." Care is the basis for attending to the needs of what has been generated.[98] This sense of care might be described as the responsible nurturing of children and youth, as well as appropriate and constructive involvement with one's community and society at large.

Integrity taken to an extreme leads to presumption. The last stage of life is reflective, providing a time for integrating all the stages of life. Such integration includes elements of despair—past failures, decisions which might have been made differently, and, of course, the inescapable fact of death.[99] When integration ignores the negatives of life, adults may move into the maladaptive disposition of presuming to be larger than life. Prejudice and lack of humility and humor characterize adults who presume to know more than they do.[100]

Despair taken to an extreme leads to disdain. With old age, the environment closes around us: the loss of old friends, the loss of freedom and mobility, the loss of physical abilities. Those who are unable to maintain involvement in the face of natural limitations—Erikson uses the term "involved disinvolvement"[101]—move toward a malignant disdain for life itself.

The healthy resolution of integrity/despair is wisdom, which Erikson defines as "the detached concern with life itself, in the face of death itself. It maintains and learns to convey the integrity of

Stage 7:
Overextension vs.
Rejectivity: Care

"Care:
Responsible nurture"

Stage 8:
Presumption vs.
Disdain: Wisdom

"Wisdom:
Satisfied reflection"

Erikson's Adaptive Strengths

Maladaptive	Adaptive Strength	Malignant
Sensory Maladjustment	HOPE	Withdrawal
Shamelessness/Willfulness	WILL	Compulsion
Ruthlessness	PURPOSE	Inhibition
Narrow Virtuosity	COMPETENCE	Inertia
Fanaticism	FIDELITY	Repudiation
Promiscuity	LOVE	Exclusivity
Overextension	CARE	Rejectivity
Presumption	WISDOM	Disdain

Adapted from Erikson, Vital Involvement, *p. 45*

experience, in spite of the decline of bodily and mental functions."[102] This sense of wisdom might be described as the satisfying perception of a life fitly lived.

A Moment of Reflection

We began this lengthy section with Erikson's fundamental precept: the prenatal interactive stimulation between infant and womb forms the basis for human personality development. We have seen how each stage of development, each crisis, revolves around personal interaction with an ever-widening environment: from womb to mother, to father and siblings, to playmates, to schoolmates, to significant role models, to intimate friends and life partners, and finally to community, society, and the world at large. The final stage revolves around positive healthy interaction with a collapsing environment.

CRITICISMS OF
ERIKSON'S THEORY

There are four aspects of Erikson's theory which have drawn criticism through the years. We have already noted the differences in identity formation between males and females. A major criticism of Erikson is that his theory focuses on male development.[103] Sprinthall explains this as a natural extension of the male-oriented culture in which Erikson developed.[104] For example, Erikson focuses on "competence" as the important outcome of the industry/inferiority stage. Research shows this is true for boys, who tend to focus on skills. It is less true for girls, who focus on relationships as well as competence.[105]

A second criticism is that the elements of Erikson's theory are vague and difficult to test. How can researchers empirically study the factors which cause conflict resolution? What is the operational definition of "initiative" or "isolation"?

A third criticism is that Erikson's theory is based more on his own subjective and personal interpretations of personality development than research data. Such subjectiveness limits empirical checks on his theory.

Finally, several stages are very similar. Autonomy, initiative, and industry all focus on "doing things on your own." Doubt, guilt, and inferiority all focus on "the need for sympathetic parental support."

Despite these criticisms, Erikson's theory clarifies important aspects of human development.[106]

Why should Christians be concerned about human growth and development? After all, Paul wrote to the Corinthians, "Therefore, if anyone is in Christ, he is a new creation; the old has gone, the new has come!" (2 Cor. 5:17). If we are a "new creation" in Christ, and if "the old" has gone, why bother with human conceptions of personality development?

The answer is found, first, in the thrust of Paul's message. What does it mean to be a "new creation"? And to what does "the old" refer? Paul is referring to the spiritual truth that one who has come into vital union with Christ has been radically transformed. Believers see the world differently. Their outlook is changed from "the old" self-centeredness and perversion of the past. Paul does not imply that believers are instantaneously transformed into healthy, whole human personalities. His letters contain explicit testimonies of his concern for Christian growth and maturing as believers take off the "old garments" and put on the "new" (Col. 3:8–12) in the social context of the church (recall the center pillar and capstone in chapter 1).

The answer is found, secondly, in practical experience. Not all bad habits are defeated upon conversion. There is faith. And then there is growth. There is the learning of self-denial and discipline, hated words to the self-centered, but words of freedom and release to the faithful. Within this context of growth, there is room for the insights which Erikson provides. Do we have difficulty trusting others? Are we shackled by shame or doubt? Do we possess a "natural"

IMPLICATIONS FOR CHRISTIANS

"Difficulty trusting others?"

"Shackled by shame or doubt?"

"Possess a 'natural' inferiority?"

"Fractured by unhealthy role models?"

"Seeking isolation not fellowship?"

"Afraid to give self away to others?"

feeling of inferiority? Have we been fractured by unhealthy role models? Do we find ourselves seeking isolation rather than fellowship? Are we afraid to give ourselves away to others? Erikson provides a way of perceiving these difficulties in the context of life experiences.

It is never God's will that children be abused. When they are, these children carry emotional, psychological, and relational scars through life. Mistrust, shame, guilt, inferiority, role confusion, isolation, stagnation, despair—all of these hinder the growth of individuals toward wholeness. Can Christ overcome these experiences? Can He heal the wounds? Of course, He can. You have most likely experienced some of the negatives in Erikson's stages. What is your testimony concerning His healing in your own life?

Part of the teaching ministry of the church is accepting people where they are and leading them to be all that God intended. Such leadership requires teachers who understand the process of growth and who, by God's grace, can help undo the damage.

IMPLICATIONS FOR TEACHING IN THE CHURCH

Let's list some of the key implications of Erikson for teaching in the local church. *As hard as some of the examples may be to believe, they are all true situations.*

1. Infants

Bed babies need to be cared for, nurtured, and loved by those who are responsible for them. They need to be held. They need to be fed when they are hungry. They need to be kept dry. Such actions, carried out in a consistent and cheerful manner, help infants trust their world. Long before children have words with which to express their feelings, they experience the world around them. The experiences of infants in church set the emotional stage, at the deepest level, for life.

Therefore, churches should endeavor to offer consistent care for infants by the same nurturing adults, rather than provide a perpetual rotation of strange faces in the nursery. Men, as well as women, should be enlisted to care for infants.[107]

A local church was experiencing a growth in young couples. Along with the young couples came several infants. The church decided to expand its nursery facilities. Several adults, not wanting to give up their ground-floor classroom, suggested that the nursery could be relocated in the basement. You investigate the basement location and find it damp and musty. You recommend that the nursery be placed in the ground-floor room, and that the adults meet in the basement. The teacher of the class remarks, "Why should adults put up with the dampness and bad smell of the basement? Babies'll never know the difference." How would you respond?

Twos and Threes need freedom to explore and experiment with their environment. Learning centers provide a wholesome environment in which to "freely" explore within limits: they provide a variety of activities, all centered on a single theme, all staffed with prepared teachers. They balance firmness and permissiveness. They set reasonable limits, but give the children freedom within those limits.[108]

2. Twos and Threes

Twos and threes should be encouraged to make choices and act on those choices.[109] But the choices should be limited only to acceptable alternatives. Compare the following scenarios of Timmy, a three year old, getting ready for church:

Scenario One:

On Sunday morning Timmy appears dressed in his favorite blue jeans and soccer shirt. (He dug them out of the dirty clothes, where they've been since last night.) "Mommy! Look! Timmy dood it! Timmy dood it!"

Mom (with angry face): "Timmy! You can't go to church dressed like that! Those clothes are *filthy*! What is *wrong* with you, anyway! Now you march yourself right back in that room and I'll be in to help you in a minute!"

Timmy hangs his head, slumps his shoulders, and walks heavily back to his room.

Scenario Two:

Mom: "Timmy, it's time to get dressed. Put this on."

Timmy: "NO . . . NO want to!"

Mom: "I don't have time to argue with you. Put this on.

And hurry! We're late for church!"

Scenario Three:

Timmy appears dressed in his favorite blue jeans and soccer shirt. (He dug them out of the dirty clothes, where they've been since last night.) "Mommy! Look! Timmy dood it! Timmy dood it!"

Mom: "Oh, Timmy, Look at you! You dressed yourself! What a big boy you're getting to be! That would be fine if you were going outside to play, but we're going to church. Let's go look at some church clothes."

Limit appropriate choices. Balance firmness and permissiveness. Set reasonable limits. Consider another case:

A couple visited a new church with their three-year-old daughter. The father accompanied her to her assigned Sunday school class. There he found fifteen children seated in two rows for "opening assembly." For forty-five minutes, the teacher led them in a Bible memory exercise, read them a Bible story, and suggested several ways they might apply the lesson to their lives. After the class, the father learned that this session was typical of her approach to teaching three-year-olds.

Knowing what you do from Erikson, how would you evaluate this teacher's approach?

3. Fours and Fives

Fours and Fives require age appropriate activities to encourage participation and success. Expect lots of questions. Help children develop a sense of accomplishment.[110] This stage revolves around the child's growth of power; that is, the ability to make things happen.[111]

Help the child experience success by teaching new activities in small steps. Be tolerant of accidents or mistakes. Use utensils that are easy to handle. Recognize the attempts of children, even if their products are unsatisfactory.[112]

Consider this case:

> A five-year-old boy is enrolled in a preschool program known for its discipline. During art class, the teacher tells the children to draw and color a picture of flowers. The boy draws a flower and colors the stem and leaves purple. When the teacher sees his picture, she exclaims, "Who in the world ever saw a flower with purple leaves?! Class, Billy thinks flowers have purple leaves!" The class laughs. "Hold out your hand!" When the boy does, the teacher raps his knuckles three times with a ruler. "The next time I give you an assignment, I expect you to take it seriously!"

What impact do you think this teacher has on her students?

4. Elementary Children

Erikson saw the industry/inferiority stage as "socially a most decisive stage" because children begin doing things beside and with others.[113] Teachers should emphasize helping children complete their learning tasks successfully. They should recognize the efforts and accomplishments of children.[114] Learning should be activity-centered, engaging as many of the senses as possible. Help children set and work toward realistic goals. Monitor the progress of learners. Give opportunities for children to show their independence and responsibility. Support discouraged learners by focusing on improvements and awarding those who are "most helpful" or "most hardworking."[115]

Examine the following case and determine what you would recommend based on Erikson's theory:

> Jeannie is a fourth-grader in Mrs. Jones' Sunday school department. Mrs. Jones has challenged the children with a Scripture memory contest. Each Sunday Mrs. Jones gives the children a key Bible verse to memorize. The next Sunday, children are given a chance to quote the verse. Each time a child successfully quotes a verse, Mrs. Jones awards him or her a bright yellow "smiley face." At the end of thirteen weeks, the children with ten or more smiley faces will be treated to a Saturday picnic.
>
> Jeannie is only able to attend Mrs. Jones department every other week because her parents are divorced—she's with her father on odd weekends. Also,

Jeannie's parents are not Christians. Neither of them encourages her Bible study activities.

At the end of the thirteen weeks, Jeannie has three smiley faces, far short of the ten required. What would you have done to help Jeannie?

5. Youth

Adolescents struggle for identity. This identity flows out of their own appearance, out of the recognition they receive from those who count, and out of their finding a meaningful direction in life. Churches can help teens deal with their role confusion by providing a wide variety of role models for them: older youth, college students, young adults in the church, parents. Help students find resources for working out their personal problems[116]—which might include the pastor, youth minister, professional counselors, and the like.

Role confusion can hinder the best efforts in the teaching ministry of the church. Adolescents are active illustrations of the Greek mindset discussed in chapter 2—trying on this role and then another, trying new fads, rebelling against church and family values, acting out their exaggerated desire for independence and freedom. Such behavior calls for the teacher's highest commitment of self-giving love, listening heart, flexibility of approach, and eagerness to help. Tolerate teenage fads unless they are offensive or hinder the learning environment.[117]

Finally, give teenagers realistic feedback on their behaviors. Focus on the consequences of their choices. Separate persons from the roles they play. For example, consider the following case:

Steve was frustrated. He had come home from a youth ministers' retreat where the role of "Youth Pastor" had been promoted. As the youth minister of his church, he thought of his youth group as a "church within a church," and he was the youth's pastor. As such, he believed he should baptize the youth who accepted Christ; he should decide on Sunday school curricula; he should basically be the center of the church's youth ministry. What is a key disadvantage of this view in light of role confusion?

Now consider this case:

A young man of seventeen visits your youth group. He gives all the signs of having no idea who he is. He attracts attention by misbehaving in class. He cuts up. He makes jokes out of the Bible study. He tries to buddy up with some of the other youth, but with little success. He has no plans for the future—after high school. One Sunday he comes to church dressed like a "roper": blue jeans, khaki shirt, cowboy boots, neckerchief, and a tin of chewing tobacco in his right hip pocket. A few weeks later he comes as a "skate boarder": crew cut, calf length cut-offs, black sneakers. A month later he shows up after church with a few friends. They are dressed in satanist trappings: black clothing, skull-and-crossbones emblems, cultic diagrams and the like. Six months later he returns with his girlfriend—fifteen and obviously pregnant—to discuss marriage. That's the last you see of him. What might have been done by the youth minister, the youth teachers, the youth leaders, to help him out of his confusion and toward identity?

6. Young Adults

Mature young adults seek intimacy with other adults. They have grown out of the dependency stage of childhood. They have properly navigated the rebellious independency of adolescence. Now they seek interdependency with other adults. A high priority in this stage concerns finding a "significant other"—one who will share life's joys and sorrows—for better or worse. But social relationships in general begin to develop during this stage. Churches can help young adults by using teaching methods that encourage discussing issues, sharing experiences, asking questions, and solving problems biblically. Smaller classes (eight to twelve members) permit better interaction than large, lecture-type classes. Social events and ministry projects outside of class deepen meaningful relationships among class members.

Young adults offer a challenge to church leaders, however. Many in this age group have yet to establish their own identity. Instability comes from clashing priorities of personal pleasure, newly acquired family responsibilities, and settling into a meaningful career. "Church" is one box among many. Unless young adults are fluent in church jargon, they may attend Bible study and worship and feel out of place, embarrassed, and confused.

"Jesus sought personal relationships with everyone, regardless of class or disposition. Paul built bridges of relationship so that he might teach others about Christ."

Jesus did not marry, nor was He sexually intimate with anyone. But He "appointed twelve . . . that they might be with him" (Mark 3:14). One day Jesus was told that His mother and brothers were outside the house where He was teaching, wanting to speak to Him. He responded, "'Who is my mother, and who are my brothers?' Pointing to his disciples, he said, 'Here are my mother and my brothers. For whoever does the will of my Father in heaven is my brother and sister and mother'" (Matt. 12:48–50). Jesus established personal relationships with many kinds of people, even when doing so was unaccepted social practice: the Samaritan woman, the Roman centurion, tax collectors Matthew and Zacchaeus, Jairus, ruler of a synagogue and Nicodemus, member of the ruling Sanhedrin. The Scriptures reflect Jesus' amazing ability to be at home with Jew, Gentile or Roman, male or female, mighty or lowly, wealthy or poor, healthy or sick, powerful or weak. He healed the deaf, the blind, the lame, and the leprous. He even healed the ear of Malchus, cut off during Jesus' arrest by the impulsive Peter. Jesus sought open, personal relationships with everyone, regardless of class or disposition.

The Scriptures also provide evidence of Paul's heart for pure intimacy in ministry. He ends his letter to the Romans with personal greetings to close friends and allies (chap. 16). But on a broader scale Paul writes, "I have become all things to all men so that . . . I might save some" (1 Cor. 9:22). Paul built bridges of relationship so that he might teach others about Christ.

> The Young Singles class needs a teacher. Several members of the Sunday school council recommend Tom for the position. When you meet with Tom to discuss this special ministry opportunity, he says, "I would love to teach the group. I've taught young singles before and just love them. The only problem is that I don't have time to plan fellowships and outings and special events. I can teach the class on Sunday morning, but that's it."
>
> How would you respond to Tom's offer, based on Erikson?

The church provides abundant opportunities to median adults for giving to others through ministry, for applying spiritual gifts to earthly needs, for participation and usefulness in God's Kingdom. Church leaders bless members when they "call out the called," helping them match personal gifts with church ministries. This is the New Testament Church, where every believer is a gifted minister, a king, a priest before God, called to service in Jesus' name.

7. Median Adults

For many church members, however, participation means little more than sporadic worship attendance. They sit in the pews and go through the motions, giving less and less, moving inexorably toward stagnation and, eventually, despair.

But generativity is at the heart of the teaching ministry of the church, where adults pass on to preschoolers, children, youth, and younger adults the principles of living in Christ. Jesus possessed integrity at the end of His life, humanly speaking, because He spent His active ministry in generativity: giving Himself away to others. Paul spent his later life not only as a "servant of Christ" (Rom. 1:1), but made himself a "slave to everyone, to win as many as possible" (1 Cor. 9:19). He gave himself away to others through teaching and preaching, through nurturing churches and training pastors. This is generativity.

On the other hand, Judas Iscariot, a zealot, joined the disciples for ulterior motives. His goal was not personal surrender but political power. He was a thief, pilfering from the treasury bag that had been entrusted to him by the disciples (John 12:6). Judas' political motivations and petty thievery demonstrated his self-absorption. King Solomon denied himself nothing. Labor, laughter, pleasure, wine, great projects, slaves, herds, silver and gold, a harem (see Eccles.

"Judas' political motivations and petty thievery demonstrated his self-absorption"

1:3–2:9). "I denied myself nothing my eyes desired; . . .Yet when I surveyed all that my hands had done and what I had toiled to achieve, everything was meaningless, a chasing after the wind; nothing was gained under the sun" (Eccles. 2:10–11). Both demonstrated stagnation in their personality development.

In your church and mine there are people who call themselves Christians, but do little more than fill a pew—and that, too often, only on special occasions. "Twenty percent of the people do eighty percent of the work," the old adage goes. Yet the New Testament tells us that every believer has gifts (Rom. 12:6–11) to be used to edify the church, and every believer is a minister, a priest (1 Pet. 2:9). The whole of the New Testament paints a picture of the Church Triumphant, full grown in Christ, giving itself away so that a lost world can find its way to the Savior. This is generativity!

Part of the teaching ministry of the church involves moving people out of stagnation and into generativity. Some ministers avoid this part of churchwork because it smacks of manipulation and arm-twisting. ("Oh, I'm sure you'll just love teaching our sixth graders.") But helping believers match their gifts with ministry needs provides an unequalled opportunity for personal growth, as stagnation and self-absorption give way to helping others. Paul focuses on this ministry—"preparing God's people for works of service"—as the heart of the work of the pastor-teacher (Eph. 4:12).

> Frank is an up-and-coming pastor. He has a charismatic personality, and makes friends easily. His view of worship is celebrative music and an upbeat message. He is evangelistic in his style, and expects the same of his staff. In an effort to reduce the bureaucracy in the church, he has eliminated most of the church committees and the church council. He has changed the approach of Sunday school from small group study (eighteen classes led by lay teachers) to large group study (two classes led by staff).
>
> Evaluate Frank's perception of pastoral ministry in light of Erikson and Paul.

8. Senior Adults

Churches would do well to remember the leaders of the past, the committed saints of God who gave their lives and substance to build the work thirty, or forty, or fifty years before. Sadly, we tend to forget the past as we look to the future. We look for new mountains to climb rather than reflect on the many mountains already conquered. Churches would do well to use seniors wherever possible, as they are able. These senior adults, once committed leaders in their churches, can languish in the pews—their positions taken by more energetic, more creative, less traditional leaders. Yet these seniors possess a lifetime of experience, a lifetime of spiritual growth, and are living longer, better, and more productively than at any other time in history.

One of the best ways to help seniors properly integrate their lives in stage eight is to help them enjoy success in giving to others in stage seven. A fruitful ministry in Jesus' name, accomplished in His power, centered on His people, founded on His Word prepares the way for integrity in the twilight years of life.

**"It is finished!"
Jesus
"I have finished
my race!"
Paul**

> Carroll retired at age sixty-five, after forty-five years in the ministry. He had served numerous churches as pastor, plus the last twenty years of ministry as an associational missionary. A popular preacher and an able administrator, Carroll had enjoyed a fruitful life in the Lord's work. But his ministry did not end at retirement. For the last eighteen years, Brother Carroll has continued to fill pulpits as needs arose, has directed his church's senior adult ministry, and has been a source of wisdom to his pastor and staff. Two years ago, at age eighty-one, he began teaching a Sunday morning Bible study class—now numbering over forty—at a nearby retirement center. He still teaches the class as I write this.

Jesus reflected integrity of personality—though He was only thirty-three when He died—when He declared from the cross, "It is finished" (John 19:30). What was finished? His work, His mission, His purpose on earth. "I have brought you glory on earth by completing the work you gave me to do. And now, Father, glorify me in your presence with the glory I had with you before the world began" (John 17:4–5).

Paul reflected integrity of personality as he approached his martyr's death. From his prison cell he writes to his beloved Timothy:

> The time has come for my departure. I have fought the good fight, I have finished my race, I have kept the faith. Now there is in store for me the crown of righteousness, which the Lord, the righteous Judge, will award me on that day—and not only to me, but also to all who have longed for his appearing (2 Tim. 4:6b–8).

On the other hand, the political intrigue of Judas led to despair and suicide (Matt. 27:5). Solomon had everything life could offer, but he could not escape the enveloping arms of despair: "Utterly meaningless! Everything is meaningless" (Eccles. 1:2). "All things are wearisome" (Eccles. 1:8). Talk about despair! Solomon is a living case study of Jesus' words: "For whoever wants to save his life will lose it, but whoever loses his life for me will find it. What good will it be for a man if he gains the whole world, yet forfeits his soul?" (Matt. 16:25–26a).

When we come to the end of life, will it be with a sense of integrity and wholeness, of dignity and satisfaction in our accomplishments?

Or will it be with a sense of despair and bitterness, of futility and desperation?

IN SUMMARY

Erikson's theory provides a structured model which demonstrates the relationship between human personality and life experiences. In general we help individuals grow a healthy personality when we focus on success rather than failure, balance security and freedom, meet emotional needs and provide competent role models.

Church leaders and lay teachers will teach and preach more effectively if they use these insights to direct their efforts to heal past neglect and prepare for future success in their learners—whatever age they teach. It is God's good will, says Paul, that we become mature (Eph. 4:13). The process of becoming mature involves getting rid of the fractured characteristics of the past and "clothing ourselves" with His characteristics (see Col. 3:8–17). By His grace, and through His power, we grow as we give Him freedom to heal our fractured selves. May He bless us as we help others do the same, even as we teach!

CHAPTER CONCEPTS

Adaptive strength	Integrity
Autonomy	Intimacy
Despair	Isolation
Foreclosure	Maladaption
Generativity	Malignancy
Guilt	Mistrust
Identity	Moratorium
Identity achievement	Psychosexual vs. Psychosocial Theory
Identity diffusion	Role confusion
Industry	Shame and doubt
Inferiority	Stagnation
Initiative	Trust

DISCUSSION QUESTIONS

1. Think of a member of your family or a close friend who reflects one of the poles of Erikson's stages. As you think over the lifespan of this individual, how does Erikson's theory fit their life experiences?

2. Which stage has caused you the greatest difficulty so far? Toward which pole in that stage did you move? Why? What influence has this had on your later development?

3. Describe your greatest discovery in reading this chapter. It may be related to your own development or your future ministry. What implications does this discovery hold for your future development?

4. James Marcia describes four identity statuses. Think back to when you were sixteen to eighteen years of age, and decide which of the four statuses best describes you at that time.

FOR FURTHER READING:

Biehler, Robert F. and Jack Snowman. "Erikson: Psychosocial Development." In *Psychology Applied to Teaching*, 7th ed., 41–57. Boston: Houghton Mifflin Company, 1993.

Clouse, Bonnidell. *Teaching for Moral Growth: A Guide for the Christian Community—Teachers, Parents and Pastors*, 121–23. Wheaton, Ill.: Bridgeport Books, 1993.

Dembo, Myron H. *Applying Educational Psychology*. 5th ed., 438-45. New York: Longman, 1994.

Eggen, Paul and Don Kauchak. *Educational Psychology: Classroom Connections*. 2nd ed., 70–77. New York: Macmillan College Publishing Company, 1994.

Erikson, Erik H. *Identity and the Life Cycle*. New York: W. W. Norton and Company, 1980.

———, Joan M. Erikson and Helen Q. Kivnick. *Vital Involvement in Old Age: The Experience of Old Age in Our Time*. New York: W. W. Norton and Company, 1986.

Gage, N. L., and David C. Berliner. *Educational Psychology*. 3rd ed., 166–170. Boston: Houghton Mifflin Company, 1984.

Gleason, John J. *Growing Up to God*. Nashville: Abingdon, 1975.

Good, Thomas L., and Jere E. Brophey. *Educational Psychology: A Realistic Approach*. 4th ed., 97–104. New York: Longman, 1990.

Hamachek, Don. *Psychology in Teaching, Learning, and Growth*. 4th ed., 42–51. Boston: Allyn and Bacon, 1990.

Slavin, Robert E. *Educational Psychology: Theory and Practice*. 4th ed., 52–58. Boston: Allyn and Bacon, 1994.

Sprinthall, Norman A., Richard C. Sprinthall, and Sharon N. Oja. *Educational Psychology: A Developmental Approach*. 6th ed., 141–162. New York: McGraw-Hill, Inc., 1994.

Woolfolk, Anita. *Educational Psychology*. 5th ed., 66–74. Boston: Allyn and Bacon, Inc., 1993.

4

HOW WE DEVELOP
AS THINKERS

JEAN PIAGET'S THEORY OF
COGNITIVE DEVELOPMENT

A basic function of teaching is helping students understand an as-signed subject. We teach more effectively when we consider the thinking capabilities of our learners. Jean Piaget provides powerful insights into how we develop thinking capabilities—how we learn, how we understand. Central to Christian growth is the proper under-standing of biblical teachings. Piaget's ideas can be of immense help to Christian teachers in their efforts to guide learners in establishing a biblical mindset.

The learner will demonstrate knowledge of Piaget's theory of cognitive development
- by matching definitions with the terms organization, adapta-tion, assimilation, accommodation, equilibration, conserva-tion, and reversibility and egocentrism;
- by identifying two components of each Piagetian stage.

The learner will demonstrate understanding of Piaget's theory of cognitive development
- by categorizing case studies of learners by Piagetian stage;
- by developing a case study of a typical learner from each stage.

HISTORICAL ROOTS

Cognitive development is the gradual, orderly process by which mental processes become more complex and sophisticated.[1] At the turn of the century, psychologists believed that intelligence was genetically determined prior to birth. Differences in intelligence were quantitative.[2] The nature of intelligence was defined in terms of how fast one could learn. That is, fast learners were more intelligent than slow learners.

Arnold Gesell was the first to postulate that intelligence was developed after birth, in an unvarying sequence of steps. As head of the Institute of Child Development at Yale University, he developed many ideas regarding cognitive development in children. Most of Gesell's ideas were later discarded as oversimplifications, but one concept lasted. The growth in cognitive abilities follows a cycle of rapid change, or reorganization, and integration, when changes are organized into the thinking process.[3] Gesell showed that differences in intelligence are actually qualitative differences, not merely quantitative. Children of different ages think differently.

Jean Piaget, a biologist and philosopher by training,[4] provided a more robust picture of cognitive development. The foundation of Piaget's theory, much like Erikson's personality theory, is that every individual functions within his environment in an interactive fashion. We know what we know as a result of the interaction between ourselves and our environment.[5] Intelligence is not simply poured into children.[6] Rather, they actively structure understanding—they help create it through their own activity.[7]

THE ESSENTIAL
VOCABULARY OF
PIAGET

Piaget developed a technical vocabulary to describe the complex process by which humans construct intelligence. These key terms produce a language which enables us to discuss Piaget's ideas with precision.

In this section we define equilibration, disequilibrium, organization, scheme, adaptation, assimilation, accommodation, operation, conservation, decentration, reversibility, and egocentrism.

Organization

Organization is the natural tendency to make sense of experiences by integrating them into cognitive structures that are logically related.[8] These cognitive structures are quite simple at first, but are built up—by combining, arranging, recombining, and rearranging behaviors and thoughts[9]—into ever more complex, coherent systems.[10] For example, infants can look at objects, and they can *grasp* objects when they happen to touch them. But they cannot coordinate the two. In time, however, infants organize these two behaviors into a higher level ability, which allows them to look at, reach for, and grasp an object.[11] This networking of behaviors and thoughts creates a complex cognitive network by which we perceive the world.

Schemes are the cognitive structures produced as a result of the development process.[12] They are organized patterns of behavior or thought, produced through interaction with the environment,[13] which represent the world as we know it.[14] All that we use to understand and function in the world are built from these building blocks. When we use the term "concept" or "idea," we are reflecting a simple understanding of Piaget's "scheme."[15] Billy, for example, has a scheme of "dogness" by which he properly calls Cocker Spaniels and German Shepherds "dogs." Figure 1 shows three simplified schemes of "dog," "horse," and "cow" in the "mind."

Schemes

Schemes change as children develop their cognitive network. They grow in number, allowing us to differentiate among similar objects, and in complexity, allowing us to see similarities among different objects. Since perception of the world depends on the level of development in the cognitive network, it is easy to see that adult concepts differ from children's. Mental processes differ. The abilities of problem solving and abstraction require a complex cognitive network, and this takes time and experience to create.[16]

The process by which schemes grow and change is called adaptation, which, in turn, consists of two related parts called assimilation and accommodation. The tendency to maintain balance between the two is called equilibration.

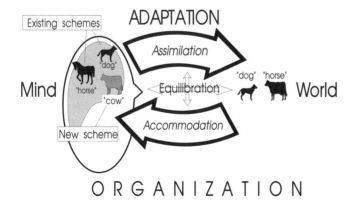

JEAN PIAGET
(1896-1980)

J ean Piaget was born in Neuchatel, Switzerland, in 1896. His father was a history professor, and Jean was raised in a scholarly atmosphere.[A]
As a boy, he was curious about nature. He spent a great deal of time observing animals. He published his first professional paper on his observations of an albino sparrow. He was ten years old.[B] He observed changes in the structure of shellfish as their environment (rough or calm water) changed.[C]

Between the ages of eleven and fifteen he worked as a laboratory assistant to the director of the natural history museum in Neuchatel.[D] At the age of fifteen he published a series of articles on shellfish, which won him the position of Curator of Mollusk Collection at the Natural History Museum in Geneva. He turned down the position in order to finish school.[E]

His godfather was a philosophy scholar and urged Jean to broaden his horizons through a study of philosophy and logic. Piaget earned his undergraduate degree in natural science from the University of Neuchatel[F] in 1914 at age eighteen,[G] and a Ph.D. in Biology[H] in 1917 at age twenty-one.[I]

Psychology captured his attention and in 1918 he went to Zurich, where he was introduced to Freudian theory. The next year, he went to Paris to study abnormal psychology. It was during this time that he worked with Alfred Binet, the developer of intelligence testing, to develop intelligence tests for children.[J] He asked questions relating to time, space, numbers, causality, and moral judgment.[K] He was fascinated by the differences in answers between younger and older children.[L] In fact, he focused more on their wrong answers,[M] finding that the same wrong answers were frequently given by children of the same age.[N] He found that older children are not simply more intelligent, did not simply know more, but differed qualitatively in their thinking processes.[O]

In 1921 he was named Director of Research at the Jean-Jacques Rousseau Institute in Geneva. This allowed him to study the cognitive behavior of children full time. For the next thirty years he quietly continued his research.[P] His regular schedule was to spend the morning with friends, take a long walk to collect his thoughts, and then spend the afternoon writing.[Q]

Piaget received honorary degrees from Harvard (1936), the Sorbonne (1946), and the University of Brussels (1949).[R] Yet he received little recognition for his theory in America until the 1960s. Sprinthall suggests two reasons for this. First, Piaget opposed Edward L. Thorndike's emphasis on laws of learning, preferring to study the child's thinking ability. Second, he wrote only in French and then in obscure language that was difficult to translate.[S] A third reason may be the fact Piaget was not interested in formal educational practice, but was fascinated with genetic epistemology, the biological basis for the growth of knowledge in a person.[T]

Piaget's work eventually overcame these obstacles, and catapulted him to fame. Slavin calls him the "best known child psychologist who ever lived."[U] Good ranks him with Sigmund Freud and B. F. Skinner as "the most influential psychologists of all times."[V]

In 1969, Piaget received the Distinguished Scientific Award from the American Psychological Association.[W] In 1975 he retired from his position at the Rosseau Institute, but continued his study until his death in 1980.[X]

Equilibrium

Equilibration is the natural tendency to maintain a balance between what one already knows, the cognitive network, and what one experiences in the world.[17] When this balance is disturbed—that is, when we experience something that does not fit what we know—we experience anxiety, discomfort, or confusion. This confusion is called *disequilibrium*.[18] Equilibration compels us to reduce the disequilibrium by restoring the balance, or *equilibrium*, between our understanding of the world and experiences in the world. Think of a rowboat on a calm lake. It is in a state of equilibrium. Now a speedboat rushes past, causing large waves which toss the rowboat up and down. This is disequilibrium. The desire of the fishermen in the boat is for equilibration, the return of calm water.

> When Billy saw a Chihuahua for the first time, he did not recognize it. He did not have a "Chihuahua" scheme, nor did his "dog" scheme include the Chihuahua characteristics. This created disequilibrium for him. "What *is* that, Dad?"

Equilibration is represented in figure 2 as arrows between our thinking and the world as it is, between assimilation and accommodation, which we'll discuss next.

Adaptation

Adaptation is the natural process of adjusting our thinking, or our environment, so that balance exists between what we know and what we experience. It is creating a good fit between one's concept of reality (schemes) and real-life experiences.[19] Adaptation is a complex process which consists of two parts. The first part, *assimilation*, is interpreting experiences so they fit what we know. The second part, called *accommodation*, is adjusting schemes so they fit our experience. Adaptation combines these two processes so that we maintain a state of equilibrium between our thinking and the world.[20]

"Assimilation: Interpreting experiences so that they fit what we know"

Assimilation. Assimilation is the first component of adaptation, that of interpreting experiences so that they fit what we know. When an experience does not fit an existing scheme, we interpret the experience[21] or relate the information[22] to the scheme which provides the closest fit. In doing so, we often modify or distort what we've experienced. When Billy first saw the Chihuahua, the only thing he could think to call it was "a cat." He was assimilating. Another child has a scheme of "fish." He calls minnows "little fish" and whales "big fish." Still another calls a skunk a "kitty."[23] In each case, experiences were (mis)interpreted by established schemes which were inadequate to perceive the world correctly. Figure 2 shows the interpreting process graphically: the subject labels the dog "dog" and the cow "horse."

Writers define the term assimilation in a variety of ways: "relating new information to existing schemes,"[24] "experience incorporated into existing schemes,"[25] "changing what is perceived so that it fits present structures,"[26] "to respond in terms of preexisting information [which] often involves ignoring some aspects to make it conform,"[27] "interpreting [an experience] in light of present schemes,"[28] and to "change the nature of reality to make it fit our cognitive structures."[29] Notice that all of these definitions have in common the changing of experience so that it fits how we think—i.e., calling a cow "horse." Other writers define assimilation in more general terms, such as: "simply taking in familiar experiences,"[30] or "using existing schemes to make sense of [the] world"[31]—i.e., calling a dog a "dog."

Assimilation does not change the structure of schemes, but it does affect the growth of schemes. Wadsworth uses the analogy of a balloon, where assimilation is putting more air in the balloon. The balloon gets larger, but does not change shape.[32] Yet we know that schemes do change. Piaget described this change as accommodation.

Accommodation. Accommodation is the second component of adaptation, that of adjusting schemes to fit what we experience. When an experience does not fit an existing scheme, we can either adjust an existing scheme so that it does fit, or we can create a new scheme. Billy's dad explained that the Chihuahua was a dog. "That's a dog?!" Billy thought for a moment as he expanded his "dogness" scheme to allow Chihuahuas to fit. The child who called minnow "little fish" and whales "big fish" created a new scheme for whales: "mammals that live in water." The unfortunate little girl who thought skunks were kitties now has a scheme called "skunk" which she'll never confuse with kitties. In Figure 2, the subject creates a new scheme "cow" to fit the new experience.

Writers define accommodation like this: "modifying schemes in order to relate to new information,"[33] "to change schemes to incorporate experience,"[34] "to adjust our own ideas to make sense of reality,"[35] "the modification or reorganization of existing cognitive structures to deal with environmental demands,"[36] "involves development of new structures and restructuring old ones,"[37] "to respond to external characteristics by changing existing structures,"[38] and "changing existing structures to respond to new situations."[39] The goal of teachers is to help students accommodate their thinking to the subject at hand.

Adaptation: Both Are Necessary. Both accommodation and assimilation are necessary.[40] Assimilation without accommodation results in our remaking the world according to our own ideas, never learning from others, filtering every conversation through our own preconceived notions.[41] A person would have a few large schemes

"Accommodation: Adjusting schemes to fit what we experience"

and be unable to differentiate well.[42] However, assimilation with accommodation allows us to better understand the world as it really is. Accommodation without assimilation remakes us into whatever we discover in the world, creating new schemes for every new experience, always accepting at face value what others say, having no filters by which to test experiences or information. A person would have a great number of small schemes and be unable to generalize well.[43]

Accommodation with assimilation provides a standard, a pattern by which we evaluate experience. We need both processes to create equilibrium between what we know and what really is. Fortunately, both occur continuously as we interact with our world.[44]

In summary, the drive to systematize our world (organization) causes us to create a mental niche for everything we experience. Creating new schemes or modifying existing schemes provides niches for experiences (accommodation). We do this so that we can put everything we experience in its place, even if we have to change the experience so that it will fit (assimilation).[45]

"The push-pull of adaptation focuses on the very fiber of teaching ministry"

I have spent considerable time focusing on the mutual processes of assimilation and accommodation because they are at the heart of Piaget's theory. But beyond that, the push-pull of adaptation focuses on the very fiber of teaching ministry: to help learners consider their own perceptions of life, and to help them accommodate their thinking to biblical themes.

One concern raised by students goes like this: "How do we keep from accommodating our thinking to worldly ideas such as homosexuality, or abortion-on-demand, or New Age religions?" They have a tangible fear that accepting the idea of accommodation may result in compromising their thinking, attitudes, and lifestyle with the world around them. But there is a difference between *understanding* and *believing*.

If I am to share the gospel with New Age devotees, I need to understand what New Agers believe. I accommodate my thinking—that is, create appropriate schemes—in order to understand New Age teachings. This has nothing to do with believing in New Age, or accepting New Age as appropriate teaching. Does understanding Hitler's *Mein Kampf* make me a Nazi, or Marx's *Das Capital* make me a Communist? For that matter, does understanding Jesus' teachings make me a Christian? Of course not.[46] Cognitive understanding and heart commitment are two different animals altogether.

Should we study evolutionary theory? If we want to be able to speak intelligently on the subject, we must. We should accommodate our thinking to evolution—to understand what evolution really teaches—rather than make it into what we think it is (assimilation). "Understanding evolution" has nothing to do with committing myself to, or even accepting, its tenets. Believers have the greatest opportunities to share the gospel with others when they understand—have accommodated themselves to—the viewpoints of others. The apostle Paul wrote,

> "Though I am free and belong to no man, I make myself a slave to everyone, to win as many as possible. To the Jews I became like a Jew, to win the Jews. To those under the law I became like one under the law (though I myself am not under the law), so as to win those under the law. To those not having the law I became like one not having the law (though I am not free from God's law but am under Christ's law), so as to win those not having the law. To the weak I became weak, to win the weak. I have become all things to all men so that by all possible means I might save some" (1 Cor. 9:19–22).

Paul accommodated himself, without compromising the gospel, to as many people as he could—in order to present the gospel. His goal was to help others accommodate their thinking to the gospel, the first step toward faith. But faith itself—believing in, committing to—is another matter entirely.

The next five terms all refer to processes by which differences in cognitive development are measured. These terms will be used to describe differences in thinking in the four stages of development.

The term "operation" refers to an action which can be carried out *Operation* mentally. This capability frees us from having to perform the actions literally.[47] An important characteristic of an operation is that it can be mentally undone, or reversed.[48] You will find the term "operation" embedded in three of Piaget's four stages of development: preoperational, concrete operational, and formal operational. We will discuss the implications of this when we explain Piaget's stages.

The term "conservation" refers to the ability to recognize that *Conservation* properties stay the same despite changes in appearance or position.[49] The most popular experiment Piaget performed involved conservation of *continuous quantity*. Two tall, narrow vials stand filled with water. The researcher pours one of the vials of water into a broad, short beaker. Then she asks the child, "Which has more water?" Younger children are unable to "conserve volume" and understand that the amount of water is unchanged. They perceive that there is more water in the tall thin vial because the water is higher than in the wide beaker. Older children understand that the amount of water is unchanged by pouring. Even though it *looks as if* there is more water in the vial, older children know better.

Piaget's experiments in conservation covered a number of topics. Take two equally-sized balls of clay. Roll one of the balls into a clay rope. Ask, "Which is more clay?" (Conservation of mass). Ask, "Which weighs more?" (Conservation of weight). Ask, "If I place these into a beaker of water, which one will make the water go higher?" (Conservation of volume). Younger children will say the clay rope is "more." Older children will recognize that the amount of clay has not changed simply by rolling it into a rope.

Conservation of number involves understanding that the number of something doesn't change because of superficial changes in appearance.[50] Take two candy bars and break one of them into eight pieces. A younger child will say the eight pieces are "more candy." An older child knows the amount of candy is the same. Show a child two equally spaced rows of five coins. Then spread out one row of coins and ask, "Which is more money?" The younger child will respond that the longer row of five coins is more money than the shorter row of five coins.[51]

Decentration

Decentration is the ability to focus on more than one aspect of a situation at a time,[52] and is a reflection of higher level thinking. The opposite of decentration is *perceptual centration*, or *centering*, which refers to the tendency to focus on one aspect of a situation to the exclusion of all others.[53] In the "continuous quantity" experiment, younger children focus on the height of the water only, not its volume (height, breadth, and depth combined). They are unable to decenter their attention from the height of the water, and so determine that the higher level equals more water.

Reversibility

The term "reversibility" refers to the ability to mentally undo an action. Older children can mentally pour the water back into the tall vial and reason that the amount of water is unchanged. Younger children cannot.[54] The inability to mentally reverse actions is called "irreversibility." Younger children do not understand that superficial changes can be undone, or reversed, to return a situation to its former state.[55]

Egocentrism

Egocentrism refers to the inability to see something from another person's point of view.[56] The term does not mean selfish or conceited. Young children simply find it difficult, if not impossible, to take another person's point of view. Their assumption is that everyone sees things the way they see them.[57] For example, a child who loves teddy bears might buy one for his mother on her birthday.

I remember studying Piaget's "Three Cone Problem" as a doctoral student. Piaget positioned two smaller cones in front of a larger cone on a table. He positioned a child at one end of the table, and chairs with stuffed animals at the other three sides. He would have the children explain or draw what they saw. Then he would ask, "What does the teddy bear [seated at a different position] see?" Young children explain or draw the same arrangement as they themselves see. Older children are able to reposition the cones in their mind and describe or draw the correct arrangement from the different perspectives.

Before we move into the actual sequence of cognitive development, test your understanding of these key concepts with the following quotes. How would you explain these quotes to someone who hasn't studied Piaget?

1. "Adaptation is the process of adjusting schemes and experiences so that we maintain a state of equilibrium."[58]
2. "It is difficult to assimilate experiences beyond the level of mental development. Thus, as teachers, we can get children to say they know, or force them to memorize, but we should not be fooled into believing that they really understand. Piaget might say, 'To know by heart is not to know.'"[59]
3. "Accommodation is the changing of existing schemes in order to incorporate experience."[60]
4. "Equilibration maintains the balance between assimilation and accommodation."[61]
5. "The ability to conserve requires reversibility."[62]
6. "An operation is a scheme whose major characteristic is that it can be reversed."[63]

If your head is spinning from all these new terms, you are over-accommodating: many new schemes, but little organization yet. Now would be a good place to take a break. When you resume, read these six statements again. See if they make any more sense than they do now. Review the key terms we've covered, and then move on to Piaget's Four Stages of Cognitive Development.

Piaget postulated that human intelligence develops from the innate reflexes of infants to the abstract logical reasoning of adults[64] through an unchanging sequence of four stages.[65] Each stage

THE FOUR STAGES
OF COGNITIVE
DEVELOPMENT

represents a qualitative difference in thinking from the other stages. Though each stage has an age range associated with it, determining the specific stage learners have attained depends on what mental capabilities they have, not on how old they are.[66] In other words, all people pass through the same four stages, but not necessarily at the same age.[67] Each given stage is seen as an advance over the previous stage and a limitation in relation to the succeeding one.[68] Abilities in a lower stage do not disappear in later stages. Rather, new abilities are added to the old ones to complete, correct, or combine with them.[69] Given these general features of stages of development, we turn our attention to analyze each of the four. They are the sensorimotor, preoperational, concrete operational and formal operational stages of cognitive development.

The Sensorimotor Stage (Ages Birth Through Two)

Newborn infants possess innate reflexes such as sucking, grasping, and the like.[70] Their cognitive activity is limited to immediate experience through the senses. They have no language by which to label experiences or symbolize events and ideas. Therefore they cannot remember.[71] The saying "out of sight, out of mind" is literally true for them.[72] They are bound to immediate experience.[73] Their thinking is limited to how the world responds to their physical actions.[74] Their responses are determined by the immediate situation, such as crying when they are hungry. Telling an infant, "Just a minute, I'm warming your bottle" has no meaning to her. She does not understand the words, does not understand time, and does not understand that she will soon receive the answer to her problem.[75] Learning *equals* experience, vivid experience. Every new discovery is exciting, because it is a first. The sensorimotor period is a continuous peak experience.[76]

Sensorimotor learning is slow, step by step, concrete and tied to immediate experience. It is private and uncommunicative.[77] But the gradually developing ability to mentally represent objects and people prepares sensorimotor children for the next stage, in which thinking shifts away from physical action to symbolic learning.[78]

"Learning equals experience—vivid experience"

These children should be taught, not merely "sat." Provide sensorimotor children a safe environment filled with a variety of toys. Teaching centers on providing basic motor skill experiences tied to God through nature, home and family, and friends at church. Activities include such things as painting with water, touching pine cones, playing with sand, helping bake bread, learning Scripture songs and thoughts, and the like. See "For Further Reading" for suggestions of books on teaching infants and toddlers.

Sensorimotor thinking and behavior do not end when children move to higher levels of thought. In fact, even college professors may demonstrate characteristics of sensorimotor thinking when they are confronted with an unfamiliar problem. Examples of this include such things as banging on a television when the reception is bad (It worked for getting milk out of a bottle!), or randomly jiggling wires and hoses under the hood of a car that won't start.

While sensorimotor learning is gradual and tied to immediate experience, preoperational learning is lightning fast and mobile. Symbolic thinking begins, in that the concrete experience of sensorimotor is replaced by the symbols of ideas. But the stage is preoperational in that thinking during this stage is limited by egocentrism, centration, irreversibility and an inability to conserve.[79]

The Preoperational Stage (Ages Two to Seven)

Preoperational thinking is egocentric. Ask why the sun is shining, and the child might say "Because I like to play outside."[80]

Preoperational thinking cannot decenter. Shown two candy bars, one whole and the other broken into eight pieces, and asked "Which is more candy?" the child points to the eight pieces, unable to decenter from number of pieces.

Preoperational thinking cannot be reversed. Ask a child, "Who is your brother?" and he will point to his brother. Ask, "Who is *his* brother?" and the child will likely say, "He doesn't have one."

The growth of language is central to this stage.[81] Vocabulary and grammar increase dramatically. The average two-year-old possesses two hundred to three hundred words. By the age of five, this has expanded to over two thousand words.[82] These words have concrete identifications, such as "horse," "tree," and "truck." Abstract concepts such as "fairness," "truth," and "democracy" have little or no meaning.[83] The development of language permits children to share ideas socially.[84] As we can see, thinking during this stage is characterized by perceptual dominance.[85] The water in the vial is "taller" than the water in the beaker, so there is "obviously" more water in the vial. To explain to a preoperational child why the water is the same accomplishes nothing more than to get the child to parrot back what you say, without any real understanding.[86] Since the words have no logical or objective meaning to preoperational children, they can make wonderfully humorous mistakes in recalling what they've "learned." A six-year-old, reciting the "Pledge of

Allegiance," says "the republic of Richard Stands and one naked individual." Another recalls what she learned in Sunday school: "Pontius was the pilot on the flight to Egypt." Still another recalled part of a worship service, in which God was addressed as "Father, Son and Holy Smoke."[87]

"Learning is intuitive, free-wheeling and highly imaginative"

Preoperational learning is intuitive, free-wheeling and highly imaginative.[88] It is filled with fantasy: talking animals, imaginary friends, wild stories, conversations with self and toys. It does not see things objectively.[89] There is no appreciation for the logical consequences of language: preoperational children talk to, rather than with, others.[90] "Hey, Daddy, look at that fat man standing next to you!"[91]

Preoperational children focus on states rather than transformations.[92] In the water problem, they focus on the height of the water before it is poured into the beaker ("the amount is the same") and after ("more water in the taller one"). They ignore the act of pouring, the transformation from one state to another. Ask preoperational children to draw a picture of an upright stick falling, and they will draw an upright stick and another stick lying flat. Older children will include intermediate positions of the stick, showing the process of falling.[93]

One other major characteristic of preoperational thought is called *transductive* reasoning.[94] Deductive reasoning flows from a general statement to particular examples. Inductive reasoning flows from specific examples to a general statement. Transductive reasoning merely focuses on particulars without touching the general. "If A causes B, then B must cause A," might express transductive thought. Piaget's daughter missed her nap one afternoon. She remarked, "I haven't had my nap, so it isn't afternoon."[95]

Though much of what we've said underscores what preoperational children cannot do (as compared to adults), cognitive development makes giant strides during this stage. Language acquisition, symbolic thought, and a wide range of conceptual abilities make this an explosive time for learning.[96] Their thinking is illogical, but not necessarily inferior. The intuitive, free-wheeling and highly imaginative nature of preoperational thought forms the basis for creativity.[97]

When teaching preoperational children, focus on what the child knows and ask questions to insure your explanations are connecting with their understanding. For example, if a preoperational child asks

"Why are clouds white?" a lecture on reflection and absorption of various wavelengths of light will be lost on him. Instead, ask him, "What white things do you know about?" After he names some things, ask, "What is the same about them?" Then say, "See, clouds are like clean, fluffy balls of cotton. They look white because of the way light shines on them and because they don't have much dust or rain in them."[98]

Children normally want to please their teachers and will respond with answers they perceive their teachers want to hear. Just because children say the right thing does not mean they understand what that right thing means. Effective teachers of preoperational children build bridges to their cognitive abilities, and instruct them in ways they can learn best. See "For Further Reading" at the end of this chapter for suggestions on teaching children ages two to seven.

Preoperational thinking is often found in adults. Three of the most common adult preoperational characteristics are egocentrism, centration, and creativity.

Human beings are innately egocentric. This means that adults do not learn how to be egocentric. Rather, they must learn *not* to be egocentric. Insufferably self-centered people (such as professional athletes, film and television stars, politicians, perhaps a next-door neighbor) did not develop this way. They failed to grow out of their self-centeredness.[99] Teaching egocentric adults requires that you build bridges to their point of view before you present them with another. Otherwise, they will dismiss you and your ideas as irrelevant or, worse, dangerous.

Adult centration is demonstrated by those who make an argument based on isolated and selective information, while ignoring information which conflicts with their view. A few years ago a woman sued a state board of education because textbooks they had approved "promoted the religion of secular humanism." When she was featured on a morning talk show, she was asked to give an example of how the textbooks promoted secular humanism. She opened one of the books and pointed accusingly to a large picture of a boy and girl standing at a stove. The boy held a spatula in one hand and a frying pan, on the burner, in the other. The girl stood beside him, watching. The caption under the picture read, "Jim cooks." "How does this promote secular humanism?" the interviewer asked. "Well, everyone knows that the Bible says that women are supposed to cook! This picture teaches little boys that they're supposed to cook. That's secular humanism!" I was dumbfounded. First, many men are single and cook for themselves. Second, married men—particularly in today's hectic world—may need to pitch in and help cook. Third, cooking is enjoyable. Why shouldn't men be encouraged to do it? Fourth, where in the Bible does the Lord lay down the theological truth "And the Man shalt not cook"? Fifth, how does a picture of a boy cooking promote "the religion of secular humanism"? And finally, I thought, who's home cooking for this woman's family while she's in New York? Who's home taking care of the family while she spends weeks at the state capitol fighting these textbooks? Her husband, that's who. Her argument was based on highly selective information and ignored the many ways her own actions violated her argument.

On the positive side, the intuitive, free-wheeling and highly imaginative nature of preoperational thought forms the basis for creativity.[100] Highly creative adults can step outside what is logically known to create something new.

In summary, preoperational children are dreamers, explorers, and magicians, dealing with illogical fantasies while they experiment with their world and their own thinking. As they experiment, they prepare the way for the next stage, in which they become logical manipulators of concrete experiences. They become literal-minded in the extreme, can deal with functional relationships (because they are specific), and test problems systematically.[101]

The Concrete Operational Stage (Ages Seven to Eleven)

Stage Three produces the beginning of operational thought.[102] Thinking is characterized by two key developments. First, children overcome the deficiencies of preoperational thought (egocentrism, centration, irreversibility, and lack of conservation)[103] and second, they begin to think logically about concrete objects.[104]

The term "concrete" refers to the actual presence of objects or events.[105] Conservation and reversibility begin to be understood in this stage so long as the materials are present.[106] Operations are tied to personal experiences.[107] Concrete operational children can mentally pour the water back into the original vial and "see" that the amount has not changed. They can mentally put the eight pieces of candy bar back together and "see" that the amount is unchanged. Thinking is less egocentric and more sociocentric—the child is more open to the views of others.[108]

Visual problems, using pictures or props, are more easily solved than word problems, involving explanations. Real conditions can be considered more easily than hypothetical situations. Asking a class of concrete operational children a hypothetical question like "Suppose the sky were green?" would most likely produce a chorus of responses: "No, it isn't!"[109]

Concrete thinking is capable of seriation: the ordering of a group of objects according to increasing or decreasing length, weight or volume.[110] This ability is required to solve problems like this: If A is greater than B, and B is greater than C, then what is the relationship of A and C? Preoperational children are stymied. Concrete operational children understand that, under these conditions, A is greater than C.[111]

Concrete thinking is also capable of classification: categorizing objects according to common characteristics.[112] Suppose we have fifteen wooden beads. Ten of the beads are brown, and five are yellow. Ask preoperational children, "Are there more brown beads, or wooden beads?" and they will likely answer that there are more brown beads than wooden beads—even though they can acknowledge that all the beads are wooden! Concrete operational children have no problem seeing that there are more wooden beads than brown beads.[113] They can properly classify the fifteen beads as "wooden," "brown," and "yellow." Children in the concrete operational stage are not "brighter" than preoperational children, but they have acquired abilities for solving problems that they could not solve before.[114]

When teaching concrete operational thinkers, use visual aids and props, particularly when discussing complex material. Let children test out what they are learning through hands-on projects. Keep verbal instructions brief and well organized. Use what children already know to bridge to new material. Confront them with logical problems which require them to use the information they are learning.[115]

Stage Four is characterized by abstraction. Learners can examine abstract problems systematically and generalize about the results.[116] They can operate with formal logic, constructing hypotheses and testing them.[117] They can isolate and control variables,[118] as well as evaluate their own reasoning and engage in introspection. They develop concerns about society.[119] They can think logically about the possible as well as the impossible.[120] Formal thinkers no longer need props or equipment to work out solutions to problems. They can manipulate objects in their minds.

"Learning involves thinking logically about concrete objects"

The Formal Operational Stage (Ages Eleven and Above)

Examples of school subjects which require formal thinking include history (relationships among trends), algebra (mathematical symbols), biology (DNA structure), chemistry (atomic structure) and literature (metaphor and symbolism). Without the ability to think abstractly, students must revert to memorizing what the teacher gives them.[121]

Summary of Cognitive Development Stages

Stage	Age	Intellectual Characteristics
Sensorimotor	0–2	thinking limited to immediate experience: pretending, miming, memory, visual pursuit, object permanence, simple reflex to goal-directed behavior
Preoperational	2–7	thinking becomes intuitive and symbolic language, begin to use symbols, logical thought in one direction, thinking remains egocentric and centered
Concrete Operational	7–11	thinking becomes literal and personal decentration reversibility conservation classification seriation can solve hands-on problems logically cannot solve abstract problems
Formal Operational	11+	thinking becomes abstract and global can solve abstract problems scientific thinking systematic experimentation complex verbal skills concern for societal problems

The formal operational stage is qualitatively different from the other three. The first three stages are tied to physical realities. Objects really are permanent. The amount of water does not change when poured from one container to another. But formal operations are less closely related to the physical environment. Practice in solving hypothetical problems and engaging in scientific reasoning may be the catalysts for formal operational thinking. These tend to be highly valued and taught in literate cultures, particularly in universities and colleges.[122]

Sprinthall makes the following comparisons between concrete and formal operational thinking. While the former is limited to the here and now, the latter extends thinking to possibilities. In the former, problem solving is dictated by details of the problem; in the latter, problem solving is governed by planned hypothesis testing. In the former, thought is limited to concrete objects and situations; in the latter, thought is expanded to ideas. In the former, thought is focused on one's own perspective; in the latter, thought is enlarged to the perspective of others.[123]

However, formal thinking is not all positive. Without a concrete foundation, abstract thinking can lead to idealistic solutions which never touch reality. "Having just discovered this boundless freedom of the mind to envisage the ideal, adolescents create their Utopias and rebel against the generation that has yet been unable to make its Utopias realities."[124]

"Learning involves formal logic and abstract reasoning"

Being Greeks, we can create images of reality in our minds, so that we think one way and live another. A television evangelist preaches against every kind of moral evil, and then cruises the red light district of his city, paying call girls for pornographic poses. A pastor preaches a "salt and light" sermon decrying "Christian Yellow Pages" and exhorting the congregation to support the public school system, while at that very moment his own children attend a private Christian school. A missionary preaches honesty and truthfulness while trading in the black market illegally—"to stretch the Lord's money." A men's mission organization meets to study missions around the world, but few ever engage in mission action. We sing "I Surrender All" with heart-felt emotion, but live for the Lord as it is convenient. We speak of the Ideal, but we live in the Ordeal. The Christ of the Book is not so concerned with abstract theologizing as He is with commitment to Him in the realities of our day-to-day experiences. "Then he said to them all: 'If anyone would come after me, he must deny himself and take up his cross daily and follow me'" (Luke 9:23). We do His work His way. No red light districts. No hypocritical preaching. No black market. Mission action more than mission talk. Living what we sing.

Formal thinking skills help us understand the "un-concrete" world of spiritual things. Concrete thinking skills help us tie spiritual truths into solving real problems in a real world. Jesus did this by way of parables. For example, "The kingdom of heaven [abstract] is like treasure hidden in a field [concrete]" (Matt. 13:44). He began with realities familiar to His listeners, then used those concrete realities to express truths about the Kingdom of Heaven. We should do the same; otherwise, we will produce religious hypocrites rather than mature disciples.

PIAGET'S VIEWS ON AFFECTIVE DEVELOPMENT

Many writers overlook Piaget's work in affective development because they see affect—feelings, values, ideals—as a separate function from intelligence—concepts, principles, reasoning. Piaget did not differentiate cognitive and affective domains this way, although he thought it quite legitimate to conceptualize them as separate for purposes of analysis.[125]

We'll save discussion of this aspect of Piaget's work for the background section of the next chapter, in which we study Lawrence Kohlberg's theory of Moral Reasoning Development.

CRITICISMS OF PIAGET'S THEORY

Though Jean Piaget has had an enormous influence on educational practice, his ideas have been criticized through the years. By analyzing these criticisms, we can better understand the scope of his work. Here are some of the most common complaints:

1. *Piaget underestimated the abilities of young children.*[126] By requiring specific criteria for inferring a specific mental ability, and by using tests which were complex and removed from real life experience, younger children were generally rated as less capable than they really are.

2. *Piaget describes lower stages in negative terms*, emphasizing what children cannot do rather than what they can.[127] The very name "pre-operational" reflects this negativism: "before-operations." Pre-operational children can't decenter, can't conserve, can't reverse, can't see things from another's point of view. Of course, Piaget was comparing qualitative differences in mental capabilities between children and adults. If adult thinking is taken as the standard of measure, then inabilities to function in adult ways will be expressed as negatives. Even so, research in the last decade has begun to emphasize what younger children can do.[128]

3. *Piaget overestimated formal thinking in adolescents.*[129] Piaget proposed that from age eleven on, children developed formal thinking skills. Research in the 1980s reveal that this is too optimistic. One study (1980) found that only nine percent of nineth graders, fifteen years of age, were mature formal thinkers. Thirty-two percent

were just entering the concrete operational stage, forty-three percent were in the concrete operational stage, and fifteen percent were just entering the formal operational stage.[130] Another study (1984) found that only twenty to twenty-five percent of college freshmen are consistently able to use formal operational reasoning.[131] A third study (1987) found that only thirty-three percent of high school seniors could apply formal operational reasoning.[132]

4. *Is Piaget's theory universal?* Studies have shown that the sequence of stages proposed by Piaget is universal, but the rate of development differs from culture to culture. Formal operational thinking may not occur in every culture.[133]

5. *Do mental abilities really develop in distinct stages?* Research has shown that the distinctness of each stage is not as clear cut as Piaget proposed. Some aspects of "number" can be achieved by two-and-a-half years of age, even though children this age cannot perform Piaget's task.[134]

6. *Biological foundation?* Piaget believed that the sequence of development derived from biological processes. The truth is that the biological implications may be superfluous to the theory.[135]

7. *Key role of motor activities?* Piaget explained that early motor experiences are the basis for cognitive growth. Yet handicapped children, who have little motor experience, show normal cognitive growth.[136]

After all the criticism, Piaget's theory is still held in high regard after sixty years.[137] It is a metaphor, based in philosophy and biology, intended to explain the development of mental capacities and functions. The explanatory strength of the theory, and its practical utility in the teaching enterprise,[138] overcomes any problems caused by minor criticisms.

IMPLICATIONS OF PIAGET'S THEORY FOR TEACHING

Piaget's view of education in general and teaching in particular is extreme in its emphasis on self-paced discovery and de-emphasis on instruction.[139] He saw the goal of education as creating opportunities for learners to create or discover knowledge, not to increase the amount of knowledge in learners. Overemphasis on instruction—teachers explaining content to learners—keeps learners from "inventing and discovering" understanding on their own. Piaget's concept of effective teaching is not transmitting content, which learners could merely learn by rote at a verbal level and not truly understand, but creating situations in which meaning could be discovered by learners.[140] Followers of Piaget, therefore, have called for a de-emphasis on transmitting knowledge by lectures and teacher-led discussions, replacing these with small group projects and problem-solving activities in which students do their own learning.[141]

Fortunately, this extremism against instruction has faded in recent years.[142] The methodology of *pure* discovery, espoused by Piaget and developed into a full-scale approach to teaching by Jerome Bruner (see chapter 8), has evolved into the methodology of *directed* discovery, which encourages greater involvement of teachers in questioning, probing, directing, and encouraging learning. More on this later.

In Christian circles, terms like "self-directed learning" and "inventing knowledge" cause quite a lot of disequilibrium. After all, don't we expect pastors to explain the Bible to their congregations? Don't we expect Bible teachers to "teach the Bible"—that is, explain to learners what to believe? Don't we expect professors in Christian colleges to "teach the truth" so that students get it right? If so, then what has Piaget to say to us?

General Implications

For me, teaching is more than talking "at" students. Teaching is more than presenting a lesson. It is more than transmitting content. Remember the Disciplers' Model of chapter 1? *The evidence of effective teaching is found in the learning which occurs.* I can talk. But do my students listen? I can present a lesson. But do my students understand it? I can transmit facts, but do those facts have meaning for those I teach? Pastors explain, but do congregations understand? Bible teachers "teach the Bible," but does their teaching ever make it into their learners' actions or attitudes? College professors talk through their notes, but do their students grasp what those notes mean?

"Teaching must deal with learners' schemes before we can help them accommodate to the Truth of Scripture"

A line from the hymn "People to People" expresses for me the problem Piaget addresses in teaching. The line reads, "How do you tell an orphan child about the Father's love?"[143] The orphan has a scheme called "father." That scheme is different from the biblical image of God as Father. The biblical image is one of protection, guidance, strength, and discipline. The child's conception? It depends on his own experiences in being orphaned. But the one who teaches this orphan about God as "Father" must deal with the child's misconception of the term. The child could easily memorize the fact that the Bible says "God is Father," but the child's understanding of that term will never be biblical until he deals with his misconception first.

Teaching in order to establish biblical understanding cannot be one-way communication only. Teacher and learner must enter into conversations in which new material is related in meaningful ways to old ideas. Bible truths collide with learner perceptions and produce disequilibrium. If we interpret (read "change") Scripture to fit our preconceived ideas (assimilation), then we are not changed by our study. This is *eisegesis*, a "reading-into" Scripture, and it's heresy. Jesus said, "The teachers of the law and the Pharisees sit in Moses' seat. So you must obey them and do everything they tell you. But do not do what they do, for they do not practice what they preach. They tie up heavy loads and put them on men's shoulders, but they themselves are not willing to lift a finger to move them" (Matt. 23:2–4).

The religious leaders worshipped "the Law" but they did not live it. Those who make the Bible fit their own man-made ideology may well worship what they've created. But it's a distortion of God's Word, and their worship is idolatry.

Now if we let the Bible speak to our students, if we help them accommodate their thinking to its message, then they grow to be like Him. This is *exegesis*, a "reading-out-of" Scripture, and in conjunction with the illuminating it provides Light to our pathway. This Light leads the bigot and the racist to learn to be "no respecter of persons" (Acts 10:34ff); the materialist to learn to put his trust in the Lord, not possessions (Hab. 3:17–19); the power-hungry to be a servant (Mark 9:35); the adulterer to be faithful (Matt. 5:27–28); the thief and liar to be honest (Hos. 4:2; Acts 6:3; 1 Pet. 2:12); and on and on, in a never-ending story, until we become as mature as the Lord (Eph. 4:11–13).

My goal as a Christian teacher is to provide situations in which learners intersect their thinking with the Lord, with Scripture and with other learners so that they might grow in the Lord. Here are some of Piaget's ideas that have helped me do this:

1. Optimal Discrepancy. If a teacher presents an idea that is well understood and accepted by learners, there will be no disequilibrium. Some learners will be bored. Little learning, if any, will happen. If a teacher presents an idea that is foreign or threatening to learners, there will be too much disequilibrium. Some learners will be fearful,

Specific Implications

others angry. Still others may dismiss the teacher's ideas as dangerous.

Optimal (the best, most effective) discrepancy (difference) between learner perception and teaching content refers to presenting ideas that challenge the thinking of learners and yet are meaningful to learners. Therefore, we should provide moderate levels of difficulty in our teaching.[144]

In order to do this we must know our learners. Optimal discrepancy is different for a preschooler and a teenager, for a day laborer and a professor. An adult "Ladies" class was studying 1 Corinthians 12 one Sunday morning when the discussion turned to the subject of "speaking in tongues." The teacher took the opportunity to express her opinion, with vivid emotion and language, that "tongues" were of the devil and that probably anyone who practiced such was not a Christian. After the class ended with prayer, one of her dearest friends lingered. When they were alone, the friend said, "I've never told you this, but I speak in tongues as part of my prayer time. It is a deeply meaningful experience for me, draws me closer to the Lord. You didn't know, but I'll be finding another class to attend." The teacher tried to make amends, but it was too late. Too much disequilibrium. It brought learning to a halt, but more than that, it destroyed a friendship. Know your learners. Frame your questions and explanations in a way that challenges their thinking without raising their blood pressure. Rock their boats, but don't sink them.

2. Direct Experience. Interaction with the environment leads to discovery.[145] Therefore, learning proceeds best through direct experiences with objects and events—experiences which are appropriate for the age of the learners. Direct experiences include activities[146] such as structured play, arts and music, and nature experiences for preschoolers; the use of visual aids and concrete props, projects, and learning centers for children; drama and role play, hypothetical situations, and small group studies for youth; and real life experiences and testimonies for adults. Much of what we do in Christian teaching is verbal—teachers telling learners about the Bible. But real understanding occurs when learners are engaged as active thinkers rather than passive listeners.[147]

3. Social Interaction. Learners may have egocentric thought patterns. They may think that things really are the way they see them. Social interaction helps them become aware of the ideas and opinions of others. This process reduces egocentrism and helps thought processes become more objective.[148] Provide age-appropriate experiences which encourage learner-to-learner interaction as well as teacher-learner interaction. For example, group projects and role play scenarios are excellent ways to intersect the thinking of older children and youth.

Small groups of learners overcome individual differences in thinking better than large classes where individual differences are easily hidden. Learners will more likely admit their confusion and lack of understanding in a small group than in a large class. More knowledgeable learners are better able to explain ideas in small groups than in large classes. This interaction helps both the knowledgeable and the unknowledgeable in ways that a large lecture class would not.

4. Thought-Provoking Questions. A thought-provoking question requires learners to consider what they know, decide what is relevant to the question, and then frame an answer based on that knowledge. Their answer is a window through which we can see their level of content mastery. Incorrect answers should receive as much attention as correct ones,[149] because they help determine where learners went wrong in their thinking.

Parroting back memorized answers to set questions does not reflect the understanding of learners. Memorized answers may hold no meaning to the learner at all, which leads to distorted memory: "and to the republic of Richard Stands."

5. Learner Responses. When a student answers a question correctly, it does not necessarily mean that he understands the answer. Focus on the process of thinking, not just the product.[150] Ask the learner to explain how she arrived at her answer? Ask him why he answered the way he did? Focus on word meanings[151]—just what does the learner mean by the words she has chosen?

Consider the common mistakes your learners make in answering questions. Anticipate these and prepare explanations that emphasize these problem areas.[152]

6. Problem Solving. Since teaching for Piaget means creating situations in which learners can make discoveries,[153] problem-solving activities provide a rich environment for learning. Problems confront learners with unfamiliar situations and create disequilibrium. Solving the problem, based on available resources, brings about equilibration and a higher level of understanding.

The methodology of problem solving encourages interaction among learners and with the teacher, discussion, questions, hypotheses, opinions, research, and teamwork. Teachers can listen to the verbalized reasoning of learners to determine how well they understand the fundamental principles involved.

7. New Material. It is difficult for learners to process new material when it is presented as packets of facts isolated from what's been learned before. Connect new material to prior learning with review. Help learners recall principles and ideas they have already mastered that are relevant to the new material. Then introduce the new material based on this previous learning. Building bridges from established schemes makes the new material more meaningful and easier to master.

8. The Teaching Environment. Learning occurs as a result of interaction between learners and their learning world. Learners accommodate their thinking to the world around them. There is sage motherly advice in the words "Choose your friends wisely" because, given time, we will begin to think like them. Accommodation will produce dramatically different results depending on whether a teenager's primary social group is the "youth group at church" or the "gang on the street."

The classroom is a "learning world." Teachers have the power to create a learning world that is safe and open, yet challenging. A learning world in which students can ask any question without fear of humiliation. Where teachers listen as well as talk. Where ideas can be challenged, defended, or refuted without harsh words or flaring tempers. Where misconceptions can be aired without condemnation. Where teacher and learner interact, sharing together questions and answers drawn from the material but anchored in real life issues. We'll discuss the specifics of this in chapter 8, when we analyze cognitive learning theory.

"Spiritual truth is revealed, not discovered"

9. The Holy Spirit as Teacher. In teaching spiritual truth, the biological mechanisms of equilibration and adaptation are not adequate to produce biblical results. Such mechanisms may help us accommodate to a particular religion, or allow us to become experts on ancient Middle East culture, or categorize the books of the Bible, or learn the major events, people, and places of Scripture. But until our thinking interacts with the Lord Himself, we produce nothing more than a biblical intellectualism. The circle of the Disciplers' Model emphasizes the role of the Holy Spirit as Teacher.

Jesus asked His disciples one day about their views on His identity. Peter responded, "You are the Christ, the Son of the living God" (Matt. 16:16). Jesus said to him, "Blessed are you . . . for this was not revealed to you by man, but by my Father in heaven" (Matt. 16:17). Spiritual truth is revealed, not "discovered."

When Jesus met with His disciples just before He died, He promised them spiritual help by way of the Holy Spirit: "If you love me, you will obey what I command. And I will ask the Father, and he will give you another Counselor to be with you forever—the Spirit of truth. The world cannot accept him, because it neither sees him nor knows him. But you know him, for he lives with you and will be in you" (John 14:15–17).

The primary work of the Holy Spirit is to teach spiritual truths. Jesus explained, "But the Counselor, the Holy Spirit, whom the Father will send in my name, will teach you all things and will remind you of everything I have said to you" (John 14:26).

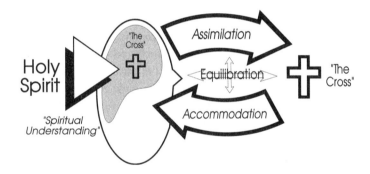

The Holy Spirit provides a spiritual context by which we may accommodate and assimilate the teachings of Jesus and grow spiritually. And *Who* is this Counselor, this Holy Spirit? Jesus identifies Himself with the Holy Spirit, His Divine Personal Presence in the lives of His disciples. "I will not leave you as orphans; I will come to you" (John 14:18). This may explain why Peter and Paul use the terms "Spirit of Christ" or "Spirit of Jesus" and "Holy Spirit" interchangeably. For examples of Paul's uses of the terms, see Romans 8:9 and Philippians 1:19; then Romans 9:1, 1 Corinthians 6:19, 2 Corinthians 6:6. For Peter's, see 1 Peter 1:11 and 4:14.

However we handle the difficulties of the trinitarian nature of God, the point is clear. Spiritual understanding requires a Spiritual

Teacher. No purely biological process can explain spiritual understanding to the satisfaction of the One Who made us to be like Him.

The Holy Spirit, the Spirit of Christ, is part of the immaterial environment in which we operate. Interaction with Him injects a spiritual underpinning to biblical studies, which leads to biblical thinking, which leads to a biblical lifestyle, which is defined as "walking with the Lord."

Jesus taught His disciples for three years. They lived together, ate together, shared ministry and miracles together. And yet, when the soldiers came to the garden of Gethsemane, they ran away. They understood a great deal from their experiences with Jesus. After all, Jesus was the greatest teacher who ever lived. But it wasn't until after the Resurrection, when Jesus appeared to them, and after Pentecost, when they were filled and empowered by the Holy Spirit, that they truly understood what had happened. It was then they became courageous concerning the Truths of the Kingdom, and by His power, turned the world upside-down (Acts 17:6).

"The Spirit of the Lord moves, not in the constrained forces of biological processes, but like the Wind"

When you teach in a church context—preaching, Bible studies, discipleship classes—you may teach for a long time without visible results. Then, without any apparent reason, you see lives transformed, attitudes changed, behaviors improved. This is the work of the Spirit of the Lord, Who moves, not in the constrained forces of biological processes, but freely like the wind: "The wind blows wherever it pleases. You hear its sound, but you cannot tell where it comes from or where it is going. So it is with everyone born of the Spirit" (John 3:8).

When your content is spiritual truth, do all you can to embrace the principles we've discussed. Develop concepts, relate materials to the thinking abilities of your learners, use small groups and interaction. Then pray for the Holy Spirit to infuse the concepts of those who know Him with His own power, His own teaching, in order to transform their understanding into spiritual growth. Remember that dependence on the Holy Spirit to teach spiritual things is not an excuse for poor methodology or faulty teaching procedures.

IN CONCLUSION

We close this chapter with a quote from Jean Piaget. It describes his goals for the educational process:

> The principle goal of education is to create men who are capable of doing new things, not simply of repeating what other generations have done—men who are creative, inventive, and discoverers. The second goal of education is to form minds which can be critical, can verify, and not accept everything they

are offered. The great danger today is of slogans, collective opinions, ready-made trends of thoughts. We have to be able to resist, individually, to criticize, to distinguish between what is proven and what is not. So we need pupils who are active, who learn early to find out by themselves, partly by their own spontaneous activity and partly through material we set up for them; who learn early to tell what is verifiable and what is simply the first idea to come to them.[154]

Piaget's language "rocks the boats" of some Christians because it is so open-ended, so man-centered, so oblivious to Scriptures' absolutes, even rebellious to the established order. All I need do is think of the Lord Who authored Scripture and Who was best known on earth as Teacher. The Lord loved people and met their needs. He began with concrete experiences of their day and led them to consider the spiritual reality of the Kingdom. He asked questions and posed problems. He used concrete demonstrations, parables, and stories. He sent the disciples on mission trips for hands-on ministry experience. He demonstrated repeatedly that the religious establishment had missed God's Truth, and gone after their own rituals.

Or think of the apostle Paul, who, as a Pharisee's Pharisee (Acts 23:6), assimilated the idea of "The Way" by condemning its early followers, hunting them down and putting them in prison. Then he met the Lord and accommodated his thinking to the reality of the resurrection. As a missionary teacher he re-interpreted the Old Testament in light of the Cross and the Empty Tomb. He understood the Pharisees in particular and the Jews in general, as well as the Greeks and the Romans. He taught in a variety of ways so each could understand and come to faith in the Risen Lord.

Jesus established the church as the base for teaching ministry (Matt. 28:19-20). Paul believed in the church as a learning environment in which the lost could find salvation and the saved grow in the Lord. The Great Commission of reaching people where they are and teaching them all things after they're reached, requires the flexibility of thinking, the open-mindedness, and the problem-solving skills Piaget so ably suggested.

CHAPTER CONCEPTS

Abstract thinking	Classification
Accommodation	Concrete operational stage
Adaptation	Concrete thinking
Assimilation	Conservation

Decentration
Disequilibrium
Egocentrism
Equilibration
Formal operational stage
Genetic epistemology
Object permanence
Operation

Optimal discrepancy
Organization
Preoperational stage
Reversibility
Scheme
Sensorimotor stage
Seriation
Visual pursuit

DISCUSSION QUESTIONS

1. According to Piaget, would better learning occur in a single large adult Bible study class, or in several small groups?

2. An associate pastor instructs a group of first- and second-grade children in Vacation Bible School on what to say to the pastor when they walk down the aisle on Sunday to make their profession of faith. Based on this chapter, is this a good thing to do? Why or why not?

3. Consider a current situation in national politics or religious news. What are the major viewpoints to this situation? How do these viewpoints reflect assimilation and accommodation?

4. Develop an example which includes "scheme," "disequilibrium," "assimilation," "accommodation," and "equilibration" using a biblical concept such as "love," "believe," or "submission."

5. Choose one of the four major age groups—preschoolers, children, youth, or adults—and develop guidelines for teaching that group. Include common mistakes you've experienced in teaching that group.

FOR FURTHER READING:

Ames, Louise B., Francis L. Ilg, and Carol C. Haber. *Your One Year Old.* New York: Dell Publishing, 1982. This is part of a series which covers child development in one-year increments through age nine.

Flavell, J. H. *Cognitive Development.* Englewood Cliffs, N.J.: Prentice-Hall, 1985.

Furth, Hans. *Piaget and Knowledge.* 2nd ed. Chicago: University of Chicago Press, 1981.

Ginsburg, Herbert, and Sylvia Opper. *Piaget's Theory of Intellectual Development: An Introduction.* Englewood Cliffs, N.J.: Prentice-Hall, Inc., 1969.

Inhelder, Barbel et al, eds. *Piaget Today.* Hillsdale, N.J.: Erlbaum, 1988.

Piaget, Jean. *Judgement and Reasoning in the Child.* Paterson, N.J.: Littlefield Adams, 1964.

Price, B. Max. *Understanding Today's Children.* Nashville: Convention Press, 1982.

Strickland, Jenell. *How to Guide Preschoolers.* Nashville: Convention Press, 1982.

Uland, Zadabeth. *Bible Teaching for Preschoolers.* Nashville: Convention Press. 1984.

Wadsworth, Barry J. *Piaget's Theory of Cognitive and Affective Development.* 3rd. ed. New York: Longman Inc., 1984.

Waldrop, Sybil C. *Guiding Your Child Toward God.* Nashville: Convention Press, 1985.

———. *Understanding Today's Preschoolers.* Nashville: Convention Press, 1982.

Chapter

5

HOW WE DEVELOP AS MORAL THINKERS

LAWRENCE KOHLBERG'S THEORY OF MORAL RAESONING DEVELOPMENT

Teaching involves more than transmitting content from instructor to student. It is a human process which involves moral issues. At a basic level, rules are necessary to insure the learning process can proceed unhindered. These include such issues as classroom discipline, fairness, equality of opportunity, and honesty. Beyond this are more personal issues that students face which can influence academic achievement and personal growth. These include issues such as drugs, promiscuity, street violence, abortion, and racism.

One might think that Christian teaching is moral in and of itself. But faith in Christ and morality are two different issues. If we do not make a conscious effort to teach our children principles of moral decision making which reflect our faith, then whose principles will they learn?

CHAPTER RATIONALE

Learners will demonstrate knowledge of Kohlberg's six stages of moral development by matching stages with definitions.

Learners will demonstrate understanding of Kohlberg's theory by explaining selected terms in their own words.

Learners will demonstrate understanding of Kohlberg's theory of moral development by creating church-related case studies which reflect a given stage.

Learners will demonstrate appreciation for Kohlberg's theory of moral development by sharing a moral dilemma they recently faced, explaining how they resolved it, and giving reasons why they took the action they did.

CHAPTER OBJECTIVES

HISTORICAL ROOTS

"A moral dilemma has no obvious clear course of action because any decision has both positive and negative consequences"

Just as children differ from adults in personality and cognitive development, so they differ in their approaches to solving moral dilemmas. A moral dilemma is a situation that requires a person to make a moral decision. The situation has no obvious, clear course of action because any decision has both positive and negative consequences. [1]

As discussed in chapter 4, Jean Piaget did not limit his studies to cognitive issues. He studied moral development as well, and used the same methodology. He began by observing children play the game of marbles.[2] How did they play? What rules did they follow? How consistently did they follow them? He found that children interpreted rules differently according to their age.[3] Below the age of two, children simply play with the marbles without regard for rules. Between the ages of two and six,[4] children show an awareness of rules—and try to go along with them[5]—but do not understand their purpose or the need to follow them.[6] Between six and ten[7], children are moving into the concrete operational stage of thinking. They begin to view rules as "sacred pronouncements" handed down by authorities—older children and parents.[8] Rules are fixed, unchangeable edicts.[9] Between the ages of ten and twelve[10] children move into the formal operational stage of thinking. They begin to understand that rules are agreements reached by mutual consent.[11] Rules exist to give direction, but they can be changed.[12]

In addition to observing children play marbles, Piaget presented moral problems to children in the form of stories. He would listen to their reactions to the stories and then ask questions to gain insight into their thinking.[13] Here's the story of Augustus and Julius: "There was a little boy called Julian. His father had gone out, and Julian thought it would be fun to play with father's ink-pot. First he played with the pen, and then he made a little blot on the table cloth. A little boy who was called Augustus once noticed that his father's ink-pot was empty. One day that his father was away he thought of filling the ink-pot so as to help his father, and so he should find it full when he came home. But while he was opening the ink-pot he made a big blot on the table cloth."[14]

Another story reads like this: "A boy named John is called to dinner. As John opens the dining room door, it hits a tray holding fifteen cups, all of which break upon hitting the floor. A boy named Henry tries to get some jam from a cupboard while his mother is out of the house. Balanced precariously on a chair, in the process of reaching for the jam he knocks over a cup and breaks it."[15]

Piaget would ask, "Are these children equally guilty? Which of the two is naughtiest and why?" Piaget found that younger children reacted differently to the stories than older children. We'll discuss how a little later. On the basis of their interpretation of rules and reactions to his stories, Piaget concluded that six-year-olds deal with moral issues differently than twelve-year-olds.

From his observations, Piaget proposed three stages of moral reasoning. The first, reflected in children below age five, he called premoral. In this stage, children are not concerned with rules. They simply want to have fun, and rules shouldn't get in the way of that.[16] Moral development begins at about age six [17]or seven[18] in Piaget's second stage. This stage is called moral realism[19] or the morality of constraint.[20] Rules simply exist. They are absolute and cannot be broken. If a rule is broken, punishment is determined by the damage done. Intentions or motivations should not be considered.[21] So, children in stage two will say that Augustus and John are more guilty than Julian and Henry because Augustus made the larger blot and John broke more cups. The fact that Augustus was trying to help while Julian was misbehaving, or that John had an accident while Henry was misbehaving, does not change the damage that was done. Piaget used the term "heteronomy" to refer to this stage because rules are handed down by an outside ["hetero-", other] authority ["-nomy"]. [22]

About age ten[23] or eleven[24] children move into Piaget's third stage, that of moral relativism[25] or the morality of cooperation.[26] Rules are flexible.[27] They were made by mutual agreement and can be changed. If a rule is broken, punishment is determined by both damage and intention.[28] Piaget used the term "autonomy" to refer to this stage because rules are internalized principles and ideals ["auto-", self].[29] Rules are what we make them to be.[30]

One day I was helping my wife at a school fair. The booth next to hers was a "Ring Toss" booth. The teacher in charge had her two children helping her, a seven-year-old daughter and a fourteen-year-old son. The son had built the booth and provided the muscle for the effort. The daughter served as ticket collector. It was late in the day. The fair was over and folks were packing up their things. The teenager walked around to the front of the booth and said to his sister, "Gimme a ring." His sister looked up at him and replied, "Where is your ticket?" "I don't need a ticket—just gimme one of those rings!" The fact that tickets were no longer being sold, that the fair was over, that people were leaving, made no difference to the sister. "If you don't have a ticket, you don't get a ring." The teenager resigned himself to another tactic. He walked around to the back of the booth where they kept the coffee can now bulging with collected tickets. He picked up a ticket, walked back to the front of the booth, and gave it to his sister. She beamed as she handed him three rings and said, "That's better!" "I only want one ring, not three." "You paid your ticket, you get three rings—that's the rule." So he took the three rings and threw them at the coke bottles. All three made "ringers." "Here's your flag," said the sister, as she handed her big brother a cheap plastic flag of Mexico. "I don't want that flag—keep it." "You made a ringer, so you get a flag." He took the flag, stuffed it in his back pocket, started to walk away, and then stopped and said, "Gimma another ring." Without hesitation, she asked, "Where's your ticket?"

"He took a ticket from the coffee can. Did he really steal it?"

This time as he walked around the booth to get another ticket from the can, his sister watched him. When she saw him reach into the can, she began to scream, "Momma, Momma, Johnny's stealing a ticket!" Did Johnny steal a ticket? The sister reflected a morality of constraint as she followed the rules her mother had given her. Ticket, three rings, a Mexican flag. She certainly believed her big brother was stealing.

The teenager followed a morality of cooperation as he took in the larger picture. He had worked all afternoon in this booth. All he wanted to do was toss a ring or two before they took the booth apart. He took the worthless ticket from the can only because his sister demanded a ticket. Tickets were no longer being sold—he couldn't buy one if he'd wanted to. The money from the ticket he used was already counted and rolled, ready to be deposited in the school's account in the morning. No, he wasn't stealing at all.

The final word in the conflict came from the mother, who, worn out from a long, hot afternoon, turned to her accusing daughter and said, "Oh Janey, be quiet—and help your brother pack this stuff in the car."

The following chart helps contrast the morality of constraint and the morality of cooperation.

KOHLBERG'S THEORY OF MORAL REASONING DEVELOPMENT

Lawrence Kohlberg was changed forever by the Holocaust of World War II. How could a moral nation, a moral people, as the Germans were, so quickly become the executioners of six million Jews? At the Nuremburg trials, leader after leader proclaimed his own innocence by saying, "I was simply following orders." Simply following

What is the source of control for our thoughts and actions?	
External Control *Heteronomous Morality* *Moral Realism* *Morality of Constraint*	**Internal Control** *Autonomous Morality* *Moral Relativism* *Morality of Cooperation*
Rules are fixed and unchangeable	Rules are flexible
Rules are imposed by higher authority and must be obeyed	Obey rules out of concern for the rights of others
Letter of the law: no exceptions	Spirit of the law: exceptions possible
Rules are literal-minded and absolute: not open for negotiation	Rules are abstract and relative: open to negotiation
Punishment required if a rule is broken	Punishment is not automatic
No allowance made for motives or intentions Punishment based solely on damage done	Consider the intentions of wrongdoer when evaluating guilt [31]

Based on Biehler and Snowman, 74, Eggen and Kauchak, 63, and Slavin, 60.

orders to machine gun naked adults and children into mass graves. Simply following orders to lead innocent people into "showers" where they were gassed. Simply following orders to work the men until they died of starvation. Isn't there a higher law than societal law? These thoughts focused Kohlberg's life's work.

Kohlberg followed Piaget's methodology by using stories to study the moral thinking of children. The stories posed a moral dilemma. Subjects were asked what the main character in the story should do, and why. The most popular Kohlberg story goes like this:

> In Europe a woman was near death from cancer. One drug might save her, a form of radium that a druggist in the same town had recently discovered. The druggist was charging $2,000, ten times what the drug cost him to make. The sick woman's husband, Heinz, went to everyone he knew to borrow the money, but he could only get together about half of what it cost. He told the druggist that his wife was dying and asked him to sell it cheaper or let him pay later, but the druggist said "No." The husband got desperate and broke into the man's store to steal the drug for his wife. Should the husband have done that? Why? [32]

As we proceed through Kohlberg's six stages, we'll suggest likely responses to this dilemma. Kohlberg grouped his six stages into three levels, each containing two stages. These levels of moral

THE LIFE OF
LAWRENCE
KOHLBERG

Lawrence Kohlberg was born in 1927 in Bronxville, New York, the youngest of four children.[A] His well-to-do parents provided a comfortable and academic life in elite private schools.[B] Kohlberg recalled that his high school years frequently found him on probation for smoking, drinking, and visiting girls in a nearby school.[C] In 1945 he enlisted in the Merchant Marines and volunteered to bring a ship of 2000 Jewish refugees through a British blockade of Palestine. The ship was rammed and boarded by British forces and in the confusion several were killed, including women and children. Kohlberg was sent to an internment camp in Cyprus, where he began to question the rules of justice and concern for people against the legal rules of society.[D] He escaped from the camp and later made his way to the University of Chicago, where he completed his undergraduate degree in two years. He enrolled in the Ph.D. program in 1949. His primary interest, prompted by the Holocaust and his internment, was moral reasoning. He studied psychoanalysis under Bruno Bettelhiem, humanism under Carl Rogers, and behaviorism under Jacob Gewirtz, but rejected these socialization theories as inadequate to deal with the moral problems people face. He then turned to Piaget's studies of cognitive development.[E] His Ph.D. thesis developed an original

reasoning are called preconventional, conventional, and postconventional.

Preconventional Morality: "What's Best for Me?"[33]

Moral decisions at this lowest level of reasoning are based on personal needs and the rules of others.[34] Moral judgements are made in one's own interest,[35] and in order to avoid punishment from those in authority.[36] The egocentric focus of this stage is on meeting my own needs.

Stage One: Punishment/Obedience: "You Might Get Caught."[37] In stage one, the determining factor in whether an action is good or bad is the personal consequences of an action to the actor. People at framework of stages of moral development.[F]

In 1962 he became assistant professor at the University of Chicago and instituted the Child Psychology Training Program.[G] In 1968 he became a full professor at Harvard, where he established the Center for Moral Development and Education. He spent the next two decades researching moral development in children and adults[H] in nine countries,[I] including Great Britain, Malaysia, Mexico, Taiwan, and Turkey.[J] Kohlberg was not interested so much in whether his subjects made the "right" or "wrong" responses, as in how they explained their judgments.[K]

In 1972 while conducting studies in Central America, he contracted a parasitic disease which left him continuously nauseated. No cure was available, and Kohlberg quickly went from a vibrant young man to a man racked with pain and depression. Though his fame spread and he was surrounded by scholars wanting to learn from him, his depression became steadily worse.[L] On January 17, 1987, he mysteriously died[M] by drowning in Boston Harbor[N] at the age of fifty-nine.

The basic principle Kohlberg espoused throughout his adult life was "to treat every person as an end in himself or herself, not as a means to some other end. Respect for every human being is the essence of justice."[O]

this stage of reasoning simply obey authority figures to avoid being punished.[38] Children are egocentric and cannot see situations from another's point of view.[39] Obedience is good in and of itself.[40] A behavior is moral if it doesn't get punished.[41] Statements like "You do what you're told"[42] and "Might makes right"[43] reflect this stage of reasoning.

Subjects at this stage of reasoning will most likely say that Heinz should not steal the drug because if he is caught, he will go to jail. On the other hand, some might reason that he should steal the drug to help his wife, if he can do so without being caught.

Consequences
to
me?

Avoid
Punishment

You and I
are both
important --
but I come first

Even
Trades

Stage Two: Instrumental/Relativist: "Let's Make a Deal."[44] In stage two, what's right is what satisfies one's own needs and occasionally the needs of others. Concepts of fairness and reciprocity with others develop.[45] People at stage two remain hedonistic[46]—still looking out for themselves[47] and for what makes them happiest.[48] There is the recognition of other's needs, but only to the extent that one can use their needs to get what one want from them.[49] The primary motivation of stage two thinking is the desire for benefit. There is no genuine concern for the welfare of others, apart from a kind of temporary mutual satisfaction.[50]

Statements like the following reflect stage two thinking: "You scratch my back and I'll scratch yours."[51] "Do for me and I will do for you."[52] "An eye for an eye, and a tooth for a tooth."[53] "Nice guys finish last."[54] "Don't bite the hand that feeds you."[55] Perhaps the clearest continuous illustration of stage two morality is in politics: "You vote for my bill, and I'll vote for yours."

Stage two emphasizes even exchanges,[56] fair deals and equal trades,[57] and manipulation.[58] Some adults never get beyond this stage. Fixing traffic tickets, bribing people, and stealing from the boss are okay if you get away with them.[59] Con artists have little *human* regard for others—they simply lack genuine empathy.[60]

Stage two reasoners would most likely say Heinz should steal the drug to help his wife. Their thinking would include ideas like "He'll feel better if his wife isn't sick"[61] or "If she dies there will be no one to cook his dinner."[62] Or, since the druggist is gouging his customers by charging an exorbitant price, Heinz is justifed in taking the drug.

In summary, preconventional moral reasoning acts on the basis of what is best for me, or what will satisfy my needs.[63] It is an egocentric orientation, in that moral consequences to oneself are the overriding considerations in making choices. It is estimated that 15 to 20 percent of teenagers are preconventional reasoners.[64]

Conventional Morality: "What Is Best for My Group?"[65]

Conventional morality develops as children move from egocentric to sociocentric thinking. They begin to see the world from others' points of view.[66] They begin to internalize the socialization they receive from parents and peers.[67] Moral decisions are increasingly based on the approval of others, family expectations, traditional values, the rules of one's social group (club, church, subculture), the laws of society, and loyalty to country,[68] regardless of the immediate and obvious consequences.[69] Conventional morality is a morality of conformity, designed to maintain the social order.[70]

Stage Three: Good Boy/Nice Girl: "Right Actions Impress Others."[71] In stage three, approval from others—particularly those in authority—is all important. This approval is gained by being "nice."[72] Good behavior is whatever pleases or helps others and is approved by them.[73] Right actions are defined as those which reflect loyalty and living up to the expectations of others, maintaining the affection and

What do you value? I'll do it to impress you

Be "nice"

approval of friends and relatives by being a "good" person. A teenage girl who keeps curfew so she won't worry her parents is reasoning at stage three,[74] where mutual trust and loyalty are evident. [75]

Statements like the following reflect stage three reasoning: "Your parents will be proud of you if you are honest."[76] "Be considerate of others and you'll get along just fine."[77] "No man is an island."[78]

The basic motivation for right action is the anticipation of the disapproval of others.[79] Stage three reasoners would likely say that Heinz should steal the drug because "good husbands care about their wives" and "people would disapprove if he let her die."[80] Others might say he should not steal the drug because people—especially community leaders and officials—disapprove of stealing. It just isn't nice.

Stage Four: Law and Order: "Know the Rules and Obey."[81] In stage four, the approval of others of stage three is translated into rules and laws—codified wisdom—which hold society together.[82] In a pluralistic society, laws must take precedence over personal wishes.[83] Moral decisions, then, are based on meeting social and religious responsibilities, upholding the law, and contributing to society and its institutions.[84]

What are society's laws and expectations?

Obey the law

"Good" acts come from knowing the rules and obeying them without question. Legal acts are good acts.[85] Right is doing one's duty, showing respect for authority, maintaining the social order for its own sake.[86] Concern for others is still the focus, but rules, order and the greater good of society for its own sake are key criteria.[87]

Statements like the following reflect stage four thinking. "It's against the law, and if we don't obey laws, our whole society might fall apart."[88] "Don't tear off the tags on pillows 'cause it says not to."[89] "We check out of the hotel at twelve noon because that's the stated check out time."[90] "Pay taxes even if the rest of the world cheats."[91]

Motivation for right action at stage four is the anticipation of dishonor[92] which would result from breaking the rules. Stage four reasoners would probably say Heinz should not steal the drug because he would break the law if he did—period.

In summary, conventional reasoning emphasizes rules which reflect the expectations of family, church, community, or nation. These rules are valuable in their own right[93] and should be obeyed. Most adults live at the conventional level[94] —"We were only following orders"—conforming to social conventions, obeying legal commands, carrying out the directives of government leaders. But this conventional thinking led to the enslavement of Europe and the horrible deaths of millions of innocent men, women, and children. Surely there had to be a higher level of moral reasoning.

Postconventional Reasoning: "What Is Best for All Mankind?"[95]

Postconventional reasoning develops as adolescents move into the fomal operational stage of thinking. Moral judgments are made in relation to abstract principles.[96] Decisions are complex and comprehensive, based on diverse points of view and general principles.[97] There is a deliberate effort to clarify moral rules and principles to arrive at self-defined notions of good and evil.[98] That is, people define their own values in terms of ethical principles they have chosen to follow.[99] Beyond personal wants or needs, beyond legal prescriptions, "principled morality"[100] is based on such overarching ideals as justice, equality, and the dignity of all human life.[101]

Agreed-Upon
Community
Rules
———
Do what is
best for
our community

Stage Five: Social Contract: "Rules Are What the Group Decides." A social contract is an implied agreement among members of society which is evaluated on the basis of "the greatest good for the greatest number."[102] At stage five there is democratic agreement on rights, standards, and the need for change. There are no legal absolutes.[103] People at stage five conform to society's laws so long as they guarantee and protect the rights of individuals in the society. But individuals can evaluate laws in terms of justice and human rights, and reinterpret or change them as needed.[104] Under certain circumstances laws may have to be disregarded, such as when a person's life depends on breaking a law.[105] Laws are not followed blindly for their own sake, but to the extent they protect life, liberty, and the dignity of individuals. [106]

So, "right" is determined by group consensus. Most writers refer to "the society at large" as the group. But Clouse refers specifically to alternate social systems in which the social contract flows out of the welfare of a smaller community.[107] We can think of several counter-culture groups that live by their own rules: street gangs like the "Bloods" and the "Latin Kings," organized crime "families," and cultic groups. We could also consider the Amish and civic organizations such as Kiwanis and Lions as more positive examples. Members of these smaller communities take on the mutually agreed upon codes and rules of their communities. Churches are social communities that set guidelines for behavior. Colleges set standards for students, who choose to follow the rules by their decision to enroll in a particular school.

Many in American society say that terminating an unwanted pregnancy is legal and therefore "right." Further, a woman must be free to determine whether or not to terminate. The State should not dictate this choice for her. Many others believe that interrupting an otherwise viable pregnancy is destroying human life, which is "wrong." Pro-choice advocates hold to one social system based on a woman's right to choose. Pro-life advocates hold to another based on an infant's right to live.

As the moral standards of American society decline, churches are becoming more active in challenging the changing mores. Churches are doing more in the fight against pornography, violence, exploitation, gambling, drugs, promiscuity, and success at any price. The church social systems, which are based on God's Word, are finding themselves increasingly in conflict with laws and standards based on society's wants.

At stage five, people will most likely say that Heinz should steal the drug because "medicine for sick people is more important than someone making a large profit."[108] Or, perhaps, he should steal it because it would be wrong for Heinz to refrain from stealing and let his wife die.[109]

Clouse makes an interesting comparison between stage two and stage five reasoning. In both stages there seems to be permission to break the law. But the *reasons* for breaking the law are very different. At stage two, laws are seen as an interference to personal freedoms. Laws prevent us from doing as we please. But at stage five, law is important and should be respected. If a law is broken in order to serve a higher good, then the individual is willing to face the consequences for it. Second, stage two reasoners experience no anxiety over breaking laws, while stage five reasoners do. Third, stage two reasoners do not ponder the difference between just and unjust laws. Stage five reasoners do. [110]

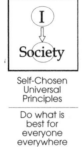

Stage Six: Universal Ethical Principle: "Right Action based on Self-Chosen Principles." [111] Reasoning at stage six is based on principles that are abstract, ethical, universal, and consistent. These principles include justice, reciprocity, equality of human rights, and respect for the dignity of individuals. [112] Stage six reasoning involves weighing all related factors and then making the most appropriate decision for a given situation. Moral decisions are based on consistent applications of self-chosen ethical principles. [113] These individually chosen ethical principles are highly abstract rather than concrete. [114] The Ten Commandments are concrete rules, but the Golden Rule—"Do to others what you would have them do to you" (Matt. 7:12)—is a stage six principle. [115] Kant's maxim—"Act only as you would be willing that everyone should act in the same situation"—is another. "Love your neighbor as yourself" (Lev. 19:18; Matt. 22:39) is another. Still another example of stage six reasoning is Socrates' refusal to alter his principles to save his life. [116]

Kohlberg found that few people actually reach stage six reasoning. Many believed stage six to be little more than a theoretical ideal. [117] Criticism grew over the years so that he eventually revised his stages by collapsing stage six back into stage five. Glover drops stage six from his treatment of Kohlberg altogether. [118]

Yet there is ample evidence of moral reasoning beyond social contract. Mother Teresa has literally given her life helping poverty-stricken Indians die with dignity. In the 1980s, Roman Catholics along the southern border hid El Salvadorans, violating U. S. law, because the nationals faced death by execution squads upon their return. Several priests and nuns were sent to prison for their participation in the pro-life action. Another example is found in a letter written by Martin Luther King from a Birmingham jail cell:

> You express a great deal of anxiety over our willingness to break laws. This is certainly a legitimate concern. Since we do diligently urge people to obey the Supreme Court's decision of 1954 outlawing segregation in the public schools, at first glance it may seem rather paradoxical for us consciously to break laws. One may well ask: "How can you advocate breaking some laws and obeying others?" The answer lies in the fact that there are two types of laws: just and unjust. One has not only a legal but a moral responsibility to obey just laws. Conversely, one has a moral responsibility to disobey unjust laws. I would agree with Saint Augustine that "an unjust law is no law at all."
>
> Now what is the difference between the two? How does one determine when a law is just or unjust? A just law is a man-made code that squares with the moral law or the law of God. An unjust law is a code that is out of harmony with the moral law. To put it in terms of Saint Thomas Aquinas: "An unjust law is a human law that is not rooted in eternal law and natural law. Any law that uplifts human personality is just. Any law that degrades human personality is unjust."[119]

At stage three, people may apply the Golden Rule to their family and close friends. But at stage six, they apply it to everyone everywhere: to the criminal as well as his victim, to the pregnant woman as well as her unborn child, to the rich and the poor, to the young and the old, to the male and the female, to Americans and to foreigners.[120]

At stage four, people obey rules and laws. At stage six they live out principles that are better than laws. The principles insure that just laws are kept, but principles have no loopholes, no legal slack.

In summary, postconventional reasoning is based on self-chosen abstract principles which can be consistently applied. Clouse estimates that only 2 to 10 percent of adults reach the postconventional level of reasoning.

While Kohlberg built on Piaget's cognitive learning theory, there are at least two substantial differences in their views on moral reasoning development. The first addresses the sequence of stages. Piaget believed that changes in reasoning ability occurred as children moved through the stages of cognitive development. But he did not believe the changes to be sequential, nor did he believe the changes could be related to biological age. Kohlberg believed his six stages were fixed and sequential.

The second difference addresses whether moral reasoning could be accelerated through education. Piaget believed moral reasoning

COMPARISON OF PIAGET AND KOHLBERG

was tied to cognitive development which was a biological unfolding of abilities. Moral relativism, Piaget's highest stage, requires formal operational thought, and schools cannot artificially advance students into this level. Kohlberg believed that progress in moral reasoning could be accelerated by confronting children with reasoning no more than one stage above their present level.[121]

KOHLBERG FROM A CHRISTIAN PERSPECTIVE

Duska and Whelan suggest that Kohlberg's theory fits well with Christian doctrine and that his six stages provide a helpful filter for various levels of Christian practice.[122] At stage one, people see God as the Determiner of good and bad, and thus He is seen primarily as Punisher.[123] Perhaps this is why Bible study materials for young children emphasize the love of God—the Gentle Shepherd—so much. It is so natural for people to fear an Angry Judge.

At stage two, God is seen as One Who cares for people's needs, as One Who wants to make us happy. Therefore, presenting the Lord as the One Who came to save us, and the kind of behavior He recommends to make us happy, would be most effective at this stage.[124]

At stage three, people desire group identification. People expand their family circle to include church membership, and begin to take on the roles and duties defined by that community. The "church family" helps define good and bad behavior in terms of what they approve. That is, the good thing to do is what the church approves. People are not self-interested in this stage, except that they would like the approval of their church.[125]

Stage four emphasizes authority, fixed rules, and maintenance of the social order. Church members at stage four show little or no egotism. Rather they demonstrate a selfless and passionate defense of the church and its authorities as the defenders of the correct order of things.[126]

At stage five, what is necessary is not mere acceptance of laws which one has always obeyed, but knowing and free choice. In order for a choice to be made, one has to have at least two options. A knowing and free choice must permit individuals the opportunity to step out of a system of values and beliefs once blindly followed, in order to compare that system with others.[127]

A college freshman grows up in church, faithful to the Lord and his youth group, a dedicated church member. He heads off to college and finds a "whole new world" of parties and priorities. He may well crash and burn as he tries new experiences and suffers the consequences.

But if his faith is real, he will one day "come to himself" like the prodigal and embrace the Lord in a whole new way. His faith will no longer be a copy handed down by loving parents. It will be his own.

At stage six, individuals evaluate systems of beliefs and values from an ideal perspective. Christ came to fulfill the Law, not to do away with it (Matt. 5:17). Time and again Jesus challenged the legalism of the Pharisees which destroyed the spirit of the Law. Time and again He appealed to a higher order, the Kingdom of God, which gave us an ideal by which to judge the real. Most important, however, were the appeals to the highest principles of all: justice and love, both based on the belief that we are all God's children, all beloved of God, and the insistence that even the highest authority should be the humblest servant.[128]

One is hard pressed to find a more consistent pattern for stage six living than in the example and teachings of Jesus. As His disciples, we should endeavor to grow, in our day-to-day behavior as well as our thinking, toward the Master, toward stage six. I once heard Francis Shaeffer remark that the profitable British slave trade was brought down by a single preacher with a Bible in his hand. One individual, convinced in his heart of hearts that slavery was unjust, changed his society.

Despite the wide-ranging influence of Kohlberg's theory, there are several criticisms of his views that need consideration as we develop our approach to moral issues.

CRITICISMS OF KOHLBERG'S THEORY

1. The Stages Sequentially Fixed? Despite Kohlberg's assertions that the six stages form a fixed, sequential pattern of development, others have found that the stages are not separate, nor sequenced, nor consistent. People reason out of several stages simultaneously, depending on the nature of the moral issue.[129] Others found that their subjects skipped stages altogether, or reverted randomly to an earlier stage. There was generally a lack of consistent response from a given stage.[130]

2. Morals or Conventions? Kohlberg is criticized for not differentiating between moral issues and social conventions.[131] Social conventions are arbitrary rules determined by a particular social group. Rules like "It's rude to eat with your hands" or "Men don't wear dresses" are not "right" or "wrong" morally.[132] Moral issues deal with fundamental rights of individuals, the general welfare of the group, the avoidance of harm. Even children as young as three can differentiate between morals and conventions. Here's an example: being noisy would be okay, if there were no rule against it. But hitting another child is wrong, even if there is no rule against it.[133]

3. Biased in Favor of Males? Kohlberg's six stages are based on principles of justice and fairness. This may be due to the fact that all of Kohlberg's subjects were males.[134] Reasoning based on caring for others and maintaining relationships is scored lower in Kohlberg's theory.[135] Since men tend to focus more on rights, and women tend to focus more on responsibilities,[136] men tend to score higher in Kohlberg's hierarchy than women—stage three for women and stage four for men at the same age.[137] In 1982, Carol Gilligan challenged Kohlberg's male bias with her own "ethic of care." Moral reasoning in women follows a three stage process from "self-interest" to "commitment to individuals" to "responsibility and care for all people."[138] Kohlberg responded by admitting that the study of the moral domain could be enlarged to include affective elements of caring, love, and responsibility, but that these should not be considered a morality separate from rational justice reasoning.[139] To assign justice solely to men and caring solely to women is to do injustice to the capacities of both sexes.[140]

More recent research on adults,[141] however, has found little or no difference in moral reasoning between men and women.[142] Both caring and justice[143] are important to both men and women.[144]

4. Decisions or Behavior? Kohlberg focused on how people make moral decisions. He did not focus on what they actually did.[145] Individuals at different stages behave the same way. Individuals at the same stage behave in different ways.[146] Kohlberg acknowledged this criticism and called for more research on predicting behavior from the stages. One such study provided an opportunity for students to cheat without being caught. Students who actually cheated in the situation were represented as follows: seventy percent (70%) of preconventional reasoners, fifty-five percent (55%) of conventional reasoners, and fifteen percent (15%) of postconventional reasoners. While members of all three groups did cheat, the percentages demonstrate a tendency to act according to one's beliefs.[147]

5. Western Bias? Postconventional reasoning may be biased in favor of Western cultures where individuality is prized. The Amish and native Americans de-emphasize individuality and place more value on cooperation, collaboration, and group orientation.[148]

Individuals in these cultures would rate lower on Kohlberg's hierarchy because of their more conventional orientation.

In cross-cultural studies, researchers have found that Kohlberg's stages exist and in the same sequence as he theorized. What varies is the rate of development and the end point of development[149] — some cultures develop moral reasoning more slowly and never reach the postconventional stage.

Lawrence Kohlberg spent his life gathering data on how children and adults deal with moral dilemmas. What are the implications of his theory for teachers? Here are nine for your consideration:

1. Expect a Variety of Responses. Recognize that younger children respond to moral dilemmas differently than older children.[150] Stress concrete actions rather than abstract principles when teaching younger children. For example, in teaching children how to treat the toys of others, we might emphasize a general principle like "You shouldn't play with toys that belong to other children." However, this principle will be lost on younger children. Better to focus on concrete actions, such as "Be careful with that toy, or it might break."[151] Further, students of the same age may operate on different levels of moral reasoning.[152]

2. Increase Awareness of Moral Issues. Discuss real and hypothetical moral dilemmas in class. Use experiences in the classroom as opportunities to heighten moral awareness. It is more effective to integrate moral issues into the regular curriculum than to provide a separate "moral education" lesson.[153] My research students consider "Research and Statistics for Advanced Studies" one of the least spiritual classes they can take. Yet I have more opportunity to teach them about the Lord's care and nurture, His desire for them to do their best, and basic character traits of honesty and integrity in that class than in any other. It may be that they are not expecting to hear about the Lord while studying two-way ANOVA allows more natural learning to happen when they do.

3. Ask the "Why?" Question. Present a specific moral dilemma and ask, "What should be done in this situation?" After a student responds, ask, "Why would you do that?" The answer to the "Why?" question will give you insight into the reasoning behind the student's response. [154]

EDUCATIONAL
IMPLICATIONS

4. Personal Choice. Ask students to make a personal choice in the dilemma: "What would *you* do in this situation?" Then have them justify their response.[155]

5. Alternatives. Analyze different courses of action by discussing the pros and cons of each choice. Encourage students to consider the perspectives of others.[156]

6. Stage Plus One. The most effective strategy in developing moral reasoning skills is to discuss alternative responses *one stage above* the student's level of reasoning. Presenting stage three reasoning to a stage two reasoner will be more effective than presenting stage two or stage four alternatives.[157]

7. Class Atmosphere. Foster an atmosphere of openness in the classroom through face-to-face groupings. Encourage interaction, practice listening and communication skills. Model the role of an accepting, open person.[158] An atmosphere of openness and trust is essential if you expect your students to discuss moral decisions they might make.

8. The Role of the Teacher. Without some form of guidance, direction, or structure from the teacher, a class of students will soon dissolve into chaos. Teachers can take several roles with regard to teaching moral reasoning:

a. The Teacher as Model. Model higher level reasoning in the classroom.[159] Demonstrate by your own thinking and behavior how to handle moral dilemmas. Lasting moral learning comes by observing teachers.[160]

b. The Teacher as Master. Advocate good behavior and a strong conscience. Teach proper values and principles. You are the source of values for your class.[161]

c. The Teacher as Facilitator. Help students develop and understand their own values. The student is the source of values in this approach.[162]

d. The Teacher as Mentor. Relate to your students as a guide, a friend, an enlightened leader from whom your students can gain moral guidance.[163]

IN CONCLUSION:
KOHLBERG

We close this part of the chapter with two instances from the life of Jesus which illustrate His conflict with the religious thinking of His day. The first revolves around a woman caught in adultery. Jesus was teaching in the temple court one day:

> The teachers of the law and the Pharisees brought in a woman caught in adultery. They made her stand before the group and said to Jesus, "Teacher,

this woman was caught in the act of adultery. In the Law Moses commanded us to stone such women. Now what do you say?" . . . When they kept on questioning him, he straightened up and said to them, "If any one of you is without sin, let him be the first to throw a stone at her" (John 8:3–5, 7).

The Law of Moses declares: "If a man commits adultery with another man's wife—with the wife of his neighbor—both the adulterer and the adulteress must be put to death" (Lev. 20:10). No gray area here. This is straightforward stage four law. Yet it is interesting to note that the Pharisees didn't bring the man with them, as stated in the Law. Perhaps this was because they were more interested in trapping Jesus than in following the Law (John 8:6).

If Jesus said to stone her, according to the Law, the Pharisees knew His popularity among the people would suffer. If He didn't agree to have her stoned, He would break the Mosaic Law and be branded a false prophet. The Pharisees believed He would lose either way.

But Jesus moved beyond their stage four thinking to stage six, and established a principle: "If any one of you is without sin, let him be the first to throw a stone at her" (John 8:7). The moral test at stage six is whether we are willing to apply the principle to self as well as others.[164] Look at the response of the mob: the men began to drop the stones in their hands, the older—and presumably wiser—doing so first, followed by the younger, more militant ones. Did Jesus break the Law? Did He demonstrate a casual regard for Scripture, changing it to fit the immediate situation? No, He did not come to destroy, but to fulfill the Law. Forgiveness based on faith supercedes arbitrary punishment, because all of us have sinned. Paul wrote that the Law was a pedagogue ("a household slave charged with accompanying a child to school,"[165] not "schoolmaster" as in the King James) put in charge to lead us to Christ. Now that we have been justified by faith, we no longer need the Law (Gal. 3:25). Jesus superimposed the Law, and made it complete.

A second example is found in the confrontation with Jesus over the Sabbath:

> And a man with a shriveled hand was there. Looking for a reason to accuse Jesus, they asked him, "Is it lawful to heal on the Sabbath?" He said to them, "If any of you has a sheep and it falls into a pit on the Sabbath, will you not take hold of it and lift it out? How much more valuable is a man than a sheep! *Therefore it is lawful to do good on the Sabbath.*" Then he said to the man, "Stretch out your hand." So he stretched it out and it was completely restored, just as sound as the other. But the Pharisees went out and plotted how they might kill Jesus (Matt. 12:10–14, author's emphasis).

The Sixth Commandment states, "Remember the Sabbath day by keeping it holy" (Exod. 20:8). The Pharisees had interpreted this rule to mean more than Scripture said. They used it as a way to control the people. But Jesus taught that "the Sabbath was made for man, not man for the Sabbath" (Mark 2:27). And He laid down the New Principle of His Kingdom: "It is lawful to do good on the Sabbath."

In fact, Jesus taught that if His followers would simply live at the principled level by loving God with all their hearts and loving their neighbors as they love themselves, that they would fulfill every rule and commandment of Scripture (Matt. 22:37–39).

May God bless you as you challenge your students not only with alternative approaches to contemporary moral issues, but also lead them to see life from the perspective of the Kingdom and its King.

JAMES FOWLER'S STAGES OF FAITH

James Fowler extends the concept of stage development to faith. Fowler sees faith as a human universal. Faith for Fowler is so

> fundamental that none of us can live well for very long without it, so universal that when we move beneath the symbols, rituals and ethical patterns that express it, faith is recognizably the same phenomenon in Christians, Marxists, Hindus and Dinka, yet it is so infinitely varied that each person's faith is unique. [166]

We are born, says Fowler, with capacities for faith. These capacities are activated and developed by the way we experience the world around us. Faith is interactive and social, requiring community, language, ritual, and nurture. Faith is shaped by significant others, as well as by initiatives of spirit and grace. [167]

Building on Erikson, Piaget, and Kohlberg, Fowler believes that "wholeness, maturity, and excellence of being come as by-products and resultant virtues of lives that are falling in love with One who intends, and is bringing, a universal commonwealth of love." [168] The overarching theme of Fowler's theory is that "we grow up and become adults in terms of some myth or image of the life-story that defines for us what it means to become a complete human being." [169] Faith is a coat against the nakedness of a soul alone. [170]

"*How* a person believes, not *what* a person believes"

Like Piaget and Kohlberg before him, Fowler emphasizes structure more than content. That is, he studies *how a person believes, not what a person believes.* This causes problems for Christians who take what one believes very seriously. He sees faith development as a natural process, while Christian faith has a supernatural cause (Eph. 2:8). He aims to demonstrate how faith develops in anyone: Christian, Muslim,

Jew, atheist,[171] while Christian faith is specific, focused on the Lord Jesus Christ—"Not all have faith" (2 Thess. 3:2, RSV).

Still, Fowler's ideas certainly shed light on the human side of faith development—the rational, social, and emotional aspects of the natural development of human faith. We'll look briefly at each stage.

During the first year of life, an infant who is properly cared for lives in an environment that produces a sense of well-being and trust. Primal faith is defined as the confidence which the infant gains from the relations, care, and shared meanings that enrich the child and offset feelings of vunerability.[174] Primal faith is closely related to the Trust/Mistrust stage of Erikson.

Primal[172] or Undifferentiated[173] Faith

Parents provide intense *preimages*[175] *of power and wisdom coupled with tender care*, "rigidity and grace, harshness and love," which are present in the images consciously formed by four- and five-year-olds.[176] Fowler uses the term "preimages" because such images are formed prior to language, prior to concepts, and coincident with emerging consciousness.[177]

Here the seeds of trust, courage, hope, and love are fused in an undifferentiated way. This fusion battles against threats of abandonment, inconsistency, and deprivation. While this prestage is largely inaccessible to empirical research, Fowler contends that the qualities developed during this first year "underlie (or threaten to undermine)" all future developments.[178]

The strength of faith at this stage is found in basic trust and the mutuality of relationship with caregivers. One danger of this stage is the formation of excessive narcissism, where self dominates and distorts mutuality. Another danger is isolation from others, if neglect and inconsistent care were experienced. The transition to stage one begins with the beginning of language and the use of symbols in speech and ritual play.[179]

Language has a profound impact on the child by age three. This language changes the relationships the child has with the world around him. As the mother mimics the efforts of the child to talk, she becomes a mirror, reflecting back to the child his own image.[181] Children of this preoperational period are making discoveries constantly. Their minds are active, free, and unhindered by preconceived notions. Their *egocentric perceptions, feelings, and fantasy transform their experiences of reality.* Symbols, stories, and the

Stage One: Intuitive/Projective Faith (Ages 3 to 7)[180]

shared life of religious tradition provide for the child a rich base of meaning—a source of guidance and reassurance.[182]

The emergent strength of this stage is the "birth of imagination, the ability to unify and grasp the experience-world in powerful images." One danger of this stage is the possible "possession of the child's imagination by unrestrained images of terror and destructiveness." Another is the exploitation of the child's imagination in the reinforcement of taboos and moral and doctrinal expectations. Movement into concrete operational thinking initiates the transition to stage two.[183]

Stage Two:
Mythic/Literal Faith
(Ages 7 to 11)[184]

About the age of six or seven, children begin moving into concrete operational thinking. They begin to form stable concepts of space, time, and causality. This means that their conceptions of the world are much less dependent on feelings and fantasy. Children at this stage work hard at sorting out the real from the make-believe.[185] I remember a discussion I had with my mother when I discovered, about age four or five, that Santa Claus didn't really exist. "Well, he's the spirit of Christmas," she said, "the spirit of giving." "But, is there a man who travels around the world in a sleigh delivering gifts?" "No, that's just a story." "Okay, then if Santa Claus is just a story, is Jesus just a story, or is He real?" "Oh, honey," she said very seriously, "Jesus is real. He's not like Santa Claus at all." "Okay, thanks!" The distinction was made, and I was satisfied.

Piaget emphasized the development of reversibility and decentration during this time. These abilities make the world "more linear, orderly, and predictable" for the child. Kohlberg emphasized reciprocity—the even exchange of his second stage—which Fowler believes leads to a strong sense of fairness. Faith at this stage is defined as "reliance on stories, rules and implicit values in the family's community of meanings."[186] This is a "conformist" stage, in which the person is tuned to the expectations of significant others. The locus of authority is in others.[187]

The strength which emerges from this stage is the "rise of narrative and the emergence of story, drama, and myth as ways of finding and giving [literal] coherence to experience."[188] The danger of this stage rises out of the literalness of concrete thinking and excessive reliance on reciprocity. This can result in an "overcontrolling, stilted perfectionism or 'works righteousness' or an abasing sense of badness which comes from mistreatment or neglect."[189] The movement into formal operational thought allows for reflective thought on meanings of stories, which ushers in stage three.

Adolescents move into Piaget's formal operational stage of thinking, in which abstract concepts and ideals are generated and used. "Systems" of ideas begin to form as adolescents restructure and reorganize their world.[191] This is the meaning of "synthesis": the pulling together of disparate elements into a new whole, a new unity. Abstract thinking (stage four, Piaget), identity issues (stage five, Erikson) and the discovery of alternative social systems (stage five, Kohlberg) provide a rich mix from which to synthesize one's own meaning. The locus of authority shifts from external to internal in this stage.[192] Fowler uses the term "synthesis" in a second way, referring to the synthesis of multiple life-stories into a "story of stories," or the meaning of life.[193]

Stage Three: Synthetic- Conventional Faith (Ages 12 to 18)[190]

The term "conventional" refers to the fact that this synthesis is drawn from significant others. It is not based on self-reflection alone. Also, this synthesis is not an object apart from self which can be evaluated. The synthesis is part of self.[194] Therefore, this stage emphasizes *internalized values and beliefs which are strongly felt but largely unexamined.*[195]

The emergent strength of this stage is the forming of a "personal myth"[196]—a personal meaning of life[197]—which incorporates one's past, anticipated future, and characteristics of personality. The danger of this stage is twofold. First, the expectations of others can be so internalized that later autonomous judgment and action can be undermined. And second, interpersonal conflicts can lead to despair.[198] Movement to stage four is initiated when one's belief system is assaulted by clashes with valued leaders or by severe changes in practices or policies once held as sacred. This disequilibrium leads to critical reflection on how one's beliefs and values have formed and changed.[199]

The synthesis of stage four becomes objectified in stage five, permitting adults to examine it and make critical choices about faith. This step requires two things. First, there must be a change in one's orientation toward external sources of authority and self. In this stage, there is a relocation of authority[201] from "the tyranny of the they"[202] to self. There must also be a differentiation between "self"—who I really am, which Fowler calls the "executive ego"— and "personae"[203]—the roles I choose to play, which Fowler calls "lifestyle." This differentiation permits the "self" to evaluate the

Stage Four: Individuative/ Reflective Faith (Ages 18 to 30) [200]

value systems of the personae. Second, there must be the objectification of values and beliefs, which requires explicit commitment and accountability for the decisions the "self" makes.[204]

These changes occur most often, if they ever do, in the midst of upheaval and radical change in adults in their thirties and forties, and point to the need of adults to take seriously their responsibilities, their commitments, lifestyle, beliefs, and attitudes.[205] Fowler's stage relates well with Erikson's Generativity versus Stagnation stage.

The strength resulting from stage four has to do with the ability to *reflect critically on one's identity (self) and outlook (ideology)*. The danger is an excessive confidence in critical thought and the tendency to overassimilate the perspectives of others into one's own world view.[206]

Transition to stage five begins with the discovery that life is more complex than stage four's logic of clear distinctions. Stories and symbols from other traditions, as well as disillusionment with one's own compromises, lead toward a multi-leveled approach to life truth.[207]

Stage Five: Conjunctive Faith (Ages 30 to 40)[208]

The synthesis of life meaning is objectified, examined, and resolved in stage four. Stage five emphasizes the integration into that synthesis of elements in ourselves and our society that are polarized, or paradoxical, or opposites. In stage four, the "self" is a conscious agent with firm boundaries. In stage six, the "self" includes the power and influence of the unconscious, with boundaries that are "porous and permeable."[209]

Middle-aged adults find themselves between their elders, who are dying, and the young, who are just beginning to take hold of life. This is one of the polarities which must be integrated—I am neither young nor old, but a little of each. Other polarities include masculine/feminine, constructive/destructive, the conscious and the subconscious. *Truth is seen as more complex, ambiguous, and multidimensioned* in this stage. And paradox becomes an essential part of truth.[210] During this stage, adults welcome the truths of traditions and communities different from their own. There is strong commitment to one's own tradition, but also humility to know that one's tradition needs constant correction and challenge from others.[211]

Adults in stage five are not ideologues. They are not wholeheartedly committed to one ideology. They do not engage in holy wars.[212] They live in tension between present reality and future possibility. They are committed to present values and institutions, and are unwilling to let go of these, even though they can see a better way in the future.[213]

The strength of stage five is the ability to "see and be in one's or one's group's most powerful meanings, while simultaneously recognizing that they are relative, partial and inevitably distorting apprehensions of transcendent reality." Stage five allows adults to see the divisions of the human family because they have discovered the "possibility of an inclusive community of being." The danger of this stage is that paradoxical truth may lead to "paralyzing inaction, giving rise to complacency or cynical withdrawal." But stage five remains divided, leaving adults suspended between the untransformed world in which they live and a transforming vision. Movement to stage six resolves this division by answering the call to "radical actualization."[214]

The fear of letting go of the present is overcome in stage six. Decentration of self is complete, and one sees the world through the eyes and experiences of others quite different from ourselves. There is an expansion of values to value the Creator and others.[216] There is an *emptying of self, a giving up of power in response to the radical love of God.*[217]

Stage Six: Universalizing Faith (Age 40 Plus)[215]

Fowler describes the characteristics of "Universalizers" in an article in *The Perkins Journal* as follows:

> Universalizers are often experienced as subversive of the structures (including religious structures) by which we sustain our individual and corporate survival, security and significance. Many persons in this stage die at the hands of those they hope to change. Universalizers are often more honored and revered after death than during their lives. The rare persons who may be described by this stage have a special grace that makes them seem more lucid, more simple, and yet somehow more fully human than the rest of us. Their community is universal in extent . . . Life is both loved and held too loosely. Such persons are ready for fellowship with persons at any of the other stages and from any other faith tradition.[218]

Fowler includes persons such as Mahatma Gandhi, Rev. Martin Luther King, Jr., in the last years of his life, Mother Teresa of Calcutta, and Dietrich Bonhoeffer as examples of stage six living.[219] However uncomfortable evangelical Christians may be with Fowler's use of terms such as "myth" and "universalism," the above quote certainly describes the life of Jesus. Raised in the Jewish faith, His vision was for the whole world. He continually challenged the authority of the religious leaders and their institutions, contrasting them with the transcendent Kingdom of God. He came as Israel's Messiah, but official Israel turned Him over to be executed as a

"Empty self, give up power"

subversive. He came to His own, but His own did not embrace Him. He was more honored after His death (and resurrection) than during His life. His teachings were powerful, yet filled with grace. Profound, yet simple. He was the Perfect Man as well as the Son of God. He loved life, yet did not hold on to it—He drank the cup of death on the cross because it was the Father's· will. He readily engaged people different from Himself for fellowship—Nicodemus the Pharisee and Sanhedrin member, the Roman centurion, the Samaritan woman at the well, the Syro-Phoenician woman, tax collectors Matthew and Zaccheus, and many others. In each instance of Fowler's quote, Jesus demonstrated stage six behavior. Yet Jesus was not a relativist, formulating His ideas of God out of His own existential experiences. The heavenly Father was His Reality and Authority: "I tell you the truth, the Son can do nothing by himself; he can do only what he sees his Father doing, because whatever the Father does the Son also does" (John 5:19).

IN CONCLUSION: FOWLER

Pluralistic society and existential philosophy have moved our thinking more and more toward relativism. This relativism emphasizes the individual's own perspective as the center of truth-seeking, a standard for decision-making. There is a sense in which this is absolutely true. Evangelical Christians hold firmly to biblical authority1 as the Truth of God. Yet holding the Bible as God's Truth will not change life until it becomes "Truth that matters to me." This is an existential event. No one can make a faith commitment for Christ in my place. I must make that choice, for myself. That is an existential event. I may believe that Christians should love their enemies and pray for those who persecute them (Matt. 5:44), but if I do not live this way, it is not Truth-that-matters-to-me. Piaget, Kohlberg, and Fowler can help us understand the natural side of human growth, and provide insight into some of the hindrances to healthy development.

"Absolute truth lies in Scripture, not in our experience"

There is another sense of relativism that undermines Christian growth, because it undermines "every source of authority to which theology can appeal . . . our evangelical faith contends that absolute truth lies in Scripture, not in our experience." [220]

Perhaps the best picture of this Truth-experience polarity is flying a kite. In order for the kite to fly, there must be a steady wind and there must be a string anchoring the kite to the flyer's hand. The wind is analogous to experience, lifting the kite into the sky. Truth remains an academic exercise for the seeker who has not experienced Truth.

The string is analogous to Scripture, anchoring the kite to the ground. Without an anchor, experience creates a multitude of truths. If the wind stops blowing, or one lets go of the string, the kite falls. I must anchor my experience in the Truth, and strive to put into practice the Truth I learn.

In this context, developmental theorists help us conceptualize our experience and differentiate among persons who live at different levels of socialization, thinking, moral reasoning, and faith. More subjectively, they help us identify our own thinking, our own position on the hierarchies, so as to better understand who we are.

CHAPTER CONCEPTS

Autonomy	Morality
Conjunctive faith	Morality of constraint
Conventional reasoning	Morality of cooperation
Good boy/nice girl	Mythic/Literal faith
Heteronomy	Postconventional reasoning
Individuative/Reflective faith	Preconventional reasoning
Instrumental/Relativist	Premoral
Law and Order	Primal faith
Moral dilemma	Punishment/Obedience
Moral realism	Social Contract
Moral reasoning	Synthetic/Conventional Faith
Moral relativism	Universal Ethical Principle
	Universalizing Faith

DISCUSSION QUESTIONS

1. Describe an experience from your childhood in which you played with children several years older than you. What do you remember from that experience related to constraint and cooperation?

2. How did you react to the story of the school fair booth? Was the teenager guilty of stealing tickets? Was the sister right in accusing him? Why or why not?

3. Choose two of Kohlberg's six stages and relate a personal experience you've had in moral reasoning. What was the conflict? How did you resolve it? How does it reflect the level of moral reasoning?

4. Differentiate among morality, moral reasoning, and Christlikeness.

FOR FURTHER READING

Biehler, Robert F. and Jack Snowman. "Kohlberg and Moral Reasoning" in *Psychology Applied to Teaching*, 7th ed. 76–85. Boston: Houghton Mifflin Company, 1993.

Clouse, Bonnidell. *Teaching for Moral Growth: A Guide for the Christian Community—Teachers, Parents and Pastors*, 229–48. Wheaton, Ill: Bridgeport Books, 1993.

Dembo, Myron H. *Applying Educational Psychology*, 5th ed., 214–23. New York: Longman, 1994.

Eggen, Paul and Don Kauchak. *Educational Psychology: Classroom Connections*, 2nd ed., 63-68. New York: Macmillan College Publishing Company, 1994.

Fowler, James W. *Stages of Faith: The Psychology of Human Development and the Quest for Meaning*. San Francisco: Harper & Row, Publishers, 1981.

_____. *Becoming Adult, Becoming Christian*. San Francisco: Harper & Row, Publishers, 1991.

Good, Thomas L. and Jere E. Brophey. *Educational Psychology: A Realistic Approach*, 4th ed., 108–15. New York: Longman, 1990.

Hamachek, Don. *Psychology in Teaching, Learning, and Growth*, 4th ed., 172–76. Boston: Allyn and Bacon, 1990.

Sell, Charles M. *Transitions Through Adult Life*. Grand Rapids, Mich.: Zondervan Publishing House, 1991.

Slavin, Robert E. *Educational Psychology: Theory and Practice*, 4th ed., 58–65. Boston: Allyn and Bacon, 1994.

Sprinthall, Norman A., Richard C. Sprinthall and Sharon N. Oja, *Educational Psychology: A Developmental Approach*, 6th ed., 177–97. New York: McGraw-Hill, Inc., 1994.

Woolfolk, Anita. *Educational Psychology*, 5th ed., 79–83. Boston: Allyn and Bacon, Inc., 1993.

Chapter

6

INSTRUCTIONAL OBJECTIVES

SETTING UP TARGETS FOR TEACHING

We have seen in the previous chapters that learners come to us with a wide range of social and intellectual skills. They sit before us at the beginning of the semester expecting us to lead them somewhere—to new discoveries, new skills, new attitudes and values—that will benefit them both now and in the future. We give them a better impression of the journey if we know where we're going and what we expect on the way. What is the end result of our study together? How will we get there? The first question will be answered in this chapter, the second in the next unit of learning theory systems.

CHAPTER RATIONALE

Learners will demonstrate knowledge of the learning domains by

CHAPTER OBJECTIVES

- defining the terms cognitive, affective, and psychomotor, and

- identifying definitions of learning levels.

Learners will demonstrate understanding of learning levels by identifying the level of learning of stated instructional objectives.

Learners will demonstrate understanding of instructional objectives by writing objectives when given a Scripture passage and learning level.

Learners will demonstrate appreciation for instructional objectives by sharing personal experiences of two classes—one that did not use objectives and one that did.

WHAT IS AN INSTRUCTIONAL OBJECTIVE?

An instructional objective is a "statement about the type of performance that can be expected of students once they have completed a lesson, a unit or a course."[1] These statements of intent focus more on students than on content,[2] more on what students will do than on what teachers will do. Objectives are not descriptions of teaching, but terminal indicators[3] that students have learned what we intended for them to learn. The term "indicator" refers to student behaviors which demonstrate learning. For this reason, instructional objectives are often referred to as "behavioral objectives."[4] Some object to this terminology because it appears to focus only on behavior and ignores equally important cognitive and affective outcomes.[5] This concern misses the point of instructional objectives. If there is no overt demonstration of learning, how will teachers know if learning has occurred? We will see in this chapter that there are specific ways students can demonstrate that they know, or that they understand, or that they value the content. "Behavioral" objectives do not limit teachers to behavioristic methods of teaching.

WHY HAVE INSTRUCTIONAL OBJECTIVES?

When I was ten years old, my family lived in El Paso, Texas. On Christmas, I received a bow and arrow set. Since it was a balmy 65° outside, I eagerly set up my target—attached to a cardboard box—and proceeded to play Robin Hood. I drew back my first shot and let it fly. The arrow missed the target, missed the box, hit the stone fence behind, and split right down the middle.

I only had two arrows left, so I decided to invent a game which would let me shoot arrows without breaking any more of them. I moved out to the center of the yard. Pulling the bowstring back as far as I could, I shot the arrow straight up. I stood and watched as it traveled higher and higher, then turned and made its way back down. I stayed under the falling arrow, watching the wind buffet it. At the last moment I positioned my foot as close to the estimated impact point as I could. It was great fun. I began to adapt the game. I'd start on one side of the yard, put some angle into my shot, then run across the yard, pick up the arching arrow, and see how close I could get my foot to the impact point. This went well until my mom saw what I was doing from the kitchen window and threatened to take my bow away. From then on I had to play my game at night—it's a lot harder in the dark! But the point is this: I never learned to be an archer.

Archers can put arrows in targets intentionally. How do they learn to do that? By shooting at a target, missing, and adjusting.

Shoot, miss, adjust. Shoot, miss, adjust. Thousands of times. And in the process of shooting, missing, and adjusting, they develop the skills needed to put an arrow in a target, and thus become archers. I never developed that skill because I refused to use targets. I did not want to fail—and break my arrows!

Later on when I began teaching a Sunday school class, I found myself following the same pattern. I would talk about the Bible (shoot an arrow into the air) and watch what the Holy Spirit did in the class (watch the wind buffet the arrow). Then, wherever we ended up was great (I moved my foot to where the arrow landed). The Lord still blessed the teaching of His Word, but I didn't grow as a teacher because I had no targets to hit, no intentional expectations to meet. My teaching was all process with no predetermined destination.

"I never learned to be an archer"

This kind of teaching is certainly not limited to Sunday school. A college professor can entertain his history classes with stories and anecdotes about the Civil War. But if, on their examination, he asks them to "describe and explain the five major causes of the Civil War," he has not been consistent in his teaching and testing. The gap between teaching and testing can be filled by instructional objectives which guide both. The subtitle of the chapter ("Setting Up Targets for Teaching") underscores the "Why?" of objectives. Before we consider the kinds of targets we can use (levels of learning) and how actually to write objectives, let's look at six major ways instructional targets strengthen the teaching-learning process.

First, classroom teaching involves many verbal activities. These activities—like lectures, films, guest speakers, projects, and readings—are often loosely organized and do not lend themselves naturally to structure learnings. Objectives focus student attention on key ideas and attitudes.[6]

Objectives Focus Student Attention

Second, objectives help clarify teachers' expectations for changes in their students.[7] Rather than surround students with foglike word magic—"to become good citizens," or "to engender the highest ideals of science"—objectives help specify the knowledge, understanding, values, and skills which teachers expect their students to achieve.

Objectives Clarify Teacher Expectations

When objectives are used as a guide for testing, students are able to demonstrate their learning more confidently. Their grades are based on their mastery of course structure rather than anwers to an arbitrary collection of test items. Not only do their grades improve,

Objectives Facilitate Better Testing

but their attitudes toward the course, their learning experience, and their professor dramatically improve as well.

Objectives Improve Session Planning

Teachers facilitate learning by providing activities and experiences that are tied to the material to be learned. In any given session, what activities should be provided? In what order should these activities be done?[8] If our aim in teaching is directed toward specific objectives, then we can select activities which move students to those objectives. Such a process provides continuity in the class sessions,[9] and a cohesiveness to learning experiences. It gives students a sense of *going somewhere.*

Objectives Improves Unit and Course Planning

Just as objectives provide a sense of going somewhere in a single session, so they can provide a road map for an entire unit or course of study. Structure a unit or course by deciding what you want students to know, understand, value, or do skillfully at the end of the study. Write instructional objectives to focus on these terminal indicators. Then plan single sessions which lead to these objectives. This "backward planning" process begins with expected accomplishments and ends with learning activities which will, progressively, move students to those ends.

Objectives Improve Teacher Performance

Archers become proficient as they shoot, miss, and adjust. Teachers become proficient as they teach, evaluate, and revise. Instructional objectives allow teachers to consider rationally how well they accomplish what they plan.[10] Are objectives too demanding? Do objectives fit student abilities? Do teaching procedures fit stated objectives? What changes need to be made so that objectives can be achieved more effectively?

No one likes to be evaluated. No one wants clear evidence that their teaching is lacking—no one, that is, except those who hunger to become skillful teachers. Archers who refuse to enter competitions for fear of losing will never reach their potential for archery. To excel in teaching, we must swallow pride and put away ego, set up targets, do our best to hit them, accept our failures, and consistently make adjustments when we miss.

KINDS OF OBJECTIVES

Objectives come in a range of flavors. Some objectives are so broad that they are worthless as instructional guides. Examples of these kinds of targets include "developing intellect" or becoming "good citizens,"[11] or "students should understand evolutionary theory."[12] Some objectives are so specific and trivial that they limit both the quantity and quality of learning. Examples of these include "recall selected definitions" or "reconstruct the flowchart,"[13] or "students should write from memory two Darwinian laws of evolution."[14]

Woolfolk suggests a middle ground for objectives which provides direction for students but allows for a broad range of learning. Here's one example she cites:

> In class, without access to notes, given three presidential elections between 1900 and 1944, write a 200-word essay describing how domestic policy might have changed if the defeated candidate had been elected. (The test specified the election years 1900, 1912, and 1940.)[15]

Students know from this objective what the teacher expects them to do. They know the range of material required to satisfy this objective. They understand the focus of study to be domestic policy of both the elected and defeated presidential candidates. Such flexible structure avoids confusion on the one hand and trivialization on the other.

Four theorists have greatly influenced the development and use of instructional objectives. These are Robert Mager (1962, 1975[16]), Norman Gronlund (1972, 1975, 1991[17]), E. W. Eisner (1967[18]) and Leroy Ford (1978, 1991[19]).

Robert F. Mager

In his book *Preparing Instructional Objectives*, Mager called for writing a three-part objective statement. The first part answers the question, "What will the student do?" The second part answers the question, "How will this behavior be tested?" The third part answers the question, "What are the criteria for acceptable performance?"[20] Here are several examples of Mager's performance objectives:

> When given a series of instances of government activities, the student can identify the instance as the proper interest of the legislative, judicial, or executive branch of government (8 of 10 correct).[21]

> Given pictures of ten trees, correctly identifies at least eight as either deciduous or evergreen.[22]

> Students should be able to define at least six of the nine Fruits of the Spirit (Gal. 5:22–23) in their own words.

Critics refer to Mager's system as being best suited for outcomes of simple recall or skill.[23] In fact, the tight specifications of Mager's work have been criticized for leading to an overly rigid system[24] of "hopelessly trivial"[25] statements of performance. This certainly was not Mager's intent, nor is this bent toward course trivia found in his writings. He includes suggestions for all levels of learning, but his broad perspective is clearly shown in his book *Developing Attitude*

Toward Learning, in which he applies his system to affective outcomes.

The problem is that none of the twenty-some-odd recent educational psychology texts I've read reference any of Mager's writings other than *Preparing Instructional Objectives*—and the majority of those reference the 1962 edition rather than the 1975 edition. The criticism may be due more to educators who use Mager's approach to write trivial objectives because they are easier to measure than higher level objectives. It may not be the system, but the improper *use* of the system, that draws the criticism. Still, Mager's insistence on performance criteria opens the door to rigidly structured courses.

E. W. Eisner

Eisner believed Mager's approach to writing objectives is too narrow. The "performance" objectives approach restricts the curriculum, discourages a range of learning outcomes, and "does not recognize student attitudes as important."[26] While Mager would not agree with these criticisms, Eisner suggested more emphasis on what he called "expressive" objectives. Expressive objectives include intangible outcomes as well as the tangible. For example, a teacher should teach reading, a measureable outcome, but should also "instill positive attitudes toward reading."[27]

But how will teachers know if positive attitudes have been instilled in their students? If Mager leads us toward the hopelessly trivial, then Eisner leads us toward the "impossibly cosmic."[28]

Norman Gronlund

Mager begins with the specific and Eisner begins with the intangible. Gronlund begins with general objective statements, followed by a list of sample behaviors which clarify how teachers know the objective has been reached. The general objective statement uses terms like *to know*, *to understand*, *to solve*, *to appreciate*. Then the sample behaviors clarify how students will demonstrate achievement of the objective. Rather than a large number of specifically targeted behaviors, Gronlund suggests a few central objectives. Research has generally favored this approach.[29]

Here's an example of Gronlund's approach for an introductory course in educational psychology.

General objective:

Students will understand how to use instructional objectives in preparing teaching procedures.

Sample behaviors:

1. Defines the levels of learning in the cognitive, affective and psychomotor domains.

2. Analyzes instructional objectives and determines which level of learning they target.

3. Given a Bible passage and a level of learning, writes an appropriate instructional objective.

4. When presented with objectives written by fellow students, evaluates the statements according to unit criteria.

Gronlund's approach targets teacher expectations for students while allowing flexibility in specific methods and evaluation procedures.

LeRoy Ford

LeRoy Ford served the Sunday School Board of the Southern Baptist Convention for seven years (1959-1966), majoring on curriculum design issues, before beginning his teaching ministry at Southwestern Seminary in Fort Worth, Texas. He chaired the Religious Education School's Curriculum Committee for years, and served as editor of the *Course Descriptions for Master's Degree Programs, School of Religious Education.* Every course offered by the School is contained in this course description guide, complete with a course rationale, course and unit objectives, major teaching procedures, and bibliography. Every student entering the School of Religious Education receives a copy of the curriculum guide so that they can choose the courses that best fit their ministry needs. Though Ford retired in 1984, the manual continues to be updated and revised every two years by the Curriculum Committee.

During my first year as a faculty member, 1981, I participated in several workshops conducted by Dr. Ford on writing instructional objectives. These workshops were offered for faculty members in preparation for writing our course descriptions. Ford's approach to instructional objectives follows Gronlund. Ford calls the general objective a "goal," which he defines as "a broad statement of learning intent which identifies the domain of learning and states the subject in a chewable bite."[30] He calls the sample behaviors "indicators" or "objectives," which he defines as a term which "states what the learner will do to prove or *indicate* achievement of a goal." The term "indicator" reflects more accurately the function of an objective.[31] Simple instructional objectives can be stated in a single statement. The goal part of the statements below is shown in normal type. The indicator is shown in *italics.*

Learners will demonstrate knowledge of the Great Commission (Matt. 28:19–20) *by writing it from memory.*

Learners will demonstrate understanding of the Great Commission (Matt. 28:19–20) *by defining the terms "go," "baptize," and "teach" in their own words.*

Learners will demonstrate appreciation for the Great Commission (Matt. 28:19–20) *by sharing a personal experience in which they intentionally engaged in teaching others the gospel.*

Ford's system also permits more complex objective statements along the lines of Gronlund's "sample behaviors." The following statements describe the course "Principles of Teaching" in the *Course Descriptions (1993-95).*[32] Notice the multiple indicator statements.

I. Course Goal and Objective

The student demonstrates understanding of principles of teaching as they relate to teaching in a Christian context.

To demonstrate achievement of this goal the student plans and conducts a Bible study using the concepts of planning and teaching presented in this course.

II. Unit Goals and Objectives

Unit 1: The Teaching-Learning Process

The learner will demonstrate understanding of the teaching-learning process in a Christian context by doing such things as these:

Defines key concepts related to teaching and learning in a Christian context

Analyzes the strengths and weaknesses of major teaching methods in terms of effectiveness for teaching in a Christian context

Evaluates past experiences with teaching in the local church in light of principles developed in the unit

Unit 2: Writing Instructional Goals and Objectives

The learner will demonstrate knowledge of instructional goals and objectives by *stating the characteristics of good goals and objectives.*

The learner will demonstrate understanding of instructional goals and objectives by doing such things as these:

Defines levels of learning in cognitive, affective, and psychomotor domains

Gives an example of an appropriate learning activity for each level of learning

Writes instructional goals/objectives for given levels of learning and assigned Scripture passages

Evaluates instructional goals/objectives using principles developed in the unit

Unit 3:   Planning for Instruction

The learner will demonstrate understanding of teaching plan development by doing such things as these:

Defines the major components of a teaching plan

Identifies teaching plan components in given sample teaching procedures

Writes a sample teaching plan on a Bible passage or topic appropriate to Christian education

Evaluates sample teaching plans on the basis of principles developed in the unit

Unit 4:   Planning for Specific Outcomes

The learner will demonstrate an understanding of teaching for knowledge, understanding, and affective response (attitude) by doing such things as these:

Defines characteristics which differentiate between knowlege, understanding, attitude, and Christian action teaching plans

Writes teaching plans which specifically target knowledge, understanding, attitude, or Christian action outcomes.

Unit 5:   Practice Teaching

The learner will demonstrate understanding of the teaching-learning process by *leading students in an actual teaching situation using one of the teaching plans developed in Unit 4.*

Unit 6:   Evaluation of Teaching

The learner will demonstrate understanding of teaching evaluation by doing such things as these:

Analyzes personal performance in the practice teaching using video tape and student evaluations

Evaluates student teachers on the basis of principles developed in the course

As you can see, students gain a clear picture of the nature and process of the course from these statements. Yet the statements are general enough to allow teachers flexibility in choosing specific content and procedures.

Ford's latest book, *A Curriculum Design Manual for Theological Education: A Learning Outcomes Focus*, applies the principles of learning outcomes to theological studies. This book is must reading for any administrator or professor involved in designing courses or leading institutional self-study efforts for re-accreditation. Appendices in the book include sample course descriptions for theological education, suggestions for creating interactive instruction in correspondence school materials, and guidelines for teaching for knowledge, understanding, skills, attitudes, and values.

**DOMAINS AND
LEVELS OF LEARNING**

In the examples of instructional objectives above, we've used general terms such as "knowledge" and "understanding," as well as more specific terms such as "define," "analyze," and "design." These terms come from various taxonomies, or classifications, of learning domains and levels.

There are three *domains* of learning. They are the cognitive domain, which refers to knowledge and understanding, the affective domain, which refers to attitudes and values, and the psychomotor domain, which refers to skills. Each of these domains of learning contains *levels* of learning. There are six levels of learning in the cognitive domain, five levels in the affective, and seven levels in the psychomotor. These domains and levels of learning provide the basis for writing instructional objectives.

The Cognitive Domain

Benjamin Bloom of the University of Chicago led a team of educators to formulate the six levels of learning in the cognitive domain in 1956.[33] The six levels of learning are knowledge, comprehension, application, analysis, synthesis, and evaluation. (Hint: you might want to review the "left pillar" in chapter 1 as an introduction to this section.)

Knowledge. The lowest level of learning in the cognitive domain is knowledge, defined as the ability to recall previously memorized facts,[34] to remember or to recognize[35] factual information. Terms which focus on

KNOWLEDGE

Cognitive Domain

this level of learning include: to identify, to recall, to recognize, to name, to state, to reproduce, to list, to quote, and to match. An example of a knowledge indicator would be: *"Learners will recall the historical context and exegetical outline of Jesus' command to 'Love your enemies.'"* Such learning need not be trivial or simple. An essay question which asks students to "list and describe the twelve causes of the fall of Rome" is difficult, but it is targeted at the knowledge level.

While rote memory is often dismissed as unimportant, the truth is that much of the Bible teaching done in churches fails to achieve this lowest level. How much of last Sunday's study do your learners remember this Sunday? How much of last Sunday's sermon do you remember today? Much of our teaching in church is information transmission. We say a lot of religious words, but how much do our learners remember? If they can't remember, how can they live out the Word? I was disappointed one day with a member of our deaf college Sunday school class. He could not remember on Wednesday much of what we had studied on Sunday. Seeing my disappointment, he remarked, "But you don't understand. You teach so much that it goes in one eye and out the other!" Information, not knowledge. Learners remember facts, definitions, and truths presented by their teachers when they learn at the knowledge level.

Comprehension. When we move from knowledge to comprehension, we also move into the domain of understanding. Understanding encompasses the upper five levels of the cognitive domain. There is a qualitative change

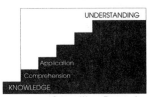

Cognitive Domain

in learning as we move from knowledge to comprehension. Texts define comprehension as "obtaining meaning from communication"[36] or "processing information."[37] Comprehension centers on the meaning of singular concepts. Learners functioning at this level of learning can give examples, or paraphrase, or translate from one form (verbal) to another (graphical), or explain something in their own words, or illustrate. Terms which focus on this level include: to draw, to explain, to illustrate, to rephrase, to translate, to convert, to infer, to interpret, and to estimate. An example of a comprehension indicator would be: *"Learners will define in their own words the terms 'love' and 'enemies' as used by Jesus in the command 'Love your enemies.'"*

What did Jesus mean by "love"? Are we to *like* our enemies? Are we to *feel warm and tingly* toward them? And who are our enemies? Terrorists who kidnap North Americans? What do these terms *mean*? Jesus used the words *agapao* (to act in another's best interest) and *echthros* (an adversary, an enemy, a foe) in His command. When someone acts against us, we are to act in their best interest. Or, as He says in clarification, "Do good to those who hate you" (Luke 6:27). "To love" in this context means "to do good" regardless of feelings. "Enemy" in this context means "those who hate you personally, those close to you." Explaining what concepts mean occurs at the comprehension level.

Application. The term "application" is often used in its broadest sense, as in

Cognitive Domain

"to apply the Bible to life." This broad sense includes learners' personal experiences and commitments. Such is not the focus of Bloom's third level. Built on comprehension, application refers to "using a concept to solve a particular problem"[38] or "using information in a novel situation"[39] or simply answering a conceptual question correctly. Terms which focus on this level include: to apply, to employ, to transfer, to use, to solve, to construct, to prepare, to demonstrate, and to calculate. An example of an application indicator would be: *"Learners will explain how agape love could be used in several case studies on family conflict."*

The levels of comprehension and application focus on singular, simple concepts: love, peace, sin, holiness, grace, walking in the light, washed in the blood and so forth. What do these words and phrases mean? How can we use these meanings to answer questions or solve problems?

Analysis. As we move to analysis, we move into what educators call the "higher levels of learning." The three higher levels—analysis, synthesis, and evaluation—focus on multiple or complex concepts.

Cognitive Domain

At the level of analysis learners "break something down into its parts"[40] or "separate something into its components."[41] This level includes classifying or categorizing according to specifications, comparing and contrasting concepts within a body of knowledge, or discovering the relationships among concepts. Terms which focus on this level include: to analyze, to categorize, to compare, to contrast, to exegete, to discriminate, to outline, and to diagram. Notice how these expressions refer to multiple or complex concepts. We can illustrate this with an outline of 1 Corinthians 13:

I. Introduction
    A.   Love vs. angelic languages
    B.   Love vs. prophecy and faith
    C.   Love vs. personal sacrifice
II. What love is
    A.   Patient
    B.   Kind
    C.   Rejoicing in truth
    D.   Protective
    E.   Trusting
    F.   Hopeful
    G.   Persevering

III. What love is not
    A.   Envious
    B.   Boastful
    C.   Proud
    D.   Rude
    E.   Self-seeking
    F.   Easily angered
    G.   Keeping a record of wrongs
    H.   Delighting in evil
IV. Conclusion
    A.   Love never fails vs. prophecies, tongues, knowledge
    B.   Childish emotions put away by mature
    C.   Faith, hope, love: love is the greatest

Notice the many singular concepts involved in this passage. Through analysis, we have identified these concepts and listed them under their conceptual headings, such as "what love is." An example of an analysis indicator would be: *"Learners will exegete five selected passages to determine their teaching on agape love as expressed by Jesus' command to 'Love your enemies.'"*

It is important to remember that *learners* must do the exegesis, the outlining. If the teacher does the analysis and simply gives it to the class, then learners do little more than receive facts. Any assignment that requires the analysis of research articles and books to determine key ideas and related concepts moves the learner to the analysis level.

Synthesis. At the level of synthesis, learners "create something new by combining different ideas."[42] Using the multiple concepts derived through analysis, learners put them back together in a new way. The smooth nar-

Cognitive Domain

rative of a term paper, built upon many articles and books, organized according to key concepts, is the result of synthesis. Terms which focus on this level include: to combine, to formulate, to organize, to produce, to integrate, to design, and to create. An example of a synthesis indicator would be: *"Learners will write an essay on God's kind of love based on a study of Jesus' command to 'Love your enemies,' 1 Corinthians 13, and 1 John 4:7–10."* In this statement we find learners analyzing three passages and then synthesizing key ideas to define "God's kind of love."

Synthesis is a dangerous level of learning because it causes learners to confront issues in a complex way. We know divorce is wrong, and yet God commanded divorce when He told the Israelites to separate themselves from their foreign wives (Ezra 10:10–11). At about the same time, Esther is praised for marrying the pagan King Xerxes (Esther 2:16–17) and saving the Jewish people from destruction (Esther 9). We know that we should not be unequally yoked with unbelievers, yet God commanded Hosea the prophet to marry a prostitute (Hos. 1:2; 2:5).

God is love and God is wrath. How can He be both? The answer is found in synthesis. The fire that warms is also the fire that burns. The difference is in our relationship to it. Those who are rightly related to God are warmed by His love. Those who refuse His love, who reject His offer of grace, are left to be burned by His wrath. He is not love or wrath. He is love-wrath, which exists like a two-sided coin.[43]

While synthesis can cause a great deal of disequilibrium in learners' thinking, such integration is essential for correct understanding. Individual Bible truths need to fit into the context of the Scripture as a whole rather than be held as unrelated bits of truth; otherwise, misunderstanding can result. Some pastors take Hebrews 13:17 ("Obey your leaders and submit to their authority") as a license to be lord over the church. This is misinterpretation because the verse is written to church members, not to church leaders. Both Jesus and Peter, writing under the inspiration of the Holy Spirit, declared that pastors are not to be lords, but servants and examples (Matt. 20:25–26; Mark 9:35; 10:44; 1 Pet. 5:2–3). As servants and examples of the Truth, they should be obeyed and followed by the faithful (Heb. 13:17). Proof-texting is a dangerous business and can lead to all sorts of error.

Evaluation. At the level of evaluation, learners objectively "judge the value of material according to specific criteria."[44] I emphasize the word "objectively" because much of the evaluation done in our humanistic society is subjective: value is judged by how

Cognitive Domain

something makes me *feel*. Bloom's highest level of learning is a thoroughly cognitive process, rationally appraising a concept or procedure according to definite standards. Terms which focus on this level include: to appraise, to argue, to assess, to judge, to evaluate, to validate, to critique, to weigh, and to examine. An example of an evaluation indicator is: *"Learners will evaluate how well they love others, using criteria established from Jesus' command to 'Love your enemies,' 1 Corinthians 13, and 1 John 4:7–10."* The criteria are established at the synthesis level and applied at the evaluation level.

In a classroom setting, students would be at the evaluation level as they judge the quality of teaching plans written by fellow students according to specific criteria synthesized from class learnings.

In summary, the cognitive domain focuses on knowing and understanding concepts and consists of six levels: knowledge, comprehension, application, analysis, synthesis, and evaluation. The first three reflect on concrete operational thinking and the last three on formal operational thinking.[45]

In 1964, David Krathwohl of Syracuse University led a team of educators, including Benjamin Bloom, to formulate a second taxonomy for the affective domain.[46] While the cognitive domain emphasizes knowledge and concept development, the affective domain emphasizes attitudes and values. Five levels comprise this domain: receiving, responding, valuing, organizing, and characterizing. (Hint: Review the "right pillar" in chapter 1 as an introduction to this section).

The Affective Domain

Receiving. The first level of the affective domain involves the "willingness to listen"[47] or "attending to something."[48] Teachers can prepare wonderful learning procedures, but if students are not tuned in, they will not learn. Part of our

Affective Domain

responsibility as teachers is to provide learning experiences which capture the interest and attention of our students. Terms which focus on this level include: to listen, to concentrate, to observe, to follow, to watch, to view (a film), to be attentive, to be focused. An example of a receiving indicator would be: *"Learners listen to an explanation of Jesus' command 'Love your enemies.'"*

Responding. Learners at the second affective level of learning engage in "active participation indicating positive response or acceptance of an idea."[49] Learners express their own opinions.

Affective Domain

They willingly answer questions. They share personal experiences related to the subject. They ask questions and participate in group discussions. Terms which focus on this level include such as these:

to share, to answer, to ask, to volunteer, to comply, to assist, and to testify. An example of a responding indicator would be: *"Learners share personal experiences in which they loved another or were loved by another as Jesus commanded."*

Moving learners to the level of responding requires effort on the teacher's part to create an environment of openness and safety for sharing. If the teacher is domineering or harsh, learners will not risk responding. I remember a teacher who asked a visitor in her Sunday school class to read a Bible verse. The visitor read from her Revised Standard Version Bible. The teacher had used the King James Version (KJV) in her study, and the word she studied wasn't in the RSV translation! The teacher *knew the (KJV) word*, but *did not understand the concept* behind it. So she did not recognize the concept when a different (RSV) word was used to express it. She panicked and sharply said, "Oh, someone with the good kind of Bible read that verse!" The visitor never returned. Not only will she not respond in that class again, she'll never attend it!

Allowing students to respond requires more class time than "sit-still-while-I-instill" receiving. But too much emphasis on receiving without providing opportunities for student response hinders learning. Further, without sufficient responding, learners will not progress to the next stage, which is critical for affective development.

Valuing. The third level of affective learning targets "personal involvement or commitment"[50] or "expressing a belief or attitude about the value or worth of something."[51] At this level

Affective Domain

students catch the importance of what is being taught. They are willing to take a position on the subject and defend it. They share class experiences with friends outside of class. Terms which focus on this level include: to justify, to commit, to defend, to initiate, to appreciate, to select, to value, and to work. An example of a valuing indicator would be: *"Learners encourage others to be loving in their behavior toward one another and speak against unloving actions within their churches."*

Values are more caught than taught. We cannot force our values on others, but we can teach in a way that encourages learners to catch our values. Dr. Bill Reynolds teaches in the School of Church

Music at Southwestern Seminary. Periodically, he leads the congregational singing in chapel. No one can promote wholehearted singing quite like Dr. Reynolds. I've never seen him berate a congregation for singing weakly. He never tells folks to sing louder. But he leads the hymns *as if they were important.* We catch his commitment, and we sing! Teaching is much the same. If we do not believe in what we're teaching, if we're merely moving ideas out of our notebooks into our students' notebooks, then they will not see the value in what we're teaching. If we teach with conviction as well as clarity, our students will catch the importance of what we teach and value it as well.

Organizing. The fourth level of affective learning emphasizes "integrating new values into one's general set of values"[52] or "organizing values into an internalized system."[53] Learners prioritize values by importance. They act in accor-

Affective Domain

dance with their convictions. They develop a cohesive system of values. Terms which focus on this level include: to prioritize, to integrate, to reorder values, to compare, and to combine. An example of an organizing indicator would be: *"Learners make 'loving enemies' a priority in their lives."* The goal for teachers is to help students move good values to a higher priority and poor values to a lower priority. In terms of Bible studies, the goal is to move biblical values higher and worldly values lower in priority. Such reordering of values requires consistent influence over a long period of time.

Once I was discussing motivation in a Doctor of Ministry seminar on educational psychology. A pastor asked, "How can I get my congregation to attend Church Training[54] instead of staying home and watching the Dallas Cowboys play football?" I asked, "If you were away from home, sitting in your motel room on Sunday afternoon, would you attend Church Training at a local church, or would you stay in your room and watch the Cowboys play?" The class responded with a serious "Hmmmmmm." "So," I continued, "it's not the value of Church Training that's in question. You're just jealous because, as pastor, you have to be at church, and your members have the freedom to stay home if they choose." "Hmmmmmm." Another pastor spoke up and said, "What we do is get all our people in Church Training, and then my education minister and I watch the game on my office television." The whole class booed the obvious hypocrisy! But the issue is one of priority. If we want people to participate in our education ministry, then that education ministry must be valuable. Over time, the programs must prove themselves worthy of our members' time. Slowly, over time, members will move these studies higher on their priority list. "Supporting church programs" is no longer valuable in and of itself. The programs must provide value in order to be supported.

Characterizing. The fifth level of affective learning involves "acting consistently with a new value"[55] or the process in which one's "value system becomes a way of life."[56] At this level learners live out their values naturally. They are

Affective Domain

known by others by those values. They actually become what they have learned. Terms which focus on this level include: to reflect, to display, to practice, to act, to demonstrate. An example of a characterizing indicator would be: *"Learners are known by others as lovers of enemies."*

It is one thing to know the Good Samaritan story, or to understand the key principles found in the story. But it is quite another to *be* a Good Samaritan, to live day by day as a Good Samaritan as a natural outflow of one's life. Or suppose a high school student develops an aversion to math because of bad experiences in his classes. He enters college dreading his first math class. But to his surprise the teacher is clear in her explanations, helpful when he runs into problems, and generally helps him to succeed in the course. At the end of the semester he has earned an "A," but beyond that, he's thinking about majoring in math—perhaps becoming a math teacher so that he can help others overcome their bad attitudes toward the subject. Not only did his teacher lead him to develop understanding of the material, but she led him to the affective level of characterizing as well.

In summary, the affective domain focuses on attitudes and values and consists of five levels of learning: receiving, responding, valuing, organizing, and characterizing.

The Psychomotor Domain

The psychomotor domain focuses on skill development and emphasizes physical actions.[57] Characteristics of psychomotor development include such things as speed, accuracy, inte-

Psychomotor Domain

gration, and coordination.[58] Adjectives that describe psychomotor learning include such terms as "correctly," "appropriately" and "efficiently."[59] The psychomotor domain receives much less attention in educational psychology texts than the cognitive and affective domains. This may be due to the perception that psychomotor learning is limited to sports, wood shop, band, or penmanship. Or it may be that cognitive and affective learning dominate classroom activities. However, psychomotor learning principles can be applied to other types of skills, such as writing teaching plans, preparing sermons, witnessing—any activity which requires a high degree of proficiency.[60]

Elizabeth Simpson of the University of Illinois developed a taxonomy for the psychomotor domain in 1972.[61] The seven levels of the domain are perception, set, guided response, mechanism, complex or overt response, adaptation, and origination.

Perception. The first level of psychomotor learning is perception, in which learners "use their senses to obtain cues to guide motor activity."[62] Learners listen to sounds made by an instrument before tuning it, or observe the proper grip on a golf club, or watch how to set up a drill press. Terms which focus on this level include: to listen, to observe, to choose, and to detect.

In learning how to share the gospel, learners would accompany a skilled witness and observe how to move from general conversation to discussing spiritual matters.

Set. The second level of psychomotor learning is set, which targets "being ready to perform a particular action." Set involves mental readiness (knowing the proper steps), emotional readiness (being willing to perform the action), and physical readiness (being properly positioned).[63] Terms which focus on this level include: to begin, to start, to proceed, to show.

In learning to share the gospel, learners would prepare mentally by learning key points and Bible passages and emotionally by practicing presentations with fellow learners.

Guided Response. The third level of psychomotor learning is guided response, which emphasizes "performing under the guidance of a model."[64] Learning at this level focuses on imitation and trial and error as the model provides skilled direction to the learner. Terms which focus on this level include: to assemble, to fix, to manipulate, to perform, to imitate.

In learning to share the gospel, learners would share part of the gospel presentation—for example, a personal testimony—during an actual evangelistic visit. A skilled witness would be present to assist if needed and to provide evaluation after the visit.

Mechanism and Complex Response. The fourth and fifth levels of psychomotor learning merely extend guided response into higher levels of proficiency. Mechanism involves the "ability to perform a task habitually with some confidence and proficiency."[65] Complex response involves "performing a task with a high degree of proficiency and skill."[66] Terms which focus on this level include: to assemble, to fix, to manipulate, to perform, to imitate—with greater skill.

In learning to share the gospel, learners continue to practice their skills in simulations and actual witnessing experiences in order to become more proficient in the process.

Adaptation. The sixth level of psychomotor learning is adaptation, which introduces the element of creativity. Learners at this level use "previously learned skills to perform new but related tasks."[67] Terms which focus on this level include: to adapt, to modify, to change, to improve, to extend, to elaborate, and to enhance.

In learning to share the gospel, learners adapt their presentation dialogue to include persons of different religious backgrounds or cultures or languages.

Origination. The seventh and final level of psychomotor learning is origination, which involves "creating new performances after having developed skills."[68] Terms which focus on this level include: to create, to develop, to invent, to design, to compose, and to devise.

In learning to share the gospel, learners at this level develop new ways to witness, or new ways to train others to witness, in order to present clearly the Old Story to an ever-changing society.

Had I known about the psychomotor domain when I was ten years old, I could have used its sequence of levels to master arrow shooting. Perception: What important cues need attention? Distance to target, windage, tension on the bow, distance of draw, elevation of aim. Set: Am I ready to shoot the arrow? Guided Response: Is there a mentor to correct my faulty efforts? Mechanism and Complex Response: Practice, practice, practice! Adaptation and Origination: What new ways can I use these skills to do new things?

Learning is complex! We have defined eighteen levels of learning in three domains. Each of these eighteen levels can serve as an instructional target. We have described eighteen possible outcomes. Now let's focus on actually writing the statements.

If you are a fan of the original *Star Trek* television series and movies, you have an inside track to understanding the three domains of learning. If you are not a fan, then you are required to go to your local video store to get the *Star Trek* movies. Watch them in light of our discussion of the three domains of learning and see if my analysis rings true.

Three Domains and a Star Trek Analogy

While I've never been able to confirm this, I believe that Gene Roddenberry, creator of the *Star Trek* concept, was a student of psychology and formed four major characters as reflections of the three domains.

Lt. Commander Spock: Cognitive Domain. Spock, half Vulcan and half human, represses his emotional human self and focuses on his rational Vulcan self. He is portrayed as a walking Cognitive Domain: rational, cerebral, objective, factual. If he were to engage in Bible study, he would be able to operate in the six levels of the cognitive domain without any problems.

Doctor "Bones" McCoy: Affective Domain. McCoy is a medical doctor and can deal rationally with medical problems. But his relationships with people are always characterized by rampant emotions: anger, frustration, joy, love, impatience. He is portrayed as a walking Affective Domain.

McCoy and Spock are often pitted against each other. Spock detests McCoy's irrational emotions, and McCoy detests Spock's "infernal logic." From time to time, the Captain is spirited away to some other planet and either Spock or McCoy is left in charge. Disaster always follows. Spock is logical, but cannot humanize his logic in order to deal with others. McCoy never can make a decision because he is too confused by mixed emotions.

Chief Engineer Scott: Psychomotor Domain. "Scottie" is a technical genius. He always knows how to coax "jest a wee bit murrr" speed out of the warp engines. He lives in schematics and technical manuals. He keeps all the systems of the *Starship Enterprise* in excellent condition, and he knows how to combine systems to do things their designers never thought about.

Captain Kirk: The Balance. Captain James T. Kirk demonstrates a balance of all three domains. He can think rationally like Spock, feel deeply like McCoy, and readjust a faulty transporter as skillfully as anyone on board. Usually it is Kirk who bursts upon the scene just in time to save the day and win the girl. A real hero!

Balance is what we need. Our students need to understand what they value; otherwise, their values are empty emotion. They need to value what they understand; otherwise, their understanding is wooden. They need to skillfully practice what they understand and value; otherwise, their learning will have no impact on themselves or the community in which they live. We speak more of this balance, this triad, at the end of Unit 3. Now we'll focus on how to actually use these domains and levels of learning to set up meaningful teaching targets.

WRITING INSTRUCTIONAL OBJECTIVES

Every semester I have Masters' students in my "Principles of Teaching" classes who majored in education in college. They are familiar with instructional objectives and the taxonomies. But few of them see the value in writing objectives or possess the ability to do so. They "know" about objectives, but many cannot "apply" that knowledge to actually write them. Since they've had little positive experience with objectives, they tend to devalue their importance.

I have found it helpful to focus student attention on four characteristics of good instructional objectives. First, instructional objectives should be written from the *learners' point of view*. What will learners do to demonstrate their learning? Second, objectives should state a general goal for learning. Is the goal to gain knowledge, or develop understanding, or change an attitude, or master a skill? Third, objectives should state how students will demonstrate the achievement of that goal? That is, what is the *indicator* which demonstrates performance at a given level of learning? And fourth, objectives should express these elements in a clearly understood format, such as this: *Learners will demonstrate (domain) of (content) by (action).*

Here are several examples of instructional objectives for John 3:16 and Ephesians 6. Study the format as well as the nature of the goals and indicators:

Knowledge

> Learners will demonstrate knowledge of John 3:16 by writing the verse from memory.

> Learners will demonstrate knowledge of the armor of God (Ephesians 6) by recalling the pieces of Roman armor and their spiritual counterparts.

Comprehension

> Learners will demonstrate understanding[69] of John 3:16 by

explaining the terms "love," "world," "believe," and "eternal life" in their own words.

Learners will demonstrate understanding of the armor of God (Ephesians 6) by explaining how faith is like a shield, how truth is like a belt, and how righteousness is like a breastplate.

Responding

Learners will demonstrate appreciation for John 3:16 by sharing their personal testimonies of salvation with the class.

Learners will demonstrate appreciation for the armor of God (Ephesians 6) by sharing a personal experience in which faith shielded them from the fiery darts of Satan.

Valuing

Learners will demonstrate a change in attitude concerning John 3:16 by committing themselves to witness to at least one person this week.

Learners will demonstrate a change in attitude concerning the armor of God (Ephesians 6) by making a commitment to strengthen the armor in their lives.

Psychomotor objectives focus on performing a task the correct way. The nature of correct performance is defined by the teacher's definition or demonstration. The phrases "as demonstrated in class" or "as illustrated in the film" are often used to guide students in seeing what is expected of them.[70]

Here are two examples:

Learners will demonstrate skill in using commentaries to explain Scripture by exegeting selected verses as demonstrated in class.

Learners will demonstrate proficiency in writing teaching plans by composing a plan on a specified Bible passage as demonstrated in class.

We have focused on writing session objectives to this point. The danger of emphasizing the session alone is that, given the limited time in a single session, objectives tend to huddle near the bottom of the taxonomies. Session by session, instructional objectives may never climb above comprehension or responding.

Teachers avoid this by using a "behavior-content matrix"[71] to identify unit or course content and levels of learning. By structuring units and entire courses this way, teachers avoid trivializing their classes and insure a range of learnings in their students. An example of a behavior-content matrix is shown on p. 154.

WRITING COURSE AND UNIT OBJECTIVES

Why write objectives? We've looked at a lot of trees. Let's move back a bit to picture the forest. We write objectives to target our

IN SUMMARY

Behavior-Content Matrix

Content Behaviors	(Levels)						Total
	K	C	Ap	An	Syn	Ev	
Area 1	1	1	1				3
Area 2			1	1			2
Area 3					1		1
Area 4					1	1	2
Area 5	2	2					4
	3	3	2	1	2	1	12

Based on Gage and Berliner, 46, Woolfolk, 447.

teaching, to improve our planning, our testing, and our evaluation of students. We write objectives to focus student learning, to structure their study, and to guide them in preparation for testing. Instructional objectives give students the sense that teachers are "going somewhere," which is crucial in establishing confidence in the course and the professor.

The cost is high. It is difficult to write good objectives, but then producing anything of quality is difficult. It is time-consuming to write objectives, yet aimless teaching wastes the time of students as well as the teacher—to what end?

Research shows that objectives improve *intentional* learning but hinder *incidental* learning.[72] While more incidental learning may occur in loosely structured discussions and projects, focused learning and subject mastery will suffer. The kind of instructional objectives emphasized in this chapter, based on Gronlund and Ford, expand opportunities for incidental learning beyond the Mager model, even while providing intentional guidelines for students. Further, Good and Brophy state that the most effective learning situations emphasize intentional learning.[73] Teachers provide a helpful mental map of their courses when they focus on a few general objectives rather than many trivial ones, avoid the temptation of being too specific and rigid, and use objectives to guide rather than dictate learning experiences.[74]

We will consider specifically how we achieve these objectives in the next unit as we study behavioral, cognitive, and humanistic learning theories.

CHAPTER CONCEPTS

Adaptation

Affective Domain

Analysis

Application

Behavior-Content Matrix

Behavioral Objectives (Mager)

Characterization

Cognitive Domain

Comprehension

Domain of Learning

Expressive Objectives (Eisner)

Evaluation

General Objectives (Gronlund)

Goal (Ford)

Guided Response

DISCUSSION QUESTIONS

1. Jesus was the greatest Teacher Who ever lived. Yet we can safely assume He never wrote an instructional objective to guide His teaching. Why do you suppose He didn't? Why do you suppose we should?

2. Read Ephesians 4:11–12 and determine what concepts, values, and skills reside there for ministers to master.

3. My dad says there are two types of people in the world: picture-people and word-people. Picture-people visualize meanings, using a variety of words and expressions to convey that meaning. Word-people demand just the proper word to express a given meaning. To properly understand the levels of learning, you must *picture* what kind of learning occurs at each level. If you tie specific *words* to levels of learning, you may write incorrect statements. For example, we can "define" a concept at three levels of learning. Describe three different meanings of "define." (Hint: focus on knowledge, comprehension, and synthesis).

4. Write complete objectives, using the suggested format given in the chapter, for the following:

    a. 1 Corinthians 13 and comprehension

    b. Revelation 2–3 and synthesis

    c. Matthew 28:19–20 and responding

    d. Colossians 3:8–12 and analysis

FOR FURTHER READING

Biehler, Robert F. and Jack Snowman. "Devising and Using Objectives." *Psychology Applied to Teaching*. 7th ed., 273–315. Boston: Houghton Mifflin Company, 1993.

Bloom, Benjamin S., ed. *Taxonomy of Educational Objectives*. New York: David McKay Company, Inc., 1956.

Dembo, Myron H. "Planning for Instruction." *Applying Educational Psychology.* 5th ed., 238–55. New York: Longman, 1994.

Ford, Leroy. *Design for Teaching and Training: A Self-Study Guide to Lesson Planning.* Nashville: Broadman Press, 1978.

———. *A Curriculum Design Manual for Theological Education: A Learning Outcomes Focus.* Nashville: Broadman Press, 1991.

Gage, N. L., and David C. Berliner. "The Formulation of Objectives and Their Justification." *Educational Psychology.* 3rd ed., 38–53. Dallas: Houghton Mifflin Company, 1984.

Glover, John A., and Roger H. Bruning. "An Introduction to Measurement [Goals and Objectives]." *Educational Psychology: Principles and Applications.* 3rd ed., 352–73. Glenview, Ill: Scott, Foresman/Little, Brown Higher Education, 1990.

Good, Thomas L., and Jere E. Brophey. "Instructional Objectives." *Educational Psychology: A Realistic Approach.* 4th ed., 142–47. New York: Longman, 1990.

Gronlund, Norman. *Stating Behavioral Objectives for Classroom Instruction.* 3rd ed. New York: Macmillan, 1972.

———. *Measurement and Evaluation in Teaching.* 6th ed. New York: Macmillan, 1990.

———. *How to Write and Use Instructional Objectives.* 4th ed. New York: Macmillan, 1991.

Krathwohl, David, ed. *Taxonomy of Educational Objectives: Handbook II: Affective Domain.* New York: David McKay Company, 1964.

LeFrancois, Guy R. "Instructional Objectives." *Psychology for Teaching.* 8th ed., 354–61. Belmont, Calif.: Wadsworth Publishing Company, 1994.

Mager, Robert F. *Analyzing Performance Problems.* Palo Alto, Calif.: Fearon Publishers, 1970.

———. *Developing Attitude Toward Learning.* Palo Alto, Calif.: Fearon Publishers, 1984.

———. *Developing Vocational Instruction.* Palo Alto, Calif.: Fearon Publishers, 1967.

———. *Goal Analysis.* Palo Alto, Calif.: Fearon Publishers, 1972.

———. *Measuring Instructional Intent.* Palo Alto, Calif.: Fearon Publishers, 1973.

———. *Preparing Instructional Objectives.* 2nd ed. Palo Alto, Calif.: Fearon Publishers, 1975.

Simpson, Elizabeth. *The Classification of Educational Objectives: Psychomotor Domain.* Urbana: University of Illinois Press, 1972.

Sprinthall, Norman A., Richard C. Sprinthall, and Sharon N. Oja. "Teaching Objectives." *Educational Psychology: A Developmental Approach.* 6th ed., 355–59. New York: McGraw-Hill, Inc., 1994.

Woolfolk, Anita. "Objectives for Learning." *Educational Psychology.* 5th ed., 437–47. Boston: Allyn and Bacon, Inc., 1993.

UNIT 3

Learning Theory Systems

In chapter 6, we presented specific guidelines for setting up targets in three domains of learning. Now we are ready to take aim and fire our educational arrows. Aiming at teaching targets is more complex than aiming at a bulls-eye, because teaching is far more complex than shooting an arrow. We will present three major learning theory systems: the behavioral, the cognitive-field, and the humanistic. We will suggest specific principles for teaching which grow out of these systems. Finally, we present a synergistic Learning Triad for teaching in a Christian context.

Chapter 10
Teaching for Attitude Change
Humanistic Learning Theory

Chapter 11
The Christian Teacher's Triad
A Dynamic Synergism of Learning Theories

Chapter

7

TEACHING FOR BEHAVIOR CHANGE

B. F. SKINNER'S
OPERANT CONDITIONING THEORY
ALBERT BANDERA'S
SOCIAL LEARNING THEORY

CHAPTER RATIONALE

Behavioral learning theory emphasizes the behavior of students, rather than their thinking or attitudes. Jesus said, "Therefore everyone who hears these words of mine and *puts them into practice* is like a wise man who built his house on the rock" (Matt. 7:24, author's emphasis). How do we help students put their studies into practice? What can we do as teachers to change the behavior of our learners? This chapter emphasizes theories of two of the most prominent behaviorists in educational psychology: B. F. Skinner and Albert Bandura.

CHAPTER OBJECTIVES

Learners will demonstrate knowledge of behavioral learning by

- recalling the origins of Associationism-Connectionism, including contributions of Aristotle, Wundt, Watson, Pavlov, and Thorndike;

- recalling distinctions among positive and negative reinforcement and two types of punishment.

Learners will demonstrate understanding of behavioral learning by

- differentiating between a conditioned stimulus and an unconditioned stimulus;

- differentiating between S-R bonds and R-S bonds;

- differentiating between primary and secondary reinforcers;

- describing the effectiveness of programmed instruction in terms of reinforcement, failure, interaction, and individualization;

- contrasting linear and branching programs;

- contrasting "reinforcement" as defined by Skinner and Bandura.

HISTORICAL ROOTS

Learning theory dates back at least to the Greeks. Aristotle established the Laws of Association to explain how learning proceeds from the associations between events. One of his examples was of seeing a boy on a bridge. If sometime later you thought of the bridge, you would also think of the boy. These two elements had been linked together, associated. This tendency is called contiguity: whenever two sensations occur together, they will be associated.[1]

John Locke

British philosopher John Locke (1632-1704[2]) held that human beings are born with minds devoid of content, like a blank slate. Experience writes on this slate, this *tabula rasa*, to create understanding and personality.[3] Circumstances, not heredity or temperament or choice, determine what is written on the slate.[4] Locke wrote that it was "In [experience that] all our knowledge is founded,"[5] and that there is "nothing in the intellect [which is] not first in the senses."[6] His writings placed emphasis on the senses and environment while deemphasizing innate knowledge, as proposed by Plato. Locke's view might be compared to a modern calculator. Its memory is empty when it is turned on, waiting for data to be entered. But the calculator has built-in functions which can be used to process the data. Such is the mind, according to Locke: devoid of data, or experience, but possessing innate capacities to process experience.[7] While later behaviorial purists would frown on his use of the terms "mind" and "intellect,"[8] he did provide a philosophical basis for behavioral thinking.

"Circumstances determine what is written on the slate"

Wilhelm Wundt

The field of modern psychology developed out of the work of Wilhelm Wundt (1832–1920), who established the first experimental laboratory in Europe in 1879.[9] Psychology is the offspring from the marriage of philosophy and physiology, and focuses on conscious experience. Wundt wanted to discover the basic elements of human experience, along the lines of an atomic table of elements in physics. These basic elements he believed were connected through association. His procedure, called *introspection*, led subjects to look within themselves to discover their feelings and sensations. Wundt's work was later criticized by behaviorists because of his use of introspection to discover internal states. Behaviorists insist on analyzing overt behavior. But Wundt underscored the existence of a basic element of human experience, fundamental to behavioral thinking. Ivan Pavlov provided evidence of what that basic element might be.

Ivan Pavlov (1849–1936[10]) was a Russian physiologist. He won the Nobel prize in 1904 for his work on digestion in dogs.[11] His experiments involved measuring dog salivation rates under differing conditions.[12] But in the process of conducting his experiments, he discovered that the salivation rates changed for unexplained reasons. Dogs would begin to salivate at the mere sight of food, or when the research assistants approached them, even if they carried no food.[13] Pavlov began a series of experiments to discover the reasons for the changes in salivation. What resulted was a theory of learning called classical conditioning,[14] which focused on stimulus-response association.

Ivan Pavlov :
Classical Conditioning

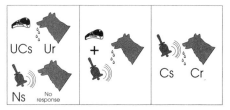

A *stimulus (S)* is a perceivable unit of the environment that may affect behavior.[15] A stimulus may be *unconditioned (UCs)* in that it affects behavior without being learned. Food is an unconditioned stimulus because it causes salivation as a reflex action. A *response* is any reaction to stimuli.[16] A *response (R)* may be *unconditioned (Ur)* in that it is a reflex action to a stimulus and is not learned. Salivation in the presence of food is an *unconditioned response*. A *neutral stimulus (Ns)* does not result in any specific behavior. A stimulus can become a *conditioned stimulus (Cs)* through the process of conditioning when it causes a given behavior. Pavlov's experiments focused on transforming a neutral stimulus into a conditioned stimulus, which produces a conditioned response (Cr). Let's see how he did this.

Pavlov presented dogs with food (UCs) along with a bell[17] or buzzer (Ns).[18] After several feedings, the dogs would salivate upon hearing the bell or buzzer alone. The bell became a conditioned stimulus (Cs) and salivation became a conditioned response (Cr) to the bell. An association had been created between a neutral stimulus (bell) and a given behavior (salivation).

Principles of Classical Conditioning. There are four basic principles related to classical conditioning. These are extinction, spontaneous recovery, generalization, and discrimination.

- *Extinction.* If the conditioned stimulus is presented without the unconditioned stimulus (if the bell is rung in the absence of food), the conditioned response will decay (salivation will decrease over time). The association between Cs and Cr weakens when Cs is presented without UCs.[19] A child who is afraid of all furry animals because he was once painfully bitten by a squirrel can disassociate pain and furry animals by playing with a well-behaved kitten.

- *Spontaneous Recovery.* Extinguished responses are not lost permanently. After a time of extinction, presentation of the conditioned stimulus will provoke the conditioned response.[20]

- *Generalization.* Once an association between the Cs and Cr is established, responses will generalize to other similar stimuli.[21] The child above was bitten by a squirrel, not all furry animals. But because the squirrel had fur, the child's response (fear) spread to other similar situations.

- *Discrimination.* Organisms can learn to discriminate between similar stimuli. When one tone of bell was linked with food and another was not, Pavlov's dogs learned to discriminate between them. They would salivate upon hearing one bell but not the other.[22]

Classroom Implications of Classical Conditioning. Classical conditioning focuses on *involuntary behaviors* which are outside of our conscious control.[23] Students who suffer from test anxiety did not consciously choose to feel this way. Their anxiety is associated with testing because of bad experiences in the past. Classroom climate provides a veritable ocean of possibilities for positive or negative associations. Whether the sea is stormy or calm depends on our teaching style. Is the classroom a warm, inviting place? Do students feel free to ask questions or share their thinking? Is the classroom a safe place to be? Then positive associations will result from the class. Or, is the classroom tense? Are student questions handled as interruptions? Is the teacher gruff in demeanor? Negative associations will result from the class, and will generalize to the teacher—and with bad experiences with others—to the school, and perhaps to learning at large.

John Watson (1878–1958[24]) coined the term "behaviorism." Critical of Wundt's emphasis on internal states, Watson insisted that psychology must focus on overt measureable behaviors. Watson believed that theorizing about thoughts, intentions, or other subjective experiences was unscientific.[25] He did, however, embrace Wundt's thinking on basic elements of human experience. How do physicists study the solar system? They observe how it behaves. If psychology were ever to gain the status of a scientific discipline such as physics, it would have to focus on how humans behave. Watson was greatly influenced by Pavlov's work[26] and was the first to use it as the basis for learning theory.[27] Watson discovered in Pavlov's S-R associations the basic element in human learning and personality development to replace Wundt's internal states.

John B. Watson: The Father of Behaviorism

Watson was an extremist. He made unsubstantiated boasts in his writing and was ethically questionnable in his reasearch on young children.[28] His best known experiment involved a young boy named Albert. Albert was given a small rat to handle. Then Watson made a loud noise by banging a metal bowl with a rod. The result was that Albert developed a fear of rats. Watson then showed this fear could be generalized to a rabbit, a dog, a sealskin coat and, for a time, Santa Claus' beard.[29]

"All behavior is established by building new S-R associations through conditioning"

Watson's contribution was demonstrating the role of conditioning in developing emotional responses such as fears, phobias, and prejudices.[30] He believed that humans were born with a few reflexes and the emotional reactions of fear, love, and rage. All other behavior is established by building new S-R associations through conditioning.[31]

E. L. Thorndike (1874–1949[32]) has been called the father of educational psychology because of the impact of his laws of learning. Thorndike's theory has been variously called "instrumental conditioning"[33]—because the learned behavior is instrumental in achieving goals; "trial and error learning"[34]—because problems are solved by trying different behaviors until the correct one is found, and "connectionism"[35]—because of its emphasis on connecting new responses with novel stimuli. Thorndike placed animals in problem-solving situations and observed how they behaved. For example, a hungry cat would be placed in a cage with a latch. A bowl of food would be placed outside. As the cat clawed at the cage attempting to get to the food, it would accidently trip the latch. After a few trials the cat became purposeful in moving directly to the latch and

Edward L. Thorndike: Father of Educational Psychology

opening the cage. Further practice allowed the cat to become proficient. Thorndike extended Pavlov's work beyond mere reflex actions, showing how new responses to novel situations were formed.[36] Further, he demonstrated that stimuli occurring after a *behavior* had an influence on future behaviors.[37] This key discovery formed the basis for the later work of B. F. Skinner.

Thorndike stated three fundamental laws of learning based on his experiments. These laws of learning have influenced educational practice ever since.

The Law of Readiness states that learning proceeds best when the learner is properly prepared to respond. If the learner is ready to respond, there is satisfaction (reward) in being allowed to respond. There is frustration (punishment) in being forbidden to respond. If the learner is not ready to respond, there is frustration in being forced to respond.[38]

The Law of Exercise states that repetition strengthens S-R bonds. This is another way of sayng that practice makes perfect.[39] This law, sometimes called the law of use and disuse,[40] led to an emphasis on drill and practice and repetition in the classroom.[41] Thorndike later modified this law to require feedback on the quality of responses that were being made.[42] Blind practice has no effect on learning.[43]

The Law of Effect is Thorndike's most important[44] law of the three. It states that any response followed by pleasure or reward is strengthened. Any response followed by pain is weakened. The law of effect holds that learning is a function of the "consequences of the act,"[45] not just contiguity.[46] One major result of this law was the use of concrete rewards such as gold stars on charts and verbal praise.[47]

Thorndike's view of learning is a mechanical process of stamping S-R bonds[48] into the nervous system through repetition.[49] His theory describes how bonds are strengthened or weakened.[50] He saw little difference between animal learning and human learning—let alone the qualitative distinctions Piaget discovered in human learning at various stages—and therefore had a decidedly dehumanizing effect on American education. Learners in Thorndike's theory are little more than robots which are mechanically programmed through conditioning.[51] Still, Thorndike's contribution was profound. His Law of Effect underscored the importance of motivation in education.[52] His theory established the basis for operant conditioning[53] and the dawn of modern behaviorism.

"Learning is a mechanical process of stamping S-R bonds into the nervous system through repetition"

Thorndike's Law of Effect states that the consequences of an act increases the probability of that act.[54] This principle of learning became the foundation of the Operant Conditioning theory which B. F. Skinner (1904-1990[55]) developed in the 1930s. By the 1950s his views dominated psychology and learning.[56] Contiguity and classical conditioning account for only a small percentage of learned behaviors. They describe how existing behaviors are paired with new stimuli, but cannot explain how new behaviors are acquired.[57] They are inadequate to explain most human learning because people consciously generate behaviors rather than merely respond to stimuli.[58] In classical conditioning, responses are *involuntary*[59] and *elicited* by specific stimuli.[60] Operant conditioning emphasizes the acquisition of new behaviors as animals or people *operate* on their environment in order to reach goals.[61] The responses are *voluntary*, and *emitted* by people or animals.[62]

Skinner did much of his research with rats or pigeons in a controlled environment, an enclosure called a "Skinner box."[63] The boxes used with rats had a metal lever and a food dispenser. With each press of the lever, the rat received a food pellet. The boxes used with pigeons had a disk to peck for the same result. In moving about the box, the rat would accidently press the lever, an emitted behavior, a response (R) to the environment. This action resulted in the rat getting a food pellet, a reinforcing stimulus (S). Earlier associationists had emphasized the S-R bond, an asociation between a stimulus and an elicited response. Skinner reversed this order to an R-S association. When a response receives a reinforcing stimulus, the probability of that response increases.[64] This reinforcing stimulus, which Thorndike called a "satisfier," is the most important component in Skinner's theory.[65] While Skinner's ideas were not new, his ability to popularize his research findings brought his ideas to the forefront of psychology.[66]

Reinforcement is the process of using reinforcers to strengthen behavior.[67] A *reinforcer* is any event that follows a behavior and increases the likelihood that the behavior will occur again,[68] or any consequence that strengthens the behavior it follows.[69] A *primary* reinforcer is a stimulus which reinforces without being learned and is related to needs or drives. Primary reinforcers include food, water, warmth, security, and sex.[70] A *secondary* reinforcer, or generalized[71] reinforcer, is a stimulus that was previously neutral, but has through conditioning been associated with other reinforcers.[72] Secondary

B. F. SKINNER

Operant Conditioning Theory

Reinforcement

THE LIFE OF
B. F. SKINNER

Burrus Frederick Skinner was born in Pennsylvania in 1904.[A] He majored in English at Hamilton College in New York.[B] He wrote poetry but was not satisfied with the result, so he entered Harvard University's graduate school in 1928 to study psychology.[C] He earned his Ph.D. in experimental psychology in 1931.[D] In 1936 he joined the faculty of the University of Minnesota, and during World War II trained pigeons to guide missiles to their targets. In 1945 he went to the University of Indiana as chairman of the Psychology Department. It was during this time he invented the "air-crib," a sound-proof, air-conditioned, germ-free, glass-encased box for infants. His daughter Deborah spent most of the first two years of her life in it. Skinner tried to market it as the "Heir-Crib," but it was not widely accepted.[E] In 1948 Skinner joined the faculty of Harvard University where he remained until his death in 1990.[F]

His interest in educational applications of operant conditioning grew out of a visit he made to his daughter's elementary school class. He saw the activities disorganized and basically a waste of

reinforcers include prestige, money, and success.[73] There are three basic classes of secondary reinforcers. *Social reinforcers* include acceptance, hugs, attention, and smiles. *Token reinforcers*, sometimes called symbolic reinforcers, include money, grades, prizes, and points. *Activity reinforcers* include free play, games, music, or trips.[74]

Positive and Negative Reinforcement

These examples reflect pleasant consequences we can give to reinforce desired behaviors. LeFrancois uses the word "reward" to describe this type of reinforcement,[75] though Skinner would disapprove.[76] Skinner called this condition positive reinforcement, because giving the positive reinforcer increases the probability of the behavior it follows.[77] Examples of positive reinforcement include the following:

> "Anyone who answers questions correctly today will get a package of Smarties candy." (Teacher tosses the candies as students answer correctly. If a student answers incorrectly, the teacher helps them work through the answer

time. He believed that children could be taught much more efficiently if their behaviors were shaped in the same way as his experimental pigeons or rats. By the 1950s he had developed "teaching machines" to lead children through their learning step-by-step with reinforcement.[G]

His best known writings include *The Behavior of Organisms* (1938), *Walden Two* (1948), *Science and Human Behavior* (1953), *Verbal Behavior* (1957), *The Technology of Teaching* (1968) and *Beyond Freedom and Dignity* (1971).

Skinner was adamant in his defense of traditional behaviorism to the end of his life. Speaking to the American Psychological Association in August 1990 he said, "[Cognitive science] is an effort to reinstate that inner initiating-originating-creative self or mind which, in scientific analysis, simply does not exist. . . . I think it is time for psychology as a profession and as a science to realize that the science which will be most helpful is not cognitive science searching for the inner mind or self, but selection by consequences represented by behavioral analysis."[H]

A few days later, he died of leukemia at the age of 86.

---

until they get it right and then tosses them the candy.)

Extra credit will be given on your term paper if more than ten references are used.

If an unpleasant stimulus is removed, then the probability of the desired behavior increases. This is called *negative reinforcement*.[78] Some writers uses the word "relief" to describe this situation.[79] Examples of negative reinforcement include the following:

	Pleasant	Unpleasant
Give	Positive Reinforcement *"You get extra credit"*	Presentation Punishment *"You get a demerit"*
Take	Removal Punishment *"No TV tonight"*	Negative Reinforcement *"No homework tonight"*

"If you complete all five problems in class today, you will not have a homework assignment."

> "Anyone who maintains a course average of ninety or better will not have to take the final exam."

The terms "positive" and "negative" do not refer to good and bad effects. In positive reinforcement we add something desired. In negative reinforcement we take away something not desired. Both of these actions increase the probability of the desired behavior.

Punishment I and II

We can discourage improper behavior by giving an unpleasant reinforcing stimuli. This is called presentation punishment,[80] or punishment I.[81] Examples of this include:

> "Anyone found fighting during recess will receive three swats from the Vice Principal."

> "If you are late for practice, you will have to run three extra laps at the end."

> "If you talk during study hour, you will remain after class and pick up the trash."

We can also discourage improper behavior by taking away a pleasant consequence. This is called removal punishment,[82] or punishment II, because it removes privileges.[83] LeFrancois calls this condition "penalty."[84] Examples of this include:

> "Since you did not clean your room, you may not watch television tonight."

> "Since you grabbed the face mask of an opposing player, your team loses ten yards."

> "If your paper is submitted late, twenty-five points will be subtracted from your grade."

The fundamental problem with punishment I and II is that they do not teach new appropriate ways to behave, but simply suppress inappropriate old ways to behave.[85] Thorndike found that pleasure was more effective in stamping new bonds in than pain was in stamping old bonds out.[86] Skinner found, similarly, that reinforcement teaches new behavior better than punishment unteaches old behaviors.

REINFORCEMENT
SCHEDULES

The way in which reinforcing stimuli are given has a direct impact on the nature of the behavior which is increased. A reinforcement schedule describes a particular pattern in the frequency and predictability of reinforcers.[87] *Continuous* reinforcement presents the reinforcing stimulus on *every occurrence* of the behavior.[88] This is the most effective schedule for learning new behavior.[89] An example of continuous reinforcement would be to walk the class through the steps in solving a statistical problem. At each step, ask a question. When the correct answer is given, reinforce it with appropriate praise.

Intermittant reinforcement presents the reinforcing stimulus periodically.[90] This approach is most effective in maintaining learned behavior[91] or making behaviors more persistent. Intermittant reinforcement can be based on time *interval* or response *frequency*, and the periodicy can be either *fixed* or *variable*. This provides four possibilities.

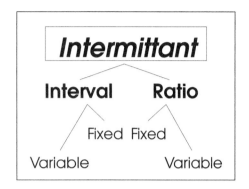

Fixed Interval. A fixed interval schedule is one in which a fixed amount of time lapses between reinforcers.[92] Examples of this include such things as a teacher checking on small group discussions every ten minutes, or scheduling a quiz every Friday. Because the reinforcement is predictable, target behavior increases just before the reinforcer.[93] As time approaches for the teacher to return, small groups become more focused in their discussions. Students cram for the quiz Thursday night. But behavior decreases right after the reinforcer.[94] When the teacher leaves, the students take a break. After the quiz on Friday, students relax until the next quiz approaches. If the teacher misses a check or two, or if a few quizzes are skipped, then study behavior declines.[95] Consider the final comprehensive examination and how many students wait until the night before to cram a semester's worth of material into their heads. Or the semester term paper, written a day or two before it's due. Fixed interval reinforcement can provide the fastest initial learning of any of the intermittant types, but the behavior is also less persistent.[96] Shorter, more frequent quizzes may be better than major, infrequent exams for encouraging more consistent effort.[97]

Variable Interval. A variable interval schedule is one in which a random amount of time passes between reinforcers.[98] Examples of this include random checks on student desk work by the teacher and unannounced quizzes. Since the reinforcement is unpredictable, work is more steady, students pause less often, and if the teacher misses a check or a quiz every now and then, study behavior continues high.[99] Persistence is much greater with variable interval reinforcement, and behaviors are highly resistant to extinction.[100]

Fixed Ratio. A fixed ratio reinforcement schedule is one in which a fixed number of responses occur between reinforcers. If students work three math problems correctly in a row, then they are allowed to start on their homework. For every ten assigned Scripture passages which are translated from the Greek, students earn one extra point on their semester grade. For every five verses committed to memory, children receive a gold star on a wall chart. Work is persistent until the break point is reached and the reinforcer received. Then behavior declines.[101]

Variable Ratio. A variable ratio reinforcement schedule is one in which a random number of responses occur between reinforcers.[102] Such a schedule produces the greatest degree of persistence, and behavior proceeds in a quick and steady manner.[103] The most common example of variable ratio reinforcement is the slot machine.[104] People deposit coins into the machine and pull the handle, over and over again. Periodically, a few coins dribble into the tray. People sit at the machines for hours, or until their money runs out. In a classroom, variable ratio reinforcement occurs as students are called on at random to answer questions.[105] Not only is this schedule effective in achieving persistence, but it is also practical to use in actual classroom discussions and question/answer sessions.

There is one other form in reinforcement which occurs when reinforcers are accidentally given regardless of what behavior is taking place. Such a schedule results in erroneous connections between results and behaviors.[106] Black cats, walking under ladders, spitting, and wearing a lucky shirt when competing in sports all reflect this kind of erroneous association.

Extinction

Extinction is the elimination of a response as a result of non-reinforcement.[107] The subject must be allowed to respond (press a lever) without receiving the reinforcing stimulus (food pellet). Under these conditions, lever pressing decreases. If the subject is prevented from responding (removed from the Skinner box), conditioning is retained.[108] Some students misbehave in order to gain the attention of the teacher. Teachers have been taught simply to ignore the misbehavior (not to reinforce it with attention) so that, in time, it will be extinguished. But it is difficult to ignore misbehavior, particularly if it is disruptive of others in the class. If the teacher occasionally reprimands the offender, then she is applying variable ratio reinforcement, the kind that produces the greatest persistence.[109] Rather than eliminating the offending behavior, she is actually strengthening it.

Generalization and Discrimination

Stimulus generalization occurs when subjects give the same response to similar but not identical stimuli.[110] Rats trained to respond to one bell tone will also respond to a different bell tone.[111] Stimulus discrimination occurs when subjects give different responses to similar but not identical stimuli.[112] Such discrimination is essential for learning how to respond in different situations. We use cues, signals or information in the environment to know when a given behavior is likely to be reinforced.[113] In a classroom situation, discrimination learning requires that feedback—information about the accuracy or appropriateness of a response[114]—be given for both correct and incorrect responses.[115] In order for feedback to be effective, it must be specific, immediate, based on the performance made, and contain corrective information.[116]

Teachers cannot wait for students randomly to hit on an appropriate behavior so that they can reinforce it. But they can provide a stimulus to encourage the proper behavior which can then be reinforced. This prior stimulus is called an *antecedent*,[117] and expands the basic R-S association to an A-R-S association. The antecedent (A) leads to a response (R) which receives a reinforcing stimulus (S). The reinforcing stimulus increases the probability that the response will occur in the future.[118] For example, after Skinner had programmed pigeons to peck a disk to get a food pellet, he introduced a light. If the pigeon pecked the disk when the light was on, it received a food pellet. If it pecked the disk when the light was off, no food pellet was given. The light was an antecedent. There are two basic types of antecedents, the cue and the prompt. A *cue* is a signal as to what behaviors will be reinforced or punished.[119] A *prompt* provides information so that learners can respond to cues correctly.[120]

Controlling Antecedants

Cueing Behavior. Cueing is providing an antecedent stimulus just before a particular behavior is to take place.[121] Without cues, students make mistakes, which require correction. This leads to frustration. By providing appropriate cues, students respond correctly and can be reinforced. This leads to satisfaction.

Antecedents

$$(P +) (C +) R - S$$

Prompt   Cue   Emitted   Reinforcing
                   Response   Stimulus

Remember that, for Skinner, the satisfaction, the consequence, the reinforcing stimulus is the most important element in the chain. But teachers can't wait until their students happen upon desirable behavior. Cueing provides a proactive way to lead students to desirable behavior. Examples include the following:

> The teacher asks probing questions until students correctly solve a problem. (Questions provide cues to the solution.)
>
> The teacher stands up at her desk in the front of the room. (The class focuses their attention on the teacher.)
>
> The teacher asks a question of the class. (Students begin thinking of an answer.)
>
> The teacher looks over the class after asking a question. (Students know he wants them to respond.)[122]

Prompting. Prompts help students respond to cues appropriately. Woolfolk gives the example of students working in pairs (cue). An effective prompt might be a checklist on peer tutoring. As students learn the steps, extinguish the list: stop using the checklist but remind the students of the steps. Continue the process until no prompt for good peer tutoring is needed. Monitor progress, recognize the good work of the pairs and correct mistakes.[123] The process of gradually removing prompts is called fading.[124]

Encouraging Behaviors

Two common approaches to encouraging appropriate behavior in students are teacher praise and the Premack principle.

Teacher Praise. When teachers recognize well-defined behavior in a sincere way, they effectively reinforce that behavior. Too often, however, teachers simply hand out compliments. This does not help change behavior.[125] Is the praise genuine? Is it immediate? Does it focus on specific behaviors? Does it include incidental answers, showing that original thinking is valued? Is it commensurate with the level of performance? Is it given with careful judgment of the situation?[126] Two cautions should be noted in praising students.

"Effective praise is more than simply handing out compliments"

First, are we teaching them to enjoy learning for its own sake, or are we teaching them to win approval?[127] Second, do we focus our praise on better answers, or on better students? Research indicates the latter.[128]

Premack Principle. David Premack (1965) suggested that an effective motivational strategy involves using what learners want to do to reinforce what the teacher wants them to do.[129] Said another way, "Of every pair of responses or activities in which an individual engages, the more probable one will reinforce the less probable one."[130] The Premack Principle is sometimes called "Grandma's Rule," because Grandma would say, "Eat your peas (what Grandma wants) and then you can have dessert (what the child wants)."[131]

Classroom examples include such things as these:

> Allow students to talk quietly with friends after they complete an individual worksheet.

> Exempt students from a homework assignment after they successfully complete a self-test.

> Exempt students from an exam if their daily average is above ninety.

Teachers who say, "We'll go to recess first so that you'll be ready to settle down to your math lessons" miss Premack's point.[132] The Premack Principle has proved to be a highly effective approach for identifying reinforcers at all age levels.[133]

Skinner saw public education as disorganized and inefficient. The goal of education for Skinner was to make students competent. As with Thorndike, Skinner saw little difference between sequentially shaping the behavior of pigeons and children. Determine the skill or competency that needs to be learned. Break the competency into small, successive steps. Design a step-by-step instructional process that moves students to those competencies.

Educational Operant Conditioning: Programmed Instruction

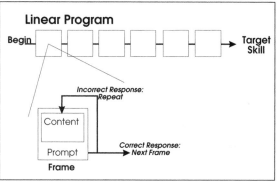

Each step, or frame,[134] presents a small amount of material and a prompt of some kind. When students respond to the prompt, they receive immediate feedback.[135] If they are correct, they proceed to the next step. If they are wrong, they receive corrective information and then are given another prompt.[136] Small steps produce maximum reinforcement and minimal failure. There is no wasted time. Students proceed according to their own abilities to learn.[137]

The series of frames which lead to a given competency is called a "program."[138] Instructional programs fall into two basic types. A *linear*-type program, developed by Skinner,[139] is one in which every student moves through every step from beginning to end.[140]

The lack of flexibility is a major problem with linear programs: the slower student may not get enough help, and the faster student may be bored. A *branching*-type program, developed by N. A. Crowder (1961),[141] eliminates these deficiencies. If students answer a prompt incorrectly, they are directed to a subprogram which enriches

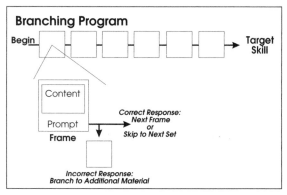

their understanding of the subject. If students answer initial questions correctly, they may be advanced several frames. Branching programs adapt to the needs and abilities of individuals. The degree to which this adaptation occurs depends on the sophistication of the program.

Computers and Programmed Instruction. There is no doubt that computers have swept over the educational scene and have become the most popular medium for dispensing programmed instruction materials.[142] The computer permits a degree of *interaction* between the student and the program that cannot be achieved with book-type programs. Students are focused on screens of information and graphics. The program has the student's undivided attention. Progress cannot be made without student response, and that response is always evaluated and feedback given.[143] Because learners receive feedback at every frame, reinforcement is maximized and failure is minimized. Compare this situation to a classroom of thirty students, where a few interact with the teacher and the rest simply listen.

Computers can track student answers and "learn" from them. This brings a new dimension to branching program sophistication. This permits the program to be *individualized* for the needs of each particular student.[144] The program can provide just what the student needs most to learn in every frame. Again, compare this to classrooms in which teachers provide some level of learning—higher or lower depending on responses they get—while some students are bored, others lost.

Computers and Education. There are a variety of ways computers impact the educational world. *Computer literacy* is the study of computers themselves, as well as computer use and programming. Computers are used as learning *tools* by providing assistance in word processing, data analysis and communication. Computers serve as *teaching machines*, providing drill and practice exercises, sophisticated audiovisual resources, and tutorials in a multitude of subjects. Computers permit *simulations* of activities that are either too costly or dangerous actually to do—flying a plane or working in a chemistry lab. Simulations can also demonstrate human blood circulation, or 4-cycle engine operation.[145] *Integrated learning* systems provide computer-based content, objectives, activities, and evaluations.[146] With the advent of artifical intelligence—programming which allows computers to simulate the learning process—*intelli-*

gent tutor systems are being developed which modify their presentations according to learner strengths and weaknesses. The cutting edge of computer technology as I write this chapter is *virtual reality simulation* environments.[147] Three-dimensional graphics, projected inside a helmet, surround the learner with a computer-generated world: a library, a plane's cockpit, a boxing ring, a battle zone. Virtual reality extends the simulation metaphor to integrate the learner inside the simulation.

While there is a wide range of possibilities in computer assisted instruction, computers are used primarily as learning tools and drill and practice teaching machines. Research has shown that programmed instruction allows for faster acquisition of material than more traditional classroom practices, but not necessarily better acquisition. Computerized materials, particularly of the drill and practice type, are best for disadvantaged learners.[148]

Do computers enhance learning? This is like asking, "Do chalkboards enhance learning?" or "Do overhead cells enhance learning?" The answer is that it depends on how these tools are used. It is the same with computerized instruction.[149] There is nothing magic about computers. Technology cannot replace good educational practice.

Proponents of computerized education see a bright future in which students will have world-wide access to libraries, universities, research centers, and government agencies. They see students developing better skills in reading, writing, and arithmetic. They envision stronger families as more people work on computers from their homes. Computer skeptics have their doubts. They see less developed skills as entertainment replaces reading and writing. They see more violence as graphic games are acted out. They see a greater gap between the haves and have nots. And finally, they see greater emphasis being placed on computer information than human advice.[150]

What has been your reaction to this chapter on behavioral learning? What statements or positions caused you the greatest discomfort? What questions were raised concerning the role of the learner in the learning process? I intentionally left these philosophical questions until now in order to give you as clear a picture of behavioral learning as possible. Now that you understand the basic positions of contiguity learning, classical conditioning, and operant conditioning, let's consider them from a Christian perspective. We'll look

IMPLICATIONS FOR CHRISTIAN TEACHING

briefly at behaviorism as a philosophy, ethical considerations for using behavioral principles, and finally suggestions for employing these principles in the classroom.

Behaviorism as
a Philosophy

Issler and Habermas clearly state the position of the evangelical Christian community. "Behavioral learning theory" is a term that refers to explanations of how we act and why. "Behaviorism" is a "mechanistic, deterministic, metaphysical view about final causes of all human behaviors. As Christians, we can use principles from the former, but we must reject the latter."[151] B. F. Skinner believed that humans are as yoked to their environment as his rats were to their experimental boxes. This is what Issler and Habermas mean by mechanistic. The environment controls behavior, not ideals or emotions or the will or profound ideas. And whoever controls the environment controls people.[152] This is what Issler and Habermas mean by deterministic. Listen to Jesus's words:

> No good tree bears bad fruit, nor does a bad tree bear good fruit. Each tree is recognized by its own fruit. People do not pick figs from thornbushes, or grapes from briers. The good man brings good things out of the good stored up in his heart, and the evil man brings evil things out of the evil stored up in his heart. For out of the overflow of his heart his mouth speaks (Luke 6:43–45).

Certainly Jesus emphasized the heart (that is, the mind, the emotions, the will) as the source of good and bad behavior. We are not helpless recipients of environmental stimuli. Jesus calls us to overcome the world (Rev. 3:21) because He has (John 16:33). Paul warns us, "Do not be overcome by evil, but overcome evil with good" (Rom. 12:21). Paul believed we have power over our environment.

"Even secular theorists
believe there are
differences between
the ways rats
and children
operate"

Behaviorism is appealingly simple,[153] an advantage in a scientific society which deems simplicity a virtue. Behavioral principles are relatively easy to master. And research has shown them to be effective.[154] But behaviorism is not universally accepted even among secular theorists. Phillips and Soltis question Skinner's suspicion of nonobservable internal states. Physics, the premier observational science, studies quarks which no one has seen. Only their effects can be measured. And gravity is invisible, though its influence is not.[155] Why rule out the intellect? Further, research has shown that behaviorism cannot explain how language develops. Young children can correctly understand sentences they've never heard before.[156] Sprinthall writes that traditional behaviorism should not be accepted at face value. There *are* differences between the way rats and children operate in the environment. Further, research has shown that conditioning is not permanent or automatic, as Skinner believed.[157]

We return, therefore, to Issler and Habermas: Christians can certainly use behavioral principles without accepting the world view of behaviorism. We are not alone in rejecting the mechanistic, deterministic philosophy underlying conditioning theory.

Ethical Considerations

If you grew up during the Cold War, you are familiar with the brainwashing techniques of the Soviets and Koreans. Classical conditioning and operant conditioning principles were used with chilling effect on military and intelligence personnel. But when we use these same principles, are we manipulating behavior? Are we brainwashing our learners? Or, to put it more positively, is there a way to use behavioral learning principles in an ethical way? The answer is yes, if we move away from Skinner's "empty box" view of learners and treat them as persons.

First, we will avoid manipulation if we use behavioral principles for justified purposes. That is, ethical use of behavioral techniques requires that the focus be helping students, not merely shaping them to teacher demands. Teaching involves beliefs and rational thought and is more than conditioning which focuses on performance.[158]

Second, changes in attitudes, beliefs, and values should occur for reasons that students accept. The rational processes of students must be engaged. Behavior changes must have student cooperation.[159]

Third, an ethical application of behavioral principles will focus more on intrinsic rewards and incentives. The term "intrinsic" refers to factors that are naturally part of the learning experience. Some writers oppose the use of external reinforcers because it reflects a kind of bribery. But use of rewards can be considered bribery only if the behaviors which are reinforced are dishonest or unfair. If the end behaviors are honest, and students are aware that reinforcers are being used, then reinforcement is not bribery.[160]

Suggestions for Using Conditioning Principles

1. Use cues and prompts to help establish new behaviors[161] or warn of impending punishment.[162]

    "It is fine to talk with your friends as you come into the Sunday school class, but when I stand with my Bible open, I need to have your attention so we can begin." Standing with an open Bible is the cue. Explaining what the cue means is the prompt.

    "If you two boys continue to disrupt the class with your talking, and I have to speak with you about it again, I will take you both to your parents."

2. Use an appropriate reinforcement schedule. When introducing new material, give plenty of reinforcement by asking questions frequently. After the new material has been learned, use an intermittent schedule to encourage persistence.[163]

3. Insure that all learners receive some praise,[164] but praise learner behaviors judiciously.[165]

4. Use the Premack Principle to identify reinforcers for your students.[166]

5. Provide clear, informative feedback on student work.[167] Remember that feedback is most effective when it involves both praise for correct answers and corrective information for wrong answers.[168]

6. Promote generalization by encouraging students to make comparisons and look for relationships among examples.[169]

    "In what ways did the actions of Barnabas reflect values taught by Jesus?"

7. Promote discrimination learning by encouraging students to look for distinctives and contrasts among examples.

    "How did Peter and Judas, both disciples, differ in their reactions to their own betrayal of Jesus?"

8. Try to use negative reinforcement ("relief") rather than punishment to curb inappropriate behaviors.[170]

    "Johnny, if you will work cooperatively with your project group for these last fifteen minutes, I won't tell your parents about your behavior today."

Key Emphases from Traditional Behaviorism

The following twelve statements summarize key distinctives of traditional behavioral learning Use these terms to compare and contrast learning as defined in chapters 8 and 9.	
1. The learner is a . . .	MACHINE
2. The focus is on the . . .	ENVIRONMENT
3. Relationship of learning "whole" to its parts . . .	WHOLE *EQUALS* SUM OF PARTS
4. Learning is . . .	MECHANICAL
5. The target learning domain is . . .	LOWER COGNITIVE
6. The goal of learning is . . .	BEHAVIOR CHANGE
7. Learning is strengthened by . . .	REPETITION
8. Learning is guided by . . .	REINFORCEMENT
9. Motivation keys on . . .	DRIVES
10. Feedback should be . . .	IMMEDIATE, ON PERFORMANCE
11. Best curriculum is . . .	SIMPLE, SEQUENTIAL
12. The Theory of Practice is . . .	PROGRAMMED INSTRUCTION

9. Try to use removal punishment ("penalty") rather than presentation punishment.[171]

   "Johnny, since you chose not to work cooperatively with your project group, please take you seat in the time-out corner."

10. Avoid reinforcing the behavior you're trying to punish.[172] A reprimand is a positive reinforcer to one who is ignored most of the time. By giving attention to misbehavior, you reinforce it. Ignore minor behavior problems. Use cues and prompts to cure behavior problems before they occur.

11. Focus on student actions, not personal qualities.[173] A common problem with teacher praise is that it goes to the "best students" rather than the best answers.

In more recent years, behaviorists have found operant conditioning to be too limited an explanation for learning.[174] While behavioral purists have held on to traditional behaviorism, most have integrated cognitive processes[175] that cannot be directly observed—expectations, thoughts, beliefs.[176] In a sense these theorists have returned to John Locke, who focused on experience as the source of all knowledge, but also spoke of the innate capacities of the intellect. Piaget emphasized the interaction between mind and environment in his concepts of adaptation and equilibration, as well as elemental cognitive structures called schemes.

These are the very internal structures and cognitive processes that Watson, Thorndike, and Skinner denied in favor of associationism and reinforcement. Still, a critical problem exists for traditional behaviorism. It cannot explain how learning occurs through modeling and imitation.[177] Basic problems confronting the purists are these: learners tend to be selective in who they imitate. They imitate models with whom they've had no previous interaction. Behavior may occur days after the observation, even without reinforcement.[178] How can this rational behavior be explained as R-S bonds in the nervous system?

The fact is that many of our most persistent habits and attitudes[179] result from simply watching and thinking about the actions of others.[180] We can learn complex behavior with a single observation without cuing or reinforcement.[181] Learning based on observation and modeling is known as Social Learning theory. Its roots are found in research in the 1940s which disputed Skinner's

ALBERT BANDURA: SOCIAL LEARNING THEORY

assertation that all behavior change occurred because of reinforcement.[182]

Traditional Behaviorism and Social Learning Theory

Albert Bandura became the acknowledged spokesman for social learning theory in 1977[183] and wrote the definitive work on the subject in *Social Foundations of Thought and Action* (1986). Bandura found that merely observing another person might be sufficient to lead to a learned response. Social learning theory moves away from traditional behaviorism in three distinct ways. First, direct reinforcement of the observer is not necessary for learning to occur.[184] Learning occurs simply by observing the model. The observer may simply want to be like the model.[185] Still, the effects are amplified if we also see the consequences of their actions.[186] Observing the effects of behaviors on others is called *vicarious reinforcement*. Succinctly stated, vicarious reinforcement occurs when we see another person's behavior reinforced.[187]

"Many of our most persistent habits and attitudes result from simply watching and thinking about the actions of others"

Second, the mental representation of observed behaviors is a departure from traditional behaviorism. This mental imagery is important if the behaviors are to be reproduced at a later time.[188] Social learning theory integrates cognitive processes into its behavioral view.

Third, there is a difference between social learning and traditional behaviorism on the nature of determinism. Traditional behaviorists hold that all behavior is controlled by the environment. Social learning theorists see learning as an interaction between personal factors, behavior, and the environment.[189] This interaction, closely associated with Piaget's adaptation, is called *reciprocal determinism:* the environment influences the learner and the learner influences the environment.[190]

In his classic experiment, Bandura placed a child at a table with a toy. Nearby was a second table. In one condition, no one was sitting at the other table. A second condition placed an adult at the table playing with Tinker Toys. A third condition placed an adult at the table playing with Tinker Toys for one minute. Then the adult moved to an inflatable clown Bobo doll and began hitting, kicking, and shouting at it. After ten minutes, the child's toy was taken away (producing mild frustration). The child was placed in a second room alone, furnished with toys, including the toys in the first room. In the first and second conditions, children showed little aggression. In the third condition, children showed considerably more aggression.[191]

Though the child was not directly reinforced for any behavior, the child's behavior changed in the direction of the aggressive model.

Just how does social learning occur? Bandura describes four components of the process: attention, retention, production, and motivation.

The Process of Social Learning

Attention. The first step in the learning process is for the model to gain the attention of an observer.[192] The learner must pay attention to the model's behaviors if learning is to occur. What determines the effectiveness of a model? Attention is attracted, intentionally or not, by high status, competence and expertise, popularity,[193] success,[194] and perceived similarity.[195] Models similar to the observer are more effective than those that are different. But competent models are more effective than incompetent ones, regardless of similarity.[196] Gender differences do not influence the modeling of academic skills, but observers tend to behave more like their own gender.[197] Observers with a negative self-concept or learning disability do better with a coping model—one who struggles and overcomes difficulties—than a mastery model—one who performs well without difficulty.[198] Parents are the most important models,[199] but teachers play a powerful modeling role as well.

Teachers are influential, competent, accessible, and have high status in the classroom.[200] We can improve our modeling influence by making clear presentations, highlighting key ideas, providing interesting cues, and using novelty and surprise.[201] Teachers must do more than simply gain attention. Attention must be focused on the critical aspects of behavior to be learned.[202] Teachers model personal traits such as values and beliefs; general academic skills, such as problem solving and creative thinking; and specific skills by step-by-step demonstration.[203]

Models need not be positive to be effective.[204] A gang leader who models murder and violence for younger members effectively teaches gang behavior. When I worked with the deaf in Irving, Texas, I met two deaf men who were leaders of their respective social groups. One was a deacon of First Baptist Church, a loving father and husband, a caring man. The other was an unemployed alcoholic who used his wife's paycheck for his drunken binges. He lied anytime it was to his advantage. He also happened to be a good bowler. Both men enjoyed the status of "tribal leader" in their respective groups. Both influenced their groups' behavior. For learning to occur, a lower status observer carefully watches the behavior of a higher status model. Notice that status, whether we're observing an outstanding deacon or drunken liar, is a relative term.

Do you have Sunday school teachers who use poor teaching methods, yet refuse to attend training conferences or teachers' meetings? Perhaps they are teaching the way their teacher taught them. Though their methods were poor, they shared themselves, their time, their love with their students. Now the students are teachers—and they teach as they observed their teacher teach, poor methods and all. When you suggest better approaches, you unwittingly criticize the teacher who loved them. The only solution to this social learning problem is to love the teachers, build bridges to them, and, over time, model better approaches for teaching. The first step in modeling new behavior is to gain observers' attention.

Retention. Observed behavior must be encoded in memory[205] so that observers remember it.[206] This encoding may be in the form of mental images[207] or a verbal description of the behavior.[208] This encoding permits learners to mentally rehearse the behavior.[209] The next time you watch downhill ski racing, notice how the skiers stand in the starting gate and mentally go through the course. They bob their heads and shift their bodies as if clearing the gates. This is mental rehearsal.

The advertising industry uses social learning principles to sell products. An image of a man and woman getting into a new car: "We build excitement—Pontiac." An image of a man and woman passionately kissing: "Ultrabrite." An image of beautiful swimsuit clad young people on the beach, laughing: "It's Miller time." An image of a woman in the 1890s being scolded by her husband, and another of a chic woman of the 1990s smoking: "You've come a long way, baby—Virginia Slims." The message is clear: "If you want excitement, passion, fun, and status, then you need our products." We'll study the specifics of how experience is encoded into memory when we discuss Information Processing Theory in the next chapter.

Production. Learners have observed new behaviors, encoded them in memory, and mentally rehearsed them. Now in the production[210] stage, learners actually practice the behaviors on their own.[211] They select and organize the response elements which have been stored in memory, perform the behavior, and then refine their performance on the basis of feedback.[212]

Motivation.[213] Bandura used the term "reinforcement" for this fourth stage, but his definition was broader than Skinner's. He included Skinnerian reinforcement which he called *direct reinforcement.* An observer watches a model, performs the action, and is reinforced or punished for the action.[214] A second type of reinforcement—the key to observational learning—is called *vicarious reinforcement.*[215] An observer watches a model

Ⓡ *Direct reinforcement*

Observer ⟩—→ Model
Observer behaves like model
and is reinforced

behave in a certain way, and further observes how the model is reinforced or punished for that behavior.[216] If the model is reinforced, the observer tends to imitate the behavior. If the model is punished, the observer tends to avoid that behavior. Vicarious reinforcement allows us to learn from how others are affected.[217] A great deal of classroom reinforcement is vicarious.[218] Praising one student for his or her good question encourages all to ask good questions.[219]

Consider the television and magazine advertisements we mentioned earlier. If you want excitment like this highly successful couple, buy a Pontiac. If you want a passionate kiss like the beautiful couple in the ad, brush your

Vicarious reinforcement **Ⓡ**

Observer ⟩—→ Model
Observer sees model reinforced
for behavior

teeth with Ultrabrite. If you want to have fun on the beach like these young people, drink Miller beer. If you want to feel equal with men, smoke Virginia Slims, and you'll be as liberated as the woman in the picture.

A third type of reinforcement is *self-reinforcement.* Learners can set personal performance standards[220] and control their own reinforcers.[221] The fact that young people tend to dress alike illustrates the point. The similarity of dress reflects a sense of belonging, which is self-reinforcing.[222] Learners are capable of observing their own behavior, judging it against their own standards, and reinforcing or punishing themselves for it.[223] The emphasis on "self" shows how far social learning theorists moved from Skinner's position. Skinner was bitterly opposed to the encroaching cognitive influence over behaviorism right up until his death in 1990.[224]

Self reinforcement **Ⓡ**

Observer ⟩
Observer behaves according to own standards
and provides own reinforcement

In summary, Bandura separated the acquisition of knowledge (learning) from the production of behavior (performance). Learning occurs through observation. Behavior based on that knowledge occurs as a result of motivation. While Skinner believed that emitted overt responses preceded reinforcement and learning, Bandura showed that learning occurs through observation before learners begin to make overt responses.[225]

Other Effects of Modeling and Imitation

The process discussed above reflects "true" observational learning in which new behaviors are established.[226] Modeling and imitation produce three other effects as well. *Inhibition* is not doing something because someone else refrains.[227] We know how, but simply don't. "Should I begin eating my salad?" Sue asks herself at the banquet. She looks at the head table to see if the hosts are eating. They aren't, so she waits. *Disinhibition* is doing something because someone else does without being punished.[228] Young people are told they may have only two slices of pizza, but John notices that some take four or five without being reprimanded. So John takes four slices. *Facilitation* is doing something that we normally would not do because we lack sufficient motivation. Mike sits quietly without asking questions in class. But several other students ask questions and are warmly received by the teacher. So Mike decides to ask a question too. Notice that these three effects motivate behavior, but new behaviors are not being learned.

Using Social Learning Theory Principles

Modeling and imitation happen whenever people are together. Those with perceived lower status learn how to behave by observing those perceived to have higher status. Whether we're in a classroom or church meeting, at a party or formal dinner, observational principles are at work. What specifically can we do, however, to enhance the learning process?

Teaching New Behaviors. Teachers are effective as models in teaching new behaviors as they demonstrate, clearly and systematically, the skills under study. We do this by focusing attention on critical elements of the skill, thinking out loud as student questions are considered,[229] using step-by-step demonstrations with verbal explanations, and contrasting good and bad examples.[230]

Strengthening or Weakening Inhibitions. Students who break rules, misbehave, turn work in late, or engage in other inappropriate behavior will encourage others to do the same if their behavior is not checked. A warm, but firm, reprimand of those who misbehave will strengthen the inhibition to misbehave in other students in the class. On the other hand, students may be inhibited in asking questions because they were humiliated by a former teacher for asking "dumb" questions. By being open to student questions and praising student willingness to ask questions, teachers weaken this inhibition. The contagious spreading of behaviors, good or bad, through imitation in the group is called the ripple effect.[231]

The central pillar in the Disciplers' Model is Building Relationships. Jesus' response to the Pharisee's question, "Which is the greatest commandment in the Law?" (Matt. 22:36) focused on relationships: Love God (v. 37), a vertical relationship, and love your neighbor as yourself (v. 39), horizontal relationships. The church is a body of Believers drawn from all walks of life and placed together in a social context because of their faith in Jesus Christ. The church is a context for social learning, in which those who are mature spiritually become the models for converts and young Christians. The Bible provides the content for learning; the life and work of the church provide the social laboratory where principles are converted to lifestyles.

Implications for Christian Teaching

Paul underscores the importance of social learning in Colossians 3:8–17. He uses the image of clothing to address the need for changed lives in the Colossian Christians. He is writing to believers (3:12) who are spiritually clean because of their faith in Christ. So here is the picture. A man has worked in the field all day. He and his clothes are dirty. He removes the old dirty clothes and bathes. Now, a clean man, he puts on the old dirty clothes. This is Paul's way of gaining attention in order to encourage a change of behavior. The dirty clothes Paul lists include "anger, rage, malice, slander, and filthy language from your lips" (Col. 3:8). Paul says they must take off those dirty clothes, and "clothe yourselves with compassion, kindness, humility, gentleness and patience" (Col. 3:12). What are these characteristics? Briefly, *anger* is the sudden explosion of temper toward another person. *Rage* is settled anger, hatred of another. *Malice* is wishing harm on someone, perhaps because they received a raise or a promotion, or asked to do some prominent work in the church. *Slander* is undermining the reputations of others, often with half-truths and innuendo. *Filthy language* certainly includes foul talk, but also refers to abusive language or coarse jesting with others. "Hey, backslider, where've ya been the last few weeks?!" These are characteristics Paul says we need to remove.

Compassion is soft-heartedness. Seeing others in need, our hearts respond with concern. *Kindness* refers to actions which spring from compassion. We see a need, we respond not only in our hearts, but we put feet to our feelings and do something to help. *Humility* is thinking rightly about ourselves. It is certainly not self-aggrandisement, in which we think too highly of ourselves, but neither is it self-deprecation, in which we think too lowly of ourselves. The believer who says, "I must have been absent when God was handing out gifts" is questioning the creative power of God and the Truth of Scripture which teaches that every believer has at least one spiritual gift (Acts 11:17; Rom. 12:6ff; 1 Cor. 7:7).

True humility is realizing that we have strengths and weaknesses. We thank God for the strengths, and use those strengths to help others in their weakness. We ask God to help us in our weaknesses, and allow others to minister to us as we need. Our strengths in the Lord allow us to be useful and have purpose. Our weaknesses keep us from becoming self-sufficient and arrogant. This allows us to put on *gentleness*—treating others, whether above us or below us, with respect. Without humility, we cannot be gentle. If we are self-important, we tend to look down on others, or worse, keep them under our control and authority. If we are self-depreciating, we tend to criticize, berate, complain, or pick at the efforts of others. Neither autocratic control nor whining criticism is gentle. But with a mental attitude of humility, we can help those weaker than we are because we know in our strength they are no threat. We can also praise those who can do things we can't, because their success does not take away from our own. Barnabas is a prime example of Christian humility. Finally, Paul says we are to put on patience, the remaining-under-the-load kind of persistent effort. These are the garments of the well-dressed Christian. They are held in place by the belt of agape-love (Col. 3:14). Again, Paul presents a picture of a first century man's apparel—an inner tunic, an outer tunic, and a cloak, all held in place by a belt.

Notice that all these characteristics are social in nature. We develop them as we relate to others. We cannot develop them sitting at home watching religious programming on television. Remember when Jesus raised Lazarus from the dead? "The dead man came out, his hands and feet wrapped with strips of linen, and a cloth around his face" (John 11:44a). But He told the people standing around him to release him from his old grave clothes. "Jesus said to them, 'Take off the grave clothes and let him go'" (John 11:44b). Jesus has given us new life. But our development as believers is a social learning process in which we rub up against each other, conflict with each other, reason together, work together, and learn from each other in

His name. The Church is the social context, and the Bible is the content.

Peter warns pastors not to be authoritarian rulers, but to be examples—models worthy of imitation by believers (1 Peter 5:3).

As the person with highest status and influence in the congregation, the pastor is the most prominent model. But all believers are called to be "perfect [full-grown], therefore, as your heavenly Father is perfect" (Matt. 5:48). As we grow and use our spiritual gifts, we become models one for the other: "Let the word of Christ dwell in you richly as you teach and admonish one another with all wisdom, and as you sing psalms, hymns and spiritual songs with gratitude in your hearts to God" (Col. 3:16). May God bless you as you become a model worthy of imitation, in Jesus' name.

> **"Peter warns pastors not to be authoritarian rulers but to be examples—models worthy of imitation by believers"**

CHAPTER CONCEPTS

Antecedent	Motivation
Attention	Negative reinforcement
Behaviorism	Observational learning
Branching program	Positive reinforcement
Contiguity	Premack principle
Continuous reinforcement	Presentation punishment
Cue	Primary reinforcer
Discrimination	Production
Elicited behavior	Program
Emitted behavior	Programmed instruction
Extinction	Prompt
Feedback	R-S bond
Fixed interval schedule	Reinforcer
Fixed ratio schedule	Removal punishment
Frame	Response
Generalization	Retention
Individualization	S-R bond
Interaction	Secondary reinforcer
Intermittant reinforcement	Spontaneous Recovery
Introspection	Stimulus
Law of Readiness	Superstitious reinforcement
Law of Exercise	Tabula rasa
Law of Effect	Variable ratio schedule
Linear program	Variable interval schedule
Modeling	Vicarious reinforcement

DISCUSSION QUESTIONS

1. Describe two specific instances of classical conditioning in your church or school. (Here's something to get you started: "The quickest way to quiet a church group is to say, 'Let's pray.'")
2. Compare and contrast S-R and R-S associations.
3. Explain the meaning of "P + C + R - S."
4. Give church-related examples of positive reinforcement, negative reinforcement, removal punishment, and presentation punishment.
5. What erroneous theology have you discovered that can be attributed to superstitious reinforcement? (Example: "I closed my eyes, opened the Bible at random, and pointed to a verse to get a word from the Lord.")
6. Differentiate between linear and branching programs. What experiences have you had with either type of program?
7. Early Christians were severely persecuted for refusing to renounce Jesus as Lord. They were thrown to wild animals, set afire as torches, and forced to fight as gladiators. Explain this behavior (1) using operant conditioning and (2) social learning theory principles.

FOR FURTHER READING

Bandura, Albert. *Principles of Behavior Modification.* New York: Holt, Rinehart & Winston, 1969.

———. *Social Learning Theory.* Englewood Cliffs, N.J.: Prentice-Hall, Inc., 1977.

———. *Social Foundations of Thought and Action: A Social Cognitive Theory.* Englewood Cliffs, N.J.: Prentice-Hall, Inc., 1986.

Biehler, Robert F., and Jack Snowman. "Behavioral Learning Theories." In *Psychology Applied to Teaching* 7th ed., 320–75. Boston: Houghton Mifflin Company, 1993.

Clouse, Bonnidell. "Moral Growth by Moral Behavior: A Learning View," and "Guidelines . . . " *Teaching for Moral Growth: A Guide for the Christian Community—Teachers, Parents and Pastors,* 148–82, 183–220. Wheaton, Ill: Bridgeport Books, 1993.

Dembo, Myron H. "Behavioral Approaches to Learning." In *Applying Educational Psychology.* 5th ed., 38–85. New York: Longman, 1994.

Eggen, Paul, and Don Kauchak. "Behavioral Views of Learning." In *Educational Psychology: Classroom Connections.* 2nd ed., 253–98. New York: Macmillan College Publishing Company, 1994.

Ford, LeRoy. *Design for Teaching and Training: A Self-Study Guide to Lesson Planning.* Nashville: Broadman Press, 1978. (Good example of a programmed text.)

Gage, N. L., and David C. Berliner. "The Definition and Varieties of Learning," "Operant Conditioning: A Practical Theory," and "Social Learning Theory. " *Educational Psychology.* 3rd ed., 250–69; 270–97; 333–49. Dallas: Houghton Mifflin Company, 1984.

Glover, John A., and Roger H. Bruning. "An Introduction to Behavioral Psychology," and "Social Learning and Modeling." In *Educational Psychology: Principles and Applications.* 3rd. ed., 268–96; 297–20. Glenview, Ill.: Scott, Foresman/Little, Brown Higher Education, 1990.

Good, Thomas L., and Jere E. Brophey. "The Behavioral Approach to Learning." In *Educational Psychology: A Realistic Approach.* 4th ed., 151–85. New York: Longman, 1990.

Hamachek, Don. *Psychology in Teaching, Learning, and Growth.* 4th ed., 17–27. Boston: Allyn and Bacon, 1990.

Hamilton, Richard, and Elizabeth Ghatala. "Classical and Operant Conditioning," and "Bandura's Social Learning Theory." *Learning and Instruction.* 25–73; 287–326. New York: McGraw Hill, Inc, 1994.

LeFrancois, Guy R. "Behavioristic Explanations of Learning" In *Psychology for Teaching.* 8th ed., 82–117. Belmont, Calif.: Wadsworth Publishing Company, 1994.

Slavin, Robert E. "Behavioral Theories of Learning." In *Educational Psychology: Theory and Practice.* 4th ed., 150–182. Boston: Allyn and Bacon, 1994.

Skinner, B. F. *Science and Human Behavior.* New York: Macmillan, 1953.

———. *The Technology of Teaching.* Englewood Cliffs, N.J.: Prentice-Hall, Inc., 1968.

———. *Beyond Freedom and Dignity.* New York: Knopf Publishers, 1971.

Sprinthall, Norman A., Richard C. Sprinthall, and Sharon N. Oja, "Learning Theory Today," and "Learning in the Classroom." In *Educational Psychology: A Developmental Approach*, 6th ed. 229–42; 258–81. New York: McGraw-Hill, Inc., 1994.

Woolfolk, Anita. "Behavioral Learning Theories," In *Educational Psychology*. 5th ed., 194–235. Boston: Allyn and Bacon, Inc., 1993.

Chapter

8

TEACHING FOR
UNDERSTANDING
(PART 1)

COGNITIVE LEARNING THEORIES
JEROME BRUNER'S DISCOVERY LEARNING

Cognitive learning theory emphasizes the *thinking* of students, rather than their behavior or attitudes. The apostle Paul wrote, "Do not conform any longer to the pattern of this world, but be transformed by the renewing of your mind" (Rom. 12:2a). Paul saw the mind as the center of activity both for conforming to world patterns and for being transformed according to God's will. How do we learn from the world around us? What role does perception play in the learning process? In this chapter we present the historical development of cognitive theory from the early 1900s through the work of Jerome Bruner.

CHAPTER RATIONALE

Learners will demonstrate knowledge of cognitive learning theory by describing the origins of Gestalt psychology, including contributions of Mach, Wertheimer, Köhler, and Lewin.

Learners will demonstrate understanding of cognitive learning by:

CHAPTER OBJECTIVES

- differentiating the views of Mach and Watson, Werthiemer and Pavlov, Köhler and Thorndike, and Bruner and Skinner;

- giving at least two examples for each law of perception from their own experience;

- explaining key elements in Bruner's discovery learning, including structure, motivation, student activity, and teacher role.

Learners will demonstrate appreciation for cognitive learning by sharing personal experiences of perception, insight, and discovery.

HISTORICAL ROOTS

Cognitive learning theories are explanations for learning that focus on the internal mental processes people use in their effort to make sense of the world.[1] Cognitive theorists believe, in contrast to behaviorists, that these nonobservable cognitive processes can be studied in a scientific manner.[2] They view learning as a reorganization of perceptions. Perception is the meaning we attach to information we receive from the world around us. Perceptual reorganization allows learners to develop a clear understanding of the subject. Cognitive theories focus on the mind rather than the nervous system, insight rather than A-R-S bonds, understanding rather than behavior. They see learners as conscious, perceiving thinkers, able to acquire meaning from the world,[3] rather than programmable robots. Certainly one can condition children to associate bits and pieces of information, but without an underlying understanding of the information, it remains virtually useless.[4] This fundamental principle of learning drives all of the cognitive theories.

"Mind not nervous system, Insight not A-R-S bonds, Understanding not behavior"

Cognitive theories grew out of Gestalt psychology. Developed in Germany in the early 1900s, it was transplanted to America in the 1920s. *Gestalt* is roughly translated as "configuration,"[5] or "pattern,"[6] and emphasizes "the whole"[7] of human experience. We will look briefly at key theorists in cognitive learning—Ernst Mach, Max Wertheimer, Wolfgang Köhler, Kurt Lewin. Then we'll focus on Jerome Bruner, who, more than any other, overcame Behaviorism's hold on educational psychology and changed the direction of American thinking in the 1950s.[8] Finally, we'll focus on constructivism, a present-day revolution in educational psychology[9] which is founded on the work of Piaget and Bruner.

Wilhelm Wundt

While behaviorists seized Wundt's concept of a "basic element" in human experience, they deplored his use of introspection as a methodology. Gestalt psychologists opposed his idea of "basic element." They believed that Wundt led psychology away from human experience as a whole as he tried to develop a concise chart of psychological elements.[10] The wholeness of experience is lost when we focus only on its smallest parts. The behavioral view, according to Gestaltists, is like studying each individual note in a musical composition rather than the composition as a whole. Music is more than notes. Wundt therefore gave birth to two widely divergent views of learning. Behaviorists focused on the "basic element" of S-R bonds (Pavlov), and Gestaltists focused on a more introspective approach to studying nonobservable human mental processes.

Both Wilhelm Wundt and John Watson wanted to make psychology a credible scientific discipline. Their assumption was: this would be accomplished if psychology were to use methods similar to other scientific disciplines, like physics. So, they emphasized basic psychological elements and observation of overt behavior.

Ernst Mach

Ernst Mach (1838–1916) rejected such thinking. Psychology is not physics. Humans perceive the world around them; planets do not. Sensations of relationship in the minds of humans do not necessarily correspond to the physical reality they see. Earlier in the text I presented three dots on the page and asked you to label what you saw. Some of you saw the dots as the three points of a triangle. Nothing in the dots suggested this. It was their configuration that prompted the relationship.[11] Thus, say Gestaltists, human learning cannot be defined by mechanical bonds. Human learning is grounded in the interaction between the world and our perception of it.

Max Wertheimer (1880–1943[12]) is the father of Gestalt psychology. The basis for Wertheimer's work came from his study of the perceived movement in a child's stroboscope. The movement cannot be explained by analyzing each picture, but only as all the pictures are taken together. Wertheimer coined the term "Gestalt" to express this "all parts together" concept.[13] It is useless, wrote Wertheimer, to to focus on the smallest parts of learning or perception.[14] The whole gives meaning to the parts. "The whole is greater than the sum of its individual parts"[15] captures Wertheimer's thrust. In 1910 Wertheimer formed a group of psychologists at the University of Frankfort and established Gestalt psychology. He formally stated its position in 1912 in a paper entitled "Experimental Studies of the Perception of Movement." Wertheimer held that the human mind gives organization to the world. The mind is not simply a connecting system but a transforming system.[16]

Max Wertheimer

Wertheimer worked with Wolfgang Köhler in 1912 and Kurt Lewin in 1916. In 1933 he moved to the United States and established the New School for Social Research at New York University. He worked there until his death in 1943.[17] Throughout his work he criticized repetition and rote memorization as blind and unproductive.[18]

Wertheimer and his followers formulated six laws of perception which explain how we attach meaning to information we receive from the world around us. These are the laws of Prägnanz [pr. prehgnahnts], similarity, proximity, closure, good continuation, and membership character. The *law of Prägnanz* states that people impose order on a disorganized perceptual field in a predictable way.[19] That is, we naturally tend to make sense of what we see. Piaget's concept

of organization refers to this same tendency. The ways people impose order on their environment follow the other five laws. The *law of similarity* states that objects which are similar in terms of form, shape, size, or color tend to be grouped in perception.[20]

How would you group these objects? (shapes, shadings)

The *law of proximity* states that objects tend to be grouped according the the nearness of their parts. How many symbols are there in this line?

| | | | | | | | | | | | | | |

Did you count fifteen lines, or did you multiply three lines by five groups? You probably "saw" five groups of three.[21]

The *law of closure* states that closed areas are more stable than open ones. Incomplete images tend to be perceived as complete. A 350° arc is perceived as a circle. Three dots are perceived as a triangle. Closure is the psychological equivalent of reward in association theory, in that it produces the "satisfying, tension-relieving end-state that terminates activity."[22] Closure may well be the psychological foundation of gossip, which "fills in the gaps" of partial stories with our own imagination!

The *law of good continuation* states that repeated reproduction of images tends to change them from distorted forms to symmetrical and balanced forms.[23] It is easier to understand a quarterly trend line in Sunday School attendance than a graph of individual Sunday attendance.

The *law of membership character* states that a single part of the whole gets its characteristics from the whole.[24] A single jigsaw puzzle piece is meaningless in itself, but taken together with all the others, it forms a complete picture. These laws form the basis of Gestalt psychology.

Köhler (1887–1940) conducted experiments with apes on the island of Tenerife, off the coast of Africa, during World War I.[25] In one experiment, an ape was placed in a cage in which a banana was hung from the top of the cage beyond reach. Two boxes of different sizes were also in the cage. Reaching the banana required moving the larger box into position, placing the smaller box on top, and then climbing to the banana.[26] The apes did not learn these steps by trial and error or by stimulus-response bonding. They "sized up the situation," understood the problem, and "saw" the solution.[27] A second experiment placed a banana outside the cage. Also outside the cage, but within reach, was a stick. The apes "studied" the situation for a moment, picked up the stick and used it to drag the banana to them.[28] Köhler's most famous chimpanzee, Sultan, was able to fasten two sticks together in order to retrieve the banana. The problems of boxes and banana and the sticks and banana were perceived and reorganized, and a solution devised. Each problem was seen as a unified whole.[29]

Wolfgang Köhler

Köhler introduced the term "insight"—solving problems by grasping relations[30]—as an alternative to Thorndike's trial and error approach to problem solving. Learning does not require "stamping in correct responses." Köhler formally presented his findings in the book *Mentality of Apes,* published in 1925.[31] But Köhler may have had more on his mind than learning as he conducted his experiments. There is evidence that he was actually using his lab as a cover for spying activities for Germany during World War I.[32]

"Insight: solving problems by grasping relationships"

Kurt Lewin (1890–1947[33]) earned his doctorate at the University of Berlin and later taught psychology and philosophy there. He came to the United States in 1932 and taught at Stanford, Cornell, Iowa and M.I.T.[34] Lewin developed Field Theory based on the principles of Gestalt psychology. He viewed persons as existing within a

Kurt Lewin

psychological field of forces, a "life space," to which they reacted. This field of forces, much like the magnetic field surrounding a magnet, is composed of persons and objects within our perceptional range, but also includes one's goals, wishes, aspirations, values, and attitudes.[35] Lewin viewed learning as a reorganization of life space, a restructuring of the cognitive structures which produce better understanding and behavior.[36] A remnant of Lewin's work is found in the Garfield cartoon where the self-assured cat says, "I need my space!" Group discussion and small group learning became popular teaching methods as a result of Lewin's work because they were effective ways to intersect the life spaces of students.

JEROME BRUNER AND DISCOVERY LEARNING

More than any other theorist, Jerome Bruner (b. 1915) changed the direction of American psychology, overcoming the hold of Behaviorism with his insights into cognitive theory.[37] Bruner saw little value in studying rats, cats, or pigeons to understand how children learn in a classroom setting. He gathered his data from children in classroom settings.[38] He believed that the goal of teaching is to promote the general understanding of a subject. Effective Brunerian teachers help students[39] form global concepts, build clear generalizations, create cognitive networks of ideas and understand these inter-relationships of ideas.[40] His view is called *discovery learning*, which consists of presenting problems and helping students seek solutions individually or in groups.[41] Bruner believed that the facts and relationships children discover through their own explorations are more usable and tend to be better retained than material they have merely committed to memory.[42] In fact, Bruner opposed Skinner's linear programmed instruction because he believed it promotes too much dependence on the program, and tends to encourage earning a reward more than learning for its own sake.[43] Bruner found that discovery learning develops better problem-solving skills and greater confidence in the ability to learn as they "learn how to learn."[44]

Bruner did not believe that discovery learning was the only kind of learning to be used in a classroom.[45] To rediscover basic facts and truths in all subjects would be time-consuming and wasteful.[46] But helping students see the relationships, principles, and concepts within the material leads to longer-lasting retention of it. Further, discovery learning leads to better self-esteem as creative thinking skills are developed and used.[47] Creative thinking involves total awareness: beliefs, desires, expectations, emotions, and intentions, not just formal logic. For the decades of the sixties and seveties, Jerome Bruner and discovery learning were to cognitive theory what B. F. Skinner and Operant Conditioning is to behaviorial theory. Some writers still make this comparison.[48] But in the 1980s, cognitive theory began to move in a different direction, using the computer as its model. We'll look closely at this new direction, called Information Processing theory, in chapter 9. Bruner opposed this new development because he believed it focused too much on the logical mode of thinking.[49]

Structure. Bruner held that any subject can be organized in such a way that it can be taught to almost any student.[50] This does not mean that details of nuclear physics can be taught to a six-year-old. It does mean that there are meaningful concepts in nuclear physics that could be taught in a way that a six-year-old would develop a general understanding of them. Determining the structure of a subject is to understand its fundamental ideas and how they relate to one another.[51] These fundamental ideas can be reduced to a diagram, or a set of principles, or a formula.[52] Structure is facilitated by three components: presentation, economy, and power.

Presentation. Unlike Piaget, who believed that qualitative differences in thinking were directly tied to biological age, Bruner believed that people possess different modes of understanding at any age. He called these the enactive, the iconic, and the symbolic. Enactive understanding is based on actions, demonstrations, and hands-on experimentation. It is wordless. One learns to ride a bike, play the piano, or conduct brain surgery by an enactive process of hands-on experience. Iconic understanding is based on pictures, images, diagrams, models, and the like. Artists and engineers emphasize iconic understanding. Symbolic understanding is based on language and the use of words to express complex ideas.[53] Mathematicians and philosophers emphasize symbolic understanding. Presenting material in the sequence of enactive (hands-on experimentation), iconic (creating diagrams and illustrations) and symbolic (expressing fundamental concepts in words) helps students develop structural understanding of the subject.[54]

Economy. Teachers confuse students when they provide too much information, or present information too quickly. The fewer the pieces of information students must keep in mind to continue learning, the greater the economy of learning. Teachers should present material in small doses. They should give time for students to process the material between doses. They can provide summaries of

Key Principles in Discovery Learning

LIFE OF JEROME
BRUNER

J erome Bruner was born in New York City in 1915. He received his undergraduate degree from Duke University in 1937 and his Ph.D. in psychology from Harvard in 1941. During World War II he led efforts in psychological warfare out of General Eisenhower's headquarters.[A] He studied propaganda techniques used by Germany.[B] After the war he returned to Harvard as professor of psychology. In 1947 he published a paper on how values and needs affect human perception. This paper laid the groundwork for an American school of cognitive psychology.[C]

Gestalt psychology and cognitive theories had flourished in Europe since 1910, but Behaviorism—guided by Thorndike and Skinner—held sway in America. The study of "thinking" was seen as subjective and unscientific.[D] Bruner changed the direction of American psychology by his prolific research and writing. He conducted studies in perception (1951) and thinking (1956).[E] His major works include *A Study of Thinking* (1956), *The Process of Education* (1962), *Toward a Theory of Instruction* (1966), *Learning about Learning* (1966), *Studies in Cognitive Growth* (1966), *The Relevance of Education* (1973), and *Beyond the Information Given: Studies in the Psychology of Knowing* (1973).[F]

In the late 1950s Bruner served as chairman of a series of conferences consisting of scientists and educators. The purpose of the conferences was to evaluate American education in light of the Soviet Union putting Sputnik I into orbit.[G] The result was his book *Process of Education* (1962), which became a classic.[H] Bruner established the Harvard Center for Cognitive Studies in 1960.[I]

The American Psychological Association presented Bruner with the Distinguished Scientific Award in 1963. His influence in the field of educational psychology came from his ability to speak intelligently about education to his fellow scholars as well as educators.[J] facts and concepts periodically to allow students to organize the material.[55]

Power. A powerful presentation is a simple presentation. Reducing large quantities of facts to formulas, models, or diagrams helps students understand the essential relationships in the material. Einstein revolutionized the world of energy with his simple $e=mc^2$ [56] (The amount of energy released in a nuclear explosion is equal to the mass of the nuclear material multiplied by the speed of light squared).

Bruner believed that external rewards were an artificial means to encourage students to learn. All children, wrote Bruner, have an innate will to learn.[57] Intrinsic, not extrinsic, motivation sustains that will to learn. Intrinsic motivation comes from the students' own curiosity, their drive to achieve competence, and reciprocity—the desire to work cooperatively with others. These are rewarding in themselves, and thus, self-sustaining.[58] The teachers' responsibility is to ensure that these natural motivators are not impaired by irrelevant and dry presentations, frustrating expectations, and unwholesome competition among students.

Motivation

Bruner's initial ideas place great emphasis, following Piaget, on *students* discovering relationships. Remember the quote of Piaget at the end of chapter 4? Here it is in part: "So we need pupils who are active, who learn early to find out by themselves, partly by their own spontaneous activity and partly through material we set up for them; who learn early to tell what is verifiable and what is simply the first idea to come to them."[59]

The Teacher

Discovery learning emphasizes student activity, student initiative, and student solutions. Bruner knew that students would learn fewer facts through this approach, but would gain a deeper understanding of the subject which could well continue beyond the classroom. It is one thing to be able to answer a teacher's questions, but quite another—better—thing for students to learn to ask questions of themselves and then find the answers.

This focus on learner-centered problem solving has become known as *pure discovery learning*. Teachers must be well-versed in the subject so that they can move easily from interconnected concept to concept. They must be models of thinking competence, weighing student questions before answering, reframing statements to make them more focused, pulling relevant examples into the class discussion, asking probing questions to further student understanding, and the like. Teachers must prepare students for discovery activities by insuring that they understand basic vocabulary and operations required for higher-level thinking. Teachers are group facilitators and presenters of problems more than tellers of facts. Teachers serve as guides for the student-centered learning process, and take care not to short-circuit the discovery process by giving students the answers.

Criticism of Discovery Learning

Pure discovery methods came under attack as being too time-consuming. Teachers began to feel they were wasting precious class time waiting for students to discover for themselves concepts and principles they could more quickly learn with teacher-structured explanations. Skinner strongly opposed discovery learning. "It is quite impossible for the student to discover for himself any substantial part of the wisdom of his culture, and no philosophy of education really proposes that he should. Great thinkers build on the past, they do not waste their time rediscovering it. . . . It is equally dangerous to forego teaching important facts and principles in order to give the student a chance to discover them for himself."[60]

There were also interpersonal problems with pure discovery. Students became frustrated with those who dominated much of the discussion time and made most of the discoveries. Often attitudes of jealousy, resentment, and inferiority were generated. In any educational setting, someone has to do the talking. With pure discovery, this someone is a fellow student. Yet most students would rather have a teacher—an expert in the subject—talk about it rather than a fellow learner who is struggling with the subject.

Finally, pure discovery methods are simply inappropriate in some settings. If the subject matter is difficult, or if students come from disadvantaged backgrounds, pure discovery is less effective than traditional approaches. Also, class time is limited and may not allow sufficient time for students to discover all the necessary links among concepts and principles.[61]

David Ausebel (1968) has been one of the most vocal critics of discovery learning.[62] Students often do not know what is important or relevant and many students need external motivation to do the work required to master school subjects. He proposed an alternative model of instruction, called *reception learning*. Teachers engage in *expository teaching* in which they provide teacher-planned, systematic instruction on meaningful information. Teachers structure the learning situation, select the appropriate materials, and then present them in an organized manner—moving from general ideas to specific facts.[63]

Thus the material is pre-processed for learners, giving them a conceptual framework to work with rather than requiring them to build the framework themselves. Such a framework allows students to "subsume" new learning—to relate it to existing concepts.[64]

In response to these criticisms, *directed*[65] *discovery methods* were developed. In directed discovery, teachers control the learning process as they direct students to make discoveries. Teachers emphasize contrast among concepts and principles. They lead students to make educated guesses and then analyze which guess is most correct. They ask conceptual questions to help students integrate the subject into their thinking. Teachers have students consider the consequences of answers they give. Finally, they help students learn by doing by making assignments to be done outside of class.

My studies of Jerome Bruner and discovery learning during seminary changed forever my approach to teaching people the Bible. For several years I taught Sunday school classes the way I had been taught growing up. I presented lessons, taught facts, told stories. Rarely did I deal with concepts, ideas, and principles in Scripture. And I did not know enough to focus on the structure, the inter-connectedness, of Scriptural truth. Bible truths existed as discrete facts, not a network of Truth. As I studied Bruner's approach to learning, and put his principles into practice in teaching deaf adults and teenagers, our Bible study sessions took on new life. If I had to choose one statement from all my seminary studies that did more to change my approach to teaching Scripture, it would be a quote from Jerome Bruner: "We teach a subject not to produce little living libraries on that subject, but rather to get a student to think . . . for himself, to consider matters as an historian does, to take part in the process of knowledge-getting. Knowing is a process, not a product."[66]

In the context of Bible study, we might paraphrase Bruner to say that we teach not to create libraries of Bible facts, but to help students think biblically, to consider real-life problems from God's point of view. The lives of my learners were transformed as they integrated biblical truth into their everyday problems and decisions. The Disciplers' Model presented in chapter one grew out of my experiences in teaching during seminary—and Jerome Bruner's ideas were a large part of that. Specific suggestions for using discovery learning are listed later under Constructivism.

Discovery Learning and Bible Teaching

"I presented lessons—rarely did I deal with concepts"

COGNITIVE THEORY
IN THE 1990S:
CONSTRUCTIVISM

There is a revolution in educational psychology and it is called constructivism. Built on the work of Piaget and Bruner, constructivism emphasizes the importance of active involvement of learners in constructing knowledge for themselves. They cannot simply be given knowledge by their teachers.[67] Constructivism emphasizes top-down processing: begin with complex problems and teach basic skills while solving these problems. Provide students math problems, then teach mathematical operations in the process of solving those problems. Assign students a composition to write. Teach writing skills—grammar, spelling, punctuation—in the process of helping them write their compositions.[68]

Constructivism involves personal discovery, experimentation, and open-ended problems. Learners are actively involved with concepts and principles, experiences, and experiments in order to discover principles for themselves. Such an approach arouses the curiosity of students, develops independent problem-solving skills, and strengthens critical thinking abilities.[69]

A Word of Caution

A recent conversation with a colleague leads me to sound a word of warning about constructivism. Some writers in educational psychology view constructivism as a process of "creating reality." That is, what is real for one student may not be real for another. Two students are watching a television evangelist. One says, "What a man of God! What faith!" The other says, "What a charlatan! Who would send that crook money?!" The "reality" of the evangelist is different for the two students—a product of what they saw and *who they are*. Here's the problem: for some writers this subjective reality is the only reality which exists. Christians believe in objective reality. There are things which are "really real." We may not know that reality, or our understanding of reality may be subjective—colored by our own personal experiences. But objective reality exists. The television evangelist is either a crook or an upright godly man. Paul writes, "Now we see but a poor reflection as in a mirror, then we shall see face to face. Now I know in part; then I shall know fully, even as I am fully known" (1 Cor. 13:12).

I have no problem with the interactive nature of learning proposed by constructivism. Every class period I see evidence of perceptual filters coloring what students hear and read. But the existential "reality is whatever I make it" carries the theme too far.

There is objective truth in mathematics which must be correctly understood. Students do not create their own math reality, though their understanding of math is colored by prior experiences. There is truth in science that should be understood as it is, not created by each learner. And there is the truth of Scripture, which should be understood for what it says and not changed according to our own perceptions or wishes. While there are differences of opinion on interpretation of Scripture, serious Bible scholars believe that the text possesses objective meaning. The text meant something specific to the writer and to his audience, and especially to the Lord Who inspired its writing. Given that caution, we move on to implications.

Drawing from Bruner's work and the more recent emphasis of constructivism, we can make the following suggestions for teaching in a Christian context:

Use explanations, demonstrations, and pictures to help students understand concepts.[70] Much of the teaching in Bible classes is verbal. We talk about biblical concepts more than we clarify their meaning. One seminary student of mine was teaching on the fruit of the Spirit. His presentation went something like this: "What is joy? Joy is God's kind of joy. It is the kind of joy we'll experience in heaven. This joy is wonderful!" He talked about joy, but never defined it. I wrote on his lesson plan "So—what is joy?" How does biblical joy differ from pleasure? From fun? From happiness? All of these are states of positive emotion, but the last three depend on surrounding circumstances. Bad experiences do not produce pleasure or fun or happiness. But joy is a spiritual characteristic that wells up from within despite surrounding circumstances. Do not merely talk about concepts. *Explain* them. Likewise, use demonstrations and diagrams to give visual support to verbal explanations.

Learning should be flexible and exploratory, allowing students to solve problems on their own.[71] Rather than telling learners what a passage says, help them discover it for themselves. List three questions on "3x5" cards and distribute them to groups of students. Give them time to study a passage of Scripture and, with the help of Bible study reference books, answer the questions. Plan time for groups to share their answers. Discuss differences in answers from the groups. Christian teachers sometimes think the term "flexible and exploratory methods" means letting everyone believe whatever they want. Such is not the case. The fundamental goal of any effective teacher of any discipline is to establish a clear understanding of that discipline. No self-

"Students do not create their own math reality"

Constructivism and Bible Teaching

respecting teacher thinks that students should "believe whatever they want" about history, geography, biology, or calculus. When educators call for "flexible and exploratory methods," they are opposing inflexible, sit-still-while-I-instill information transmission. Telling Bible students five key truths from Colossians 3 is far less effective than asking questions and having the students construct those five truths from the Scripture themselves.

Arouse curiosity, minimize risk of failure, and maximize relevance of the subject to students.[72] Such actions enhance the natural motivation that flows out of learning. At the beginning of a Bible study session, ask a question or two which directly relates both to key concepts to be studied and to needs of the students. Write student responses on the blackboard, and then say something like, "This is what we're going to study today. [Bible writer] has something specific to say to help us answer these questions. Let's see what it is. Open your Bibles to [passage]." The questions focus minds on the key concepts under consideration. Answers have been given. Curiosity over what the Scripture says has been established. If the questions are correctly written, then the study will produce relevant learning for the students. Minimize risk in the classroom so that students will feel free to suggest answers, ask questions, and generally participate in the learning process.

Periodically return to important concepts.[73] Keep a log of key biblical concepts studied week by week. Use terms from past studies to emphasize their meaning and to reinforce the knowledge structure of your students.

Encourage informed guessing.[74] Constructivists encourage students to make educated guesses in answering questions. Then they lead students to analyze those answers and determine whether they are correct or not.

Use a variety of materials and games.[75] Since motivation is based on the intrinsic value of curiosity, teachers need to provide a variety of learning experiences. Nothing kills curiosity like ritualistic teaching which follows the same pattern session by session.

Let students satisfy their own curiosity, even if the ideas are not directly related to the lesson.[76] This increases student motivation and interest. It also helps students know that their teachers care about their own interests and questions. A teacher asks a question and instructs the class to answer it from several passages of Scripture. After a moment, a student says, "The answer to your question

is [such and so], but I saw something here that really spoke to me."
The effective teacher will respond, "And what is that?" The ineffective teacher will say, "That's fine, but we really need to stay on the
lesson. Who'll read verse five?" The latter teacher undermines student motivation to learn because he does not realize that the learner
is more important than the lesson.

*Use examples that compare and contrast the subject matter to re-
lated topics.*[77] When studying the free will of man, balance it with
some discussion of the soveriegnty of God. When studying "God is
love," discuss the fact that God is also holy. When studying grace,
balance it with some discussion of justice. When encouraging students to be strong in their convictions, remind them that they are also
to love others. Without balancing related truths, biblical concepts
are learned as unidimensional and rigid. We are not to speak lovingly without truth or speak truthfully without love—we are to speak
"the truth in love" (Eph. 4:15).

Key Emphases from Cognitive Theory

The following twelve statements summarize key distinctives of cognitive learning. Use these terms to compare and contrast learning as defined in chapters 7 and 10.	
1. The learner is a . . .	MIND
2. The focus is on . . .	PERCEPTION
3. Relationship of learning "whole" to its parts . . .	WHOLE *GREATER THAN* SUM OF PARTS
4. Learning is . . .	RATIONAL AND INTERACTIVE
5. The target learning domain is . . .	HIGHER COGNITIVE
6. The goal of learning is . . .	CHANGE IN UNDERSTANDING
7. Learning is strengthened by . . .	INSIGHT INTO RELATIONSHIPS
8. Learning is guided by . . .	APPLICATION TO LIFE
9. Motivation keys on . . .	ACHIEVING DELAYED GOAL
10. Feedback should be . . .	DELAYED, ON PERFORMANCE
11. Best curriculum is . . .	PROBLEM-SOLVING
12. The Theory in Contemporary Practice is . . .	CONSTRUCTIVISM and DIRECTED DISCOVERY

IN SUMMARY   In this chapter we introduced you to cognitive learning theory. We
                              traced its development through the work of Ernst Mach, Max Werthi-
                              emer, Wolfgang Köhler, and Kurt Lewin. We focused on Jerome
                              Bruner and his discovery learning as the pinnacle of cognitive learn-
                              ing. We introduced the newest form of discovery learning called con-
                              structivism. Finally we suggested specific techniques for using these
                              ideas in Bible teaching. In the next chapter, we focus on the current
                              giant among cognitive theories, Information Processing Theory.

CHAPTER CONCEPTS

Cognitive learning theory	Law of Prägnanz
Constructivism	Law of Proximity
Directed discovery	Law of Similarity
Discovery learning	Life Space
Economy	Perception
Enactive Mode	Power
Gestalt psychology	Presentation Modes
Iconic Mode	Pure discovery
Insight	Reception learning
Law of Closure	Structure
Law of Good Continuation	Symbolic Mode
Law of Membership Character	

DISCUSSION QUESTIONS

1. Discuss how Gestalt psychology differs from stimulus-response psychology. Include differences
   relating to the mind, the outcome, and the focus.
2. Compare and contrast the ideas of the following paired theorists: Watson and Mach, Pavlov and
   Werthiemer, Thorndike and Köhler, and Skinner and Bruner.
3. Choose three of the laws of perception. Define each law and give an example of it from your own
   experience.
4. How does Lewin's concept of life space apply to the teaching ministry of the church. That is, how
   does "church" promote growing in spiritual understanding.
5. Choose a favorite Bible passage, at least a chapter in length. Explain how Bruner's approach to
   teaching would differ from a verse-by-verse study of the passage. (Focus on structure.)
6. Differentiate between pure discovery, directed discovery, and reception learning methods.
7. Survey the suggestions for teaching. Have your teachers used any of these approaches? What was
   your reaction to them. (Select a minimum of three.)

FOR FURTHER READING

Biehler, Robert F., and Jack Snowman. "Bruner: The Importance of Structure and Discovery." In *Psychology Applied to Teaching*. 7th ed., 425–28. Boston: Houghton Mifflin Company, 1993.

Bruner, Jerome S. *Toward a Theory of Instruction*. New York: Norton Publishers, 1966.

Clouse, Bonnidell. "Guidelines from Cognitive Psychology." In *Teaching for Moral Growth: A Guide for the Christian Community—Teachers, Parents and Pastors*, 257–76. Wheaton, Ill: Bridgeport Books, 1993.

Dembo, Myron H. "Discovery Learning." In *Applying Educational Psychology*. 5th ed., 270–74. New York: Longman, 1994.

Eggen, Paul, and Don Kauchak. "The Importance of Discovery Learning: The Work of Jerome Bruner." In *Educational Psychology: Classroom Connections*. 2nd ed., 409–16. New York: Macmillan College Publishing Company, 1994.

Gage, N. L., and David C. Berliner. "Bruner's Theory of Cognitive Growth," In *Educational Psychology*. 3rd ed., 145–47. Boston: Houghton Mifflin Company, 1984.

Good, Thomas L. and Jere E. Brophey. "The Cognitive Structural View of Learning." In *Educational Psychology: A Realistic Approach*. 4th ed., 186–205. New York: Longman, 1990.

Hamachek, Don. "Encouraging Learning by Discovery." In *Psychology in Teaching, Learning, and Growth*. 4th ed., 222–30. Boston: Allyn and Bacon, 1990.

LeFrancois, Guy R. "Bruner's Theory: An Overview." In *Psychology for Teaching*, 157–60. Belmont, Calif.: Wadsworth Publishing Company, 1994.

Slavin, Robert E. "Discovery Learning." In *Educational Psychology: Theory and Practice*. 4th ed., 228–30. Boston: Allyn and Bacon, 1994.

Sprinthall, Norman A., Richard C. Sprinthall, and Sharon N. Oja. "Jerome Bruner and the Process of Thought." In *Educational Psychology: A Developmental Approach*. 6th ed., 243–49. New York: McGraw-Hill, Inc., 1994.

Woolfolk, Anita. "Discovery Learning." In *Educational Psychology*. 5th ed., 318–22. Boston: Allyn and Bacon, Inc., 1993.

Chapter

9

TEACHING FOR UNDERSTANDING (PART 2)

INFORMATION PROCESSING THEORY

This chapter continues our focus on teaching for understanding begun in chapter 8. Here we highlight *Information Processing Theory*, today's giant among learning theories. Information Processing uses the computer as its model for how humans learn. How does the mind make sense of the world? How do we learn what we learn? Why do we forget? How can we improve our ability to remember? How do we create the cognitive structure Piaget wrote about? How can we improve the learning process for ourselves and for our students? More space is given to Information Processing Theory in recent educational psychology texts than any other theory.

CHAPTER RATIONALE

Learners will demonstrate knowledge of the information processing by
- identifying four reasons why we forget;
- identifying four ways to improve memory recall;
- defining attention, perception, recognition, rehearsal, and retrieval.
- comparing the IPT model with a computer system;
- explaining how information moves from SR to STM to LTM and back to STM;
- describing the role of metacognition in learning;
- developing three different mnemonic devices based on material in the chapter.

CHAPTER OBJECTIVES

Learners will demonstrate appreciation for information processing by sharing personal experiences related to meaningful learning.

HISTORICAL ROOTS

E. C. Tolman is the "ancestral hero"[1] of Information Processing Theory. His experiments with rats and mazes led him to the conclusion that the animals were creating an internal representation of the maze—a cognitive map of the environment. Though he was a behaviorist, he broke ranks with behaviorism in discounting trial-and-error learning of S-R bonds in favor of cognitive maps.[2] Tolman's ideas were not widely accepted because he was unable to translate his findings into a form that teachers could use in teaching.

"Cognitive learning theory, Tolman's cognitive map theory, and the computer combined to provide a new way of looking at learning"

Disenchantment grew with the learning theories of the 1940s and 1950s. Training programs for pilots in World War II demonstrated that pilots were complex information receivers and processors. Communication research in radio and television provided better models for human thought. But the advent of the computer provided a powerful model for human symbol-manipulating.[3] Cognitive learning theory, Tolman's cognitive map theory, and the computer combined to provide a new way of looking at learning. Today, educational psychology texts give extensive space to Information Procession Theory, while most have relegated Jerome Bruner and discovery learning to a small section or footnote.

Information Processing Theory (IPT) does not reject conditioning theory. There is ample evidence that Edward Thorndike and B. F. Skinner discovered powerful ways to enhance association of ideas. But IPT is interested in *how* a pigeon learns to discriminate, *how* a rat learns to run a maze, and *how* a child learns to recognize words on a page.[4] IPT did not return to Wundt's introspection because it was proven to be subjective, unreliable, and inconsistent. But IPT does focus on mental events in terms of behavioral effects which can be reliably measured.[5] IPT is a cognitive theory because it defines learning as the result of interaction between learners and their environment.[6] Theorists have found that we operate in two different modes as we process information. The first is called automatic[7] or incidental[8] processing. This unconscious process records every experience and event in our lives without intention or attention. The second is intentional[9] processing, which is the result of attention and study. While we will briefly mention automatic processing, we will focus our attention on intentional processes.

Four components make up a basic computer system. The first is an *input device*. This is usually a keyboard, but can also include a mouse, light pen, or digitizing tablet. Input devices permit information to be entered into the computer's working memory. The second component is the working memory of the computer. Random-Access Memory (RAM) holds information entered into it. The computer's processor can manipulate this information, whether it be words or numbers. The working memory is volatile—if the computer is turned off, all the information in RAM is lost. The third component of the computer is long-term storage. This is usually a hard disk, but it can also be a floppy diskette, or tape. When information is written from RAM to the hard disk, it is stored in a more permanent fashion. If the computer is turned off and later turned back on, information can be read back into RAM from the hard disk. The fourth component is a monitor, a televisionlike display often called a screen, which displays the information being held in the working memory. In summary, we have *input* to the working memory from the keyboard, *output* to the screen, *storage* to hard disk, and *retrieval* from the hard disk. Information Processing Theory mirrors these elements in describing human learning.

THE COMPUTER AS A MODEL OF LEARNING

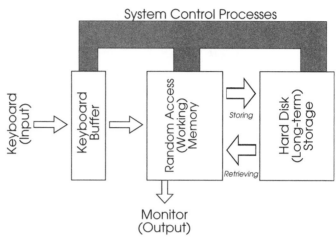

Computer Processing Model

A model is a representation that helps us describe and visualize what is impossible to observe directly.[10] The IPT model shown below is a model reflecting the interaction of cognitive structures and cognitive processes which control learning. The cognitive structures, or information stores, are data storage units. Cognitive processes are internal, intellectual actions that transfer information from one unit to another. These processes include attention, recognition, rehearsal, encoding, and retrieval. Metacognitive processes are the "executive control processes" which govern the operation of the other cognitive processes.[11] Our first step in understanding IPT

THE INFORMATION PROCESSING THEORY MODEL

is to define each structure and process. We will then demonstrate how this model can help us improve the understanding and retention of our students.

Sensory Registers

The environment bombards our senses with hundreds of stimuli—sounds, smells, sights. In a classroom, we're surrounded by the stimuli of lectures, overhead cells, films, and group discussions. These elements constitute the information we must process in order to learn. Even though stimuli are present, we are not aware of all of them. Music can play in the background but not actually be heard.[12] The first stage in the process takes place in the various sensory registers—the sense organs or receptors—of the stimuli. Sensory memory holds data for a brief period of time, from one-half to four seconds. Iconic memory holds visual images very briefly. Echoic memory holds sounds for a longer time, allowing us to piece together sounds for speech or music. If the data is not attended to within this time, the sensory data is lost.[13] Receiving too much information at once, without help as to what is most important, makes learning any of the information difficult.[14] A deaf college student attending my Sunday School class once told me that I taught so much and so fast that "it goes in one eye and out the other!"

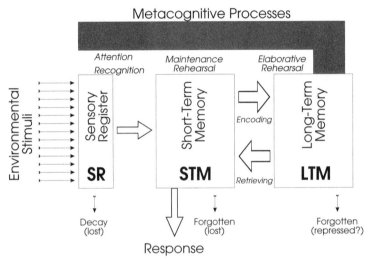

Information Processing Model

The sensory register might be thought of as a buffer or way station between the environment and internal memory.[15] As soon as stimuli are received by the sensory receptors, the mind begins working on them. This is where perception enters the picture. Perception, the meaning we give to what we receive, is part objective reality and part our own cognitive structure.[16] "The eyes look but the brain sees . . . we see what the brain decides is in front of our eyes."[17]

Still, much of what goes into this first stage is lost permanently. We remember various stimuli because we pay attention to them long enough to move them into short-term memory.[18]

If stimuli are attended to, they are moved to short-term memory. This data storage unit, sometimes called "working memory"[19] or "active memory,"[20] retains information as we consciously work on it. It contains all that is in our immediate awareness.[21] Its counterpart in a computer is RAM memory, which temporarily stores the programs and data in use. Short-term memory screens stimuli coming in from the sensory registers and decides what to do with them. The basic choices are to ignore them, retain them by repeating them, or process them for permanent storage in long-term memory.[22] STM could be thought of as our conscious mind. It is here our thinking is done, where details are held until a problem is solved.[23]

Short-Term Memory (STM)

Storage in STM is limited to five to nine items for up to a minute for adults.[24] Three-year-olds can hold about three items, seven-year-olds about five items, and teenagers from five to nine items.[25] If you look up a telephone number for a local repair shop, you can say it to yourself a few times, turn to the phone and dial the seven digit number correctly. If the line is busy and you wait a minute or so to redial, you will probably have to look at the number again. STM has discarded the number.

The limited storage of STM can be increased by combining separate items into larger, more meaningful units. The number 3478913 is harder to remember than 347-8913. The social security number 538427639 is harder to remember than 538-42-7639. The letters "u n r" require three units of storage. Putting them together as "unr" makes them easier to remember, but still requires three storage units. But putting them together as "run" makes them much easier to remember because the word has meaning for us, and takes up only one storage unit. This process of combining individual items into related groups is called "chunking."[26]

Because of limited storage, the STM can be a bottleneck for processing information. It is easy to overload students with so many details and facts that they have difficulty thinking and solving problems.[27] We will discuss ways to avoid overloading students a little later. In short, STM is the conscious part of the information processing system in which we deal with a limited number of bits of information. Without rehearsal and use, this information is lost in a

Long-Term Memory
(LTM)

matter of seconds. If, during these seconds, we are able to make sense of the information, we can encode it for long-term storage.[28]

Long-term memory is our permanent information storage device.[29] Its counterpart in a computer is the hard drive, which holds programs and data for retrieval even when the computer is turned off. LTM is capable of holding encoded information for a lifetime.[30] It is virtually unlimited in capacity[31] and contains a permanent record of everything[32] an individual has experienced (automatic processing) or learned (intentional processing). The interests, skills, attitudes, and knowledge stored in LTM influence what we perceive, how we interpret our perceptions, and whether we choose to process information at all.[33] Though encoded information remains in LTM forever,[34] it does not follow that we can retrieve or decode it all.

LTM provides three basic types of memory. *Episodic* (episode, event) *memory* records life events just as they happen. These autobiographical images of life[35] are similar to a videotape which records our personal experiences,[36] such as our first day of school, sixteenth birthday party, or first best friend. *Semantic* (semantics, meaning[37]) *memory* records facts, concepts, principles, generalizations, and rules, problem-solving strategies, thinking skills, and the like.[38] This memory is not connected to any particular event. It is organized in networks of connected ideas or relationships.[39] Some writers use the term "declarative" knowledge to refer to what is stored in semantic memory.[40] *Procedural* (procedure, sequence) *memory* refers to knowing *how* rather than knowing *that*: riding a bike, playing the piano, or typing. This memory is stored in a series of stimulus-response pairings.[41] *Procedural* knowledge is stored in procedural memory.[42] The learner who says, "I know it, but I just can't do it" reflects declarative knowledge without procedural knowledge. *Background* knowledge—Piaget's "cognitive stucture"—includes all prior learnings and experiences. The richer and more varied one's background knowledge, the easier it is to relate new information to it.[43] The more one learns, the easier it is to learn.[44]

The smallest element which resides in LTM is called a scheme—a concept very similar to Piaget's term. A scheme is an *abstract structure* of information. It is *abstract*, because it summarizes information about many different cases or examples. It is a *structure*, because it represents the interrelatedness of information components. When a well-formed scheme and an event match, comprehension occurs.[45] There is no disequilibrium. But if the scheme is faulty, or lacking, then new information creates confusion, or disequilibrium.

We have defined each major component in the information processing model. Now let's look at how environmental stimuli make their way through these components to be stored in long-term memory. We will focus on SR to STM (attention), STM to LTM (learning), and LTM to STM (remembering) operations. We must discuss these processes sequentially, but remember that they can happen simultaneously.[46] When you see (SR) a cocker spaniel, an image is transmitted to STM. Images of dogs are retrieved from LTM until a match is found. But along with the identification information for cocker spaniel also come memories of past cocker spaniels and the feelings that were associated with those events. Still, we cannot study the processes simultaneously. So let's begin with moving information from sensory registers to short-term memory.

INFORMATION PROCESSING OPERATIONS

Information in sensory registers might be described as a series of snapshots which are retained from one-half to four seconds. These registers hold an exact copy of the stimuli, just as they are perceived.[47] Hold your index finger in front of your face and wiggle it back and forth rapidly. As your finger moves left and right, you will notice a blur in between. This is a residual trace of the finger on the sensory register.[48] Visual images fade much more quickly than sounds. The longer fade times of sounds permit us to piece together and

Moving from Sensory Register to Short-Term Memory

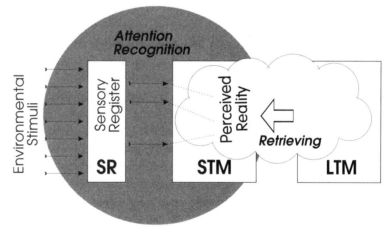

make sense of music or language. If the snapshots are not recognized or attended to within that time, they fade and are lost. If they are attended to, then they are processed and passed on to short-term memory.[49] Paying attention to specific stimuli results in selective focusing. We process what we pay attention to and lose what we ignore.[50] *Recognition* refers to matching an incoming stimulus with stored information in LTM.[51] We will process what we recognize much better than what we don't. Consider this scene: You are standing in the airport waiting for a friend to arrive. Passengers are moving through a doorway as they enter the terminal. You scan each person just enough to determine whether he or she is your friend. That is, you pay attention to each person individually until you determine that person is a "no match." Finally, one of the passengers "fits" whom you're looking for—a match is made and you've found your friend. Attention and recognition are two key elements in moving information from SR to STM.

As soon as stimuli are received by the senses, the mind begins working on some of them. This means that the sensory images that we consciously process are not exactly the same as what we saw, or heard, or felt. Sensory images are what our senses perceived.[52] STM contains perceived reality, not objective reality.[53] Further, what we choose to attend to and what we recognize is a function of prior learnings, the network located in LTM.[54] Our mind acts as a filter which tends to change what we receive in order to fit what we already know. Piaget called this assimilation. As we process new information, build new networks of ideas, pattern our schemes in different ways, we learn. Piaget called this accommodation.

Implications for Teaching

What implications can we draw from attention and recognition? First, lesson beginnings are very important. Teachers have a natural motivation in sharing new ideas and explaining concepts. But *students may not be interested* or motivated toward learning the day's subject. We must focus on lesson beginnings that gain the attention of our students. Demonstrations, displays, overhead cells, pictures, maps, graphs, questions, and stories are examples of elements that help gain the attention of learners.[55] Second, *bad experiences* in the past can dull students' attention. We will facilitate better learning if we can convince students that what they are studying will be useful, enjoyable, informative, and meaningful.[56] Third, if teachers begin class the same way every day, students will become used to it and attention will suffer. Variety is important in the classroom.[57]

We have seen that the STM is a processing bottleneck. It is easy to overload the STM with details and facts so that the ability to think and solve problems is limited.[58] There are two major ways to solve this problem. First, help students *overlearn basic information and operations* so that they can be used with little mental effort. This is called *automaticity*. In math, help students overlearn required math operations so they can be done without much thought. Overlearning word meanings and grammar helps in language courses. Overlearning grammar rules and punctuation helps in writing courses. Second, *change your presentation style* to help students process information more efficiently. Present information more slowly. Provide regular summaries of key ideas and principles. Use visual aids. Engage students with questions and problems. If students are unable to answer your questions, or if they are unable to frame a question, they are suffering from STM overload.[59]

You will remember that STM can hold up from five to nine pieces of information for as long as a minute.[60] If we do not do something to extend the life of this information in STM, there will be nothing for us to encode for long-term storage. We have already discussed the role of chunking in accomplishing this. Another method for extending STM information storage is called *maintenance rehearsal*,[61] or rote rehearsal, or repetition.[62] By repeating the information over and over, without altering its form,[63] either out loud or mentally,[64] students can hold it longer. The longer learners can hold information in STM, the more likely it is that they will encode it for long-term storage.[65] *However, such repetition has no direct effect on LTM* (see endnote for an important exception).[66] It simply increases the time students hold information in STM. For example, when entering numbers into a calculator, students might enter numbers one at a time—look at the number, enter it, look at the next—or, they might look at five numbers, repeat them aloud once or twice, and then enter all five into the calculator.[67]

Moving Information from Short-Term Memory to Long-Term Memory

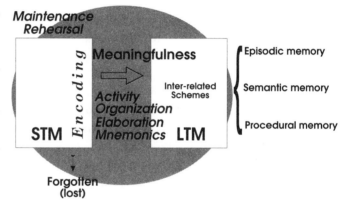

Transferring information from STM to LTM[68] requires that the information in STM be encoded. We encode information by forming mental representations of the information, called schemes, based on its essential features.[69] Forming schemes requires relating the new information to concepts already stored in LTM.[70] In order for information to be encoded, it must possess the quality of *meaningfulness*, which describes the number of connections between one idea and another in LTM.[71] There are four basic approaches to insuring information is meaningful to students: activity, organization, elaboration, and mnemonics.[72]

Activity. Piaget demonstrated that learners are not passive recipients of information. Rather, they are active participants in the learning process. Teachers will facilitate meaningfulness in what their students learn by putting them into an active role, working with them until the teachers' explanations make sense to them.[73] So how do we put students into an active role? Have them write out questions about the material. Have them paraphrase explanations from their notes or textbooks. Let students analyze examples, solve problems, write essays, engage in hands-on experimentation, take application-oriented (rather than simple recall) tests.

Organization. Organization refers to clustering information into categories or patterns which reflect the built-in connections. These connections help create meaningfulness.[74] Students learn better when they create their own organization of material (Bruner's pure discovery), but teachers who present information in preorganized forms will accelerate the move toward meaningfulness (as in directed discovery and reception learning). Examples of ways learners can organize information include charts, matrices,[75] hierarchies, tables, flowcharts, and chronologies. Older students organize better than younger students. Skilled students organize better than unskilled students. Familiar material is easier to organize than new or unfamiliar material.[76]

Elaboration. Elaboration, or elaborative rehearsal,[77] is relating new information to concepts already in LTM.[78] It is the process of increasing the number of associations among concepts either by forming additional links or by adding new information.[79] Learners *elaborate new information* with previous learnings.[80] The goal in the process of elaboration is to create logically interconnected information, so that any part can be used to retrieve the other parts.

Mnemonics. Mnemonics (pr. neh-MON-ix) are strategies to aid the process of encoding by forming associations that don't normally exist in the content.[81] Mnemonics provide an artifical basis for organization and meaningfulness.[82] Whenever possible, we should help students see the structure, the interrelatedness, that naturally exists in our material. But when the material to be learned is difficult to structure naturally, mnemonic devices provide ways to establish meaningful associations. Mnemonic devices include the loci (low-sigh) method, rhymes, acronyms, acrostics, pegwords, and key-words.

The *loci method* of association, sometimes called the place meth-od,[83] is the oldest known mnemonic, dating from classical Greek times.[84] It is also the most popular.[85] Consider rooms in a building, or buildings on campus, or stores along a street. Order these loca-tions sequentially in your mind, so that you can "walk through" them. Then place items that you want to remember in these places. You can include furniture and boxes as well as other objects that help you locate the items to be remembered. Cluster similar items in the same room or building. In order to recall the items, walk through the rooms and retrieve each one from its place.

Simple *rhymes* can make recalling arbitrary rules simpler. Two of the most well-known are "i before e except after c" and "30 days hath September, April, June, and November."[86]

An *acronym* is a first-letter mnemonic[87] that forms words from the first letter of each item. HOMES is an acronym for the Great Lakes: **H**uron, **O**ntario, **M**ichigan, **E**rie, and **S**uperior. ROYGBIV (pr. roy-gee-biv) are the colors of the spectrum: **R**ed, **O**range, **Y**el-low, **G**reen, **B**lue, Indigo, and **V**iolet. Acronyms are effective for re-calling short lists.[88] Some acronyms have become words in their own right, such as SCUBA (**s**elf-**c**ontained **u**nderwater **b**reathing **a**ppara-tus), LASER (**l**ight **a**mplification by **s**timulated **e**mission of **r**adia-tion), and RADAR (**r**adio **d**etecting **a**nd **r**anging).[89]

An *acrostic* is a sentence mnemonic[90] that forms sentences from the items to be learned. An acrostic for ROYGBIV might be "**R**ich-ard **O**f **Y**ork **G**ave **B**attle **I**n **V**ain." In helping to recall the naval equivalents of left and right, one might use these sentences: "The ship *left port*" and "The *star boarder* is always *right*."[91] My mother won a promotion and citation of merit for developing acrostic stories to help postal employees learn how to categorize postal zones by street names. (See the accompanying example of one of her stories.) While you may wonder how anyone could memorize such a strange story, compare that to memorizing seventy-seven street names in al-phabetical order, and keeping that list separate from twenty other lists! The New York Post Office system adopted this system for all their sorting trainees. Failure rates decreased significantly.

A list of previously memorized *pegwords*, usually based on rhymes (1=bun, 2=shoe, 3=tree, etc.), is used to compose interacting images with items to be remembered.[92] Let's say you need to go to the store for fish, roses, and a carton of Cokes. Picture a bass—head, scales and all—wrapped in a hamburger bun, roses growing out of a shoe, and the carton of Cokes wedged up in a tree. By recalling the pegwords bun, shoe, and tree, you will remember the grocery list.

The *keyword* is the newest mnemonic device developed to aid in foreign language study.[93] The first step is to isolate part of a foreign word that, when spoken, sounds like a real English word. This is the keyword.[94] The Spanish word for postal letter is "carta." Isolate part of the word that sounds like an English word: "cart." "Cart" is the keyword.[95] Second, form an interacting visual image between the keyword and the English translation.[96] Picture a shopping cart holding a giant postal letter. This forms an acoustic link between the keyword and the English translation. Research has shown this method to be effective for learners from preschool to college.[97]

Cautions in Using Mnemonics. Do not use mnemonic devices as a substitute for clarifying the actual interconnectedness of Scripture. While mnemonics can help memorize disjointed pieces of information, the Bible is filled with interrelated pieces that make up the whole. Focus first on meaningful relationships across writers and Testaments. Resort to mnemonic devices only when the material cannot be naturally structured, and when remembering the material is important for future studies.

Second, take care in choosing the images you use with mnemonic devices. While zany images are easier to remember, they will do more damage than good if they make fun of or mock the very truths we're attempting to teach. A seminary student of mine was teaching our class six characteristics of Jesus as He made His way to Jerusalem to die on the cross. He formed a mnemonic of the six principles with the letters M-O-N-K-E-Y, and had the class picture Jesus walking toward Jerusalem with a monkey on His back. I don't remember any of the principles that student taught that day, but I've never been able to get the image out of my mind. Often youth ministers use "funny little songs" in an attempt to teach deep spiritual truths. Be careful. Choose wisely. Or you may be teaching your youth that "deep spiritual truths" are little more than funny little songs.

Retrieval from Long-Term Memory to Short-Term Memory

It is the nature of LTM that information encoded there, whether intentionally or incidentally, remains there for life. If this is true, then why do we forget? The problem is not in losing encoded information, but in being unable to retrieve it for use in STM. The ability to retrieve information depends on how well the information was

When the New York Area Post Office hired me as a letter sorting clerk, I learned that I was expected to memorize four different sorting schemes. The most difficult of the four involved sorting the 700 named thoroughfares, such as 2525 Juno Street or 11825 Deepdene Road, into the nineteen Post Office Stations. This was extremely difficult. Many new employees were being fired after failing their third testing. This is where mnemonics saved my job.

I will use the Forest Hills area as an example of the nineteen stories we wrote. There were seventy-three named thoroughfares in the Forest Hills. Many of them were names of Pilgrims and Indians. So we used the names in silly sentences that brought to mind something about Pilgrims and Indians. This made the connection between the Forest Hills Post Office and its named thoroughfares.

In making the mnemonic sentences, I used these basic rules:

1. Street names should be used "as is" if possible, corrupted if necessary, but in any case they should be directed to the one common thought or theme.

2. The street names should tell a story.

3. Use a maximum number of street names and a minimum number of connecting words.

4. The phrases should be catchy and rhythmic—the more absurd the greater their value.

In the following story, names of thoroughfares are capitalized. The word in brackets explains the meaning of the street name as used in the sentence, but we focused on memorizing only the street names.

AN EXAMPLE OF MNEMONICS IN ACTION

BY AUDREY YOUNT

JUNO DEEPDENE DANE, WHITSON BOW and HARROW, UPSHAW ATOM and
Do you know DEEPDENE DANE, with his BOW and arrow, pulled up, shot a 'm and

ASCAN MANSE SLOCUM SEMINOLA's? 'McINTOSH'!!! STANDISH WENDOVER in
ash canned many slow Seminoles? "My gosh!!" STANDISH went over in

the APEX of the ARCHWAY with SYBILLA and EXETER , 'Did you SEASONGOOD the
the APEX of the ARCHWAY with Sybilla and asked her, "Did you SEASONGOOD the

WALNUT pudding in DEKOVEN?' 'LOUBET I did' she replied. INGRAM HOLDER IVY
WALNUT pudding in the oven?" "You bet I did" she replied. Ingram holds IVY

CLOSE! THERESA BALDWIN WANDA was WAILING because of an OCCIDENT.
CLOSE! THERESA bawled when WANDA was WAILING because of an accident.

'NOME', said SELFRIDGE NORDEN NANSEN, ROMAN BYE. OLCOTT OLIVE
"No ma'am," said selfish NORDEN NANSEN, roamin'by. Al caught OLIVE

OVERHILL so they'LL PARK END KESSEL in KEW FOREST LANE. MARKWOOD
over the hill so they'LL park and kiss in KEW FOREST LANE. MARKWOOD

MARTELL played TENNIS with ROCKROSE RUSSELL on the FAIRWAY CLOSE to the
MARTELL played TENNIS with ROCKROSE RUSSELL on the FAIRWAY CLOSE to the

STRATFORD hotel in the MIDDLEMAY. In the SUMMER at HARVEST, the COLONIAL
STRATFORD hotel in the middle of May. In the SUMMER at HARVEST, the COLONIAL

PURITANS LIVINGSTON at PORTSMOUTH ate CONTINENTAL BORAGE, but in the
PURITANS living at PORTSMOUTH ate CONTINENTAL porridge, but in the

WINTER when the UNDERWOOD GREEN went a WAY, times became PILGRIM.
WINTER when the UNDERWOOD GREEN went a WAY, times became pretty grim.

HERRICK up' cried VIOLA SHELBOURNE, 'EUCLID CRANFORD'! GUILFORD
"Hurry up!" cried VIOLA SHELBOURNE, "You crank the Ford!" The old ford

GROTONupttheSHORTHILLonBEECHKNOLLROADtoaPLACEnearSTATIONSQUARE.
*groaned up the SHORTHILL on BEECHKNOLL ROAD to a PLACE near STATION
SQUARE.*

The stories proved so helpful with other employees, that my scheme teacher submitted a set to the Postal Service. I received a Superior Accomplishment Award certificate, and $250, and was promoted to the position of Scheme Instructor. The mnemonic stories made the class time fun rather than a boring lecture time. Trainees challenged each other and the number of new employees passing the test improved dramatically. Instead of approximately 30% passing, nearly all of the new employees now passed. Turnover rates decreased and training time was saved. Also, trainees retained the sorting schemes much better. Even many of the older employees heard about the mnemomic stories and requested copies to improve their retention.

The mnemonic stories not only saved my job as a letter sorter, but opened the door to promotion and influence as a trainer of others.

Audrey Yount is the author's mother and lives with her husband and mnemonic writer Bill Yount in Fort Worth, Texas.

encoded. There are four basic reasons why we have difficulty retrieving encoded information, or why we forget. These are disuse, distortion, repression, and interference.

Disuse. The old adage is "Use it or lose it." If encoded information is never used, never retrieved, then retrieval becomes increasingly difficult. We spent hours in high school learning to diagram sentences, solve quadratic formulas, and master the laws of physics. How much of that can we still use? To overcome the problem of disuse, we must use the information we've learned. In the classroom setting, review prior learnings as you study new material. Have you noticed my periodic mention of Piaget's ideas in this chapter? If I had not tied cognitive theories to Piaget's work, would you have remembered what assimilation, or accommodation, or disequilibrium means? Have you found these elaborative Piagetian links helpful in learning cognitive theory? Use the concepts and principles learned yesterday in learning new concepts today.

Distortion. If information is encoded incompletely—as a result of confusion or lack of organization—then it will be retrieved incompletely. In trying to make sense of what we recall, we tend to fill in the gaps with other, sometimes unrelated, information. The result is distorted recall. In order to overcome the problem of distortion, we must emphasize the *meaning* of the material to our students. They must *understand* the material—its structure and its organization— not just know facts. Elaboration, the integrating of new information with previous learnings, reduces distortion. Mnemonics relate unfamiliar material with the familiar,[98] making it more meaningful.

Taken together, we can say that undistorted retrieval requires undistorted encoding.

Repression. Bad experiences are painful. Memories of bad experiences are painful as well. In the classroom students can experience humiliation and embarrassment when they fail in a learning task or become confused in a subject. Harsh criticism from teachers and ridicule from fellow students can make school a series of bad experiences. Learners tend to repress these experiences, along with the subjects they were studying. In a sense, students choose to forget these painful times. The antidote for repression is to make the learning environment as pleasant as possible. Avoid harsh attitudes. Soften negative student reactions to wrong answers from fellow students. Protect less skilled students from abusive attacks by others. Make learning experiences as enjoyable as possible.

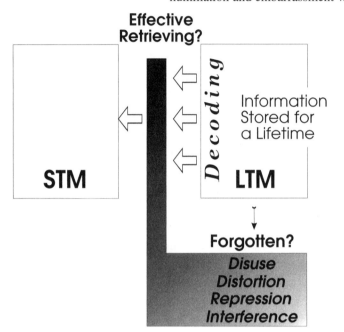

Interference. Interference is the loss of information because something else learned detracts from it,[99] or when information gets mixed up with or pushed aside by other information.[100] There are two basic types of interference: proactive inhibition and retroactive inhibition. *Proactive inhibition* occurs when previous learnings interfere with new learnings. When learning two verses of Scripture, having learned verse one makes learning verse two more difficult. *Retroactive inhibition* occurs when the new learnings interfere with prior learnings. In the process of learning verse two, we tend to forget verse one. The solution to the problem of interference is to insure proper organization of the material[101] and to overlearn those elements[102] most likely to cause interference. Use review and comparison[103] to encode the material correctly.

In summary, solve the problem of disuse by using the material periodically in future studies, of distortion by emphasizing meaning, of repression by building a warm classroom atmosphere, and of interference by review and comparison. These approaches to teaching will help students retrieve the essential elements of their subjects.

Metacognition is the knowledge of and control of cognitive processes[104] such as attending, recognizing, rehearsing, encoding, and retrieving. Metacognition, defined by John Flavell in 1976,[105] moves our consciousness up one level. On level one, we attend to specific stimuli. We elaborate material in order to encode it in long-term memory. On level two, we "watch ourselves" attending to stimuli, or encoding. We can evaluate how well we process information. On level three we can analyze how well we evaluate our thinking process. On level one, students learn subjects. This might be called "tactical learning." At level two, students learn how to learn. This is called "strategic learning."[106] Eggen and Kauchak list three types of metacognition: meta-attention, meta-communication, and meta-memory.[107]

Metacognitive Processes

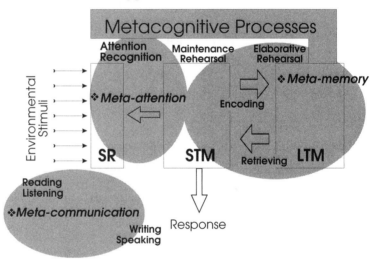

Meta-attention is the awareness and regulation of attention. What helps students attend to their studies better? Drinking coffee? Sitting toward the front of the classroom? Reviewing assigned reading before coming to class? Encourage students to monitor study habits when they're alone. Do they study with the stereo on? Does the stereo help their concentration, or does it distract them?

Meta-communication is the awareness and regulation of communication: speaking, listening, writing, and reading. A student answers a question, pauses, and then says, "Wait, let me rephrase that." She has listened to her own answer, judged it incomplete, and asks to try again. Another student misses part of a lecture and says, "I didn't quite hear that. Would you repeat it?" These examples reflect meta-communication.[108] Teachers who model good speaking and listening skills help focus student attention on them.[109]

Meta-memory is the awareness and regulation of memory strategies, of ways to remember better. Younger children rely on rote memorization and remain unaware of better strategies even when the strategies are suggested to them. By the age of ten, children are more effective in using efficient memory strategies.[110]

IMPLICATIONS OF INFORMATION PROCESSING THEORY

Metacognitive processes permit us to evaluate our own learning process and improve it. Effective teachers help students do more than learn subjects. They help students become more effective learners regardless of the subject matter.

Attract and hold attention[111]

Unless students are attending to what you are saying, they will not be able to process it. Sudden changes in rhythm and tone of speech, moving to a chalkboard and writing a word or drawing a simple diagram, asking a question—anything that stands out draws attention. Be careful not to overdo the spontaneous, however, or you may frighten or offend some students.

Engage students' thinking about their learning[112]

Ask questions about their work such as "How did you get your answer?" Or, "Why did you choose that process?" Or, "Why do you think [historical event] happened?" Then have students search for the answer.

Encourage student self-attention[113]

Help students control their own attention behaviors. Help them focus on objectives, or consider the rewards of good study habits, or isolate themselves from other students who distract. Help students ask themselves what prevents them from paying attention. Then show them ways to overcome these problems.

Emphasize organization in your teaching

Organize your presentations.[114] Use devices such as outlines, flowcharts,[115] or advance organizers[116] to provide students with preprocessed organization. An advance organizer is a general statement given before instruction that relates new information to existing knowledge.[117] Encourage students to develop concept maps[118]— translating text to diagrams[119]—of the material. Make assignments that require older students to organize a body of material on their own.[120] Minimize memorization of facts[121] and maximize understanding of relationships between concepts.

Give feedback to students on their quality of thinking.

Help them understand the limitations of their current learning strategies so that they will try other approaches.[122]

Use elaboration to increase meaningfulness of the material.[123]

Build on previous learnings. Relate new material to old. Ask questions that require comparisons, relationships, and patterns: "How does [this] compare with [that]? How are they different? Give an example." Review the main points and key ideas at the beginning and end of the session. Explain the relevance of present studies to life issues of students.[124] Ask students to think of connections between the present study and their own lives.[125] Allow time at the end of class for students to review their notes and ask clarifying questions.[126] Ask for and use a variety of examples. Have students summarize your lectures.[127]

Provide mnemonic devices to help students remember easily confused terms.[129] Teach students how to create various types of mnemonics.[130] However, use mnemonics only when the material does not lend itself to the natural organization of concepts and principles. Also, use care when using mnemonic images so that they do not undermine the seriousness of what is being learned.

Help students develop mnemonic devices[128]

Teach closely related ideas together, stressing similarities and differences.[131] For example, when teaching the meaning of *agape* love, always mention the terms *phileo* (friendship love) and *eros* (romantic or erotic love). When teaching on the sovereignty of God, mention how this relates to the free will of man. When teaching about God's holiness (wrath), mention God's grace and mercy (love). Take care not to teach single-dimension concepts but rather the multidimensioned truths of Scripture. Use active review—students recalling for themselves—to summarize key distinctions between closely related ideas.

Overcome interference

Use concrete analogies to make abstract information more meaningful.[132] Analogies are more effective when students are familiar with them. It is less important that the analogy itself be closely related to the concept.[133] Jesus used sheep and goats to illustrate two kinds of character. His listeners readily understood what He was saying because they knew about sheep and goats. When we use these analogies, we have to teach most of our members about sheep and goats. Our teaching is more effective when we use analogies that our students have experienced.

Stress meaningfulness in your teaching

Jerome Bruner said that one cannot learn everything about anything. Yet many teachers—especially in college and seminary classrooms—expect beginning students to master subjects they themselves have studied for years: "You are expected to know it all." This is unrealistic. Be specific in important task assignments. Focus attention on required learnings in the course. Give students key questions to consider as the content is presented.[134]

Help students know what they are expected to retrieve

Younger children have less stored in LTM[135] and therefore less ability to relate logically what they know to the task at hand. Provide clear, complete, and explicit directions and materials for them. Identify basic terms students should memorize.[136]

Help students improve their recognition ability

*Lead students
to rehearse
important concepts*

Rote rehearsal is one of the earliest tactics learned in school, and is used by everyone occasionally.[137] By the age of eight, children can begin rehearsing *sets* of facts rather than lists of individual facts. Use elaborative rehearsal—emphasize meaning and chunking[138]—to help students encode key ideas clearly.

*Guide students
in metacognitive
processes*

Teach students how to think about ways they learn and remember.[139] Help students to set goals for themselves, to describe steps they take in solving problems, to keep a log of terms that are clear and unclear, and to describe procedures in completing an assignment.[140] Such assignments help them think about *how* they think and will improve their learning in the future.

*Encourage
self-questioning*

Have students write questions about the content under study. Writing conceptual questions—questions which focus on concepts and ideas rather than simple recall of facts—helps students understand the material.[141] This process is more effective when students possess sufficient prior knowledge of the subject to know what is more and what is less important. The clarity of instructions concerning types of questions, the amount of practice writing questions, and the amount of time given to digest the material and write questions, all have a bearing on the effectiveness of the learning experience.[142]

*Assist students with their
note-taking skills*

Teach students how to improve their skills in taking notes from lectures or assigned readings.[143] While research is unclear about what makes note-taking effective (Should notes be brief or detailed? Should notes focus on facts or ideas? Should notes be kept in verbatim form, or reorganized later?) evidence suggests two basic benefits. First, taking notes leads to better retention and comprehension of material than listening or reading alone. Second, reviewing notes provides opportunities to recall and comprehend the material.[144]

Provide skeletal outlines of lectures to students,[145] but take care to balance detail with structure. Giving students too much detail makes lectures predictable and boring. Giving too little structure causes confusion. Skeletal outlines help prepackage the material so that students can readily see its organization. This organization is essential for long-term learning because taking notes without making sense of them—without an elaboration process—does not aid the learning process.[146]

When I was in seminary, I found that taking quality notes on lectures was essential for my success. On each page, I drew a vertical line which created a two-inch margin on the right. I wrote down key ideas and supporting material in the large area on the left—often employing diagrams to help cluster related ideas together—and used the two-inch margin for questions, unfamiliar vocabulary, and connections with other subjects. If the professor gave us an opportunity to ask questions during class, I'd ask one or two from my margins. I'd study terms the professor used that I did not know. I'd re-read assigned text material to discover answers to my questions, or ask the professor or fellow students. At home I reorganized my notes, synthesized key ideas, added explanatory material gleaned from answering my own questions. The resulting notebook provided a study resource that was clear, focused, and organized.

Information Processing theory receives more attention in recent educational psychology texts than any other learning theory. In this chapter we have introduced the basic components and processes in the Information Processing model. Suggestions for teaching derived from the IPT model have been given.

IN SUMMARY

CHAPTER CONCEPTS

Acronym

Acrostic

Activity

Attention

Automatic processing

Automaticity

Background knowledge

Chunking

Cognitive map

Cognitive process

Cognitive structure

Declarative knowledge

Distortion

Disuse

Echoic memory

Elaborative rehearsal

Encoding

Episodic memory

Iconic memory

Intentional processing

Interference

Keyword

Loci, or place, method

Long-term memory (LTM)

Maintenance rehearsal

Meta-attention

Meta-communication

Meta-memory

Metacognitive process

Mnemonics

Organization

Pegword

Perception

Proactive inhibition

Procedural knowledge

Procedural memory

Recognition

Repression

Retrieval

Retroactive inhibition

Rhymes

Scheme

Semantic memory

Sensory register

Short-term memory (STM)

DISCUSSION QUESTIONS

1. Define each of the following components and give examples of their operation from your own experience: sensory register, short-term memory, long-term memory, and metacognitive processes.

2. Create a chart comparing short-term and long-term memory on the following characteristics: speed of acquisition, accessibility, length of retention, stability, and capacity.

3. Define the following types of memory and give two examples of each from your own long-term memory: episodic memory, semantic memory, and procedural memory.

4. Describe how you take notes during lectures or while reading assigned passages. Be as specific as possible. Share your notes with at least two other students. How does your note taking compare with others? How does it differ?

5. Scan the chapter again and write at least three conceptual questions from the material. Then determine how effective this was in helping you understand the material.

FOR FURTHER READING

Biehler, Robert F., and Jack Snowman. "Information Processing Theory." In *Psychology Applied to Teaching*. 7th ed., 376–421. Boston: Houghton Mifflin Company, 1993.

Case, Robbie. "The Process of Stage Transition: A Neo-Piagetian View." In R. J. Sternberg (ed.), *Mechanisms of Cognitive Development,* 19–44. New York. W. H. Freeman.

Clouse, Bonnidell. "Guidelines from Cognitive Psychology." In *Teaching for Moral Growth: A Guide for the Christian Community—Teachers, Parents and Pastors.* 257–76. Wheaton, Ill: Bridgeport Books, 1993.

Dembo, Myron H. "Cognitive Approaches to Learning." In *Applying Educational Psychology.* 5th ed., 86–143. New York: Longman, 1994.

Eggen, Paul, and Don Kauchak. "Cognitive Views of Learning." In *Educational Psychology: Classroom Connections.* 2nd ed., 301–57. New York: Macmillan College Publishing Company, 1994.

Gage, N. L., and David C. Berliner. "The Cognitive Processing of Information." In *Educational Psychology.* 3rd ed., 298–331. Boston: Houghton Mifflin Company, 1984.

Good, Thomas L., and Jere E. Brophey. "The Information Processing View of Learning." In *Educational Psychology: A Realistic Approach.* 4th ed., 206–43. New York: Longman, 1990.

Hamachek, Don. "Information Processing: A Model of How Learning and Memory Occur." In *Psychology in Teaching, Learning, and Growth.* 4th ed., 187–214. Boston: Allyn and Bacon, 1990.

Hamilton, Richard, and Elizabeth Ghatala. "Information Processing Theory I, II, and III." In *Learning and Instruction.* 74–205. New York: McGraw-Hill, Inc., 1994.

LeFrancois, Guy R. "A Basic Information Processing Model." In *Psychology for Teaching.* 122–43. Belmont, Calif.: Wadsworth Publishing Company, 1994.

Slavin, Robert E. "Cognitive Theories of Learning Basic Concepts." In *Educational Psychology: Theory and Practice.* 4th ed., 184–220. Boston: Allyn and Bacon, 1994.

Sprinthall, Norman A., Richard C. Sprinthall, and Sharon N. Oja. "Information Processing." In *Educational Psychology: A Developmental Approach.* 6th ed. 285–320. New York: McGraw-Hill, Inc., 1994.

Woolfolk, Anita. "Cognitive Learning Theories." In *Educational Psychology.* 5th ed. 236–81. Boston: Allyn and Bacon, Inc., 1993.

Chapter

10

TEACHING FOR ATTITUDE CHANGE

HUMANISTIC LEARNING THEORY

Humanistic learning theory emphasizes the values and attitudes of students rather than their behavior or thinking. Solomon wrote, "Lay hold of my words with all your heart; keep my commands and you will live" (Prov. 4:4). Jesus said, "Love the Lord your God with all your heart and with all your soul and with all your mind" (Matt. 22:37). The "heart" is the seat of conviction, values, attitudes, and ideals. It is not enough simply to do the right things (ritual), or think the right thoughts (orthodoxy). Scripture teaches us to *be* right, as people of God—to integrate God's truth into who we are. How do we establish values? How do we help learners change their attitudes toward spiritual truths? How do we help students develop Christian ideals? In this chapter we present the arm of educational psychology which deals with the affective, the emotional, and the personal aspects of education: humanistic learning theory.

CHAPTER RATIONALE

Learners will demonstrate knowledge of Humanistic Learning Theory by

CHAPTER OBJECTIVES

- recalling the distinctions among secular humanism, classical humanism, and Christian humanism.
- identifying a key contribution of the following theorists to the teaching-learning process: Brown, Rogers, Combs, Gordon, Patterson, and Purkey.

- explaining the usefulness of educational humanism to the Christian teaching process;
- contrasting the extreme claims of humanistic educators with recent research findings.

Learners will demonstrate appreciation for Humanistic Learning Theory by sharing at least three classroom experiences which helped shape their present value system.

WHAT IS HUMANISM?

Few words evoke resentment and anger among evangelicals like the word "humanism." It has been the rallying cry, the call to arms, of conservative Christians for three decades. The word elicits tangible fear and provokes quick commitment to "defend the faith." Why then should I devote an entire chapter in a Christian textbook to the subject? The answer lies in the definition of the term, whether we speak of "small-h" humanism or "capital-H Humanism." The American Heritage Dictionary defines "humanism" (small h) as a "system of thought that centers on human beings and their values, capacities, and worth," or, "concern with the interests, needs, and welfare of human beings."[1] Evangelical Christians should have little difficulty seeing the importance of "little-h" humanistic learning in the church. We could use the phrase "personalizing the classroom" or "making Bible study relevant" and be confident no one would object. Christ died and the Church was established because God loves learners. The Church-at-its-best concerns itself with the needs of learners. The teaching ministry of the Church focuses on establishing biblical values in learners. The right side of the Disciplers' Model emphasizes meeting the needs of learners and improving openness and willingness to share in the classroom. These are the "small-h" humanistic emphases of this chapter.

"We could use the phrase 'personalizing Bible study' and be confident no one would object"

The American Heritage Dictionary further defines "Humanism" (capital H) as "a cultural and intellectual movement of the Renaissance that emphasized secular concerns as a result of the rediscovery and study of the literature, art, and civilization of ancient Greece and Rome."[2] "Capital-H" Humanism presents a problem for Christians because of its secular foundation.

In order to delineate clearly the various kinds of humanism, we will look at secular humanism, classical humanism, and educational humanism. We will conclude with a discussion of the personal dimension of Christian education.

Secular Humanism

Humanism emphasizes man. "Secular" refers to "worldly rather than spiritual" matters, "temporal," "profane."[3] Secular humanism, therefore, emphasizes man and excludes God. In 1882, German existential[4] philosopher Friedrich Neitzsche (pr. NEAT-chee) wrote that "since God does not exist, man must devise his own way of life."[5] In 1946, John Paul Sartre wrote that man must work out his own values by making choices.[6] The Russian Christian Dostoyevsky once wrote that "If God did not exist, everything would be permitted." This was Sartre's beginning point: God does not exist. Individuals define themselves by making choices and working out their own values.[7] In 1970 John Randall wrote that "men should place their faith in man himself—in man's infinite possibilities . . . [as well as in] a realistic recognition of man's finite limitations."[8] Each of these existentialists focuses on man and excludes God. Such is the nature of secularism, the "religion of humanity." Secularism has four major tenets. First, secularism emphasizes the self-sufficiency of man's own natural powers to direct destiny. Second, secularism rejects supernatural religion as little more than superstition. Third, secularism accepts the scientific method as a substitute religion. And fourth, the priority values of secularism are academic freedom and civil liberties.[9] It is no wonder that secular humanism is anathema to Christianity—and vice versa. The term "humanism" is often used as an abbreviation of secular humanism. It would be more correct to use the term "secularism."

Classical Humanism

Classical humanism has two forms. The first grew out of southern Europe in the Renaissance and is secular. Man was placed at the center of all things. This "new horizon" of life was culturally rich, purely human, easily attainable, without much restraint. It appealed to the emotions and emphasized living for the present. This world view focused on success, stressing fame and pleasure, gratification of human craving, and satisfaction of sensual desires.[10]

The second form of classical humanism grew out of northern Europe in the Reformation and had a biblical foundation. The authority for teaching was not Man, nor even the Church, but the Bible, which was placed at the center of the curriculum. This "Christian humanism"[11] emphasized the sovereignty of God as well as the worth of the individual. Reformation leaders, such as Luther and Calvin, stressed living a life worthy here as well as in the hereafter. Schools emphasized high educational standards, including trained teachers, discipline, pleasant methods, and attractive classrooms and materials.[12]

Such a view fits perfectly with Christian education today, where learner needs are met through the study and application of God's Word. Don't we want warm, friendly classes? Don't we want to integrate the needs and interests of our learners into our studies? Don't we stress contacts, visitation, and ministry to members and prospects because we care about them as people? Aren't we interested in helping learners apply their studies to their own life situations? Of course we are. And each of these desires is "humanistic" in the sense that it focuses on the person, the learner, rather than the "lesson." This is the thrust of educational humanism.

Educational Humanism

Humanistic Learning Theory[13] developed, not in opposition to the Church, but in opposition to the mechanically rigid approach to learning fostered by Skinner's programmed instruction and Freudian psychoanalysis.[14] Research in the 1940s—pursued by clinical psychologists, social workers, and counselors—focused on the affective side of learning.[15] Educational humanism, or affective education, emphasizes the affective domain we introduced in chapter 6: receiving, responding, valuing, organizing, and characterizing. Christian teachers desiring to hit these kinds of targets do so with affective methods, which we will discuss a little later. Learners are more than learning machines to be programmed by teachers or computers. In fact, true human learning involves more than knowledge and content. Life-changing learning involves attitudes, emotions, and values. The goal of educational humanism is to *personalize the classroom.*

How do we teach Scripture so that our learners personally integrate it into their lives and life situations? It is one thing to know that it is wrong to cheat. It is quite another to live honestly. It is a good thing to know the Good Samaritan story. It is quite another to be a "Good Samaritan." In Christian education, "knowing the right answer" isn't enough. Jesus calls us to a Kingdom lifestyle. This requires the integration of affective elements in the teaching process.

Educational humanism is concerned with the uniqueness, the individuality, the humanity of each individual learner.[16] It is most concerned with the affective needs of students: emotions, feelings, values, attitudes, predispositions, and morals.[17] Emphases include personal freedom and growth, choice, and self-determination in the educational process.[18] The focus of the humanistic teacher is on the total person—intellectual, emotional, and interpersonal—and how these factors affect learning and motivation.[19]

Abraham Maslow, Carl Rogers, and Arthur Combs are three leading psychologists who influenced humanistic methods of education more than any others.

Abraham Maslow is considered to be the father of humanistic psychology.[20] Maslow believed that children will make wise choices for their own learning when given the opportunity. Such a principle leads to "free education," in which teachers arrange attractive learning situations. Students then select from the offerings those they find personally valuable. In this climate, teacher-directed classroom management becomes secondary to the motivating power of self-chosen activities. The learning experience itself becomes its own reward.[21] Maslow is best known for the "heirarchy of needs" theory of motivation, which we will discuss in chapter 12.

Abraham Maslow

Carl Rogers wrote, "In my view education should evoke *real* learning . . . not the lifeless, sterile, futile, quickly forgotten stuff which is crammed into the mind of the poor helpless individual tied to his seat by ironclad bonds of conformity!"[22] As if behavioral and cognitive educators embraced this kind of learning! Rogers developed person-centered methods for his work as a counselor-therapist. The term "person-centered" refers to the idea that counseling should revolve around the client, as opposed to directive therapy, which revolves around the counselor. Roger's ideas were not based on objective data but rather on personal answers to questions about individuals. How do they feel? How do they perceive their relationships with others? He transferred his ideas into the classroom where he led graduate seminars in psychology and counseling. He focused more on phenomenology, the world as it is perceived by individuals, than reality, the world as it may actually be.[23]

Carl Rogers

"Center the learning process not in the lesson, nor in the teacher, but in the learner"

As a graduate professor, he transferred his counseling methods to the seminar room. His principles of teaching emphasized "learner-centered education."[24] In Rogers' view, teachers should trust students to do their work to the best of their ability and provide opportunities for learning.[25] Teachers should be "real persons" before students and not present a facade. They should be sincere and transparent facilitators.[26] Teachers should respect their students as well as their students' feelings and frustrations.[27] Teachers should view learning from the student's point of view.[28] The result of these efforts, according to Rogers, is that students take responsibility for their own learning.[29]

CARL ROGERS
(1902–1987)

Carl Rogers was born in Oak Brook, Illinois,[A] a suburb of Chicago,[B] in 1902.[C] His father was a civil engineer, and his mother was a deeply religious woman. Rogers' family life centered around family prayers, church attendance, and hard work. Additionally, there were strict rules against dancing, playing cards, attending movies, smoking, drinking, or showing any sexual interest. At the age of twelve, Rogers' family moved to a farm thirty miles west of Chicago in an effort to keep him and his five brothers and sisters from the temptations of suburban and city life.[D]

In 1919 Rogers went to the University of Wisconsin to study scientific farming.[E] During his college years, he attended a conference on evangelism and decided to go into Christian ministry. A series of events caused him to question the fundamentalism of his parents, and after obtaining a degree in history, he decided to study at Union Theological Seminary—precisely because it was more liberal in theology.[F] During his studies at Union, he focused more clearly on the special nature of "personhood."[G] He decided he could no longer espouse religious faith and began taking courses in clinical and educational psychology at Columbia Teachers' College. He earned his Ph.D. in 1931 with a dissertation on personality adjustment in children ages nine to thirteen.[H]

Rogers' professional career was spent at the University of Rochester, Ohio State University, the University of Chicago, and the University of Wisconsin.[I] In 1945 while at University of Chicago, Rogers developed a laboratory for client-centered counseling and began a base of research to support counseling methodology. He was the first to tape record counseling sessions and challenged other therapists to examine their methods and attest to their effectiveness.[J] In 1968 he and several colleagues established the Center for Studies of the Person in LaJolla. Rogers was one of the founders of the Association for Humanistic Psychology and served on the board of directors of the *Journal of Humanistic Psychology* since its beginning in 1961.[K] In 1987, after an exhausting trip to Russia, Rogers died during surgery for a broken hip at the age of 85.[L] Carl Rogers is best known for his person-centered, nondirective approach to counseling in which the counselee directs the counseling process.[M]

Arthur Combs

Arthur Combs wrote, "I am not a humanist because I want to go about being nice to people. I am a humanist because I know that when I apply humanist thinking to my teaching, students will learn anything better."[30] Combs stressed the role of facilitator for teachers. Much of his emphasis parallels Jerome Bruner's discovery learning, but Combs placed more emphasis on sharing personal views and less on objective problem solving. Effective facilitators, according to Combs, are well-informed, sensitive, believe in their students' ability to learn, have a positive self-concept, and use many methods to engage students in the learning process.[31]

For Combs, meaning is not inherent in the subject matter; it is the individual who instills subject matter with its meaning. The dilemma in teaching, for Combs, is not how to present subject matter, but how to help students derive personal meaning from subject matter."[32] This emphasis of relevance over meaning has saturated teaching both in the church and the classroom. Simply stated, "meaning" refers to the objective understanding of the subject: *What does this mean?* "Relevance" refers to the subjective understanding of the learner: *What does this mean to me?* These statements concerning the importance of "personal meaning"—that is, relevance—undermine Combs' own assertion that "students will learn anything better" using humanistic methods. Research has shown that such methods may improve attitudes toward school, and may improve students' self concepts, and may even improve cooperation among students because subjects are made more relevant. But academic achievement suffers[33] as objective meaning is de-emphasized.

"Combs emphasized personal relevance over objective meaning"

The Disciplers' Model calls for balance between meaning and relevance. The Thinking Pillar (cognitive meaning) stands on the Foundation Stone of the Bible. The Feeling Pillar (affective relevance) stands on the Foundation Stone of Learner Needs. Both are necessary for growth. Cognition without affect produces dry abstraction. Affect without cognition produces warm fluff. Taken together, Christian teachers help learners understand clearly and discover personal relevance in that which they understand.

Other Important Humanistic Psychologists

Four other psychologists are mentioned for their influence in humanistic learning theory. C. H. Patterson saw affective education as an antidote to an overemphasis on educational technology. He advocated characteristics in teachers and teaching techniques similar to those of Rogers and Combs. George Brown's confluent education stressed the combination of cognitive and affective factors in the learning process, but emphasized the affective as more important for long-term learning. Thomas Gordon studied with Carl Rogers and applied person-centered therapy to parent-child relationships in his book *Parent Effectiveness Training* (1970). The success of that book led him to write *Teacher Effectiveness Training* (1974) in which he stressed the affective relationship between teachers and students. This relationship is enhanced by openness, honesty, caring, and interdependence. William Purkey's invitational learning encourages teachers to transmit messages consistently, both verbal and nonverbal, to students that they are responsible, able, and valuable. In *Inviting School Success* (1984), Purkey suggests four student factors that are likely to lead to school success: relating (students to relate to fellow students), asserting (experiencing self-control of the learning process), investing (personally participating in learning), and coping (meeting school expectations successfully).[34]

HUMANISTIC APPROACHES TO EDUCATION

Humanistic teaching methods focus on learner experiences, emotions, values, and choices, and are better suited to situations where *appreciation* of subjects is the primary goal.[35] The emphasis in humanistic learning is on relevance to the learner rather than cognitive understanding of the subject.

Group Processes. The heart of humanistic methodology in the 1970s involved sensitivity training and encounter groups. Groups of learners spent large portions of class time expressing feelings, exploring interpersonal relationships, and sharing personal values. Simulation games and role-playing activities are still used to help participants intensify their sharing.[36]

Self-Regulated Learning. Humanistic educators emphasize self-directed and self-motivated learning in which students control their own learning. Such control includes selection of topics and resources, setting goals, and evaluating outcomes with little teacher guidance.[37]

Warm Classroom Climate. Humanistic educators emphasize a relaxed and safe class atmosphere[38] where teachers demonstrate care for learners as individuals. Present are such factors as open communication, willingness to share, genuine empathy, and warmth.[39]

Priority on Affective Outcomes. Humanistic educators believe that providing an environment of freedom, responsibility, caring, and interpersonal sharing is more important than achieving a few additional points on standardized tests.[40] Achieving personal growth, enhanced and clarified values, and better interpersonal skills take priority over standard curricula, testing, and academic achievement.

"Authentic" Assessment. Humanistic educators avoid grades, standardized testing, and formal evaluations. They prefer to evaluate learners on a pass/fail basis, and emphasize written evaluations for individual students.[41] Value is placed on the individual, not performance.[42]

Individualized Instruction. Humanistic educators mold instruction to student abilities. Each student progresses at his or her own pace. Students are given responsibility to identify needs, plan activities, and evaluate mastery. A wide variety of activities are offered for achievement of academic goals. Teachers encourage peer assistance—learners helping each other—and cooperative learning experiences.

THREE TYPES OF HUMANISTIC EDUCATION

Much of the content of humanistic theorists focuses on attitudes more than specific methods. However, three basic types of educational practice have grown out of humanistic theory. These are the Open Classroom, Learning Styles, and Cooperative Learning.

The Open Classroom

My seminary Philosophy of Education class, circa 1974, visited an elementary school which had moved to the Open Classroom concept. The school had no walls. Learning areas were separated by bookshelves. Bean bag chairs and pillows provided comfortable areas for reading and study. There were no "classrooms" and no "classes." Each student had an individual educational plan which detailed agreed-upon goals, objectives, and activities. Teachers moved from area to area, providing individual help as needed. Time in school was measured by learning goals accomplished rather than subject matter periods. I remember one young girl who was involved in a research project. Part of her educational plan included viewing a film. On her own, she moved to the film area, set up the projector, threaded the film, watched the movie—taking notes relevant for her project—and then put the equipment away. At no time did she require teacher help.

The "open classroom" concept focused on the student, not the teacher. Learning stations, projects, and individualized workbooks were used in place of direct instruction. Teachers helped students individually to set specific learning goals.[43] There was no rigid curricula or age-grading. Teacher-student relations were relaxed. Emphasis was placed on learner experiences and the role of emotions. Students were given freedom to move, explore, and discover on their own. There were few formal tests.[44]

For all their popularity in the 1970s, such schools are now rare in North America.[45] The walls have been put back. Children have been organized into classes with teacher-teams who work to achieve specific content objectives. Research has demonstrated that open education methodology did succeed in affective learning but produced lower achievement in cognitive outcomes.[46] Students learned less and were less motivated to learn than in traditional classrooms.[47]

Learning Styles

"If students have difficulty learning the way we teach, perhaps we should teach the way they learn." This is the central principle of learning styles. Research in the late 1970s and early 1980s demonstrated that learners could be classified by differing abilities to learn. Some learned best through sharing personal experiences. Others learned best through well-organized lectures. Still others learned best through problem solving and experimentation. Others learned best through projects and hands-on activities, others through music, and so on. In traditional classrooms, students succeed when their preferred learning style matches the predominant style of the classroom. Learning styles emphasize the need to provide learning alternatives so that all students can experience a "best fit" environment.

In a learning styles classroom, students have many options for learning, including individualized activities, group activities, lectures, and multimedia presentations. Core subjects are rotated throughout the day to ensure that all students have a turn at their best subject first. Exams are scheduled according to each student's own internal clock. Students are generally more involved in classroom activities because they fit student choices better.[48]

While the humanistic "learner-centered" focus is clear, the Learning Styles approach places more emphasis on cognitive and academic growth than open classroom structures. Research has shown that schools employing Learning Styles principles produce high academic achievement along with positive attitudes toward school.[49]

While Learning Styles has received enthusiastic support in recent years, I have misgivings about how far teachers can go in being all things to all students. While teachers should avoid an overly rigid emphasis in one learning style alone—say, all group discussion or all lecture—there are limits to what a single teacher can do to provide unique learning opportunities for each student in the class. How do we keep track of each person's work? How does writing a poem compare to producing a term paper? How does composing a song compare to leading a group to develop a valid checklist for observing teaching skills? Too much emphasis on personal talents and interests moves us away from measures of mastery, performance, and excellence in the classroom. Several years ago a local university experimented with learning styles by offering multiple sections of courses geared to identified styles. The experiment came to a quick end as soon as it was discovered what an administrative nightmare this caused. Providing options for students geared to different learning styles is certainly possible. But providing as many versions of a course as there are students in the class is unrealistic.

The newest manifestation of humanistic theory is Cooperative Learning. The term *cooperative* stands against *competitive*. Cooperative Learning classrooms refrain from grading systems that pit individual students or student teams against each other in a race for limited high grades. In cooperative learning, high grades can be earned by every student or student team that meets the requirements for excellence. Students are encouraged to help each other learn. Emphasis is given to active participation in achieving both cognitive and affective outcomes. Cooperative Learning places more emphasis on academic achievement. It provides less unstructured freedom than the Open Classroom and does not cater to individual student preferences as in Learning Styles. Research has shown that Cooperative Learning increases achievement, motivation to learn, higher thinking skills, and interpersonal relationships in students.[50]

Cooperative Learning

The following quotes represent humanistic thinking two decades ago when educational existentialism was in full bloom. Each of these statements is analyzed in light of educational realities and more recent research:

ANALYZING
HUMANISTIC
APPROACHES

"Trust children and let them make their own decisions. Instruction should be learner-centered" (Maslow, Rogers).[51]

Humanistic educators placed too much responsibility for educational decision making on students. What other requirements do students have besides those in your class? If they have a major exam in another class, will they spend time reading twenty pages of material for your class—particularly if they receive nothing for this preparation beyond the "joy of learning?" What is to prevent students from making wrong choices? Shouldn't teachers provide some direction for student learning? How important is subject mastery? Is it important for students to understand the subject, or is it enough simply to experience something about it? The move from Bruner's pure discovery, a more humanistic approach to cognitive learning, to directed discovery, Ausebel's reception learning, and Information Processing theory is evidence that educational psychology found trusting learners too much led to mediocre performance.

"Effective teachers are trusting, sincere, empathetic, and confident" (Rogers, Combs).

This is an important principle because teaching is a highly personal, deeply interactive social process which requires a warm relational bridge. Look for the best in students. Empathize with their problems. Try to see the course work load from their point of view. However, do not allow individual students to short-circuit course requirements because of personal difficulties or irresponsibility. ("My hard disk crashed at 3 this morning as I was printing my term paper. Will I still be docked for lateness?") If we excuse the student's irresponsibility and procrastination, we are being unfair to other students in the class who submitted their papers on time.

"Affective factors in education are as important as cognitive factors" (Brown).

Contemporary educators have moved away from this principle. Affective responses may come after the subject is mastered. Personal involvement should enhance, but not replace, cognitive learning. Students in my research class have few positive affective responses during the course. Their emotions range from fear to anger to frustration to defeat. And yet at the end of the semester, when it all comes together and most of the class has earned an "A," there is celebration. If I gave in to their protests and anguish a third of the way through the course, they would never achieve the victory or experience the exhilaration they do at the end of the semester. Affective elements should enhance, not replace, the cognitive.

Key Emphases from Humanistic Theory

The following twelve statements summarize key distinctives of humanistic learning. Use these terms to compare and contrast learning as defined in chapters 7 and 8.	
1. The learning is a . . .	PERSON
2. The focus is on . . .	EXPERIENCES/VALUES
3. Relationship of learning "whole" to its parts . . .	WHOLE *GREATER THAN* SUM OF PARTS: INCLUDES EMOTIONS
4. Learning is . . .	PERSONAL AND INTERACTIVE
5. The target learning domain is . . .	AFFECTIVE
6. The goal of learning is . . .	CHANGE IN ATTITUDES/VALUES
7. Learning is strengthened by . . .	PERSONAL SHARING
8. Learning is strengthened by . . .	PERSONAL SATISFACTION
9. Motivation keys on . . .	PERSONAL VALUES
10. Feedback should be . . .	PERSONAL, ON EFFORT
11. Best curriculum is . . .	ELECTIVE
12. The Theory in Practice is . . .	LEARNING STYLES

"Teachers should have positive relationships with students" (Gordon).

Teachers who exhibit an attitude of harshness and rigidity impair the learning process. Students learn better when they feel accepted by their teachers. Still, teachers are not mere friendly colleagues. They are assigned the task of equipping students in a given area. They will be required to assign a grade to students based on the student's objective performance in their courses. Assigning grades is not always a friendly act! Furthermore, making friends with every student is emotionally draining. When I first started teaching I made every effort to learn the names of all of my students each semester. I would call them by name throughout the semester. But year by year I discovered that learning 250 to 300 names was growing more difficult, and more than that, many of my students really didn't care whether I knew their names. So more recently I've focused on learning the names of students who show they really want to know their professor personally. On a positive note, building warm relationships is the bedrock for effective discipleship through the church. In the over-scheduled world we live in, time to build relationships is hard to find. But *koinonia* grows as people spend time with people— with Jesus in the middle.

"Encourage learners to explore their feelings and emotions" (Purkey).

The right pillar of the Disciplers' Model encourages teachers to help learners "remove masks" and "share themselves" with others. These activities help build a warm, trusting atmosphere in the classroom. Small group sharing was very popular in the 1970s. Often these encounter experiences had little to do with the subject matter. But sharing experiences and feelings should not be an end in itself. It should be a means to the end of integrating subject matter into life. In the context of Bible study, it should be the means to spiritual growth as Bible truths become personalized and integrated.

HUMANISM
IN THE 1990S

The 1970s Encounter Group phenomenon and Open Classrooms are gone. Clouse explains the decline of humanistic thinking in the 1980s as having three major causes. The first was its association with the drug counter-culture and its affinity with the occult. The second was a decline in attacks by the Christian Right. During the 1970s a number of Christian leaders and groups vociferously attacked humanism. Tim LaHaye wrote in 1980, "Most of the evils in the world today can be traced to humanism, which has taken over our government, the UN, education, TV and most of the other influential things in life."[52] Such attacks caused humanists to redouble their efforts to explain their position. In the 1980s such attacks declined, and the prominence of the movement dwindled. Clouse states the third reason for a decline in humanism was the increased prominence of cognitive psychology,[53] as we saw in the chapters on Cognitive Learning and Information Processing.

Research demonstrated that learning and motivation require more than freedom of choice. Existential individualism leads directly to chaos as each one does what is right in his own eyes. The chaos in American society today can be laid at the feet of existential extremes in education through the 1960s and 1970s. "Choice" has become the

banner cry of individuals who believe their own wants and comforts
are more important than community standards. Even the secular press
has dedicated issues and articles to the excess of self-concept and
self-esteem. *Newsweek*'s cover story of February 17, 1992, was
"Hey, I'm Terrific: The Curse of Self-Esteem." *Newsweek* presented
an in-depth analysis of the fact that our society has gone overboard
with the idea of self-esteem and positive self-concept. In one telling
example, they reported a research study that showed American high
schoolers significantly *more confident* in their math and science
skills than their Japanese counterparts. The only problem is that the
Japanese high schoolers proved significantly *more capable* in math
and science than American students.[54] For thirty years we have worshipped "feel good" at the expense of "think right" and "do well."
The result is more self-esteem problems than ever.

But why should we be surprised at the breakdown of academic
achievement at the hands of humanistic educators? How long would
a business exist if every worker did as he or she pleased? How effective would a military unit be if it depended solely on the choices of
each soldier to do his or her duty? What organization could function
as an effective community if every member did as they pleased?
When employees submit themselves to work for the good of the
business, they help themselves. An effective military unit, submitted
to the command and direction of its leader, is more likely to survive
than an ineffective one. Organizations are as strong as the commitment of their individual members to that organization. And it follows that teachers should know better what their students need to
understand than students do. Teachers can better organize curricula
and learning activities than students can. Teachers can explain and
illustrate difficult topics better than students can. Let the teachers
teach! And let the students learn!

On the other hand, business leaders who ignore the needs of
workers, military commanders who exploit their soldiers, and organizations that take volunteers' efforts for granted will soon fail. In
the same way, teachers who teach lessons rather than learners and
who demonstrate an uncaring and disinterested attitude toward students will soon find that meaningful learning has stopped.

In the 1970s most educational psychology textbooks devoted
whole chapters to "humanistic learning theory." In the 1990s few
textbooks do.[55] Humanistic principles have been moved to chapters
on motivation and classroom climate. Humanistic educators have

drawn back from the extremes of the past and espouse cooperative learning strategies that emphasize both cognitive and affective outcomes, employ *guided* discovery methods, and focus on helping students understand, as well as love, a given subject.

HUMANISTIC LEARNING IN THE CHURCH

Then why did I include humanistic learning in this unit on learning theory systems? The answer is that humanistic principles are central in Christian education. Much of the learning that goes on in our churches reflects "small-h" humanism: a "concern with the interests, needs, and welfare of human beings."[56] Effective churches are those that care about people, that minister to the needs of people, that take seriously the perceptions and problems of the people they serve. Effective Bible study classes are warm, inviting, open, sharing groups of believers who structure their convictions according to God's Word and love each other freely. See "The Right Pillar" of chapter 1 for specifics on using affective principles in a Christian context.

Jesus said, "Love the Lord your God with all your heart and with all your soul and with all your mind" (Matt. 22:37). The "heart" is the seat of conviction, values, attitudes, and ideals. It is not enough simply to do the right things (ritual), or think the right thoughts (orthodoxy). Scripture teaches us to *be* right, as people of God—to integrate God's truth into who we are. This chapter gave principles of affective education, emphasizing values, and changed attitudes. May God bless your teaching efforts as you love your students and care for them one by one, even as you help them understand.

CHAPTER CONCEPTS

Affective learning
Confluent education
Cooperative learning
Existentialism
Humanism-secular
Humanism-classical
Humanism-educational
Learning Styles

Meaning
Open Classroom
Person-centered learning
Phenomenology
Relevance
Secularism
Self-regulated learning
T.E.T.

DISCUSSION QUESTIONS

1. Discuss the similarities and differences among the secular humanism of the Renaissance, the "Christian humanism" of the Reformation, and educational humanism.

2. Describe one or more contributions to humanistic learning by Brown, Rogers, Combs, Gordon, Patterson, and Purkey.

3. Explain why principles drawn from educational humanism (affective learning) are useful in Christian teaching.

4. What educational experiences have you had that shaped your present value system?

5. Identify the following questions or activities as cognitive or affective.

   a. Read 1 Corinthians 13. How does this passage make you feel?

   b. Compare the responses of Peter and Judas to their betrayal of Jesus.

   c. What does the term "agape" mean?

   d. What experiences of witnessing have you had?

   e. If you had been Nicodemus, what would you have asked Jesus?

   f. Explain "sanctification" in your own words.

   g. Have you experienced the joy Philip must have felt as he led the Ethiopian to faith in Christ? What was it like?

6. Compare and contrast humanism and Humanism. How are they alike? How do they differ?

FOR FURTHER READING

Biehler, Robert F. and Jack Snowman. " Humanistic Approaches to Education." In *Psychology Applied to Teaching*. 7th ed., 470–561. Boston: Houghton Mifflin Company, 1993.

Brown, George I. *Human Teaching for Human Learning: An Introduction to Confluent Education*. New York: Viking Press, 1971.

Clouse, Bonnidell. "Moral Growth by Moral Potential: A Humanist View." In *Teaching for Moral Growth: A Guide for the Christian Community—Teachers, Parents and Pastors*. 296–333. Wheaton, Ill: Bridgeport Books, 1993.

Combs, Arthur W. "Affective Education or None At All." *Educational Leadership* 39(7), 494–97.

Dembo, Myron H. "The Humanistic Perspective." In *Applying Educational Psychology*. 5th ed., 198–233. New York: Longman, 1994.

Eggen, Paul, and Don Kauchak. "Humanistic Views of Motivation." In *Educational Psychology: Classroom Connections*. 2nd ed., 431–33. New York: Macmillan College Publishing Company, 1994.

Gage, N. L., and David C. Berliner. "Open and Humanistic Approaches to Teaching." In *Educational Psychology*. 3rd ed. 556–81. Boston: Houghton Mifflin Company, 1984.

Good, Thomas L., and Jere E. Brophey. "The Humanistic Perspective." In *Educational Psychology: A Realistic Approach*. 4th ed., 463–87. New York: Longman, 1990.

Gordon, Thomas. *TET: Teacher Effectiveness Training*. New York: McCay, 1974.

Hamachek, Don. "Humanistic Psychology: Key Ideas and Concepts." In *Psychology in Teaching, Learning, and Growth*. 4th ed., 27–34. Boston: Allyn and Bacon, 1990.

LeFrancois, Guy R. "Humanistic Approaches to Teaching." In *Psychology for Teaching*. 238–61. Belmont, Calif.: Wadsworth Publishing Company, 1994.

Patterson, C. H. *Humanistic Education*. Englewood Cliffs, N.J.: Prentice-Hall, 1973.

Purkey, W. W., and J. M. Novak. *Inviting School Success*. 2nd ed. Belmont, Calif.: Wadsworth, 1984.

Rogers, Carl R. *A Way of Being*. Boston: Houghton-Mifflin, 1980.

———. *Freedom to Learn for the 80's*. Columbus, Ohio: Merrill, 1983).

Slavin, Robert E. "How Do Humanistic Approaches Differ from Direct Instruction?" In *Educational Psychology: Theory and Practice*. 4th ed., 296–301. Boston: Allyn and Bacon, 1994.

Smith, M. Daniel. "Humanistic Learning Environments." In *Educational Psychology and Its Classroom Applications*. 185–208. Boston: Allyn and Bacon, 1975.

Sprinthall, Norman A., Richard C. Sprinthall, and Sharon N. Oja. "Model Three: Interpersonal Learning," and "Carl Rogers." In *Educational Psychology: A Developmental Approach*. 6th ed., 340–42. New York: McGraw-Hill, Inc., 1994.

Chapter
11

THE CHRISTIAN
TEACHERS' TRIAD

THE DYNAMIC SYNERGISM
OF CHRISTIAN TEACHING

Over the past four chapters we have investigated three systems of learning theory. Each system has its advocates. Indeed, you probably found yourself in agreement with one of the systems more than the others. But like tools, each designed for a specific purpose, learning theory systems address different types of problems in the teaching-learning process. The most effective teacher is the one who can draw from all three systems to solve a variety of problems in learning. This chapter describes the three-circled Christian teachers' triad, describes imbalance that can result from too much attention to any one system, and relates specific principles of teaching to each component.

CHAPTER RATIONALE

Learners will demonstrate knowledge of the Christian teachers' triad by drawing and labelling the complete diagram from memory.

Learners will demonstrate understanding of selected principles of teaching by identifying them as behavioral, cognitive, or humanistic.

Learners will demonstrate understanding of the Christian teachers' triad by developing examples in which imbalance impairs the learning process.

CHAPTER OBJECTIVES

Learners will demonstrate appreciation for the triad by sharing personal experiences they've had in classrooms where either an imbalance (negative) or balance (positive) existed.

We have spent four chapters describing three major learning theory systems. As we have seen, each has its proponents. Yet we cannot focus on one system alone in the real world of the classroom if we really want to help our students learn. Educational problems do not fall neatly into any one system: some are behavioral, some cognitive, and others affective. Effective teachers move freely from system to system, engaging learners where they are, helping them master the subject and grow as a result. The Christian Teachers' Triad helps me balance my approach to teaching in this way. Let's use this framework to integrate all three systems of learning theory we've discussed.

THE TRIAD OF HUMAN EXPERIENCE

The three intersecting circles in the Venn diagram represent three areas of human experience. Each circle is independent of the other two. Each circle can be any size. The diagram at left represents an *ideal balance*: all three circles are the same size, and all three intersect equally. The three areas of human life represented by this triad are "what I think," "how I feel or value," and "what I do." Let's look at each of these.

What I Think

The first circle represents the rational side of life: knowing, conceptualizing, problem solving, analyzing, synthesizing, evaluating. Without a clear focus on "correctly handl[ing] the word of truth" (2 Tim. 2:15), we open ourselves and our learners to deception and delusion.

John 3:16 says, "For God so loved the world that he gave his one and only Son, that whoever believes in him shall not perish but have eternal life." What did God do when He loved the world? And who is the world that He loved? What does it mean to believe in His Son?

What kind of life do we obtain through this belief? And what does eternal add to this life?

Jesus said, "Do not judge, or you too will be judged" (Matt. 7:1). What did Jesus mean by judge? Are we not to have an opinion? Are we to go through life without evaluating our teachers and preachers? No. John writes, "Dear friends, do not believe every spirit, but test the spirits to see whether they are from God, because many false prophets have gone out into the world" (1 John 4:1). So what did Jesus mean?

I grew up singing the hymn "Come Thou Fount of Every Blessing." I love that hymn. Even the second verse, which begins "Here I raise mine Ebenezer.' But it wasn't until I began interpreting our worship services for deaf people that I ever asked myself what an "Ebenezer" is! The answer is found in 1 Samuel 7:12 where Samuel builds an altar of thanksgiving to God and names it "Ebenezer, saying, 'Thus far has the LORD helped us.'" The second phrase of the verse captures this very meaning: "hither by Thy help I'm come." In others words, *I am building an altar to the Lord because He has been faithful in helping me get as far as I've come.* I translated it into sign language something like *Here I raise my praise to Jesus. Up til now you've helped me a lot.* I've loved singing this hymn for years, but until I studied the meaning of the words, I didn't know—much less understand—what I was singing!

If our learners are to grow in the Lord, they must go beyond simplistic facts and pat answers. They must go beyond words to meanings. For unless these learners understand what Paul meant when he wrote under inspiration of Holy Spirit, they will never make proper application of God's message to their own lives. We will not grow up into Christ (Eph. 4:15) without a clear understanding of what God's Word means. This kind of learning outcome results from cognitive learning.

What I Feel

The second circle represents the emotional, or affective, side of life: feelings, attitudes, values, and priorities. If the rational represents what we think (our "head"), we might consider the affective representing what we value (our "heart"). Actually, the biblical use of "heart" involves the entire triad: mind, emotion, actions, and will. But often the Bible uses the term "heart" to refer to the affective elements of life. "A happy heart makes the face cheerful, but heartache crushes the spirit" (Prov. 15:13). This verse refers to feeling happy or depressed.

Several passages refer to proper values or commitments. "Only be careful, and watch yourselves closely so that you do not forget the things your eyes have seen or *let them slip from your heart* as long as you live. Teach them to your children and to their children after them" (Deut. 4:9, author's emphasis). "From your heart," not "from your head." The command was for Israel to value what the Lord had done. Or, another, "I have *hidden your word in my heart* that I might not sin against you" (Ps. 119:11, author's emphasis). The writer had made a commitment to live by God's Word. Finally, John writes, "Blessed is the one who reads the words of this prophecy, and blessed are those who hear it and *take to heart* [i.e., value] what is written in it, because the time is near" (Rev. 1:3, author's emphasis). Commitments.

Still other passages use the term "heart" to refer to proper priorities in living. "Whatever you do, *work at it with all your heart*, as working for the Lord, not for men" (Col. 3:23, author's emphasis). And another, "But if from there you seek the LORD your God, *you will find him if you look for him with all your heart* and with all your soul" (Deut. 4:29, author's emphasis). Or another, "There is, however, some good in you, for you have rid the land of the Asherah poles and have *set your heart on seeking God*" (2 Chron. 19:3, author's emphasis). Proper priorities.

If our learners are to grow in the Lord, we must help them personalize Bible truths. They must move from doctrine to lifestyle. For unless these learners *value* what Jesus said, they will never put His words into practice. We do not grow up into Christ (Eph. 4:15) without personal commitment to live according to God's Word. These kinds of learning outcomes result from affective learning.

What I Do

The third circle represents the behavioral, or action, side of life. We may have the greatest understanding of "love," but do we love? We may value missions, but do we support missions with our time, or talent, or money? We can believe "with all our hearts" in forgiveness, but do we forgive? What I do with my life, what I do in my life, is a window on who I am. Jesus said, "Watch out for false prophets. They come to

you in sheep's clothing, but inwardly they are ferocious wolves. *By their fruit you will recognize them*. Do people pick grapes from thornbushes, or figs from thistles? Likewise every good tree bears good fruit, but a bad tree bears bad fruit" (Matt. 7:15–17). "Make a tree good and its fruit will be good, or make a tree bad and its fruit will be bad, for a tree is recognized by its fruit" (Matt. 12:33). Jesus underscored the importance of *doing* this way:

> Therefore everyone who hears these words of mine and *puts them into practice* is like a wise man who built his house on the rock. The rain came down, the streams rose, and the winds blew and beat against that house; yet it did not fall, because it had its foundation on the rock.
>
> But everyone who hears these words of mine and *does not put them into practice* is like a foolish man who built his house on sand. The rain came down, the streams rose, and the winds blew and beat against that house, and it fell with a great crash (Matt. 7:24–27, author's emphasis).

The day I realized what Jesus was saying in this passage, I got down on my knees and asked His forgiveness for the many times I had "taught the Bible" but never given a hint to my learners how they might live out its precious truths. I was sending them out as fools, not the wise.

What is the work of the pastor-teacher? "To prepare God's people for works of service, so that the body of Christ may be built up" (Eph. 4:12). Preparing involves teaching people to think correctly (head). Preparing requires personal commitment to the task (heart). But the proof, the verification, the witness, the confirmation that true preparation has been made is in the service, in the ministry, in the doing of what God has called His people to do. Skillful execution of truths results from behavioral learning.

THE DISTORTION OF IMBALANCE

The problem, of course, is that we are called to prepare *people*. People do not come to us prepackaged and preequipped to serve. They do not come spin-balanced and ready to roll. Every person tends toward one of the three elements of the triad. Some emphasize the rational, others the emotional, and still others the behavioral. But imbalance in life, just as in wheels, causes vibration and eventual breakdown. Let's look at the consequences of imbalance.

Intellectualism

Learners who emphasize the rational over emotional or behavioral elements are thinkers. They like theologically sound hymns rather than foot-tappin' choruses. They prefer factual and conceptual questions over personal ones. They tend to like well-organized lectures more than group discussion—particularly if the group emphasizes people's feelings and personal experiences more than the Scripture. Their emphasis is more on meaning than relevance.

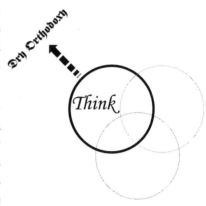

The problem with this emphasis is that it can result in a Bible study which is purely academic. The Word of God is relevant! Too much emphasis on meaning can degenerate into "meaning for meaning's sake." When we focus on the rational to the exclusion of the emotional and behavioral, we open ourselves to a dry, impersonal, abstract head-knowledge that makes little or no difference in our lives. Just consider the person who is unbiblical in his defense of the Bible! It is one thing to understand honesty, but quite another to be honest. One thing to understand the plan of salvation, quite another to be saved. One thing to understand Matthew 28:19–20, quite another to support and engage in missions. Bible knowledge, doctrinal understanding, Christian principles, and spiritual concepts will lead to spiritual pride unless we integrate them into our own lifestyles (1 Cor. 8:1–3).

Emotionalism

Learners who emphasize the emotional over rational or behavioral elements are feelers. They focus on feelings, attitudes, values, and personal experiences. They prefer free-wheeling discussions over structured lectures. They love to sing celebrative choruses and spiritual songs, repeating them enough so they no longer need to think about the words. Hymns—particularly hymns of deep theological significance—bore them.

They enjoy giving testimonies and hearing the testimonies of others. They aren't interested in explanations of terms or historical background; they're eager to move into personal application. Their emphasis is more on relevance than meaning.

The problem with this extreme is that it can result in a Bible study that is purely subjective. "The Bible means what it means *to me*. What does it matter what I believe so long as it feels right?" What feels right, however, may not *be* right. My self-centered speculations about what Jesus meant may not be what He meant. When we focus on the emotional to the exclusion of the behavioral and rational, we open ourselves to a groundless, personal perception of Scripture—warm fluff. This leads, eventually, to deception and delusion.

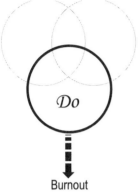

Do

Burnout

Learners who emphasize the behavioral over rational or emotional elements are doers. They prefer to be involved in activities and projects, mission programs, and organizations. They are not interested in analyzing the deep meanings of Scripture, and even less interested in sharing their feelings about it. They are utilitarian in their study—"What are we going to do with this? How can we use it?"

Burnout

The problem with this emphasis is that it can result in an approach to Bible study that leads to busyness, overwork, guilt and, eventually, exhaustion. The residue of this extreme are learners who will not pray, do not ask or answer questions, will not do assignments, refuse to accept any position of responsibility in the class or the church at large, and may well leave the church. Without understanding the *why* of doing, without personally valuing the doing, learners simply go through the motions until they burn out and give up.

So here is our dilemma as teachers and teacher-trainers: an effective teaching ministry requires thinking, but too much focus on thinking leads to a dry, cold, idealistic, intellectualism. An effective teaching ministry requires positive feelings toward the class, the content, and the teacher, but too much focus on feelings leads to mindless, sentimental, impractical fluff. An effective teaching ministry requires doing, but too much focus on doing leads to mindless, unfeeling ritual.

The Dilemma

The answer to this dilemma is to balance the rational, emotional, and behavioral elements of our own Christian growth as teachers as well as in our teaching. Develop biblical concepts, embrace

So What's the Answer?

Christian values, engage in spiritual activities. Proper understanding, through cognitive learning, provides the foundation for biblical values and ministry. Personally embracing biblical values, through affective learning, injects life into biblical exegesis and practice. Competent Christ-centered activities, through behavioral learning, build the bridge between Bible study (concepts and values) and the world of people in need.

THE TRIAD OF JESUS THE TEACHER

Jesus reflected this triad of rational, emotional, and behavioral elements in His own ministry. Jesus was a prophet (Matt. 13:57; Matt. 21:11; Luke 24:19; John 6:14), proclaiming the Kingdom of God. He used stories and illustrations to explain the Kingdom of Heaven. He represented God the Father to the people, and

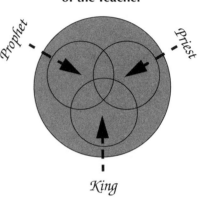

The External Influence of the Teacher

proclaimed the Word of God. As prophet, Jesus focused on the objective element of Kingdom living.

Jesus was a priest (Heb. 3:1; 4:14). He loved people and gave His own life for others. He healed their sicknesses and calmed their fears. He ministered to them. He moved among the people and lifted them to the Father. As priest, Jesus focused on the subjective element of Kingdom living.

Jesus was King (Mark 15:2; Luke 23:3; John 18:37; Acts 17:7). He chose twelve apprentices and trained them for action (Matt. 10). He sent His followers into the whole world to "make disciples of all nations, baptizing them . . . and teaching them to obey everything I have commanded you" (Matt. 28:19–20). He is our Leader, our Lord. He calls us to action (Matt. 5–7; John 17:20). He emphasized that our fruit (actions) exhibits our roots (concepts, values) (Matt. 7:16–17). Our spiritual wisdom is shown in how we *practice His words*—not by how well we understand them or value them (Matt. 7:24–27). As King, Jesus focused on the action element of Kingdom living.

Jesus demonstrated in His own teaching ministry, in His own life, the balance we raise as our standard. He is our Model, our Guide, and our Helper as we seek to emulate this balance in our own life and ministry.

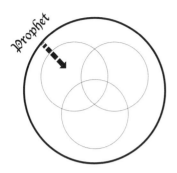

So how do we do this? How do we provide a learning environment that permits balanced growth in these three elements of life? How do we help learners think? Or feel? Or put into practice? Here are some practical suggestions.

A little boy sat in his Sunday School class listening to his teacher intently. She asked, "What is gray, has a furry tail, and stores nuts for the winter?" The little boy thought for a moment and then said, "Well, it sounds like a squirrel—but I'll say Jesus Christ." He was not being irreverent. He was doing his best to answer the teacher's question. And it seemed to him that "Jesus Christ" was the answer to most of her questions.

How can we help our learners to think clearly? We will do well if we focus on the meaning of concepts, ask questions, pose problems, and share examples. Let's look more closely at each of these.

Concepts vs. words. Take a moment and write down eight definitions of the word "run." (It will mean more to you if you really stop reading and do this exercise first). Here are some sentences which use various meanings of the word "run":

- Johnny runs (moves swiftly) to second base.

- Judy runs (manages) her business efficiently.

- Tim runs (operates) the printing press well.

- Susie has a run (defect) in her hose.

- Peter's team scored a run (score) in the second inning.

- Water always runs (flows) downhill.

- Members of Congress run (campaign) for office.

- Fido was kept in a nice dog run (an outdoor enclosure).

The word is singular: "run." The meanings are multiple: move swiftly, manage, operate, and so forth. These meanings reflect the concepts referenced by the word "run."

THE TEACHER'S TRIAD

Helping Learners Think: Cognitive Approach

Earlier in the chapter I asked you several questions about Jesus' statement: "Do not judge, or you too will be judged" (Matt. 7:1). Jesus was condemning the nagging, carping, censorious spirit of the Pharisees and religious leaders of His time. He was saying that when we live like this, we will be criticized by others. Citizens of the kingdom are to avoid the hypercritical, judgmental spirit of religious bigotry. It is not enough to say "Jesus said, 'Don't judge.'" Unless you explain what Jesus *meant* by "judge," you leave your learners to define the word out of their own imaginations. *Their* definition of "judge" may not agree with Jesus'.

Focus on Bible meanings, concepts, principles. Don't stop with knowing words. You may be reading your own definitions of these words into Scripture, and then reading out of Scripture your own ideas. This is *eis*egesis (reading into) rather than *ex*egesis (reading out of), and it is heresy!

Questions vs. answers. You help learners think by asking questions more than by giving prepackaged "pat" answers. When you hand out answers to your learners, they may hear little more than noise in the air because they haven't invested any brainpower in it. In one ear and out the other. Forgotten by Monday lunch. But when you ask a question, you drive learners into the Bible for answers. You confront them with a dilemma: they must process facts, develop concepts, relate those concepts to your question and formulate an answer. Along the way they may develop questions of their own—a sure sign that thinking is happening! How do they answer? Mold their responses into clear understanding. Help them discover God's answers to your questions. Ask more questions and give fewer "pat" answers.

Problems vs. reasons. You will help learners think more by posing problems than by giving reasons. Giving five reasons why Christians ought to forgive will do less to develop an understanding of "forgiveness" than confronting them with problems which can be solved by a forgiving spirit. "Here's a case study. Based on our study this morning, how would you handle it?" Listen to their answers. Correct misunderstandings. Suggest alternatives. Lead the class to see the relevance of "forgiveness" to a contemporary situation.

Examples vs. facts. Love is patient, kind; it does not envy, boast; it is not proud, rude, self-seeking, easily angered; it keeps no record of wrongs; does not delight in evil but rejoices with the truth (see 1 Cor. 13:4–6). These are facts. What do they *mean*? What is an example of "patient, kind." Illustrate "envy" and "boasting." Explain "proud, rude, self-seeking, and easily angered." How might I keep a "record of wrongs"? Why would anyone "delight in evil," and what is the "truth" that I am to rejoice with? Even with the modern New International Version translation, we must clearly explain the meanings of the biblical words. But even more so with the King James Version, which uses language unfamiliar to the 1990s layman: "Charity suffereth long, and is kind; charity envieth not; charity vaunteth not itself, is not puffed up, Doth not behave itself unseemly, seeketh not her own, is not easily provoked, thinketh no evil; Rejoiceth not in iniquity, but rejoiceth in the truth" (1 Cor. 13:4–5, KJV).

Whatever translation of Scripture we use, we must focus on correctly translating the words on the page so that the Word, the message, comes through clearly. Paul said it this way: "Do your best to present yourself to God as one approved, a workman who does not need to be ashamed and *who correctly handles the word of truth*" (2 Tim. 2:15, author's emphasis).

Concepts more than words. Questions more than pat religious answers. Problems more than reasons. Examples more than sterile facts. These distinctions will enable you to help learners *think*.

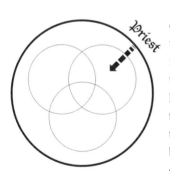

One day years ago I was having a cup of coffee with a pastor acquaintance, listening to him tell about his ministry with Children's Church. He told me of a ten-year-old boy who had come forward during the invitation to get some help. When they retired to a room for counseling, the boy began sharing his story. His parents were getting a divorce, he had no friends at school, his grades were bad—he just didn't know what to do. The pastor responded something like this, as I recall his story, "Son, I really don't care to hear about your problems. Do you know that you are a lost sinner? Do you know that if you die tonight without Jesus, you'll spend eternity in Hell?" The boy, according to the pastor, looked at him with ever-widening eyes. His mouth fell open, and tears ran down his cheeks. Then he stood and ran out of the church. "So I guess I put the fear of God in him!" was the pastor's conclusion.

Helping Learners Respond and Value: Humanistic Approach

I never think of that boy without praying that the Lord will send someone to share the love of Jesus with him. For you see, the pastor was doctrinally correct. But he had not one ounce of care, concern, or compassion for the heartfelt needs of this ten-year-old boy.

Do you remember "Joan" and her "Oh, somebody with the good kind of Bible read that verse for us." This is no way to create an atmosphere of openness, warmth, and trust in the class. So how *do* we create such a climate—a greenhouse for Christian values? We will make good progress toward emotional warmth in the classroom if we focus on sharing ourselves, sharing the experiences of class members, accepting them as they are (while helping them grow), using humor appropriately and building trust. Let's look at each of these more closely.

Personal Experiences vs. Wooden Stories. An effective way to begin a Bible study session is to tell a story related to the subject. Teaching materials provide good suggestions for doing this: "Joan is a single mother. . . ." and the like. Good, yes, but they may not be the best material for your class. Fictitious testimonies, contrived case studies, and artificial anecdotes may do little to warm up your class. They are wooden, stilted, forced—no matter how good they are—because they are not related to the life experiences of you or your class.

Far better are stories which flow out your own experience, or the experiences of class members. All of us have experiences of success and growth and victory in the Lord. As these experiences are shared, to the glory of God, the class is warmed by His presence and our praise of Him. Use the suggestions to direct your thoughts to living stories of the class—and use these as a way of leading the class to ready their hearts and minds for God's Word.

Earn the Right vs. Put on the Spot. Teachers do not have the right to call on learners to confess their sins in front of the group. This "group confession of sin" was a primary tactic in brainwashing our military prisoners of war in the Korean and Vietnamese conflicts. Christian teachers "prepare God's people for works of service, so that the body of Christ may be built up" (Eph. 4:12). It is not for us to tear down our learners through guilt, but to correctly handle God's Word (2 Tim. 2:15). The Holy Spirit convicts of sin (John 16:8), not teachers. And yet the natural tendency is to put learners on the spot. A seminary student of mine began his ten-minute MicroTeach exercise this way:

"Okay, how many of you haven't had a daily time of prayer and Bible study this week? (Pause.) Just lift your hands. (Uncomfortable pause.) Well, now I know that in a class this size there's someone who hasn't had a regular time of Bible study and prayer this week. (Tension building.) Remember, God is watching, and He knows who you are." (Angry pause.)

Finally, a young man in the back of the room bowed his head and slowly lifted his hand. The student teacher then proceeded to talk about quality quiet times. The student teacher had no right to do this. It humiliated this learner. It angered the class. It certainly killed any sense of openness toward the student teacher.

If the student had "earned the right" to ask that question by sharing his own struggles with having a daily quiet time, there would have been no problem. Look at the difference:

> "This past week I've not spent time in prayer and Bible study as I normally do. I mean, things have gotten so busy and hectic—and I've let them push my devotional time aside. Any of you struggling with this problem? (Several heads nod in agreement.) Let's see what we can discover that will help us give top priority to the Lord."

Such an approach increases openness. It warms the class because "we have a common struggle" and "we're working together" to find answers from God's Word. Share yourself before you ask others to share. Earn the right.

Acceptance vs. Judgment. We discussed Jesus' command "Judge not, lest ye be judged" earlier in the chapter. Jesus was condemning the carping, nagging, nit-picking, censorious spirit of the Pharisees. We need to pray through our own attitudes toward those we teach, or we will move in this same direction. "Oh, my people never want to pray." Or, "I can't get anyone in my class to answer a question." Or, "Projects? Are you kidding?! I can't get anyone to do anything in my class!"

Hmmmm. I wonder if these teachers tell their classes these things? The disciples failed in many ways, but Jesus forgave them, and loved them, and continued to teach them. Accept those you teach where they are. Then love them and teach them and allow them to grow in the Lord. Some will take longer than others. The commitment level of a few may never please us. But that is not our concern. Our concern is to be faithful in our loving ministry toward those we teach. If your focus is on acceptance rather than judgment, openness and warmth will grow in your class or church.

Humor vs. Solemnity. Paul was a great Christian philosopher. His writings are deep and often hard to understand. Even Peter had trouble understanding him sometimes! (See 2 Peter 3:16.) But for Paul, the evidence of Christ in our lives is not philosophical reasoning or theological expertise, it is the joy and gratitude we have from the in-dwelling Christ.

"Be *joyful in hope*, patient in affliction, faithful in prayer" (Rom. 12:12, author's emphasis).

"For the kingdom of God is not a matter of eating and drinking, but of righteousness, *peace and joy in the Holy Spirit*" (Rom. 14:17, author's emphasis).

"May the God of hope *fill you with all joy and peace* as you trust in him, so that you may overflow with hope by the power of the Holy Spirit" (Rom. 15:13, author's emphasis).

"Convinced of this, I know that I will remain, and I will continue with all of you for your progress and *joy in the faith*" (Phil. 1:25, author's emphasis).

"Being strengthened with all power according to his glorious might so that you may have great endurance and patience, and *joyfully giving thanks* to the Father, who has qualified you to share in the inheritance of the saints in the kingdom of light" (Col. 1:11–12, author's emphasis).

"Do not be anxious about anything, but in everything, by prayer and peti-tion, *with thanksgiving*, present your requests to God" (Phil. 4:6, author's em-phasis).

The Bible is a solemn book, with a solemn message. We must ap-proach Scripture and Scripture study with reverence. But this rever-ence differs from the stoic, stern, dispassionate logic of those false teachers which Paul wrote against in Colossians. Where the Spirit is free to produce fruit, there is joy (Gal. 5:22).

The super-serious has little warmth. The super-silly has little depth. But the proper use of humor can both warm up and settle down a class. Humor can enhance the openness of the class, not just to one another, but to God's Word as well. People who honestly laugh together can also honestly share together, or pray together, or weep together. (See Roman 12:15.) If you can use humor naturally, you will find an effective technique for building openness in the classroom.

One last word on humor. Be sure that the humor is positive and uplifting. Avoid crude or vulgar jokes, stories with double mean-ings, and even lighthearted pranks or gags. Humor is wrong when it denigrates others, or demeans the sacred task at hand. "Nor should there be obscenity, foolish talk or coarse joking, which are out of place, but rather thanksgiving" (Eph. 5:4).

Trust vs. Guilt. One last suggestion on improving the warmth of a class is this: avoid guilt and strengthen trust. Guilt is a strong motivator. Perhaps that is why so many immature leaders use it. It produces quick results but undermines the glue that holds human relationships together: trust.

B. F. Skinner conducted many experiments in which he taught rats to run mazes. In some cases he used a positive reinforcer: food. In others he used punishment: electric shock. He found that electric shock motivated the rats to learn the maze faster than food. But the shock also taught the rats to fear the maze. Eventually, rats would refuse to move, regardless of the degree of shock applied, even to the point of death. Guilt is like an electric shock to the personality. It produces quick results, but leads to fear of the cage, be it a Sunday school class, seminary class, or congregation. Such motivational techniques are toxic to learners.

Where do you find Jesus, the Lord of lords, teaching this way? "For God did not send his Son into the world to condemn the world, but to save the world through him" (John 3:17). Where do you find Paul, strong personality that he was, teaching this way? Paul counters his enemies in Corinth, who claimed Paul was strong in his letters but weak in person (2 Cor. 10:10), by saying "In fact, you even put up with anyone who enslaves you or exploits you or takes advantage of you or pushes himself forward or slaps you in the face. To my shame I admit that we were too weak for that!" (2 Cor. 11:20–21a).

Rather, Paul loved the church at Corinth, and grieved over their problems: "For I wrote you out of great distress and anguish of heart and with many tears, not to grieve you but to let you know the depth of my love for you" (2 Cor. 2:4). By his clear teaching, and his firm but loving exhortation, he led the church at Corinth away from her problems and into a more focused relationship to Christ.

Trust grows among people as they live and work and pray together, as they share needs together, as they forgive one another. Paul underscored this social element of the Christian faith this way:

> But now you must rid yourselves of all such things as these: anger [fury toward another], rage [settled hatred toward another], malice [wishing harm on another], slander [demeaning another's character], and filthy language [abusive talk] from your lips. . . .
>
> [But] . . . clothe yourselves with compassion [soft-heartedness toward others], kindness [kind actions toward others], humility [right thinking toward others], gentleness [tenderness toward others] and patience [long-suffering with others].
>
> Bear with each other [put up with each other] and forgive whatever grievances you may have against one another. Forgive as the Lord forgave you. And over all these virtues put on love [*agape*: caring for others in need], which

binds them all together in perfect unity.

Let the peace of Christ rule in your hearts, since as members of one body you were called to peace. And be thankful. Let the word of Christ dwell in you richly as you teach and admonish one another with all wisdom, and as you sing psalms, hymns and spiritual songs with gratitude in your hearts to God.

And whatever you do, whether in word or deed, do it all in the name of the Lord Jesus, giving thanks to God the Father through him" (Col. 3:8–17). *[Note: the words in brackets are mine. RY.]*

If we were to take Paul's words as marching orders for our classrooms, we would find a great increase in the trust level among its members. Experiences more than wooden case studies, earning the right, accepting more than judging, humor more than supersolemnity, trust more than guilt: These distinctives will help you create a climate for the growth of Christian values.

Helping Learners Do: Behavioral Approach

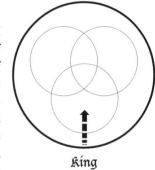

ᚴíng

Years ago as I've mentioned, I taught a Sunday school class for deaf college students. One day I met one of the members of my class on campus and, after a few minutes of conversations, asked him what discoveries he'd made during our study the previous Sunday. "Ohhh," he said, "that was a long time ago." Yes, I agreed. This is Wednesday and our study was Sunday, but what did he get out of the study? "Well, ummmm, we were studying the Old Testament, right?" Well, no, actually, we studied a passage out of Ephesians. "Ephesians! That's right! I remember now!" So what did he discover? What did he learn? "Ohhhh, well, I don't remember. That was a long time ago!" I had spent five or six hours preparing to teach. I had given the presentation all I had. Now, on Wednesday, he couldn't remember the first thing about what we'd studied. What a discouragement! How could he possibly *act* on what we had studied if he couldn't *remember* what we had studied?

How can we help our learners put what they learn into practice? Let me suggest two general ways and then focus on a third specific way to do this. The first general way is to *engage learners in thinking* through concepts and implications of Scriptural truth. We discussed this under "Helping Learners Think." Learners cannot transfer truths from classroom to life unless they clearly understand those truths. Solving real-life problems in class, based on the Scripture study, is an excellent way to build bridges into the daily lives of learners.

The second general way to lead learners to put truth into practice is to *lead them to value Scriptural truths and their implications*. We discussed this under "Helping People Feel, Respond, and Value." When learners see for themselves the value of biblical truth, they are far more likely to use it in facing situations in their own lives.

The third, and most specific, way to encourage learners to put biblical truths into practice is by way of *assignments*. These assignments can vary in their intensity and scope: selected verses to read, specific questions to answer, projects to do, journals to keep, words to analyze, and the list goes on. By making an assignment to be done outside of class, you prompt learners to think of Sunday school (and the content of the study) during the week. You share part of the teaching responsibility with learners as they share the results of their study the following Sunday. Assignments can be done individually, or in pairs, or in groups of various kinds. By focusing learners on things to be done during the week, you open learners to be taught by the Lord, on their own.

When you make assignments in class, be sure to *use* them in class next time. Provide time for learners to share what they did and what the Lord taught them. Do not chastise learners who forget the assignment—this is toxic teaching, remember? Simply focus on the results of the learners who remembered. Let them shine by sharing what they learned during the week. This will encourage learners to do the assignments in the future. Consistent bridge building between Sunday school class and the "real-life" of learners pays rich dividends for Christian growth!

The Center of the Triad

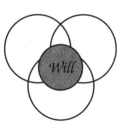

The Christian teacher provides an environment for healthy, balanced growth by emphasizing thinking, valuing, and doing activities and by setting the example as a thinking, committed, doer of the Word. But there is another element of Christian growth that far outweighs all that we've discussed up to this point. You'll notice in the diagram at left that the three circles overlap in the center of the triad as indicated by the gray circle. Let's consider this area as the will, the ego, the "I" of the personality. Those without Christ determine the course of life for themselves:

what *I* think, what *I* value, what *I* choose to do. This I-centered view is a philosophy called existentialism, and it has been a central force, as we saw in the last chapter, in American thinking for three decades now. Existentialist's view any outside authority—parent, teacher, government, church, Bible—that attempts to bend me to its views impinges upon my personhood and makes me less human. They believe that I must define myself by making choices. Paul writes, "The man without the Spirit ["the natural man", KJV] does not accept the things that come from the Spirit of God, for they are foolishness to him, and he cannot understand them, because they are spiritually discerned" (1 Cor. 2:14).

When we accept Jesus Christ as our Lord and Savior, He takes up residence within us (Col. 1:27). The struggle of spiritual growth centers on who will be in charge. If *I* continue to reign, determining what *I* think, what *I* value, and what *I* do, there will be little perceptible difference between my way of life and that of one who isn't saved. Paul suffered this battle and described it this way:

> I know that nothing good lives in me, that is, in my sinful nature. For I have the desire to do what is good, but I cannot carry it out. For what I do is not the good I want to do; no, the evil I do not want to do—this I keep on doing. Now if I do what I do not want to do, it is no longer I who do it, but it is sin living in me that does it. So I find this law at work: When I want to do good, evil is right there with me. For in my inner being I delight in God's law; but I see another law at work in the members of my body, waging war against the law of my mind and making me a prisoner of the law of sin at work within my members. What a wretched man I am! Who will rescue me from this body of death? Thanks be to God—through Jesus Christ our Lord! So then, I myself in my mind am a slave to God's law, but in the sinful nature a slave to the law of sin. Therefore, there is now no condemnation for those who are in Christ Jesus, because through Christ Jesus the law of the Spirit of life set me free from the law of sin and death (Rom. 7:18–8:2).

Who will be on the throne in my life? Do I call the shots, or do I humble myself under the gracious hand of the Lord? Spiritual growth comes as I learn to surrender my life to Him. Jesus said, "If anyone would come after me, he must deny himself and take up his cross daily and follow me" (Luke 9:23). Deny self. This is anathema to existentialists. It is the destruction of all they hold most sacred: the exalted free choice of an individual to do as he or she judges right. Not much has changed. Three thousand years ago, the writer of Judges noted, "In those days Israel had no king; everyone did as he saw fit" (Judg. 17:6). One need only read today's newspaper to learn the result of everyone doing as they "see fit." Rampant divorce, child abuse, rape, murder, gang violence, suicide, drugs, pornography, and so on *ad nauseam.*

As we give over the control of our lives to the Spirit of Christ, He gives us power to become all we were created to be. Spiritual growth is learning how to let Jesus be Lord, not just in my theology, but in my life. Paul said it this way: "I have been crucified with Christ and I no longer live, but Christ lives in me. The life I live in the body, I live by faith in the Son of God, who loved me and gave himself for me" (Gal. 2:20). The most important thing we can do to help our learners grow in the Lord is to teach them to depend on Him. Let's see how.

CHRIST, THE CENTER OF THE TRIAD

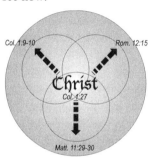

As we have seen, the key to spiritual growth is surrender. Jesus is the Way. Jesus is the Truth. He is the Life (John 14:6). But He does not force His way into our lives, nor does He dominate us. "I stand at the door and knock. If anyone hears my voice and opens the door, I will come in and eat with him, and he with me" (Rev. 3:20). He gives us the freedom to invite Him in or lock Him out. As we invite Him to lead us, to teach us, to mold us into what He desires, He helps us think and feel and do according to His will.

Christ-ian Thinking

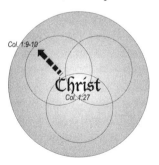

Paul spent three years in Ephesus (Acts 19) preaching and teaching. One of his converts was Epaphras, a prominent man from Colossae, a city in the Lycus Valley, about a hundred miles to the east. Epaphras returned home and ministered to the church there (Col. 1:7). Later, after Paul was imprisoned in Rome, Epaphras visited him and shared a growing concern: Greek ideas of "mystery," and secret "knowledge" and special "wisdom" were undermining the faith of the Colossians in Christ. In his letter to them, he uses these very terms to refocus their minds on the Lord:

> For this reason, since the day we heard about you, we have not stopped praying for you and asking God to fill you with the *knowledge* of his will

through all spiritual *wisdom* and *understanding*. And we pray this in order that you may live a life worthy of the Lord and may please him in every way: bearing fruit in every good work, growing in the knowledge of God, being strengthened with all power according to his glorious might so that you may have great endurance and patience, and joyfully giving thanks to the Father, who has qualified you to share in the inheritance of the saints in the kingdom of light (Col. 1:9–12, author's emphasis).

The knowledge Paul prays for the Colossians is not secretive, special head knowledge (*gnosis*), which puffs us up with pride (1 Cor. 8:1), but an intimate heart knowledge (*epignosis*) of the Lord's will which comes through our relationship with Him. As we walk with the Lord, He teaches us what His will is. Not only do we grasp the Lord's will, but His will grasps us—gets a hold on us. This is part of the meaning of *epignosis*. In the context of Bible study, Jesus teaches us what the Bible *says*. Not what society says, nor parents, nor friends, nor our own reasoning. But what God says to us through Scripture.

Further, the Lord helps us understand what Scripture *means*. If I rush to interpret Scripture on the basis of my definitions, rather than learn the writer's definitions, I may read my own thinking into Scripture rather than read God's out of it. As I walk with the Lord day by day, He leads me into a proper understanding of Scripture, just as He did with the disciples on the road to Emmaus (Luke 24:13, 32).

Further, the Lord helps us *put His teachings into practice*. We've already noted that Jesus declares this as wisdom (we'll talk more about this under "Christ-ian Doing" below).

From knowing to understanding to doing. Doing begets broader knowledge, which begets deeper understanding, which begets more effective doing. All of this under the direction of the Lord Who lives within and teaches us. This cycle of knowing, understanding, and doing results in a change of thinking. I think less like my culture, my background, and my upbringing—and begin to think more like the Lord Himself. "*Do not conform* any longer to the pattern of this world, but be *transformed by the renewing of your mind*. Then you will be able to test and approve what God's will is—his good, pleasing and perfect will" (Rom.12:2, author's emphasis). How do our learners renew their minds? By knowing what the Bible says, understanding what the Bible means, and putting it into practice—as Jesus leads.

Christ-ian Feeling

The affective component of the personality is so important in spiritual growth because so much revolves around openness, values,

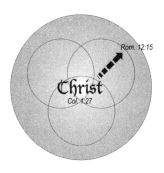

priorities, and commitments. And yet, many Christians have emotional problems and value defects just like unbelievers: hatred, anger, instability, harshness, insecurity, bitterness, selfishness, and the like. Scripture underscores the importance of progression in removing the negative and growing the positive. Love, not hate. Forgiveness, not anger. Steadfastness, not instability. Gentleness, not harshness. Courage, not insecurity. Sweetness, not bitterness. Generosity, not selfishness. Paul underscored this to the Romans. Watch for the focus on priorities and values, and compare them to the "natural behavior" of people.

> Be joyful in hope, patient in affliction, faithful in prayer. Share with God's people who are in need. Practice hospitality. Bless those who persecute you; bless and do not curse. *Rejoice with those who rejoice; mourn with those who mourn.* Live in harmony with one another. Do not be proud, but be willing to associate with people of low position. Do not be conceited. Do not repay anyone evil for evil. Be careful to do what is right in the eyes of everybody. If it is possible, as far as it depends on you, live at peace with everyone. Do not take revenge, my friends, but leave room for God's wrath, for it is written: "It is mine to avenge; I will repay," says the Lord. On the contrary: "If your enemy is hungry, feed him; if he is thirsty, give him something to drink. In doing this, you will heap burning coals on his head." Do not be overcome by evil, but overcome evil with good (Rom. 12:12–21, author's emphasis).

As we walk with the Lord, He teaches us within each day's struggle how to put off the negative and put on the positive. He shows us that seeking His values produces positive results, not only in our own lives, but in the lives of those around us. His priorities, not mine. His values, not my society's.

Christ-ian Doing

Much of what we've discussed regarding thinking and feeling, understanding and valuing, flows into doing. We've discussed "doing" all along. It is difficult to understand Scripture, yet fail to act on it. Likewise, it is difficult to be committed to scriptural values, yet not to live them. This is part of the natural balance of Christian growth. Therefore, as I grow in understanding of and commitment to the Lord, my actions also change. Old habits die; new habits grow.

How do we refine those habits? How do we learn the skills of spiritual living? We are saying that Jesus lives within, and He teaches us. Here is His own illustration of the process: "Take my yoke upon you and learn from me, for I am gentle and humble in heart, and you will find rest for your souls. For my yoke is easy and my burden is light" (Matt. 11:29–30).

First, let's define terms. "Take" denotes a voluntary action. I can take the yoke or I can leave the yoke. "Yoke" refers to a wooden bar which tied two oxen together. Two oxen can pull a load more easily than one, and the yoke ties them together. "My" refers to whose yoke it is. The yoke Jesus is calling us to accept is His yoke. Not my parents' nor my pastor's nor my friends'. The yoke of the Lord is my ministry—what does the Lord want me to do? All believers are gifted (Eph 4:7) in order to help strengthen the church (Eph. 4:12). Where should I serve? What should I do? "Take my yoke," Jesus says.

What kind of yoke is it? That's all church people talk about—work, work, work. Why should I give up what I want in order to do what the Lord wants? Because His yoke is the place where we find real refreshment ("rest"). Remember when Jesus was talking to the woman at the well? The disciples had gone to town for food. When they returned, they urged Him to eat. He said, "I have food to eat that you know nothing about" (John 4:32). Had He gotten food somewhere else? No, Jesus' food was "to do the will of him who sent me and to finish his work" (John 4:34). In the same way, when we take on Jesus' yoke, it isn't "church work"—it's His work. And that makes all the difference in the world. Why? *Because Jesus Himself pulls in the yoke with us*. He says, "Learn from me." He teaches us how to pull. Just as a young unbroken colt is hitched to a seasoned plow horse to teach the colt how to pull, so we hitch ourselves to the Lord and learn how to minister from Him.

Is His yoke harsh and cutting like the yoke of the law? Does it irritate and chafe? No, His yoke is "easy," comfortable, and His burden is "light," easy to be carried. Jesus the carpenter had carved yokes for oxen and had custom fit the wooden beams to the shoulders of the animals. In the same way He custom fits our ministry to who we are. When we are in His will, when we are pulling with Him, when we are doing at His direction, there will be no burnout. For in His yoke, there is rest.

My first lesson in ministry yokes came with the call into deaf ministry. The Lord helped me learn sign language and understand deaf culture. I had no one in my family or background who was deaf, but He gave me a heart for deaf people. Through my years of working with deaf people, Jesus taught me things about teaching, and listening, and communicating that permeate my efforts at Southwestern today. *Now* my yoke is the seminary classroom. I sense it every time I step into the room; it is confirmed every time I leave. To teach, equip, shape, challenge, mold, and learn from young ministers is an indescribable joy. The Lord's yoke leads to fulfillment and joy.

As Christ grows in our lives, the center of the triad expands. Notice how the circles overlap much more, reflecting a more balanced approach to learning. This integration of learning—thinking, valuing, and doing—is not limited to spiritual things. Secular theories have moved a long way toward integration of the three learning systems in the past ten years. Increasingly, secular theories present a synergistic approach to learning.

A Dynamic Synergism

The triad represents a dynamic synergism of the three learning systems. It is "dynamic" in that the three components individually push us toward the imbalances of cold intellectualism, warm fluff, and burnout. The triad represents the struggle to maintain balance among thinking, valuing, and doing. It is a "synergism" in that all three *together* do far more than any one system alone. Bandura's social learning theory is a behavioral theory which integrates cognitive elements. Information Processing Theory is a cognitive theory that blends behavioral elements. The recent emphasis on self-regulation in behavioral theory (self-reinforcement) and cognitive theory (personal goal setting) integrates humanistic elements in both systems. Even in the world of educational psychology—a scientific discipline which strives to separate and analyze—theorists are recognizing the need for an integration of all three systems of learning theory. The prophet-priest-leader triad which reflects effective teaching in a Christian context appears to be the direction educational psychology has taken in the last ten years—though secular theorists would certainly use different words to describe it.

IN SUMMARY. . .

The goal of Christian teaching is Christlikeness in our learners—regardless of the subject matter. The teacher helps by balancing thinking, feeling, and doing components in the classroom, and leading learners to depend on the Lord day by day. We, of course, cannot produce Christlikeness. Only the Lord can teach us how to live as He does. But we are instruments in the Master's hand. We can cooperate with Him in the process and succeed. Or we can do things our own way and fail.

In the end, those who honor Jesus as Teacher and Lord, who teach as He teaches them, who loves as He loves them, will be the teachers who influence others toward Christlikeness. May God richly bless you as you spend your life pursuing this wondrous task.

Only let us live up to what we have already attained (Phil. 3:16).

CHAPTER CONCEPTS

Acceptance vs. judgment	Exegesis
Assignments	Experiences vs. stories
Balance	Feeling
Burnout	Humor vs. solemnity
Concepts vs. words	Intellectualism
Doing	King (leader)
Dynamic synergism	Priest
Earn the right	Problems vs. reasons
Ebenezer	Prophet
Eisegesis	Questions vs. answers
Emotionalism	The triad
Epignosis	Thinking
Examples vs. facts	Trust vs. guilt

DISCUSSION QUESTIONS

1. Read the following statements and determine whether they reflect **B**ehavioral, **C**ognitive, or **H**umanistic principles of teaching. Place the appropriate letter (B, C, or H) on each line:

_____ 1. *Teach learning strategies.* Instruct your students in how to study, how to take notes, how to organize, and how to remember what they need to know. Don't assume they know how to study, nor leave them to their own devices.

_____ 2. *Encourage openness.* Develop a relaxed, open class atmosphere. Avoid negative tones and moralizing, as this hinders learner participation. Focus on the positive.

_____ 3. *Provide factual foundation.* Provide an adequate foundation of terminology, concepts, and examples to support the main focus of learning: the discovery of meaning.

_____ 4. *Clarify learning task.* Use objectives, tests, outlines, or other advance organizers to provide clear direction for the student. Know where you're going, and share it with your learners.

_____ 5. *Correct responses.* Avoid erroneous teaching ("sharing of ignorance"). Explain, then question. Teach, then test.

_____ 6. *Call on volunteers.* Let those who wish to share positive experiences do so. Do not call on learners to confess failures publicly.

_____ 7. *Gain and retain attention.* Work to gain and retain the attention of your students. Vary the level of intensity in the class through the use of mands (verbal emphasis), visual aids, and personal enthusiasm. Create surprise by using a variety of learning activities.

_____ 8. *Discussion of concepts.* Provide time in class for large-group or small-group discussion of key ideas and principles.

_____ 9. *Permit deviation from the routine.* Avoid "the same old thing" every class. Add some spontaneity to the class process. Allow learners to ask questions, make comments, share experiences, and even "chase rabbits" within reason.

_____ 10. *Elaborative rehearsal.* Help learners relate new material to what they've already learned. Conversely, don't make each class hour separate and distinct from the next. Help learners bridge from the known to the unknown. Elaboration strategies include paraphrasing, creating analogies, answering questions, and describing how new material relates to existing knowledge.

_____ 11. *Simplicity.* Take small steps. Move from simple to complex. Move from concrete (experienced truths) to abstract. Teach in a logical sequence.

_____ 12. *Model the role.* How you live speaks louder than what you say. Be an "example to the flock" (1 Pet. 5:3).

_____ 13. *Chunking.* Divide material to be learned into meaningful chunks. Either present material "prechunked" or encourage (older) learners to "chunk" for themselves.

_____ 14. *Practice.* Use active, rather than passive, recall. Distribute drills throughout session to reduce boredom. Teaching is more than telling and learning is more than listening.

_____ 15. *Contrast.* Help learners more clearly define concepts and principles by comparing and contrasting terms. ("Must I *like* the people Jesus commanded me to *love*?")

_____ 16. *Structure.* Help learners discover the structure of the course material and major and minor points. Focus on the meaning of the material more than discrete bits of information.

_____ 17. *Use small groups.* Subgroups within the class provide for greater participation and volunteering, because they are less intimidating.

_____ 18. *Delayed feedback.* Help learners evaluate their performance. Ask questions. Pose problems. Give short self-graded quizzes. Make specific comments on written work.

_____ 19. *Organize material.* Clearly present what you expect your students to learn. Use advance organizers, outlines, pretests, or key words to structure the material to be learned.

_____ 20. *Build relationships.* React positively to positive responses. React in a neutral manner to negative responses. Avoid criticizing or embarrassing learners. Don't "lose the war" over a single battle. Use natural humor to relieve tension.

_____ 21. *Reward.* Provide tangible rewards for good performance and good effort. Personal rewards (smiles, hugs, pats on the back) are more enduring than stars or candy.

_____ 22. *Guessing and mistakes.* Allow learners to make guesses and risk answering with incomplete information. Then allow the class to evaluate their responses. Provide explanations and allow the class to critique your views.

_____ 23. *Provoke thinking.* Your task is to help students think creatively: to comprehend, illustrate, devise, examine, sift, condense, summarize, synthesize, evaluate, compare and contrast, integrate. Your task is to help change your learner's mental structure to better reflect life as it really is.

_____ 24. *Worthy learners.* Treat each learner as a person of worth, as a worthwhile individual. Love (for students) covers a multitude of sins (in teaching). The learner is more than a computer to be programmed. Encourage learners to probe their own personal experiences with the topic under consideration.

_____ 25. *Empathize.* Your task is to empathize with your students. Be open and sincere with them, particularly when they ask questions or express confusion and frustration. Handle learner comments with care and respect. Strive to see the learning situation from the *learners'* point of view.

_____ 26. *Sequence material.* Properly sequence course material for optimum learning. Set goals, order learning experiences, provide feedback, test, motivate, and reward successful accomplishments.

2. Draw the Christian Teachers' Triad from memory. Include the following elements: Christ, priest, thinking, warm fluff, prophet, doing, feeling, intellectualism, burnout, king (leader), Col. 1:27, Col. 1:9–10, Rom. 12:15, and Matt. 11:29–30.

3. Which of the three circles of the triad best reflects your preferred teaching/learning style? Which of the three circles least reflects your preferred teaching/learning style? List three things you will do to strengthen your weakest area. Before the next class session, share these answers with at least two other classmates.

UNIT 4

The Teacher as Motivator

Unit 3 presented key principles from learning theory systems which govern the learning of facts, concepts, attitudes, and skills. Learning theories help teachers understand *how* students learn. But what can we do to arouse interest or make the attainment of educational goals attractive? What effect do grading structures have on learning? What effect do teacher personality factors have on classroom climate? How do teacher behaviors influence the atmosphere in the classroom? How do evaluation practices help or hinder learning? These kinds of questions focus on *why* students learn. In Unit 4 we present an introduction to motivation and answer each of these key questions in four chapters.

Chapter 12
Motivation Defined
    Motivation as Direct Reinforcement
    Motivation as Providing Desirable Models
    Motivation as Creating Curiosity
    Motivation as Enhancing Meaningfulness
    Motivation as Meeting Needs
    Motivation as Providing Successful Experiences

Chapter 13
The Teacher and Classroom Climate
    Teacher Personality and Classroom Climate
    Teacher Behaviors and Classroom Climate
    Competitive and Cooperative Learning

Chapter 14
The Teacher as Evaluator
    Teacher Evaluation: Testing
    Using Peer Evaluation
    Using Self-Evaluation

Chapter

12

MOTIVATION DEFINED

Learning theory focuses on behaviors, attitudes, and concepts. Motivation focuses on the *energy, vitality,* and *intensity* of learning. Why do some students desire to learn while others do not? Why are some students persistent in their efforts while others quickly give up? Why do some students attribute their success to effort while others attribute it to luck? If our desire is to help students achieve certain learning goals, how do we energize them so that they can succeed? This chapter defines motivation as applying direct reinforcement (traditional behaviorism), providing appropriate models (social learning theory), creating curiosity (cognitive theories), enhancing meaningfulness (information processing theory), promoting personal growth (humanistic theories), and encouraging achievement through successful experiences (aspiration and achievement theories).

CHAPTER RATIONALE

Learners will demonstrate understanding of motivation by

- explaining motivation in the classroom according to the three systems of learning theory;
- explaining motivation according to achievement and attribution theories.

Learners will demonstrate appreciation for proper motivation principles by sharing personal classroom experiences related to behavioral motivation, cognitive motivation, humanistic motivation, achievement motivation, and attribution theory.

CHAPTER OBJECTIVES

INTRODUCTION

Consider the following teaching situations. What factors in these situations affect the motivation level of the students?

Situation One

Students are required to take an introductory course in mathematics as part of their degree plan. Most of the students dislike math and some admit to an outright fear of the course.

Situation Two

You teach a class entitled "The Teaching Ministry of the Church." The aim of the class is to prepare ministers of education and Christian education directors for the practical problems they will face when they are called to their first church. Since most of them haven't experienced local church ministry, they really do not understand the problems they'll face. Your challenge is to make the answers you are giving credible and "real world."

Situation Three

A "Church History" course requires a hundred pages of difficult reading a week and the lectures "augment," rather than explain, what students read. They are falling farther behind and becoming frustrated.

Situation Four

A median adult class gathers to study the story of the Good Samaritan. As you enter the classroom you overhear one of the members sarcastically remark, "Oh boy, the Good Samaritan story again. I can't wait!" Several folks laugh in agreement.

Situation Five

You are teaching a class in introductory Hebrew. Most of your students have no background in the language. The curious alphabet, the unfamiliar grammar, even reading from right to left have students nervous.

Each of these situations calls for a different approach to motivation. What would you do to create a positive climate for learning in them? Take a few moments and jot down your thoughts before moving into the chapter.

WHAT IS
MOTIVATION?

Motivation is a "hypothetical construct used to explain the initiation, direction, intensity, and persistence of goal-directed behavior."[1] It is a "force that energizes and directs behavior toward a goal."[2] It is a "directive, sustaining quality that energizes and maintains learning activities."[3] In short, motivation focuses on the *intention* to learn.[4] Research has shown that proper motivation for learning results not only in better achievement, but also in better student attitudes and fewer classroom problems.[5]

*General and
Specific Motivation*

Motivation can be general or specific. *General motivation* toward learning is an enduring and broad disposition to master a variety of learning situations. It is closely related to the "industry" trait in

Erikson's "Industry/Inferiority" stage of personality development. General motivation is stable over time and situation. It resides in the learner rather than the teacher or class.

Specific motivation, however, energizes a student toward a particular class or topic. It is more unstable, changing from class to class and topic to topic. It resides primarily in the teacher and the particular content to be learned.[6]

Motivation can be extrinsic or intrinsic. *Extrinsic motivation* is impersonal and is based on rewards that originate from outside the learner.[7] Students achieve in order to win parents' approval, or to gain the praise of their teacher, or to earn high grades.[8] Under an extrinsic system of motivation, learners are passive players. They engage in appropriate behavior only when offered attractive incentives or to avoid aversive consequences.[9] Excessive use of extrinsic motivation can make learners dependent on the rewards. When the rewards stop, so does the behavior.[10]

Extrinsic and Intrinsic Motivation

Intrinsic motivation is based on the personal satisfaction derived from achieving learning goals. Students achieve because of their own personal desire to learn. They enjoy the subject, or they are personally interested in mastering it.[11] *Intrinsic motivation* depends on the learner being an active player in the learning process. Such students engage in appropriate behavior because they want to grow, and learn, and master their subjects.[12]

"Motivation focuses on the *intention* to learn"

Both are important. Extrinsic motivation may be required to get students started in a new subject and initially to direct them down the right path.[13] Students who do not enjoy learning for learning's sake, who are not interested in a given subject, or are disadvantaged in some tangible way may need the motivational boost of external rewards to initiate their learning. If successfully tied to the quality of students' performances, these rewards can actually raise the level of their intrinsic motivation.[14]

Learning is complex—and *motivating* students to learn is complex as well. In summary, we will present motivation as a matter of reinforcing desired behavior (traditional behaviorism), providing appropriate models for behavior (social learning theory), creating a sense of curiosity (cognitive learning theory), making material meaningful (information processing theory), meeting personal needs (humanism), and encouraging achievement through successful experiences (aspiration and achievement theories).

MOTIVATION
AS DIRECT
REINFORCEMENT
(Traditional Behaviorism)

You will recall from chapter 7 that behaviorism is concerned with how the consequences of behavior regulate and control future actions.[15] Behaviorists are most interested in discovering the cues that elicit desired behaviors as well as the reinforcers that sustain them.[16] Behavioristic motivation is extrinsic and majors on rewards which learners can earn through proper behavior. Rewards include things such as teacher praise, "happy faces," high test scores, and so forth.[17] The consequences of past behaviors, called the learner's "reinforcement history,"[18] produces the present level of motivation.[19]

Behavior Modification

The motivational theory which developed out of behaviorism is called *behavior modification*. Teachers select appropriate reinforcers for each student and then tie those reinforcers to desired behaviors. An appropriate reinforcer is an activity that a particular student enjoys doing: reading a book, working on a computer, or talking quietly with a friend. When students successfully complete required assignments, they are rewarded by being allowed to spend time in their preferred activities.[20] Selectively using reinforcement strategies to move students toward particular goals is called *shaping*. One particular system which uses reinforcers to shape behavior is called a *token economy*. Tokens or tickets are given to students for specific behaviors. These tokens are saved and exchanged for desired activities or items.[21]

*The Decline of Direct
Reinforcement*

Direct reinforcement strategies were most popular in the 1960s. Educational theory and practice have moved away from excessive use of behavior modification strategies for several reasons. First, direct reinforcement decreased intrinsic motivation in students.[22] If a student is interested in a particular subject, providing rewards in that subject actually decreases interest. Students who were given rewards for correct solutions to problems chose less difficult problems than students who received no rewards at all. Worse yet, giving rewards simply for completing an assignment, rather than meeting some standard of performance, resulted in decreased motivation.[23]

**"Interested in a
subject? Providing
rewards decreases
the level of interest"**

Second, educators found that direct reinforcement narrowed student focus in the learning process. Interesting class discussions were short-circuited by the simple question, "Will this be on the test?" Rewards gained through "passing a test" became more important than learning.[24] Other types of motivation were sought to broaden the learning spectrum.

Third, the logistical problems associated with selecting, using, and tracking reinforcers for each student became an administrative burden. Token economies were developed to help ease the burden, but eventually the system was discarded as too tedious and time consuming.[25]

Fourth, and most important, direct reinforcement ignored important aspects of learning. These were the perceptions and beliefs of students.[26] The rise of Bruner's discovery learning and Information Processing Theory moved educators away from behavior modification systems of motivation.

Suggestions for Using Behavioral Principles

Direct reinforcement is effective in motivating behavior in disadvantaged learners as well as in students who are not intrinsically interested in the subject at hand. By clearly explaining course requirements and expectations you set up specific targets for students to hit. Using frequent, consistent, specific, and immediate reinforcement will direct students toward achieving course skills.[27] Praising student achievements appropriately increases their level of effort.[28] Encouraging student efforts for completing course tasks increases their expectation of success.[29] By engaging student attention on specific course tasks and providing successful class experiences through the semester, not only will many of your students master the required skills, but they will also develop positive feelings about you, the subject, and themselves.

Teacher Praise

Research has demonstrated that the most effective reinforcer is teacher praise. Praise is more than objective feedback on performance. It also provides information on the student's personal worth. This last element is a powerful motivator.[30]

"Praise should be more than warm and fuzzy positive reactions"

Yet praising students effectively is a complex skill. Praise should be contingent on specific tasks[31] because random or indiscriminant praise is ineffective.[32] Praise should be given in moderation because too little is ineffective and too much is meaningless.[33] Praise should be perceived as credible, believable, and sincere. Praise should provide informative feedback and not simply be warm and fuzzy positive reactions.[34] Praise should focus on student performances and not teacher perceptions.[35] Praise should be given for student performance and not mere participation.[36] Praise should be individual— that is, not given to everyone all the time.[37] Use prior performances as a benchmark for a student's improvement rather than the performance of peers.[38]

Let's review Situation 1 as stated at the beginning of the chapter: Students are required to take an introductory course in mathematics as part of their degree plan. Most of the students dislike math and some admit an outright fear of the course. The course is required. Students are enrolled because someone outside themselves has determined the course is "good for them." In addition, most of the students dislike math as a subject. Some are afraid of the course because of previous bad experiences in math classes. How would direct reinforcement be effective in motivating students to master the course content?

Complex reinforcement schedules popularized in the 1960s have given way to other approaches to motivation. Teacher praise, however, remains a powerful reinforcer.

MOTIVATION AS PROVIDING APPROPRIATE MODELS
(Albert Bandura's Social Learning Theory)

In more recent years, behaviorists have found direct reinforcement to be too limited an explanation for learning.[39] While behavioral purists have held on to traditional behaviorism, most have integrated cognitive processes[40] that cannot be directly observed—expectations, thoughts, beliefs.[41]

As we saw in chapter 7, Bandura used the term *reinforcement* for his fourth stage of learning, but his definition was broader than Skinner's. He included *direct reinforcement*. An observer watches a model, performs the action, and is reinforced or punished for the action.[42] A second type of reinforcement—the key to observational learning—is called *vicarious reinforcement*.[43] An observer watches a model behave in a certain way, and further observes how the model is reinforced or punished for that behavior.[44] If the model is reinforced, the observer tends to imitate the behavior. If the model is punished, the observer tends to avoid that behavior. Vicarious reinforcement allows us to learn from how others are affected.[45] A great deal of classroom reinforcement is vicarious.[46] Praising one student for his or her good question encourages all to ask good questions.[47] A third type of reinforcement is *self-reinforcement*. Learners can set personal performance standards[48] and control their own reinforcers.[49] The fact that young people tend to dress alike illustrates the point. The similarity of dress reflects a sense of belonging, which is self-reinforcing.[50] Learners are capable of observing their own behavior, judging it against their own standards, and reinforcing or punishing themselves for it.[51]

In general, then, students are motivated to achieve when they are presented models who demonstrate mastery of desired skills.[52] Teachers are effective as models in teaching new behaviors as they demonstrate, clearly and systematically, the skills under study. We do this by focusing attention on critical elements of the skill, thinking out loud as student questions are considered,[53] using step-by-step demonstrations with verbal explanations, and contrasting good and bad examples.[54] Students who break rules, misbehave, turn work in late, or engage in other inappropriate behavior will encourage others to do the same if their behavior is not checked. A warm, but firm, reprimand of those who misbehave will strengthen the inhibition to misbehave in other students in the class. On the other hand, students may be inhibited in asking questions because they were humiliated by a former teacher for asking "dumb" questions. By being open to student questions and praising student willingness to ask questions, teachers weaken this inhibition. The contagious spreading of behaviors, good or bad, through imitation in the group is called the *ripple effect*.[55]

The fact is that many of our most persistent habits and attitudes[56] result from simply watching and thinking about the actions of others.[57] We can learn complex behavior with a single observation without cuing or reinforcement.[58]

Teachers are influential, competent, accessible, and have high status in the classroom.[59] We can improve our modeling influence by making clear presentations, highlighting key ideas, providing interesting cues, and using novelty and surprise.[60] Teachers must do more than simply gain attention. Attention must be focused on the critical aspects of behavior to be learned.[61] Teachers model personal traits such as values and beliefs; general academic skills, such as problem solving and creative thinking; and specific skills by step-by-step demonstration.[62]

"Teachers *are* models: influential, competent, accessible, and high status"

Finally, we can provide appropriate models for our students. Mr. Art Herron, now with the Southern Baptist Sunday School Board, served with me as Minister of Youth at Columbia Baptist Church in the late 1970s. Art made a significant impact on our young people by bringing in teams of college students from Baptist Student Union[63] organizations for summer programs. One team focused on junior high and the other on senior high students. Art met with the college students for Bible study and planning each week. The teams were responsible for planning and executing specific programs aimed at growing our young people. Young people were assigned to each college student for one-on-one time as well.

I've never been called to be a minister of youth, but if I were, I'd want to begin a practice of choosing and training spiritually mature high school seniors in the church to become teachers and leaders for the seventh and eighth graders. Such a ministry would give selected seniors an outlet for what they'd learned. It would help them to grow in a whole new dimension. Beyond that, it would provide effective Christian models—similar in age and experience—for the younger teens.

Let's review Situation 2 as stated at the beginning of the chapter: you teach a class entitled "The Teaching Ministry of the Church." The aim of the class is to prepare ministers of education and Christian education directors for the practical problems they will face when they are called to their first church. Since most of them haven't experienced local church ministry, they really do not understand the problems they'll face. Your challenge is to make the answers you are giving credible and "real world."

How might you apply principles of Social Learning Theory to enhance the real world emphasis of this course? Be sure to consider vicarious and self reinforcement approaches.[64]

MOTIVATION AS CREATING CURIOSITY
(Cognitive Learning Theories)

We saw in chapter 8 that cognitive learning theory is concerned with how we know, think, and remember.[65] Basic to cognitive theories is the idea that thought processes control behavior.[66] In chapter 4 we introduced you to Jean Piaget and his concept of equilibration. Equilibration is the *natural tendency to maintain a balance* between what one already knows, the cognitive network, and what one experiences in the world.[67] When this balance is disturbed—that is, when we experience something that does not fit what we know—we experience anxiety, discomfort, or confusion. This confusion is called *disequilibrium*.[68] Equilibration compels us to reduce the disequilibrium by restoring the balance, or *equilibrium*, between our understanding of the world and experiences in the world.

Motivation for cognitive theorists, therefore, is creating disequilibrium, or curiosity, in the minds of learners. Specific suggestions were made in chapter 4 for cognitive teaching which are motivational in nature. Review optimal discrepancy, direct experience, social interaction, thought-provoking questions, and problem-solving activities.

Further, ask open-ended questions which create a sense of surprise, or cause discussion, or provide contradictory points of view, or allow discovery.[69]

Let's review Situation 3 as stated at the beginning of the chapter: a "Church History" course requires a hundred pages of difficult reading a week and the lectures "augment," rather than explain, what students read. They are falling farther behind and becoming frustrated. How might you apply cognitive learning principles to enhance this classroom environment? Be sure to consider optimal discrepancy, direct experience, social interaction, the use of questions, and discussion.

MOTIVATION AS INCREASING MEANINGFULNESS *(Information Processing Theory)*

Organization, according to Piaget, is the *natural tendency* to make sense of experiences by integrating them into cognitive structures that are logically related.[70] This natural tendency to make sense of the world is the cognitive definition of motivation.[71] We saw in chapter 9 that information processing theory focuses on how humans process information from the environment through sensory registers and short-term memory to long-term storage. We suggested several ways to approach motivation from this perspective. Attract and hold attention with attractive displays, voice changes, or simple diagrams. Encourage students' thinking about their own learning. Teach students how to learn in order to place more control in the hands of students. Organize presentations with outlines, flow charts, advance organizers, and the like to provide information in a preprocessed form. Avoid confusion and information overload which hurt motivation. Use elaboration to increase meaningfulness. (Do this by building on previous learnings, relating new material to old, and asking questions that require comparisons, relationships, and patterns.) Use analogies and illustrations to make explanations more clear. Teach students how to use mnemonic devices to make learning tedious material more enjoyable. Provide clear expectations for retrieval so that learners know what they must remember. Teach students the skills of self-questioning and notetaking so that their probability for success in the classroom increases.

Let's review Situation 4 as stated at the beginning of the chapter: A median adult class gathers to study the story of the Good Samaritan. As you enter the classroom you overhear one of the members sarcastically remark, "Oh boy, the Good Samaritan story again. I can't wait!" Several folks laugh in agreement. Obviously several class members are so familiar with the story that it has lost its meaningfulness. How might you apply information processing principles to enhance this classroom environment? Be sure to consider the role

**MOTIVATION
AS MEETING
PERSONAL NEEDS**
*(Humanistic
Learning Theory)*

of gaining attention, as well as the use of elaboration, self-questioning strategies, and retrieval of previous learnings or experiences related to the study.

Humanistic psychology is concerned with the autonomy, dignity, and worth of the self,[72] as well as personal growth.[73] The basis for humanistic motivation is the learner's self-concept and how the school contributes to that self-concept.[74] Regarding motivation, Arthur Combs wrote in 1962, "People are always motivated; in fact, they are never unmotivated. They may not be motivated to do what we would prefer they do, but it can never be truly said they are unmotivated."[75]

The key to motivation toward learning for humanistic educators is to allow learners to choose what they desire to learn. As we saw in chapter 10, however, too much freedom of choice leads to mediocre performance and decreased achievement.

Abraham Maslow, considered the father of humanistic psychology,[76] believed that all human beings have an innate drive for self-realization, or self-fulfillment, or self-actualization.[77] This self-actualization can be defined as the unfolding and fulfillment of one's personal potential.[78] Because Maslow believed that gratification of needs is the most important factor in human development,[79] he proposed his "Hierarchy of Needs" as a description of how persons move toward fulfillment.

The Hierarchy of Needs consists of seven levels. Maslow called the first four levels *deficiency*, or *basic, needs*.[80] These include survival, safety, belonging and love, and self-esteem. The lack of these traits prevents people from growing and drives them to satisfy these lower needs.[81] Maslow called the higher four levels *growth needs*, or *being needs*.[82] These include knowing and understanding, aesthetic appreciation, self-actualization, and transcendence. These higher needs are never satisfied like deficiency needs are, but expand as people grow.[83]

Deficiency Needs

Survival, or physiological, needs include the need for shelter, warmth, food, water, and sleep.[84] They involve concern for immediate existence.[85] If they are satisfied, then the door opens to the next level: *safety* needs. This level is concerned that tomorrow be assured,[86] and includes the desire for security[87] and freedom from threat in a predictable, orderly environment.[88] If these needs are satisfied, then people move to the third level: *belonging and love*. This third level includes receiving love and acceptance from family and peers, feeling wanted, being a member of a group, enjoying reciprocal affection, and establishing relationships.[89] The fourth level is *self-esteem*, which includes the need for recognition and approval, self-respect, competence and mastery, a high opinion of one's self,[90] achieving some sense of social status,[91] feeling unique, special, and different.[92]

The fifth level of need and the first growth need is *intellectual achievement*,[93] or the need to know and understand.[94] Included here are the needs to know how to do things and to understand the meaning of things, events, and symbols.[95] It is obvious that the primary function of a school—to help students know and understand their world—will falter if students have deficiency needs. While teachers cannot undo the negative influences of a sinful world, they can provide a classroom environment which encourages survival, safety, belonging, and self-esteem. To the extent this is achieved, students will be motivated to learn "naturally." The sixth level is *aesthetic*

Growth Needs

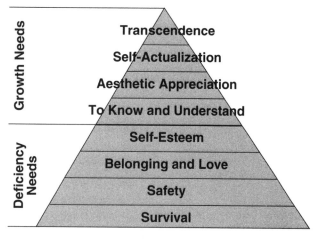

Maslow's Hierarchy of Needs

appreciation:[96] the need to experience and understand beauty, order, truth,[97] justice and goodness,[98] and positive humor.[99] The seventh level is *self-actualization*, the need to develop full use of one's talents, capacities and potential.[100] It is, according to Maslow, "the desire to become everything that one is capable of becoming."[101] Characteristics of the self-actualized person include such things as acceptance of self and others, spontaneity, openness, democratic relations with others, creativity, positive humor, and independence.[102] Clouse includes these characteristics as well: self-actualized persons are realistic, resist conformity, have a high sense of ethics, and center on work rather than themselves.[103]

Some texts rearrange the order of levels, so that intellectual and aesthetic needs lie above self-actualization.[104] Most texts, however, place self-actualization at level seven as shown in the diagram. In fact, there are several variations in the way you'll see Maslow's hierarchy presented.[105]

Maslow's later work (1968) included an eighth level called *transcendence*, or *spiritual needs*, which he defines as the spiritual need for broader cosmic identification.[106] Hamachek, the only text author I've found to include this level in the hierarchy, writes: "It seems an important addition, one consistent with what the religions of the world have always talked about."[107]

Implications for Teachers

In light of the hierarchy of needs model, teachers should help students satisfy their deficiency needs. If students are tired or hungry or abused, their desire to learn is diminished. If there is a threat of embarrassment in the class, achievement will suffer.[108] Avoid frequent competition among students.[109] Be conscious of self-esteem factors in the classroom.[110] Take advantage of student interests.[111] Promote feelings of success by making appropriate assignments and providing positive feedback and credible rewards.[112] Make learning attractive and meaningful.[113] Display a caring attitude toward students.[114] Personalize the content so that students can integrate it into their own experience.[115] Help students set their own goals.[116] Provide alternative learning activities from which students can choose.[117] Make sure that you provide a safe, supportive classroom climate and set high, but attainable, standards.[118]

Let's review Situation 5 as stated at the beginning of the chapter: You are teaching a class in introductory Hebrew. Most of your students have no background in the language. The curious alphabet, the unfamiliar grammar, even reading from right to left have students nervous. How might you apply humanistic principles to enhance this classroom environment? Be sure to consider the role of safety and belonging.

MOTIVATION AS PROVIDING SUCCESSFUL EXPERIENCES (Achievement and Attribution Theories)
Achievement Motivation

H. A. Murray in 1938 defined achievement motivation as the "need to accomplish something difficult, to excel oneself, to rival oneself and others."[119] People who strive for excellence in a field for the sake of achieving and not for a reward have a high achievement need.[120] More recently (1964), John Atkinson proposed a theory of achievement motivation. His research discovered that students could be classified as *success-oriented* or *anxiety-ridden*. Success-oriented students are motivated to achieve and might be called "success-seekers." Anxiety-ridden students are motivated to avoid failure and might be called "failure-avoiders."[121] Success seekers have a history of success, are self-confident, reflect achievement motivation, and have an internal locus of control.[122] They tend to set *intermediate* goals which challenge, yet offer a high probability of success.[123] When success-seekers fail, they see that failure as an underestimate of how much effort was required. They try harder the next time.

Failure-avoiders have a history of failure. They have little confidence, reflect weak achievement motivation, and depend on external sources of control—praise or approval.[124] They tend to set goals either too low or too high. If the goal is too high and failure results, then there is no blame because the task was too difficult. There is no negative outcome—"What could I do? It was just too hard." But if the goal is too easy, success is assured. And there is no positive result—"Awww. Anybody could have done that!" Blame for failure has been avoided, but pride in achievement has been lost.

"Provide a safe, supportive classroom climate"

The development of the need for achievement occurs in families and cultures which encourage initiative and competition, where failures are not criticized, and students are allowed to solve problems on their own.[125] Achievement motivation is influenced by our own perceived causes for success and failure.[126] The study of this aspect of achievement motivation is called Attribution Theory.

Attribution Theory is an attempt to systematically describe students' explanations for their successes and failures in classroom situations.[127] Successful students might say, "I really studied hard for that exam—I deserved an A!" or "Man, I sure lucked out. His questions came directly from the material I studied!" Failing students might say, "I just don't have what it takes for this class!" or "I guess I just didn't study hard enough this time." Motivation for future achievement is affected by the attributions students give to their successes and failures.

Attribution Theory

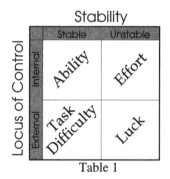

Table 1

Bernard Weiner has done extensive study in attribution theory.[128] His model deals with four perceived causes of success or failure in achievement situations: ability, effort, task difficulty, and luck.[129] These four causes are shown in Table 1.

The table shows stability and locus of control variables.[130] Stability refers to whether the perceived cause remains the same over time or can change. Locus of control refers to whether the perceived cause is internal or external to the student.[131]

Stability

	Stable	Unstable
Internal	I just can't do statistics! *ability*	I didn't study enough! *effort*
External	That was a tough test! *task difficulty*	I guessed wrong on what to study! *luck*

(Locus of Control along vertical axis)

Failure Explanations
Table 2

Stability

	Stable	Unstable
Internal	I'm good at statistics! *ability*	I studied hard for this exam! *effort*
External	That was an easy test! *task difficulty*	I guessed right on what to study! *luck*

(Locus of Control along vertical axis)

Success Explanations
Table 3

Achiever Status

	High Achiever	Low Achiever
Success	Ability and Hard Work	Luck
Failure	Laziness	Lack of Ability

(Outcome along vertical axis)

Persistent Attributions
Table 4

If students make a low score on a test, they will tend to explain their failure in one of four ways, as shown in Table 2:

"I just can't do statistics!" (ability)

"That was a tough test!" (task difficulty)

"I didn't study enough." (effort)

"I guessed wrong about what to study." (luck)

If students make a high score on a test, they will tend to explain their success in one of four ways, as shown in Table 3:

"I'm good at statistics!" (ability)

"The test was easy!" (task difficulty)

"I really studied hard for this exam!" (effort)

"I guessed right about what to study." (luck)

Stable attributions (ability and task difficulty) build expectations for future successes or failures.[132] That is, perceptions of low ability or high difficulty tend to increase expectations of future failure. Perceptions of high ability or low difficulty tend to increase expectations of future success.

Internal attributions (ability and effort) produce feelings of pride or shame in students.[133] That is, perceptions of low ability or lack of effort produce feelings of shame. Perceptions of high ability or diligent effort produce feelings of pride.

Over a period of time, repeated success or failure can lead to rigid attributions by high achievers and low achievers. High achievers see success as a result of hard work and failure as a result of laziness. Student failure does not diminish expectancy of success. It simply encourages high achievers to work harder.

Low achievers see success as a result of luck and failure as a result of lack of ability. Therefore, successes produce little pride or motivation for further achievement, since they are a matter of luck. Failures reinforce the perception in low achievers that they lack the ability to succeed.[134] (See Table 4.)

College professors are persons who achieved their positions by working hard to earn high grades and secure the respect of their teachers. They are high achievers and tend to attribute the successes and failures of their students to hard work and laziness respectively. Students, being novices in a given subject, may be seen by their professors as lacking either ability or sufficient initiative to master their courses. These two perspectives can impair teacher-student relationships as professors demand more from students and blame student failures on lack of effort.

Such attitudes can be passed on to ministerial students, who reflect them in the churches they serve. The ministers are trained in theology, Bible, Christian education, and church organization. Ministers who have had successful ministries tend to attribute their success to ability and hard work. Without being aware of it, they can begin to attribute the lack of progress in church growth and ministry to lack of ability or laziness. Pastors and staff ministers can demand more from church members and blame lack of results on laziness, spiritual immaturity, or lack of proper zeal. "If the members of this church were more committed, we could really accomplish something here!"

Such frustration on the part of high achievers, in colleges or churches, does little to help low achievers excel. The fundamental goal in changing attributions is to move students to *attribute their success to the personal effort* they make in learning.[135] Help them to understand that their achievement is not a matter of luck or faith, but strictly a matter of personal effort. Help them develop learning skills and strategies.[136] Emphasize progress in a given area by reviewing previous material to show how "easy" it was, or by encouraging students to redo projects when they have learned more.[137] Challenge high achievers with assignments and problems that offer a mix of potential success and failure. The possibility of failure motivates high achievers to work harder.[138] Support low achievers with assignments that offer mostly success, particularly at the early stages of learning.[139] Model a mastery orientation for learners. Persons who have a mastery orientation value achievement for its own sake, believe they have the ability to improve, do not fear failure, are willing to take risks, are self-confident and energetic, and welcome feedback.[140] These suggestions will help low achievers to build a history of successes tied to their own effort.

"Ultimate goal: help learners attribute success to effort"

Each of these approaches to motivation can be used by Christian teachers to help energize students in their classrooms and churches. So often we hear pastors and denominational leaders condemn, carte

IMPLICATIONS FOR CHRISTIAN TEACHING

blanche, the use of behavioral or cognitive or humanistic principles in Christian teaching. But as we saw in chapter 11, we can use these principles effectively to solve educational problems in a Christian context, without accepting the secular perspectives of their proponents. Christians are people, after all, people with problems in behavior, understanding, and attitude. Accepting Jesus Christ as Savior redeems us from sin and gives us new life. But old habits and worldly perceptions, and sinful attitudes give way to godly habits, biblical perceptions, and spiritual attitudes only through a process of growth. Central to this growth is effective motivation and teaching.

Leon Marsh charted the motivational principles of Jesus in his book *Educational Psychology for Christian Education*.[141] Here are some of his key points.[142]

Jesus Used Rewards

Jesus promised eternal life to those who put their faith in Him (John 3:16). He promised abundant life to those who seek first God's Kingdom (Matt. 6:33). Certainly these are spiritual rewards, but He gave temporal rewards as well. He healed the centurion's servant (Matt. 8:10, 13) and Jairus' daughter (Mark 5:35–42) because of their faith. He healed the woman with a hemorrhage because of her faith. He forgave the woman caught in adultery because of her faith (John 8:3ff). While this is certainly not the mechanical pellet-dropping conditioning of a Skinner box, it did produce dramatic changes in behavior. These incidents reflect behavioral motivation.

Jesus Called for Imitation and Personal Application

Jesus taught by example. He not only talked of love, but He loved those to whom he talked: "As I have loved you, so you must love one another" (John 13:34). He not only talked of humility, but washed His listener's feet like a common household slave (John 13:3–15). The disciples became interested in prayer one day after they watched him "praying in a certain place" (Luke 11:1). Jesus was the supreme model. Paul called for Timothy to learn from his own experience in life (2 Tim. 3:10–11). Peter calls on pastors and ministers everywhere to be "examples to the flock" (1 Pet. 5:3). These examples reflect social learning theory.

Jesus Used Questions

There are over one hundred questions recorded in Scripture which Jesus asked. These were used successfully in motivating His followers. Here are just a few of them, along with their purpose: to awaken conscience (Matt. 23:17); to elicit faith (Mark 8:29); to rebuke criticism (Mark 10:3); to introduce and follow up a story (Luke 10:25–37); to compel a thought (Matt. 21:28–32), and to bring conviction (Mark 3:4). This is a cognitive approach to motivation.

Jesus gained attention by calling for it, using such expressions as "Behold!" (Matt. 13:3). He maintained attention through the use of stories, and attached kingdom principles to common place objects like sheep, goats, dogs, eagles, leaven, tares, fig trees, mustard seeds, light, soil, fishing nets, and hidden treasure. Because the stories were framed around experiences familiar to His listeners, they were able to integrate His stories into their thinking. They were able to easily remember His teachings and pass them on to others. Such activities reflect principles of information processing theory.

Jesus Was Able to Gain and Maintain Attention

Jesus transformed the negative "Thou shalt nots" of the Old Testament into positive demands of life under grace. While He did not hesitate to condemn the rigid religiosity of scribes and Pharisees, He cared for the people of Israel, and of the whole world, who were like sheep without a shepherd (Mark 6:34). He healed them and fed them, encouraged them and supported them, blessed them and taught them. His whole life was focused on the salvation—the making whole—of individual believers. For "the Son of Man did not come to be served, but to serve, and to give his life as a ransom for many" (Matt. 20:28). His care for people and emphasis on the positive reflect humanistic principles of motivation.

Jesus Emphasized the Positive

CHAPTER CONCEPTS

Ability	Luck
Aesthetic appreciation	Ripple effect
Behavior modification	Safety
Belonging and love	Self-actualization
Deficiency needs	Self-esteem
Direct reinforcement	Self-reinforcement
Disequilibrium	Shaping
Effort	Specific motivation
Extrinsic motivation	Stability
General motivation	Survival
Growth needs	Task difficulty
Intellectual achievement	Token economy
Intrinsic motivation	Transcendence
Locus of control	Vicarious reinforcement

DISCUSSION QUESTIONS

1. Choose any two of the five situations presented at the beginning of the chapter and apply princi-ples of motivation from a different system than that given in the text. For example, the text ap-plied behavioral principles to situation one. Discuss this situation with any other system.

2. Consider recent experiences of success or failure in your studies. What attributions did you make to explain them? Did you focus on ability, effort, task difficulty, or luck?

3. Discuss examples of motivation (or lack of motivation) in classes you've taken. What type of mo-tivation was applied? Was it effective in motivating you to achieve? Why or why not?

4. Jesus reflected behavioral, cognitive, and humanistic principles of motivation in his teaching. Does this mean He was a behaviorist? A cognitive theorist? A humanist? Why or why not?

FOR FURTHER READING

Biehler, Robert F., and Jack Snowman. "Motivation." In *Psychology Applied to Teaching*. 7th ed., 508–60. Boston: Houghton Mifflin Company, 1993.

Clouse, Bonnidell. "Moral Growth by Moral Behavior (Reasoning, Potential)." In *Teaching for Moral Growth: A Guide for the Christian Community—Teachers, Parents and Pastors*, 148-82, 221–56, and 296–333. Wheaton, Ill: Bridgeport Books, 1993.

Dembo, Myron H. "Motivation and Learning." In *Applying Educational Psychology*. 5th ed., 144–97. New York: Long-man, 1994.

Eggen, Pau,l and Don Kauchak. "Increasing Student Motivation." In *Educational Psychology: Classroom Connections*. 2nd ed., 422–85. New York: Macmillan College Publishing Company, 1994.

Gage, N. L., and David C. Berliner. "Section E: Motivation." In *Educational Psychology*. 3rd ed., 369–444. Boston: Houghton Mifflin Company, 1984.

Good, Thomas L., and Jere E. Brophy. "Part Five: Motivation." In *Educational Psychology: A Realistic Approach*. 4th ed., 56–487. New York: Longman, 1990.

Hamachek, Don. "Motivational Dynamics and Human Learning." In *Psychology in Teaching, Learning, and Growth*. 4th ed., 258–302. Boston: Allyn and Bacon, 1990.

Hamilton, Richard, and Elizabeth Ghatala."Traditional and Current Views of Motivation." In *Learning and Instruction*, 327–68. New York: McGraw-Hill, Inc., 1994.

LeFrancois, Guy R. "Motivation and Teaching." In *Psychology for Teaching*, 264–89. Belmont, Calif.: Wadsworth Pub-lishing Company, 1994.

Maslow, Abraham H. *Toward a Psychology of Being*. 2nd ed. Princeton: Van Nostrand, 1968.

———— *Motivation and Personality*. 3rd ed. New York: Harper & Row, 1987. Revised by Robert Frager, James Fadiman, Cynthia McReynolds, and Ruth Cox.

Rothstein, Pamela R. "Motivation." In *Educational Psychology*, 136–52. New York: McGraw-Hill, Inc., 1990.

Slavin, Robert E. "Motivating Students to Learn." In *Educational Psychology: Theory and Practice*. 4th ed., 344–85. Boston: Allyn and Bacon, 1994.

Smith, M. Daniel. "Motivating the Student." In *Educational Psychology and Its Classroom Applications*, 327–74. Boston: Allyn and Bacon, 1975.

Sprinthall, Norman A., Richard C. Sprinthall, and Sharon N. Oja. "Motivation in the Classroom." In *Educational Psy-chology: A Developmental Approach*. 6th ed., 527–54. New York: McGraw-Hill, Inc., 1994.

Woolfolk, Anita. "Motivation and the Individual Learner." In *Educational Psychology*. 5th ed., 334–65. Boston: Allyn and Bacon, Inc., 1993.

Wlodkowski, Raymond J. *Motivation and Teaching: A Practical Guide*. Washington, D.C.: National Education Associ-ation, 1986.

Chapter 13

THE TEACHER AND CLASSROOM CLIMATE

James writes, "Not many of you should presume to be teachers, my brothers, because you know that we who teach will be judged more strictly" (James 3:1). Why should teachers be held to a higher standard? It is because we deal in human personality. Any mismanagement or misdirection of persons entrusted to our care carries the heaviest condemnation.

The motivation to learn blooms in a classroom that both challenges and nurtures learners. Effective teachers create just such an environment; ineffective teachers do not. What makes the difference? This chapter looks at teacher variables such as personality traits, teaching behaviors, and reward structures which facilitate a positive learning environment. Finally, we will view classroom climate from the perspective of the Christian teachers' triad.

CHAPTER RATIONALE

Learners will demonstrate understanding of classroom climate by
- explaining the influence of various factors related to teacher personality on classroom climate;
- defining structuring, signal giving, "mands," organization, wait time I, wait time II, directing questions, redirecting questions, probing, and positive and negative reactions.
- comparing and contrasting the following grading structures: individual competition, group competition, group reward, individual reward.

Learners will demonstrate appreciation for the importance of teacher variables in setting classroom climate by sharing personal experiences with effective and ineffective teachers.

CHAPTER OBJECTIVES

TEACHER PERSONALITY AND CLASSROOM CLIMATE

This text is dedicated to helping you understand the teaching-learning process so that you can be a more effective teacher. But what does being "effective" as a teacher mean? Some would define effectiveness in terms of student ratings. "Dr. Jones' classes are always full—he's the most popular professor in the school!" Others would define effectiveness in terms of actual student learning. "Dr. Smyth is really tough—but I come out of his classes with an understanding of the subject that *means* something to me!" Some of the characteristics we'll discuss in this chapter enhance student attitudes. Others enhance student achievement. Both are important, yet they are independent. Research suggests that how students rate a teacher has little to do with how much they actually learn in a class.[1] Still, positive student attitudes are important to the classroom climate. And, classroom climate has an influence on learner achievement. Effective teachers succeed in helping students master their courses with positive attitudes. Let's look at some of the factors involved in this complex task.

"Personality" is a global concept that refers to persons as they are seen by others. The term suggests "distinctive qualities of a person, especially those distinguishing personal characteristics that make one socially appealing."[2] Teaching is a social enterprise. It follows that persons who are socially appealing—who can relate to others in a positive way—can create a better climate for learning than persons who are socially inept. Think of teachers in your educational past whom you loved and respected. Now think of teachers you feared. How were these teachers' personalities different? How did these differences impact classroom climate? Let's look at four critical personality factors: warmth, enthusiasm, flexibility, and emotional maturity.

Warmth

Teachers who are warm, caring, and friendly set a positive emotional tone in the classroom. In fact, Hamachek writes that this characteristic is the one most strongly linked to positive student attitudes.[3] Contrast this with teachers who are cold, uncaring, and aloof. The former concentrate on students as persons, the latter on lessons to be taught. The former concentrate on thinking and sharing and learning, the latter on deadlines and punctuality and performance. The former engage all students in an effort to help them learn, the latter confront students in an effort to combat ignorance. It is clear which kind of classroom produces openness, curiosity, and freedom to ask questions.

Consider the warm words of Jesus the week before He died: "O Jerusalem, Jerusalem, you who kill the prophets and stone those sent to you, how often I have longed to gather your children together, as a hen gathers her chicks under her wings, but you were not willing" (Matt. 23:37). In the face of Jerusalem's violent history and his own impending death, Jesus spoke words of warm embrace, of togetherness and love. Later, when Judas the betrayer approached Jesus in the garden, Jesus accepted his kiss of greeting and called him "friend" (Matt. 26:49–50). He had chosen twelve men to "be with him" (Mark 3:14).

Jesus did not think of these learners as servants, but friends (John 15:15). These students were loved by their Teacher, and encouraged, commanded, to love each other (John 13:34). What a classroom climate!

"These students were loved by their Teacher, and encouraged, commanded, to love each other—what a classroom climate!"

Enthusiasm

Enthusiasm refers to "great excitement for or interest in a subject or cause."[4] Teacher enthusiasm brings life and energy into the classroom. Enthusiasm manifests itself as intensity, vigor, movement, joy, surprise, frustration, and delight.[5] Such elements reflect an intense interest in the subject as well as zeal for communicating that subject to others. Contrast this with teachers who move through their material methodically and monotonously, with little change of pace. Their focus is on their own notes, often yellow with age, rather than the newness of the material as it stirs their students' thinking. Students have difficulty generating excitement for subjects that seem boring to their teachers. Such was the contrast between the teaching of the scribes and Pharisees who quoted prominent rabbis and the teaching of Jesus, Who spoke with authority: "You have heard that it was said to the people long ago . . . but *I tell you* that . . ." (Matt. 5:21–22, author's emphasis). Jesus' teaching had such intensity that "the crowds were amazed at his teaching" (Matt. 7:28–29).

Flexibility

"Teaching flexibility" means using appropriate methods, whether direct or indirect, according to classroom needs. Direct methods include lecturing, explaining, and correcting. Indirect methods include questioning, listening, and accepting students' opinions and feelings.[6] Flexibility is the most repeated adjective used to describe good teachers.[7] Such teachers are more positive and more democratic than rigid teachers. Rigid teachers tend to use the same procedures in the same way, regardless of student outcomes.[8] They hold stereotypical views of students and tend to have low expectations of student ability. They are more authoritarian and prone to bias and

"Flexibility is the most repeated adjective used to describe good teachers"

prejudice. They depend more on first impressions and past records than do flexible teachers.[9] In short, research has found that students in all subjects learned more with flexible teachers.[10] Matthew 23 reflects the distinctive difference between the flexibility of Jesus' understanding of the Law and the rigidity of the Pharisee's religion. Jesus understood Kingdom principles and used them appropriately to teach and minister. The Pharisees held rigid traditions and religious formulas, and burdened their followers with them (Matt. 23:4). Flexible teachers focus on their students and employ whatever means are necessary to secure their learning.

Emotionally Mature

Emotionally mature teachers display a sense of humor, have a pleasant manner, and are fair and disciplined.[11] Such teachers work well with others, manage their impulses, express good feelings without embarrassment, refrain from worry, and can accept constructive criticism.[12] Contrast them with immature teachers, who tend to be unpleasant, impulsive, irritable, rash, anxious, and short of temper.[13] College and seminary students may be able to avoid such teachers by choosing others. But for elementary and secondary students, required by law to attend school with little or no choice in their teachers or subjects, immature teachers can make school an unbearable experience. The experience of Jesus and Lazarus reflects the difference in emotional maturity between Jesus and the Pharisees. Jesus was late. Lazarus was dead (John 11:17). Martha was distraught (John 11:21). Jesus' response, in word and action, was measured and calm. He raised Lazarus from the dead. And the response of the Pharisees upon hearing of the miracle? "If we let him go on like this [performing miracles, v. 47], everyone will believe in him, and then the Romans will come and take away both our place and our nation" (John 11:48). Immature teachers always consider their *position* more important than their *mission*, which is helping students learn.

"Immature teachers consider their *position* more important than their *mission*"

Warmth, enthusiasm, flexibility, and emotional maturity are powerful influences in creating a positive classroom climate. If we want to increase our perceived effectiveness in the classroom, we would do well to focus more on personal attributes than on teaching functions and activities.[14] Still, what teachers actually do in the classroom influences classroom climate.

TEACHER BEHAVIORS AND CLASSROOM CLIMATE— GLOBAL BEHAVIORS

There are several key teacher behaviors that affect classroom climate. We will consider both global and instructional behaviors.

Global behaviors refer to overarching activities which provide structure for classroom climate. These include content-communication balance, preparation, organizational clarity, scholarship, responsibility, and self-evaluation.

Some teachers believe that teaching is nothing more than telling students what one knows. The key to good teaching for these teachers, then, is to know a subject well, to develop a command of the subject matter.[15] "Sit still while I instill." This is a necessary but insufficient basis for effective teaching. Unless teachers can convey their knowledge in a way that is recognizable to students, confusion, not learning, will result. Other teachers believe that teaching is primarily lesson-planning, pace, explanations,[16] and activities. The key to good teaching for these teachers, then, is planning goal-oriented activities that engage students with teachers and with one another. "Choose two from column A and one from Column B." This is a necessary but insufficient basis for effective teaching. Unless the activities convey real content, warm fluff, not learning, will result.

I experience this difference every semester in my "Principles of Teaching" classes. Theology students exegete a passage of Scripture, jot down two or three points on an outline, and think that they are prepared to teach (i.e., tell what they know). Christian Education students plan a learning readiness activity, two questions for group work, large group sharing and a concluding comment, and think they are prepared to teach—without even cracking a commentary or Bible dictionary (i.e., choose two from column A). The former is deep and cold, the latter warm and shallow.

Effective teachers know their subjects, and plan meaningful activities—lecture, discussion, projects, questions, and problems—to help students integrate the new material into their thinking. Effective teachers balance subject knowledge and course structure, so that their scholarship can be communicated in an understandable manner, and learning activities can provide a meaningful challenge to serious students. Serious scholarship provides depth. Proper planning provides warmth. Together these provide a winning combination in effective learning.

Skilled performance in any endeavor requires years of behind-the-scenes practice, effort, and hard work. Listen to Olympic athletes describe the years they sacrificed to practice in order to skate, swim, ski, or dive in the Games. Years of effort for a moment of excellence. Teaching is a complex social skill. Hamachek recalls

Content-Communication Balance

"Preparation gives students confidence that teachers are going somewhere."

Preparation

telling one of his favorite teachers, "You make teaching look easy." His professor replied, "Perhaps, but you have no idea how many hours I worked to make it appear easy."[17] Effective teachers work hard behind the scenes to make their teaching "natural."

Preparation includes speaking skills, platform skills,[18] explaining skills, questioning skills, listening skills, discipline skills, and long-range planning skills. All of these factors give students the confidence that teachers are *going somewhere*—and that where they are going is important.

Organizational Clarity

Learning in a confusing classroom is like hunting for a favorite shirt in a darkened closet: all the shirts look alike—dark shapes in the shadows. Organizational clarity is like turning on the closet light: suddenly one can see the distinctive colors and patterns of the shirts—and can easily find the favorite. It follows from our discussion of Information Processing Theory in chapter 9 that organization and clarity are essential for meaningful learning. The result is higher morale, more positive student attitudes, and higher achievement.[19]

Scholarship

Effective teachers are well-informed, not only in their own subjects, but also in supplementary areas such as literature, painting, and music. These supplementary areas provide fertile sources of analogies, relationships[20] and illustrations to enrich classroom learning. My classes focus on practical ministry in local churches as well as scriptural foundations and principles of Christian education. Yet examples drawn from the fields of physics, philosophy, and computer science provide students a different context in which to consider principles and problems. The day I stop learning is the day I'll stop teaching. Times change. Students change. Needs change. Effective teachers blend new studies, new theories, new discoveries into their class structure in order to keep current. Such on-going scholarship not only enhances teaching directly but also provides a model of academic achievement for students as well.

Responsibility

Effective teachers accept responsibility for how well their students learn. Good teachers see low achievement as a problem to be solved rather than a burden to bear. They build relationships with problem students and work to help them out of their learning problems. Less effective teachers do not accept responsibility for student underachievement. They tend to blame students and use threats and demands to motivate better performance.[21]

Self-evaluation

Champions push themselves in order to excel. They study videotapes of their performances and reflect on strengths and weaknesses.

In short, they evaluate themselves regularly in order to reduce their weaknesses and polish their strengths. Effective teachers are thoughtful about their work and monitor their instruction. They reflect on the relationship between their planning and the actual instruction in class.[22] They use this analysis to improve plans for future sessions.

Instructional behaviors refer to specific behaviors which influence classroom climate in the actual practice of teaching. We can consider these behaviors as structuring, questioning, and reacting behaviors.[23]

TEACHER BEHAVIORS AND CLASSROOM CLIMATE— INSTRUCTIONAL BEHAVIORS
Structuring Behaviors

Structuring is defined as setting the context for classroom behavior. Teachers do this with advance organizers, objectives, and course outlines. Too much structure limits student freedom and produces a rigid atmosphere. Too little structure magnifies student freedom and produces a chaotic atmosphere. Both extremes decrease achievement.[24]

Challenge and encourage. Effective teachers balance challenge and encouragement.[25] On the one hand, they push their students to achieve at increasingly higher levels. On the other, they nurture and support student efforts, encouraging them when they fail. Poor teachers reflect frustration, futility, and impatience with student failures. "Oh dear! Don't you know that?"[26]

Provide personal feedback. Effective teachers provide specific, informative feedback to individual students. Such teachers give help to individuals when help is really needed. Ineffective teachers tend to provide global feedback to the class as a whole.[27] Review the section on "Teacher Praise" in chapter 12.

Relate and expect. Effective teachers establish positive rapport with their students. Rapport is a relationship, a bond, between teacher and student which provides the interpersonal medium for teaching and learning to happen. Teachers do this by nurturing the self-esteem of their students, by emphasizing cooperative learning activities and by focusing on the learning process more than the learning product.[28] Along with the rapport, effective teachers establish high, yet achievable, expectations for students.[29] The combination of rapport and high expectations produces a positive classroom climate.

Manage time for learning. Allocated time refers to time planned for specific activities. In a Sunday morning Bible study program, the allocated time might be 9:30 to 10:30. Engaged time refers to the

"Fifty minutes of meandering discussion resulted in no significant learning, no new discoveries, no explanations. Too much freedom. Too much fluff."

actual time spent on a given learning task. In Sunday School, the engaged time excludes time given to greetings, announcements, prayer requests, and refreshments. The effectiveness of learning is directly related to the amount of time students actually engage in learning.[30]

Follow a specific outline. Effective teachers follow an explicit teaching format. This format includes such components as review of the previous day's work, goals, guided practice, feedback on performance, and time to practice.[31] These components provide structure to class time and underscore to students that the class is going somewhere.[32] Such a structure limits tangential "rabbits" that move class discussion off the subject. There was nothing more frustrating for me in college and seminary classes than professors who began class by asking, "So, what would you like to talk about today?" I found it insulting that these professors cared so little for their subject that they would open the floor to follow whatever thoughts came to any student's mind in the moment. Fifty minutes of meandering discussion resulted in no significant learning, no new discoveries, no explanations. Too much freedom. Too much fluff. I promised I'd never waste the time of a classroom full of students like that if ever I had the opportunity to teach. Perhaps I've overcompensated since I'm told from time to time that my classes cover a lot of ground in a semester. But my students never leave a class wondering what they were supposed to learn.

Signal giving. It is one thing for a teacher to have an explicit plan. It is another for students to recognize that class time is organized. Signal giving refers to the skill of providing definite starts and stops throughout the class time to emphasize transitions in the organization of the material. "We have discussed the concept of justification. Now let's move to sanctification." Signal giving includes the use of "mands" or verbal emphasis.[33] "Listen! Curiosity is an essential concept in cognitive motivation." Signal giving attracts attention and helps students separate more important from less important material.

Orchestrate activities. An orchestra is composed of various instruments playing many notes. Unless the instruments play in a coordinated way and the notes are played in harmony, under the direction of the conductor, the result is noise. Compare the cacophony of an orchestra warming up—each musician playing notes without regard for any other instrument—with the melodious sound of that same orchestra playing a symphony. In the same way, effective teachers orchestrate the pace and tempo in the class in a harmonious way to bring about learning. Boredom results if the pace is too slow. Confusion results if the pace is too fast. Balance is essential.

Wlodkowski suggests three ways to orchestrate a proper pace.[34] First, let students control the pace with the use of questions, input, and discussion. Such feedback helps teachers maintain a pace appropriate for their learners. A second suggestion is to use movement, voice, body language, and pauses[35] to control pace. "Movement" can range from a rigid pose rooted behind a podium or overhead projector to exaggerated pacing. "Voice" can range from dull monotone to emotional outburst. "Body language" can range from dull stiffness to frenetic gesture. "Pauses" refer to the timing and duration of breaks in classroom pace, and can range from too few/too short to too many/too long. In each of these, the former produces boredom, the latter uneasiness and apprehension. Wlodkowski's third suggestion is to shift class interaction from teacher-student to student-student and back again.[36] Too much teacher-student interaction produces overdependence on the teacher. Too much student-student interaction produces shallow socializing. Teachers who conduct their classes so that all these factors exist in harmony, in line with student needs and course goals, produce an effective learning environment.

"Use movement, voice, body language, and pauses to control pace"

Classroom climate, as well as student achievement, is affected by how teachers ask questions. Key issues in questioning include frequency, cognitive level, pausing after the question, directing, redirecting, and probing.

Questioning Behaviors

Frequency of Questions. In general, the more questions teachers ask, the more students learn.[37] Questions should be asked after material is presented in order to evaluate how well students understand the presentation. Teachers often ask a question before presenting material. Students have difficulty making a sensible reply. Then teachers explain. If this is done often, teachers make students feel incompetent. Teach, then test. Explain, then question. This allows students to demonstrate their learning in a positive way, and it provides feedback to teachers concerning the clarity of their presentations.

Cognitive Level of Questions. In general, the higher the cognitive level of question, the more students learn.[38] Comprehension questions, which deal with concept meanings, are better than knowledge questions, which focus on recall of simple facts. Comprehension questions call for students to interpret, compare, and explain. Words such as describe, illustrate, and rephrase characterize this level.

Application questions, which call for students to use material to solve problems, produce higher achievement than comprehension questions. Words such as "apply," "solve," "classify," "choose," and "employ" reflect this level. Analysis questions call for students to identify causes and motives, as well as the internal structure of a subject. Words such as analyze, conclude, infer, distinguish, exegete and outline reflect this level. Synthesis questions require students to create something new or develop new ideas. Words such as "predict," "construct," "originate," "design," and "plan" reflect this level. Evaluation questions call for students to judge or appraise something. Words such as judge, argue, and decide reflect this stage.[39] Simplistic, leading, or rhetorical questions undermine classroom climate and student achievement.

"Can you keep quiet for three seconds?!"

Pausing After the Question. Effective teachers give learners enough time to answer their questions. Craig Pearson studied the amount of time several hundred elementary teachers paused after asking a question. The average pause was nine-tenths of a second! Teachers were instructed to wait three seconds after asking their questions. Student behavior changed significantly as a result. Pearson reported that student answers were longer (they had more to say). More students volunteered answers (they were more confident). Inflected answers—those that end with a "?"—decreased.

Students worked together more. More students *asked* questions. Finally, students considered "slow" showed considerable improvement.[40] Gage and Berliner call this pause "Wait Time I" and state that it gives students time to consider the question, process relevant information and formulate an answer. The higher the cognitive level targeted by a question, the longer Wait Time I needs to be.[41]

Directing Questions. Every child in an elementary or secondary classroom should have an equal opportunity to succeed or fail. This requires some system of directing questions to all children evenly. Research suggests this systematic patterning of questions reduces anxiety and increases achievement. Randomly asking students questions increases the level of anxiety in the classroom. Further, teachers tend to call on more knowledgeable students when they have no system to insure even distribution of questions. This tendency deprives less able students of an equal chance to respond.[42]

When teaching adults, I prefer to allow *volunteers* to answer questions. Some adults learn from listening. Others fear embarrassment. I can generate better rapport in the classroom when I remove the anxiety of randomly calling on individuals to answer. Quiet students can be engaged before or after class or during small group work. As their trust in the teacher and confidence in their mastery grow, they will more likely volunteer to answer future questions in class.

Redirecting Questions. There will be times when you ask a question and receive a wrong answer in reply. Poor teachers simply give the correct answer and move on. Effective teachers redirect the question to keep it before the class. This means asking the question again to another student or to the class as a whole.[43] Teachers can also redirect questions asked by students back to the class. This not only engages student thinking but gives the teacher time to consider how best to answer.

Probing Questions. Often a student's initial response to a question is shallow. Poor teachers accept shallow responses and move on, or they may provide more explanation themselves. Effective teachers help students consider issues at a deeper level by asking a second, more detailed, question. Probing needs to be done sensitively. When I was taping the Disciplers' Model video series, my mother and father were part of the studio class. At one point I asked a question of the group. My mother, caught up in the presentation, raised her hand and answered the question. Her answer was good, but I wanted her to clarify part of it—so I asked a probing question: "And what do you mean when you use the term 'believe'?" She gasped and froze. She was willing and able to answer my first question. Her inability to answer the probe shocked and embarrassed her. Be ready to rescue students when they are trapped by a probing question. (By the way, we cut Mom's segment out of the video.)

We have discussed how effective teachers structure class time and solicit responses. When students respond, teachers react. The manner in which we react influences the climate of the classroom.

Reacting Behaviors

Pausing After Student Response. Question and answer periods can take on the feeling of the Inquisition if the pace of questions is too fast. By pausing after students respond, teachers slow down the pace and encourage others to consider the question. Gage and Berliner call this pausing after student response "Wait Time II." Achievement increases as teachers slow down.[44]

Using Positive Reactions. Effective teachers praise correct answers and follow up incorrect answers with probing questions to help students find the correct response. They encourage students by warmly accepting them.[45] Warm is always better than cold, and accepting is always better than rejecting.

Avoiding Negative Reactions. Effective teachers do not criticize, humiliate or embarrass students for their incorrect responses. Research shows that as criticism increases, achievement decreases.[46] I once knew a professor who sometimes reacted to student questions like this: "That is the dumbest question I've heard in a long time. I refuse to spend even a moment of our class time responding to it." Needless to say, students learned very quickly not to ask questions in his classes! How would you describe the climate in his classroom?

"A theology student rattled the class as he angrily shouted out *You're wrong!*"

Using Neutral Reactions. Effective teachers react to negative responses such as complaining, criticizing, or arguing in a neutral manner. They do not get hooked into angry responses that invariably hinder future teaching opportunities. My worst experience with a student happened as a "Teaching Ministry" class was discussing church growth—the capstone of the model described in chapter 1. I had asked students to evaluate my view on church growth individually. Then I put them in pairs to share views, then in groups of four. Finally I asked the class as a whole, "So now that you've had time to consider the capstone, how would you evaluate my view of church growth?" A theology student, seated in the rear of the class, rattled the class as he angrily shouted out, "You're *wrong!*" My first reaction was that, if I'd had a gun, I'd have blown him away. Perhaps it's my Texas upbringing. But that thought was gone in an instant, replaced by concern for why this young man was so angry. I calmly turned toward him and said, "Okay, you believe I'm wrong. Convince me. Where exactly am I wrong?" A mixture of words and venom spewed from his mouth. With great animation and hyperbole he accused me of manipulation and distortion, of improper motives and subtle untruths. For thirty seconds he railed out at me while the class sat in stunned silence. About a minute into his outburst, he began to slow down. Words came more deliberately. His emotional state grew calmer. After a few more seconds, he ground to a halt. I turned to the class at large and asked, "Okay, you've heard Tim's evaluation of the material. How would you respond?" Six students proceeded to take his accusations and characterizations apart. Because I did not personally attack him—in fact, I made it a point to be open to him in the class sessions that followed—I finally won him over and helped him grow in his understanding of the teaching ministry of the church. Had I "put him in his place," I would have lost any chance of reaching him.

Effective teachers are able to balance responsibility to the teaching task with concern for students. We said it in the preface, but it bears saying again: the best teachers weave together content and communication, grace and justice, nurture and control in order to help learners grow. Teaching is art in that this weaving of elements happens spontaneously, in the very process of teaching: framing the right question on the spot, responding appropriately to learners "in the moment," using humor appropriately to dispel tension or drive home a sensitive point. This is art, and flows out of the personality of the teacher. Now let's focus on the effects of competition and cooperation in the classroom.

COMPETITION

Competition means to "strive with another or others to attain a goal, such as attaining an advantage or winning a victory."[47] There is no doubt that competition produces excitement. Just consider the frenzy surrounding football's "Super Bowl," basketball's "Final Four," or the Olympic Games. In the classroom, competition is based on grades, test scores, projects, and debates. Hamachek reports it is almost impossible to find research studies that praise competition as a motivator in the classroom. While competitive methods may produce a few winners, they produce many more losers—and this causes problems in school.[48] Other studies have found that competitive methods produce higher anxiety, lower self-esteem, and less responsibility for and value toward fellow students.[49] While students readily and aggressively compete on the playground, it is a different situation in the classroom. Students *choose to compete* at recess. There is no choice in the classroom. They are *free to quit* a game anytime. They cannot quit the classroom. Being locked into competitive learning activities can make school feel like a prison, especially to low achievers.

Destructive Competition

My wife has a pleasant alto voice, but she will never sing in public. Why? Because in the third grade her teacher placed her before the class and made her sing. When she finished, the teacher laughed and told her she'd never ask her to sing again. Hmmm. I wonder if her teacher *intended* to scar this nine-year-old for life?

My first college, was considered the Cal Tech of the East when I entered as an electrical engineering student in 1966. The school always accepted more students than they could accommodate and used the "Introductory Physics" course as the means to cull the less serious students from the ranks. It was common for half the students to fail this class—and failure meant dismissal from the school. At the end of the semester, grades were posted by name, ranked by grade, in the hallway outside the main office. A line was drawn across the list separating "pass-ers" from "fail-ers." I can remember reading down the list—my heart pounding—looking for my name. There were shouts of joy when we found our names above the line. Others left in tears and anger.

These two examples show how destructive competition can be. Learning is de-emphasized, becoming a means to an end—to be better than others[50]—rather than an end in itself. Further, public failure is worse than private failure because of its impact on interpersonal relationships among students. It is bad enough for Johnny to fail a test, but worse when everyone else knows how badly Johnny did. Finally, an emphasis on ranking and relative performance reduces the quality of learning for most students. Students begin to avoid failure more and strive for success less. Since they believe they cannot win (only the top few can "win"), they work to avoid failure.

Constructive Competition

Some measure of competition always exists in the classroom even if teachers don't plan for it. "Whadjaget?" is a common question after tests are returned. The key is to use competitive methods in a constructive way. Competition motivates students when they are prepared to compete on an equal basis.[51] Help students focus more on their personal improvement than on their relative standing in the class. Encourage them to beat their last test score rather than the test score of the brightest student in the class. Keep grades confidential. Allow students to demonstrate their learning in a variety of ways.[52]

COOPERATION

Cooperation means to "work or act together toward a common end or purpose."[53] In chapter 10 we introduced you to cooperative learning and reported that it increases achievement, motivation to learn, higher thinking skills, and interpersonal relationships in students.[54] It also improves student self-esteem and acceptance of handicapped students.[55] Let's look at some specific examples of cooperative learning strategies.

Learning Together. Students are placed in four- or five-member heterogeneous teams. That is, groups consist of students of different ability levels, races, and genders. Each team is given a single assignment which is produced as a group. Teams are stable, working together for several weeks.[56]

Group Investigation. Students are placed in two- to six-member heterogeneous groups. Each group is given a subtopic to research, discuss and prepare for presentation. Groups then present their findings to the whole class.[57]

Teams-Games-Tournaments (TGT). Students are assigned to four- or five-member heterogeneous groups to study materials in preparation for competition against other teams. Study groups discuss the material, answer questions, and take daily quizzes. At the end of the week, students of similar abilities are assigned to three-member tournament teams to compete. The study groups are stable over several weeks. Tournament teams change weekly.[58]

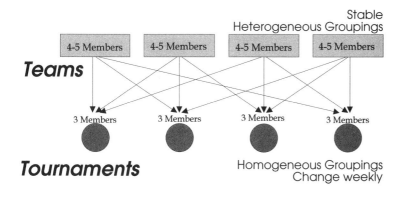

Student Teams-Achievement Divisions (STAD). STAD is set up very much like TGT, but substitutes fifteen minute quizzes, taken individually, for the tournament competitions. Study teams are changed periodically.[59]

Jigsaw. Students are assigned to heterogeneous groups. Each student in the group is given individual study materials and assignments which form part of a learning whole. When these are completed, groups meet together to share what each member has learned. Students are tested individually on the whole material.[60]

Cooperative learning is not intended to be a replacement for direct instruction and traditional entire-class learning. It is a supplement which yields numerous benefits in classroom climate. These include interactive learning, reduction of anxiety, interpersonal skills development, as well as many more winners.[61]

Reward Structures and
Academic Achievement

The diagram at right, developed by Michaels,[62] combines individual/group structures with the availability of rewards to produce four classroom climates. "Individual" and "Group" refer to who receive the rewards. An individual reward is earned by a student's own efforts. A group award is given to every member of the group as a result of the group's efforts. "Limited" and "Unlimited" refer to the availability of rewards. "Limited awards" means that only the best students or groups can earn rewards. "Unlimited awards" means that any student or group achieving a given standard earns rewards.

Task Focus

	Individual	Group
Limited	Individual Competition *Dog-eat-dog*	Group Competition *Tribal warfare*
Unlimited	Individual Reward *Every man for himself*	Group Reward *True cooperative learning*

(Reward Type)

Individual Competition. Students compete individually for a limited number of A's. Grading-on-the-Curve is the primary example of this approach. I'll never forget one of my "higher education" experiences. One of my first classes had one hundred students. On the first day the professor announced that only ten of us would earn A's during the semester. I had never formally studied the subject before. Yet I was competing with a dozen students who had not only taken the subject before, but had used the same textbook! That made no difference when the class averages were computed. I achieved a 90 average during the semester, but this translated into a "B" for the course because "the grader wasn't hard enough in his evaluations, and too many students were in the A category." I resented the fact that I spent sixteen weeks studying a subject that was new to me only to be arbitrarily demoted because too many others did better.

Worse than my demotion in grade was the spirit this competitive structure created in the class. I was out of class for a week with the flu and asked several classmates if I could borrow their class notes. I had to ask six students before I found one willing to share his notes with me. The first five were afraid I might outscore them and bump them out of an A. *And we wonder why pastors trained under such a system have difficulty working cooperatively with other pastors.* They have been trained to compete, to overcome, to win, to outdo others, to succeed. Such attitudes do not foster a cooperative spirit.

Group Competition. Students are assigned to groups which then compete for grades. The top group will receive an A for all its members. The second and third groups may receive B's for all their members. Groups four, five, and six—given completed assignments—will be given C's. This structure is better than individual competition because the "losers" can at least comfort one another. But the classroom climate under this type of grading structure might be described as tribal warfare.

Individual Reward. When the available rewards are unlimited, student achievement is based solely on their quality of work. In an individual reward structure, students work individually to accomplish course goals according to stated expectations. Every student who meets the stated criteria earns the reward—such as an A. Since students are not competing against each other for limited rewards, they are much more likely to help each other learn.

Group Reward. Students work together in groups to achieve, as groups, the stated course goals and expectations. Every group that meets the stated criteria earns the reward for its members. Research has shown that group reward structures produce higher achievement, higher self-esteem, and better interpersonal relationships among students than does any other structure. This structure constitutes true cooperative learning, illustrated by cooperative methods discussed earlier. Most of my Christian Education courses in seminary were structured as group reward. The school had just completed a research project among Southern Baptist pastors concerning the skills of our graduates. The number one need, according to the study, was for graduates to know how to work with people. As a result of this finding, most of my professors structured their classes around group projects. I admit that I was often frustrated by the group process. There were always students who did not do their share of the work. In order for the group to meet course expectations, a few of us did most of the work. Many times I complained out loud, "Why can't I just do my own work? " It was not until the end of my first year as minister of education at Columbia Baptist Church that I realized the importance of the group process and interpersonal skills I'd developed. The cooperative learning strategies I'd experienced carried me through that first year on church staff.

Consider these words of Paul in relation to our discussion of classroom climate and the Christian teacher. Paul expected believers

IMPLICATIONS FOR CHRISTIAN TEACHING

to "live a life worthy of the calling" they had received (Eph. 4:1; see also Col. 1:10). Their faith was not some appendage to add to their own system of values and lifestyle. "You are not your own; you were bought at a price. Therefore honor God with your body" (1 Cor. 6:19–20). Believers are to be "completely humble and gentle; be patient, bearing with one another in love" (Eph. 4:2). Not arrogant, not mean-spirited, not hot-tempered. We are to bear with, or in today's language, "put up with," other believers in love (Col. 3:13). Believers are to "make every effort to keep the unity of the Spirit through the bond of peace" (Eph. 4:3). Struggle to keep peace. Wrestle with the forces that would divide believers into camps. Warfare among believers never comes from the Holy Spirit, but is always of the flesh (Gal. 5:19–23). This unity belongs to the body, or the community of believers (Eph. 4:4), and is based on our unified hope in Christ: "one Lord, one faith, one baptism; one God and Father of all, who is over all and through all and in all" (Eph. 4:5–6). What is the purpose of Christian unity? To permit each of us to use our personal ("to each one of us," v. 7) gifts ("grace," v. 7) together, so that we will no longer live like "Gentiles" or hardhearted, sensuous, ignorant pagans (see vv. 17–19).

Since believers are expected to live in a manner worthy of the Lord—to be humble, gentle, patient, forbearing, loving, peaceful and united—then believers who are leaders and teachers should reflect these characteristics even more. "Not lording it over those entrusted to you, but being *examples* to the flock" (1 Pet. 5:3, author's emphasis).

The classrooms of Christian teachers should exemplify cooperation, mutual support, *koinonia*, and mutual love. Christian classrooms should challenge students to be their very best because our mission is so important. Christian teachers should integrate their maturing faith into the very woof and weave of classroom performance. The seminary professor who labeled his student's question "the dumbest I've ever heard" separated his "love for the brethren" (1 Thess. 4:10, KJV) from his classroom behavior. He had compartmentalized his faith from his teaching. Beloved, this ought not to be!

IN SUMMARY

Using the Christian Teachers' Triad from chapter 11, let's synthesize this chapter into three key principles regarding classroom climate: Light rather than Dark; Warm rather than Cold; and Active rather than Passive.

"Light" refers to clear presentations, organized lectures and meaningful activities. "Dark" refers to confusing, chaotic meandering. Cognitively, classroom climate is improved when teachers and their teaching make sense. It is the cognitive side of teaching that challenges, confronts, stretches, and probes.

Light Rather than Dark

"Warm" refers to feelings of openness, safety, and rapport. "Cold" refers to feelings of aloofness, fear, and being alone. Humanistically, classroom climate is improved when teachers and their teaching are inviting, accepting, and reassuring. It is the humanistic side of teaching that supports, encourages, nurtures and cares for students.

Warm Rather than Cold

"Active" refers to students being personally engaged in the learning process. "Passive" refers to students being dormant receptacles of whatever teachers deem important. Behaviorally, classroom climate improves when students are actively engaged in learning. It is the behavioral side of teaching that trains, reinforces, and models effective learning skills.

Active Rather than Passive

Hamachek concludes his excellent discussion of effective teaching by writing,

> Good teachers are good for many reasons, and one of those reasons might be that they are basically good people to begin with. If I interpret the research correctly—and read a bit between the lines—I infer that good teachers rather like life; are firm but fair; expect a lot from themselves and their students; have a sense of humor; and enjoy, at least most of the time, their work.
>
> To be a good teacher means that we not only know our subject area and something about our students, but that we also know something about ourselves.[63]

Lord, teach us about ourselves. Help us to integrate the fruit of the Spirit—love, joy, peace, patience, kindness, goodness, faithfulness, goodness, and self-control—into our teaching. Help us make our classrooms spiritual arenas in which we stretch yet support, confront yet care, persuade yet permit, lecture yet listen, and challenge yet charm those whom God has sent us to teach. Help us grow beyond being Christians who teach. Enable us to become Christian in our teaching. That our students might grow to become all You would have them to be. For Your Kingdom's sake we ask it. Amen.

CHAPTER CONCEPTS

Allocated time

Body language

Competition

Content-communication balance

Cooperation

Directing questions

Engaged time

Enthusiasm

Explicit format

Flexibility

Group competition

Group reward

Group investigation

Individual reward

Individual competition

Jigsaw

Learning together

Mature

Movement

Organizational clarity

Preparation

Probing questions

Questioning behaviors

Rapport

Reacting behaviors

Redirecting questions

Responsibility

Scholarship

Self-evaluation

Signal giving

Student Teams-Achievement Divisions
  (STAD)

Structuring behaviors

Teacher personality

Teams-Games-Tournaments (TGT)

Voice

Wait time I

Wait time II

Warmth

DISCUSSION QUESTIONS

1. Choose two of the four teacher personality factors discussed in the chapter. Define each factor in your own words. Describe teachers you've had who possessed these factors. Describe teachers you've had who did not possess these factors. How did these four teachers affect classroom climate?

2. Choose any five of the following terms: structuring, signal giving, mands, organization, Wait Time I, Wait Time II, directing questions, redirecting questions, probing, and positive and negative reactions. Define each term and give an example of its use in class.

3. Dr. Yount shared examples of individual competition and group reward structures in his seminary education. Have you had similar experiences in college or seminary? Identify the type of reward structure and describe its impact on your learning.

4. Think of the both the best teacher and worst teacher you've ever had. Write their names at the top of a sheet of paper, separated by a vertical line down the page. Review the chapter and identify the characteristics which differ between the two teachers you selected. At the bottom of the page, summarize in four or five sentences what you learned about teachers and classroom climate from this exercise.

FOR FURTHER READING

Biehler, Robert F., and Jack Snowman."The Impact of Classroom Atmosphere and of the Teacher." In *Psychology Applied to Teaching*. 7th ed., 524–33. Boston: Houghton Mifflin Company, 1993.

Dembo, Myron H."The Grouping Dimension [Cooperative Learning]." In *Applying Educational Psychology*. 5th ed., 170–76. New York: Longman, 1994.

Gage, N. L., and David C. Berliner. "The Recitation." In *Educational Psychology*. 3rd ed., 627–49. Boston: Houghton Mifflin Company, 1984.

Hamachek, Don. "Psychology and Behaviors of Effective Teachers," "Understanding Oneself: A Key to Enhancing Teaching Effectiveness," "Toward Making Teaching Meaningful, Relevant, and Lasting." In *Psychology in Teaching, Learning, and Growth*. 4th ed., 391–424; 425–60; 461–504. Boston: Allyn and Bacon, 1990.

Kagan, S. *Cooperative Learning*. 8th ed. San Juan Capistrano, Calif.: Kagan Cooperative Learning, 1992.

Michaels, James W. "Classroom Reward Structures and Academic Achievement." *Review of Educational Research*. 47 (1977): 87–98.

Slavin, Robert E. "Motivating Students to Learn." In *Educational Psychology: Theory and Practice*. 4th ed., 344–84. Boston: Allyn and Bacon, 1994.

———. *Cooperative Learning: Theory, Research and Practice*. Boston: Allyn and Bacon, 1990.

Smith, M. Daniel. In "Characteristics of Effective Teachers," *Educational Psychology and Its Classroom Applications*, 128–158. Boston: Allyn and Bacon, 1975.

Sprinthall, Norman A., Richard C. Sprinthall, and Sharon N. Oja. "Motivation in the Classroom." In *Educational Psychology: A Developmental Approach*. 6th ed., 527–54. New York: McGraw-Hill, Inc., 1994.

Woolfolk, Anita. "Classroom Management and Communication." In *Educational Psychology*. 5th ed., 398–433. Boston: Allyn and Bacon, Inc., 1993.

Wlodkowski, Raymond J. *Motivation and Teaching: A Practical Guide*, Washington, D.C.: National Education Association, 1986.

THE TEACHER
AS EVALUATOR

As far as we can gather from Scripture, Jesus never administered a formal examination. But He did evaluate His disciples. He assessed them *by their actions* when they were caught in a storm on the sea of Galilee (Matt. 8:26; Mark 4:40). He assessed their *understanding* of His mission: "Who am I?" (Matt. 16:15; Mark 8:29). He assessed the kingdom *values and personal devotion* of Peter when He asked him, "Do you love me?" (John 21:15ff). Jesus "knew what was in man" (John 2:24–5, KJV). Yet He asked questions and posed problems to reveal what His listeners understood and believed. This chapter will help you consider ways to sharpen your evaluative skills, whether you teach in an academic setting or not. Teaching is a process of leading learners to a specific destination. Evaluation determines whether they've arrived.

Learners will demonstrate understanding of proper principles of writing test items by:
- determining whether selected test items are correctly written;
- writing two questions of each type on the material contained in *Created to Learn*;
- evaluating the questions of at least three classmates.

Learners will demonstrate appreciation for writing clear test items by sharing experiences of good and bad testing experiences with the class.

WHY EVALUATE?   We defined "education" in the preface as the process of developing the innate capacities of learners, especially by schooling or instruction. How do we know whether our students have developed their innate capacities? How do we know whether our educational efforts produce meaningful learning? We must periodically check student learning[1] for several reasons. Evaluations provide information on student progress toward instructional goals[2] and—in elementary situations—form a communication bridge between the school and home.[3] They reveal which students need additional help.[4] Evaluations provide a basis for honors, promotion, graduation, and probation.[5] They provide feedback on the quality of instruction.[6] Evaluations in the form of tests and quizzes produce incentive for greater efforts[7] because research has shown students learn more in courses that use tests than in those that do not.[8] Measuring student performance and assigning grades for student achievements cause anxiety and stress. But evaluation is necessary because too much depends on the information it provides.[9]

Evaluations usually focus on academic achievement (cognitive learning), but some schools also include behaviors and attitudes in their evaluations.[10] Daniel Smith makes a strong case for evaluating learning in all three domains:

> [In the "evaluation game"] . . . you find learning evaluated primarily on the basis of what has been acquired cognitively . . . whereas teaching is often evaluated on the basis of whether students *like* it or not. Actually, to be thorough, evaluation of learning and teaching both should include affective, cognitive and behavioral dimensions . . . and teaching should be assessed on the basis of the learning that it brings about—including affective and behavioral domains in the definition of learning.[11]

Teachers gather a great deal of information *incidentally* as they interact with students. This *informal* evaluation consists of comments, answers to questions, body language, and facial expressions. These evaluations are unsystematic because the information is not the same for every student. Assuming an entire class understands because a few respond correctly means that some may not be able to move to the next stage of learning.[12]

Formal (systematic) evaluations, such as those made by tests, quizzes and performance observations, are essential to help teachers make decisions regarding learning activities and time allotment.[13] Systematic evaluations prevent making assessments based on activity level (active or passive) or appearance (attractive or unattractive).[14] We will discuss evaluations in all three domains, but spend most of the chapter focusing on academic (cognitive) testing. In an academic setting, nothing affects student attitudes more than the quality of the tests they must endure. Poorly written test items, subjectively graded essays, and unclear requirements make evaluation unsettling. Grades—and future opportunities—hang in the balance. Toy with students in the way you evaluate them, and you will suffer poor student ratings. Formal evaluations are rarely made in non-academic settings, such as Sunday school classes. Still, principles which govern the writing of test items help teachers frame questions more clearly.

Cognitive learning is defined by the six levels of Bloom's taxonomy, which we introduced to you in chapter 6. In that chapter we outlined the use of broad domain-related goal statements ("Learners will demonstrate understanding of John 3:16") and specific level-related indicator statements ("by explaining the terms "love," "world," "believe," and "eternal life" in their own words") to set up targets for teaching. We introduced the concept of a behavior-content matrix, sometimes called a table of specifications,[15] to track subject content areas and levels of learning addressed in class. The behavior-content matrix provides a clear and specific basis for writing test items and constructing examinations.

Tests which provide systematic, unbiased information on student achievement must possess three characteristics: validity, reliability, and objectivity.[16] A test is "valid" if it measures what it says it measures. There are several types of test validity[17] but we'll focus on content validity here. When the content of a test matches the universe of learnings the test covers, it is said to have *content validity*. That is, a test designed to cover "unit 4" of a course should contain items that reflect the major learnings from unit 4 and no others. Including test items from unit 3 ("testing recall") or from footnotes or optional reading assignments ("the better students will have studied these") violates content validity unless students are specifically told these areas will be tested. A behavior-content matrix assures content validity, because the test items match the outcomes targeted by the unit or course. *Reliability* refers to the precision of the test or how accurately the test measures student achievement. Arbitrary, poorly written questions inject random noise into student scores and lower test reliability. The principles we'll soon discuss on writing test items will improve the reliability of your tests. *Objectivity* refers to

MEASURING
COGNITIVE LEARNING

absence of personal bias in answering questions or scoring answers. Even essay questions, which are notorious for their subjectivity, should be graded as objectively as possible—otherwise, the scores are not systematic assessments of student achievement.

OBJECTIVE TESTS

An objective test is a test made up of questions which can be answered with a word or short phrase, or by circling an answer. Answers to objective questions are either correct or incorrect. Graders do not need to interpret student responses.[18] Different graders will award the same score for each student.[19] Objective tests have several advantages over essay tests. Asking one hundred objective questions over a given content field provides a much better sampling of student knowledge and understanding than asking three or four essay questions. With objective tests, grading is easier and the scores are a more reliable measure of what the student knows.[20] However, writing good objective questions is more difficult and time consuming than writing essay questions.[21]

The most common types of objective questions[22] are multiple-choice[23] or changing alternative[24] question; the true-false[25] or constant alternative[26] question; the supply,[27] fill-in-the-blank,[28] or completion[29] question; and the matching question.[30]

The True-False Item

The true-false item presents the student with a factual statement which is judged to be either true or false.[31] For example:

> T F According to chapter 14 in *Created to Learn*, students are more concerned with the quality of lectures and classroom activities than they are with the quality of examinations. (false)

Advantages. True-false test items are efficient and potent. They are efficient in that a large number of items can be answered in a short period of time.[32] They are potent because they can directly reveal common misconceptions and fallacies.[33] Scoring true-false items is fast and easy.[34]

Disadvantages. A good true-false item is hard to write.[35] An item that makes good sense to the writer may confuse even a well-informed student. Statements require careful wording, evaluation and revision. Also, true-false items encourage guessing.[36] A student can earn fifty percent on a test by chance simply by guessing the right answer.[37]

Writing
True-False items

The following guidelines will help you avoid major pitfalls in writing true-false test items.

Focus on one central idea.[38] Each statement should focus on one central idea in order to minimize confusion:

> Poor: T F　　Skinner developed operant conditioning principles and Bruner developed the hierarchy of needs.

> Better: T F　　Skinner developed operant conditioning principles.

Avoid specific determiners.[39] Specific determiners are words like "only," "all," "always," "none," "no," or "never." True-false items containing these words are usually false. On the other hand, items containing terms like "might," "can," "may," or "generally" are usually true. Write items without using these terms:

> Poor: T F　　Consistent use of instructional objectives will always improve teaching quality.

> Better: T F　　Consistent use of instructional objectives improves teaching quality.

Call for an absolute answer.[40] Base true-false items on statements that are absolutely true or absolutely false.[41] Avoid statements that are true under some conditions but not others, unless the conditions are specifically stated. Well-informed students will have greater difficulty answering obscure or confusing statements correctly because they have more information to process in trying to understand what the item is asking:

> Poor: T F　　Christians are "complete in Christ," and therefore have no need for secular theories of development.

> Better: T F　　Christians can learn from secular development theories without compromising their faith.

The first statement mixes spiritual truth ("complete in Christ") with human growth. Christian students would be hard pressed to respond "False" to such a statement. Yet, educational theories do help us understand the teaching-learning process better.

Minimize the use of negative statements.[42] State items in the positive rather than the negative to reduce confusion.[43] Avoid double negatives altogether:[44]

> Poor: T F　　It is not infrequently observed that three-year-olds play in groups.

> Better: T F　　Three-year-olds play in groups.

The latter item tests knowledge of three-year-olds and social development. The former requires knowledge plus an ability to perform mental gymnastics.

Use precise language.[45] Avoid using terms like "few," "many," "long," "short," "large," "small," or "important" in test items. These terms are ambiguous. How much is enough for a true-false answer? How big is "big"? How many is "many"?

> Poor: T F   Writing clear test items is important in motivating students to study for exams.

> Better: T F   Students are motivated to study for exams when teachers write clear test items.

Avoid direct quotes.[46] Do not use direct quotes from class notes or required readings. Quotes taken out of context are too ambiguous to use as test items. Using them overemphasizes rote memory.[47] It is better to focus on the sense of class notes or readings rather than on exact words:[48]

> Poor: T F   Maslow wrote, "It is quite impossible for the student to discover for himself any substantial part of the wisdom of his culture." (false: Skinner)

> Better: T F   Maslow opposed Bruner's discovery approach to education on the grounds of self-initiated learning.

Attribute opinion to a source. Give the source of an opinion statement. Doing this informs the student that the statement is asking whether or not the source, and not the student, holds that opinion:[49]

> Poor: T F   It is not possible for students to discover for themselves any substantial part of their culture's wisdom.

> Better: T F   Skinner believed that it is not possible for students to discover for themselves any substantial part of their culture's wisdom.

Watch item length. Avoid making true statements longer than false items. True statements often require qualifications to insure they are absolutely true.[50]

Avoid complex sentences. Complex grammatical constructions and obscure language confuse students. Write items that are simple statements of truth or misconception.[51]

Use more false items.[52] When developing a True-False test, make about sixty percent of the items false.[53] False items discriminate between students better than true items. You can improve the reliability of true-false test scores if you have students correct false items to make them read correctly. These two techniques help reduce guessing and increase reliability of scores.

Multiple-Choice Items   The multiple-choice, or changing alternative, item is the most popular type of objective question.[54] It consists of a sentence or question stem and several responses.[55] One response is correct. The others, called distractors,[56] are incorrect but plausible. The most common form of this type is the multiple-choice question with four or five responses.[57] For example:

> The measurement characteristic most related to the precision or accuracy of a test is
>
> > a. validity
> > b. subjectivity
> > c. reliability
> > d. objectivity

Advantages. The multiple-choice question, with its multiple responses, can be written with less ambiguity and greater structure than true-false or short answer questions.[58] Guessing is reduced[59] since the probability for selecting the correct answer by chance is one in four (25%) or one in five (20%) instead of one in two (50%) for true-false items. Multiple-choice items demand more discrimination than other forms of objective questions. Lastly, one can write multiple-choice items which test at higher levels of learning than other question types.[60] Because multiple-choice questions can be processed faster, they allow for better sampling of student mastery than is permitted by short-answer essays.[61]

Disadvantages. Writing good multiple-choice questions is both time consuming[62] and difficult.[63] Distractors are hard to create,[64] particularly if you are providing a fifth or sixth alternative response.[65] Secondly, multiple-choice tests are less efficient because students can process fewer multiple-choice items than other objective types.[66]

The following guidelines will help you avoid major pitfalls in writing changing alternative items.

Writing Multiple-Choice Items

Pose a singular problem. The stem of the question should pose a clear, definite, singular problem.[67] A common mistake in multiple-choice questions is the use of an incomplete stem.[68] Make the stem a complete sentence or a direct question,[69] rather than an sentence fragment:[70]

Poor: Behavior modification is

> > a. punishment
> > b. classical conditioning
> > c. self-actualization
> > d. reinforcement contingencies

Better: Which of the following alternatives best characterizes the modern clinical use of behavior modification?

> > a. punishment
> > b. classical conditioning
> > c. self-actualization
> > d. reinforcement contingencies (correct)[71]

One and only one correct answer.[72] Be sure that one and only one response is correct. Avoid using synonyms or overlapping responses:[73]

Poor: Which of the following types of research describes a current
               situation?

               a. experimental
               b. descriptive (overlaps c)
               c. correlational (overlaps b)
               d. ex post facto

Correlational research is descriptive. Either b or c could be considered a correct answer.

Better: Which of the following types of research describes a current
               situation?

               a. experimental
               b. base-line design
               c. correlational (correct)
               d. ex post facto

Minimize negative stems.[74] Avoid negative stems if possible. Negative items can confuse some students who might otherwise know the material. If you must use a negative in the stem, underline or italicize it:[75]

Poor: Which of the following is not an example of an objective type
               item?

Better: Which of the following is *not* an example of an objective type
               item?

Make responses similar. Avoid making the correct response systematically different from the others (grammar, length, construction). Responses should be written in parallel form so that the form of the response is not a clue to the correct answer:[76]

Poor: The boiling point of water is

               a. 424°F
               b. 282°F
               c. 212°F at sea level, in an open container
               d. 98°F

Better: The boiling point of water at sea level, in an open container, is

               a. 424°F
               b. 282°F
               c. 212°F
               d. 98°F[77]

Make responses equally plausible.[78] All responses in an item set should be equally plausible and attractive to the less knowledgeable student.[79] Each response should be credible and logical: [80]

Poor: Which of the following is *not* an objective-type question?

             a. constant alternative
             b. essay
             c. completion
             d. large-group discussion (not credible)

Better: Which of the following is *not* an objective-type question?

             a. constant alternative
             b. essay
             c. completion
             d. changing alternative

Randomly order responses.[81] Teachers unwittingly place the correct answer in the middle of the set more often than in the first (a.) or last (d.) positions. Responses should be randomly ordered for each question.[82]

Avoid sources of irrelevant difficulty.[83] Avoid irrelevant sources of difficulty in the stem and responses. Some teachers confuse students by using complex vocabulary.

Eliminate extraneous material.[84] Do not include extraneous material in a question. That is, do not attempt to mislead students by including information not necessary for answering the question.

Avoid responses such as "none of the above."[85] Alternative responses such as "none of the above," "all of the above," and "both b and d" should be eliminated if possible. These responses reduce the number of possible correct choices.[86]

Test at higher cognitive levels.[87] Multiple-choice items can set a complex case (political, educational, or social situation) and present alternative explanations for the case. One of our doctoral students developed a pastoral leadership inventory which involved ten cases of church conflict and four ways to handle each. Pastors were to read the case and select the approach he would most likely take to solve the problem. Each alternative was linked to a leadership style. By analyzing the pastors' choices, their predominant leadership style was defined. Charts, maps, or graphs can be used in conjunction with a series of multiple-choice questions which call for analysis, synthesis and evaluation. Avoid testing predominantly at the knowledge level—recall of facts.

Supply Items

Supply items, sometimes called "completion"[88] or "fill in the blank"[89] items, present a statement with one or more blanks. The student fills in the blanks with the most appropriate terms—consisting of a name, word, or phrase[90]—in order to correctly complete the statement. This question type should be used when the correct re-sponse is a single word or brief phrase.[91] For example:

> When different graders obtain the same scores for a given test, it is said to have _____. (objectivity)

Advantages. Supply items are relatively easy to construct.[92] They are efficient in that a large number of statements can be processed in a given length of time.[93] Since recalling a term is more difficult than recognizing it, supply items discriminate better.[94] Supply items offer little opportunity for guessing.[95]

Disadvantages. Supply items are notorious for being ambiguous. It is difficult to write a supply item that is clear and plainly stated. Grading can be arbitrary and unfair, depending on how synonyms—different words with the same meaning[96]—are handled.[97] This is because more than one word may adequately fill the blank. Finally, misuse of completion items can lead to overemphasis on memoriza-tion.[98]

Writing supply items

The following guidelines will help you avoid major pitfalls in writing supply items.

Limit blanks. Use only one or two blanks in a supply item. The greater the number of blanks, the greater the item ambiguity.[99] Dembo describes supply items with too many blanks as being "mutilated:"[100]

> Poor: Piaget wrote that _____ consists of _____ and
>   _____.
>
> Better: Piaget wrote that adaptation consists of _____ and
>   _____.

Allow for only one correct answer. Write the item in such a way that only one explicit term or definite word[101] will correctly com-plete the statement.[102] If there are equally acceptable terms for a given concept (i.e., "true-false" and "constant alternative"), then credit should be given for either answer.[103]

Omit important terms.[104] Leave only important terms blank. Blanking out minor words makes the item trivial.[105]

Place blank at the end. In most cases, it is preferable to place the blank at the end of the sentence. This gives the student the entire sen-tence as a basis for supplying the proper term. Placing the blank at the beginning reverses this natural process and confuses prepared students as well as the unprepared.[106]

Avoid irrelevant clues.[107] Do not provide irrelevant clues to the correct answer. An example of an irrelevant clue is to make the length of the blank equal to the number of characters in the word. Make all blanks the same length.[108] Another irrelevant clue is the use of "a" or "an" rather than "a(n)" just before the blank.

Avoid text quotes.[109] Do not use directly quoted sentences out of required reading as supply items. Sentences taken out of context are usually ambiguous. Write the supply item based on a clear concept, not a specific quote.

Matching items present students with two columns[110] of items which relate to each other. A common version of a matching question has a numbered item list on the left and a lettered response list on the right:[111]

Matching Items

_____ 1. Programmed Instruction	a. Erikson
_____ 2. Life Space	b. Kohlberg
_____ 3. Equilibration	c. Levine
_____ 4. Trust-Mistrust	d. Maslow
_____ 5. Hierarchy of Needs	e. Piaget
	f. Skinner
	g. Thorndike

Advantages. The matching item can test a large amount of factual material simply and efficiently.[112] Response pairs can be drawn from various texts, class notes, and additional readings to form a summary of facts. Grading is easy.[113]

Disadvantages. A good matching item is difficult to construct. As the number of response pairs in a given item increases, the more mental gymnastics are required to answer it. Matching items are restricted to measuring factual information[114] and simple concepts.

The following guidelines will help you avoid major pitfalls in writing supply items.

Writing matching items

Limit number of pairs. Do not include too many pairs to be matched in a given item. The list should contain no more than eight[115] to ten[116] pairs. Design the test so that the entire question is contained on one page.[117]

Make response list longer. If each response is used once and only once, then the response list should contain more responses than are needed to match all the items (see the example above). This prevents students from answering the last item simply by elimination.[118]

Opinions vary on how much longer to make the response list. Suggestions range from two to three items[119] to fifty percent[120] longer. However, if responses can be used more than once, then both lists can be the same length.[121]

Only one correct match.[122] It is important to ensure that each item (left column) matches only one word or phrase in the response list. Response options may be used more than once, however.

Maintain a central theme.[123] A matching item should contain matched pairs that all relate to one central theme. Avoid mixing names, dates, events, and definitions in a single matching item. If this is not possible, construct several matching items, each with a central theme: dates-events, terms-definitions, authors-writings, and so forth.[124]

Keep responses simple.[125] It is better to place longer statements in the item list and the shorter answers in the response list. This helps subjects rapidly scan the response list for the correct match.

Make the response list systematic.[126] Arrange the answers in the option column in some systematic way, such as alphabetical or chronological order.[127] This makes the task of searching through the responses less taxing and allows students to concentrate on answering correctly. Notice in the example above that the response list is ordered alphabetically.

Give specific instructions.[128] Be sure to explain clearly how the matching is to be done. Specifically indicate whether answers can be used more than once.[129] Show an example, if necessary. This eliminates "test-wiseness" as an extraneous variable in the scoring.

Essay Tests

Essay tests are constructed from unstructured or "open-ended" questions which require students to write out their response. For example: "Discuss educational motivation from the perspective of the three major learning theory systems."

Advantages. Essay test items are easy to construct.[130] They allow much greater flexibility and freedom in answering. Since grammar, structure, and content of the answer are left to students, teachers gain insight into students' ability to organize, integrate, and synthesize.[131] Essay items permit testing at higher levels of learning than most types of objective questions.[132] Finally, answers to essay questions permit a greater range of answers than objective items. Guessing is eliminated.[133]

Disadvantages. The greatest disadvantage of essay items is that they are difficult to score consistently.[134] The answers are more ambiguous and subjective than objective responses.[135] The reliability of scores is lower than those produced by objective tests over the same content because of the variability of response.[136] Essay items produce a smaller sample of material because of the amount of time required to analyze and understand the question, develop the answer, and write it out in complete sentences. This poses content validity problems.[137] Finally, essays are tedious and time consuming to grade.[138]

The following guidelines will help you avoid major pitfalls in writing essay items.

Writing essay items

Use short-answer essays.[139] It is much better to use several short answer essay items than one or two long ones. Nunnally suggests that a "short answer" cover a half page.[140] If your testing period is one hour, it would be better to ask for six ten-minute essays than two thrity-minute essays. This improves sampling of material, focuses the essays sufficiently to increase reliability of grading, and produces a better measure of what students know.[141]

Write clear questions.[142] Write essay questions that give sufficient information to guide students toward your intended response.[143] A student shared with me an essay question he'd recently faced: "Explain the doctrine of God (10 points)." Scholars have devoted lifetimes to answering this question. It is much too broad and vague:

Poor: Discuss learning theory and its role in Christian education.

Better: Describe the three major learning theory systems and explain how each system can be used in a Christian teaching context.

Require all students to answer all questions.[144] A common practice, given the strong influence of "student choice" from humanistic educators, is to list six to eight essay questions and allow students to choose any four to write on. This reduces the systematic nature of the scores on the test since students are not being evaluated on the same questions. It is better to set course objectives, teach according to those objectives, and systematically test whether students achieve those objectives.

Develop a grading key. Develop a specific grading key[145] or model answer[146] for each essay item. Award points for each element in the key. Major elements should receive more points than minor ones. A point or two should be awarded for grammar, punctuation, organization, and the like.[147] A grading key provides a systematic guide for objectively grading an essay answer. Without such a key, the score is as much a result of the perception of the grader as it is a measure of the knowledge of the subject. In addition, grade each paper without knowing its author[148] and grade one question at a time for all papers.[149] These practices increase the reliability and objectivity of the scoring.

Consider assigning essays as homework.[150] Rather than confronting students with essay-type questions on an examination, assign essays as homework. The lack of time pressure and availability of resources will permit students to write better papers. Use objective tests to systematically evaluate student understanding.

Item analysis

Item analysis is a procedure for determining which items in an objective test discriminate between informed and uninformed subjects. A test's purpose is to separate students along a scale of achievement. It is important that *this separation be done fairly*. Every item in a test should contribute to this separation process. Those that do not should be revised or eliminated. A popular method of item analysis is a procedure called the discrimination index. After administering and grading the exam, the procedure is applied as follows:[151]

Rank order subjects by grade. Rank order students high to low by their overall grade on the exam. The rank position of each student is a reflection of the student's overall preparation for the examination.

Divide students into top and bottom groups. Identify top and bottom proportions of students to compare. You can choose a percentage ranging from ten to forty percent. Twenty-five percent is common and gives you the top and bottom quarters of the class. The number of students in *one* of the groups (NUMBER) is used to compute the discrimination index.

Count correct answers. For each question in the exam, count how many students in the top group answered correctly (HIGH) and how many in the bottom group answered correctly (LOW). If the question is fairly separating students by their level of preparation, more of the top group should answer it correctly than of the bottom group.

Compute the discrimination index. The index is computed by subtracting LOW from HIGH and dividing by NUMBER. Let's say you have a class of forty students who take an exam. After grading the exam, rank the students by their overall test score. Select top and bottom quarters (25%) for computation of the discrimination index. In this case, you'll have the ten highest scoring students in group one and ten lowest scoring students in group two. Begin with question one and count how many students in the groups answered it correctly. Let's say that in our case, eight of the top ten subjects answered #1 right (HIGH=8) and three of the bottom ten answered #1 right (LOW=3). The discrimination index for item one is "(8 - 3)/10," or +0.500. Repeat this for every item.[152]

Interpret the index. A discrimination index ranges from -1.00 to +1.00. *Negative indices* indicate faulty questions. More "bottom" students answered these right than "top" students. These questions should be rewritten. *Positive indices* indicate good questions. The more positive the index, the more discriminating the question. A question that produces positive values close to zero does not discriminate between upper and lower groups, but it may pinpoint important learnings that you want every student to know. This kind of question is called a barrier question.

Using indices to revise tests. Rewrite or eliminate all questions that produce negative indices. Consider the mix of discrimination and barrier questions in your exam. A good starting place is sixty percent barrier items and forty percent discriminating items. Tests can be made *legitimately* more difficult by increasing the percentage of discriminating questions and by selecting questions with higher discrimination indices.

A Word of Caution. Discrimination index values should be based on as many students as possible. In classes of less than forty students, indices become less reliable. While the discrimination index is an extremely helpful tool in evaluating test items, it should be used with caution and in conjunction with student feedback. Still, the use of the discrimination index by teachers helps solve one of the most frustrating aspects of schooling: arbitrary testing. The discrimination index provides a way to develop examinations which yield valid measurements of student learning.

The overarching theme of our present unit is motivation. Shoddy or arbitrary testing practices undermine student motivation. No matter how well students understand their assigned subjects, poorly written tests prevent them from demonstrating what they've learned. Teachers may assign grades based on these faulty measurements, but the grades are not valid indicators of student learning. This is bad enough in secular settings, but it is sin when Christian teachers unfairly evaluate their students. It calls to mind Jesus' warning about causing "little ones who believe in me" to sin: "It would be better for

Testing as a Motivational Tool

him to have a large millstone hung around his neck and to be drowned in the depths of the sea" (Matt. 18:6).

Slavin describes seven characteristics that enable tests to be motivational tools. Tests should focus on "important" subject matter.[153] That is, relate test items to unit objectives. Tests should be "soundly based."[154] That is, tests should fairly and accurately focus on actual performance. Tests should set "consistent standards."[155] Requirements should be the same for all students. Tests should be based on "clear criteria."[156] Students should know what is required to earn a high grade. Tests should have "reliable interpretations."[157] Tests scores should be interpreted in terms of objectives and the subject matter. Students often make self-defeating interpretations along the lines of "doing *some* homework is better than doing none," or "a C is at least better than failing." Students should receive "frequent evaluations."[158] Brief, shorter quizzes maintain higher achievement than longer, less frequent examinations. And finally, students should receive "challenging evaluations."[159] Motivation is highest when tests are challenging for all, impossible for none.

MEASURING OTHER OUTCOMES

Affective learning focuses on attitudes, values, and ideals. Psychomotor learning focuses on skills. The discussions of the affective and psychomotor domains in chapter 6, behavioral learning theory in chapter 7, and humanistic learning theory in chapter 10, provide general suggestions for observing student attitudes and skills. Attitude scales, self-report papers, role play simulations, and observations of student choices and performances all fit into affective and psychomotor measurement. Academic achievement, measured by cognitive outcomes, is primary in an educational setting. But affective and psychomotor learning are important as well, particularly in spiritual matters. Understanding the Great Commission (Matt. 28:19–20) is laudable. But we also want our students to embrace the Great Commission, to value it, be committed to it. This requires more than rote memorization of it or being able to paraphrase it. We want our students to develop skills in sharing the gospel. Understanding Scripture is a cognitive outcome, but it also involves a heart-felt desire, a commitment to "rightly divide the Word of Truth," and the skills to use study helps to accomplish this.

Even in secular subjects such as research and statistics, I want students to value good research design and effective analysis procedures (affective) so that they can speak the language of science as

DESIGN FLOWCHART

The following diagram presents the process of developing sound tests.

1. Analyze the subject matter in relation to the age and background of students. What major and minor learnings from the content are appropriate for your students? Given Bruner's admonition that "one cannot teach everything about anything," what learnings—facts, concepts, attitudes, skills—are most relevant for your students?

2. On the basis on your analysis in step one, write goal statements targeting major learnings.

3. Write learning outcomes, or indicators, to establish what students will do to show they've achieved the stated objectives. Construct a behavior-content matrix to reflect the balance of teachings in a given unit.

4. Develop instructional sequences and assignments to guide students in learning facts and concepts and developing positive attitudes and skills related to goals and outcomes.

5. Write high-quality test items on the basis of the behavior-content matrix. Be sure every test item reflects targeted learnings for the unit of study. Write test items according to guidelines given in this chapter.

6. Assemble the test items into a clearly organized format. Write clear instructions for each question type.

7. Administer the examination to your students.

8. Score the examinations. Perform an item analysis on the test.

9. Evaluate each step of the process on the basis of the test results and student feedback:

(1) Were learning goals appropriate? Was there too much emphasis on one domain or another?

(2) Were learning outcomes appropriate? Too easy? Too difficult?

(3) Were the instructional sequences—lectures and activities—appropriately selected? Were students properly prepared for the examination? (If the class as a whole does poorly on an exam, the problem lies either with the instruction or the examination. Be willing to accept responsibility for poor student performance unless you have clear evidence that the class as a whole is unmotivated.)

(4) Which test items produced a negative discrimination index? Analyze each item. Is it poorly written? Does it target trivial material? If so, revise the item. If the item appears solid, was the material it tests not emphasized in class?

(5) Did the format of the test confuse students? How can it be improved?

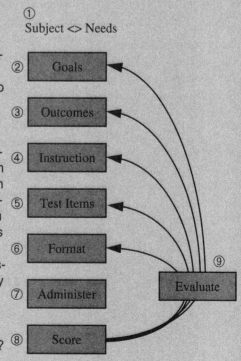

Christian researchers. I want them to develop expertise in research (skill) so they can make an impact for Christ in the scientific community. Knowledge, understanding, attitude, and skill provide a solid educational foundation for life. See suggested readings for specific suggestions in measuring affective and performance outcomes.

IN SUMMARY

In this chapter we looked at procedures for developing various types of tests. We have considered four kinds of objective items: true-false, multiple-choice, supply, and matching. We have discussed the use of essay questions. Finally, we described item analysis, which allows test developers to determine whether objective test items are valid.

As Christian educators, we are held to higher standards than our secular counterparts (James 3:1). We deal with the "little ones" of the Lord—young adults who look to us as representatives of Christ to teach them. There is no greater damage done to these little ones than that from arbitrary, unfair, and shoddy examinations—which determines their future opportunities in the Lord's service. The Old Testament is clear: "Do not use dishonest standards when measuring length, weight, or quantity. Use honest scales and honest weights, an honest ephah and an honest hin. I am the LORD your God, who brought you out of Egypt" (Lev. 19:35–36). And Isaiah writes, "Woe to those who make unjust laws, to those who issue oppressive decrees, to deprive the poor of their rights and withhold justice from the oppressed of my people . . ." (Isa 10:1–2a). Jesus warns us that, as we evaluate others, we will be evaluated: "With the measure you use, it will be measured to you—and even more" (Mark. 4:24).

It is a matter of simple ethics that our evaluations of students—believers who look to us for learning in a Christian context—should be as accurate and fair as possible. We must challenge our students toward excellence, but the measurement of their accomplishments must be made with honest scales and standard measures. Christian teaching is far more than scholarly discourses. It includes nurture, guidance, and support, not only in learning, but in measuring that learning in a fair manner.

CHAPTER CONCEPTS

Barrier question   Item analysis
Changing alternative   Negative index
Constant alternative   Objective test
Content validity   Objectivity
Discriminating question   Positive index
Discrimination index   Reliability
Distractors   Specific determiners
Grading key   Supply question
Informal evaluation   Systematic evaluation
Irrelevant cues   Validity

DISCUSSION QUESTIONS

1. Explain why objective tests produce more reliable scores than essay tests.

2. Evaluate the following questions based on material in the chapter. Write the letter "G" if you believe the question is good, "P" for poor, and "?" for not sure.

   _____ 1.   _____ and _____ are major influences on identity formation (Erikson).

   _____ 2.   T F   Carl Rogers, one of the founding fathers of humanistic psychology, grew up in a conservative, Bible-believing home.

   _____ 3.   Jean Piaget

   a. founded the Behaviorism School in America.

   b. understood human thinking to be stable from childhood to adulthood.

   c. laid the foundation for humanistic psychology.

   d. developed principles of affective, as well as cognitive, development.

   _____ 4.   Kohlberg's fourth stage, related to society's need for organization and harmony, is called _____.

   _____ 5.   T F   Piaget is to humanism what Skinner is to cognitive theory.

3. Write out two questions of each type (five types) relating to material in *Created to Learn*.

4. Write out your best and worst testing experience. Consider each one and describe what made these experiences as good/bad as they were.

FOR FURTHER READING

For an in-depth study:

Kubiszyn, Tom, and Gary Borish. *Educational Testing and Measurement: Classroom Application and Practice*. Glenview, Ill.: Scott, Foresman and Company, 1987.

Nunnally, Jum C. *Educational Measurement and Evaluation*. New York: McGraw-Hill Book Company, 1972.

Payne, David A. *The Assessment of Learning: Cognitive and Affective*. Lexington, Mass.: D. C. Heath and Company, 1974.

For general information:

Biehler, Robert F., and Jack Snowman. "Measurement and Evaluation of Classroom Learning." In *Psychology Applied to Teaching*. 7th ed., 562–619. Boston: Houghton Mifflin Company, 1993.

Dembo, Myron H. "Classroom Assessment," and "Analyzing Test Results and Reporting Student Progress." In *Applying Educational Psychology*. 5th ed., 546–95; 596–633. New York: Longman, 1994.

Eggen, Paul, and Don Kauchak. "Part Five: Assessment." In *Educational Psychology: Classroom Connections*. 2nd ed. 640–711. New York: Macmillan College Publishing Company, 1994.

Gage, N. L., and David C. Berliner. "Section G: Measurement and Evaluation." In *Educational Psychology*. 3rd ed. 651–751. Boston: Houghton Mifflin Company, 1984.

Glover, John A., and Roger H. Bruning. "Part Four: Educational Measurement and Evaluation." In *Educational Psychology: Principles and Applications*. 3rd. ed. 350–481. Glenview, Ill.: Scott, Foresman/Little, Brown Higher Education, 1990.

Good, Thomas L., and Jere E. Brophey. "Part Eight: Measurement and Evaluation." In *Educational Psychology: A Realistic Approach*. 4th ed., 680–764. New York: Longman, 1990.

Hamachek, Don. "Measurement and Evaluation of Learning Outcomes." In *Psychology in Teaching, Learning, and Growth*. 4th ed., 345–90. Boston: Allyn and Bacon, 1990.

LeFrancois, Guy R. "Measurement and Evaluation." In *Psychology for Teaching*. 8th ed. 348–86. Belmont, Calif.: Wadsworth Publishing Company, 1994.

Slavin, Robert E. "Assessing Student Learning." In *Educational Psychology: Theory and Practice*. 4th ed., 482–527. Boston: Allyn and Bacon, 1994.

Smith, M. Daniel. "Part Five: Evaluation and Measurement of Learning. In *Educational Psychology and Its Classroom Applications*. 469–537. Boston: Allyn and Bacon, 1975.

Sprinthall, Norman A., Richard C. Sprinthall, and Sharon N. Oja. "Measurement and Individual Differences," In *Educational Psychology: A Developmental Approach*. 6th ed., 425–56. New York: McGraw–Hill, Inc., 1994.

Woolfolk, Anita. "Part 6: Evaluating Student Learning." In *Educational Psychology*. 5th ed., 504–74. Boston: Allyn and Bacon, Inc., 1993.

UNIT 5

Jesus, the Master Teacher

Jesus was the greatest teacher who ever lived. In His thirty-three years of life and three years of ministry, He so transformed His disciples and wider circle of followers that within a generation they had turned the known world upside down. In the person of the Holy Spirit, Jesus as Divine Personal Presence continues to draw men and women to faith and grow them into spiritual maturity. As we began the text with the Disciplers' Model, so we end it with a reverent analysis of Jesus' teaching—both when He walked the earth and now as He indwells His disciples. May God bless you as you step onto holy ground and learn from the Master.

Chapter 15

THE EDUCATIONAL PSYCHOLOGY OF JESUS

CHAPTER RATIONALE

We began this text with the Disciplers' Model—an approach to teaching that helps learners grow in the Lord. We have spent the last fourteen chapters integrating the latest thinking of educational psychologists into that model. In this last chapter, we reverently and carefully analyze how Jesus taught, for "all the people . . . were amazed at his teaching" (Luke 4:36, 32). This chapter is less technical than the others—and more devotional. It is my hope and prayer that reading this chapter may give you a sense of sitting at the Master's feet, observing Him, listening to Him, learning from Him. May God bless you as you seek to model your teaching after His.

CHAPTER OBJECTIVES

Learners will demonstrate understanding of Jesus as Teacher by writing at least three positive and three negative examples of Jesus' personal characteristics you've seen in teachers.

Learners will demonstrate understanding of Jesus' approach to teaching by writing at least three positive and three negative examples of Jesus' methods you've seen in teachers.

Learners will demonstrate understanding of educational psychology by identifying which component of the Christian teachers' triad relates to each of the personal characteristics and methods of Jesus.

Learners will demonstrate appreciation for Jesus as Teacher by committing themselves to at least four changes you will make in your approach to teaching as a result of Jesus' example.

INTRODUCTION

Sherwood Eddy, in his book *Maker of Men* writes,

> [Jesus] was allowed less than three years in which to do His work; little more than a year in His public ministry, and a year in retirement training His pathetic remnant. He was cut off in His young manhood, a little past the age of thirty. Socrates taught for forty years. Plato for fifty. Aristotle had lived long and filled libraries with his learning. Buddha and Confucius had fulfilled their three score and ten. He was among a crushed people, under an oppressive legalism, zealously opposed and hated by scribes and Pharisees, betrayed by Jews and crucified by Gentiles. He left no book, no tract, or written page behind Him. He bequeathed no system, no philosophy, no theology, no legislation. He raised no armies, held no office, sought no influence, turned His back forever on might, magic, and cheap miracle.

> Yet He transformed the bigoted Jew and universalized his religion; He showed the philosophizing Greek the highest truth; He won the proud Roman to plant the cross on his standard instead of the eagle; He stretched out His hand to the great continents and transformed them—to Asia, to savage Europe, to darkest Africa, to America.[1]

We have much to learn from this greatest-of-all teachers. First, we'll look at the kind of students Jesus had. In what condition did Jesus find them? Second, we'll focus on the characteristics Jesus displayed. What kind of Person was this Master Teacher? Finally, we'll consider the major teaching methods Jesus used.

As we begin this journey, consider one word of warning. There is danger in such a study. Botanists destroy delicate plants as they analyze them; zoologists destroy living organisms as they dissect them. We must approach our study of Jesus as Teacher with a proper sense of awe and reverence. He is our Lord and Master and not a case study to be played with for the sake of academic exercise. And so we honor Him as Lord and Teacher even as we look to Him as a Model of how we should teach.

THE STUDENTS
OF JESUS

We take them as they are and lead them to become all they can.

A friend of mine, a fellow minister of education, invited me to join him for a cup of coffee at a local cafe. He was as depressed as any minister I'd ever known. As he poured out his heart, he returned again and again to the same lament: "If I only had some committed people to work with!" or "If I had some members with the leadership skills to direct our programs!" Seminary had taught him about programs for children and youth and adults; singles and seniors; outreach and in reach; organization and enlistment; Church Council, Weekly Workers' Meetings and Appreciation Banquets. But where do you find the people to make these programs come to life? Where do lay leaders come from? Seminary had exposed him to a wide variety of Christian ministry *ideals*. He now found himself in the *ordeal* of local church ministry. And he was sinking fast.

His experience is not unique. I suppose every minister has had feelings like these from time to time. Even seminary professors fall prey to the idea that we could teach so much better "if only" our students were more creative or motivated or something. It is a fantasy of the imagination. We are not called to some abstract ideal. We are called "to prepare God's people for works of service" (Eph. 4:12). We take them as they are and lead them to become all they can. That is our calling. And that is exactly what Jesus did with His disciples.

We tend to think of the disciples—especially Peter, James, and John—as great men of faith. This they became. But as "great men of faith" is not how they began. They were chosen carefully, after much prayer (Mark 6:2–16), but they were very human. Let's look at some of the basic characteristics of the twelve men Jesus chose as His closest students.

Scripture provides us ample evidence that the Twelve were rough in character and demeanor. James and John, the sons of Zebedee, were short-tempered—so much so that they were nicknamed the "Sons of Thunder" (Mark 3:17). James and John wanted to call fire down from heaven to destroy a Samaritan town because they did not welcome Jesus. Jesus rebuked them for their outburst and went on to another village (Luke 9:54–55).

The Disciples Were Imperfect

Simon, son of John, was impetuous and unstable. Though Jesus gave him the name Peter (Petros, "the rock"), Peter gave little evidence of stability. Jesus told the disciples about His impending death in Jerusalem, but Peter protested. When the guards came for Jesus in Gethsemane, Peter drew a sword and cut off Malchus' ear. Though Peter had bragged that he would die for Jesus (John 13:37), he denied being a disciple to a servant girl, to one of the men standing by the courtyard fire, and to one of the high priest's relatives (John 18:17, 25–27). Peter was impetuous and unstable, even after three years of living with the Master.

Thomas was a realist. He wanted cold hard facts. He had been absent the first time Jesus had appeared to the disciples (John 20:24). When he heard that the others had seen Jesus, Thomas exclaimed, "Unless I see the nail marks in his hands and put my finger where the nails were, and put my hand into his side, I will not believe it" (John 20:25). Where had he been the last three years? He had witnessed many miracles at the hands of Jesus. He had lived and worked with these men. He doubted the resurrection, but he was an honest doubter. A week later when Jesus stood before Thomas and invited him to test his wounds, Thomas' reaction was immediate and absolute: "My Lord and my God!" (John 20:28).

Then there were the political power-brokers, Judas Iscariot and Simon the Zealot. These two saw in Jesus a chance to overthrow Roman oppression. They sought to use Him in their political struggle. Beyond this, Judas was a petty thief. He pilfered money from the disciples' common purse which he was responsible to keep (John 12:4–6). No, the disciples were far from perfect.

The Disciples Were Slow to Learn

Jesus chose the Twelve during His first year of ministry.[2] These disciples followed and observed Jesus for nearly three years. They traveled with Him, ate with Him, laughed, and prayed with Him. They witnessed numerous miracles of healing, feeding, and restoring. But they were so slow to understand the essence of the Kingdom Jesus came to proclaim. A father brought his son, tormented by seizures, to the disciples, but they could not heal him. (Jesus had given them the "authority to drive out evil spirits and heal every disease and sickness" earlier. See Matt. 10:1.)

> Jesus rebuked the demon, and it came out of the boy, and he was healed from that moment. Then the disciples came to Jesus in private and asked, "Why couldn't we drive it out?" He replied, "Because you have so little faith. I tell you the truth, if you have faith as small as a mustard seed, you can say to this mountain, 'Move from here to there' and it will move. Nothing will be impossible for you" (Matt. 17:18–20).

The disciples still had a lot to learn.

Perhaps the strongest evidence of their slowness to learn was their reaction to Jesus' death. He had talked plainly to them of His impending death and resurrection (John 16:5–33), and yet they were shocked when He actually died, and surprised by His resurrection.

> [The angel said to the women,] "He is not here; he has risen! Remember how he told you, while he was still with you in Galilee: 'The Son of Man must be delivered into the hands of sinful men, be crucified and on the third day be raised again.'"
>
> *Then they remembered his words.* When they came back from the tomb, they told all these things to the Eleven and to all the others. It was Mary Magdalene, Joanna, Mary the mother of James, and the others with them who told this to the apostles. But *they did not believe* the women, because their words seemed to them like nonsense" (Luke 24:6–11, author's emphasis).

Even when He appeared to them after His resurrection, some of them doubted!

Then the eleven disciples went to Galilee, to the mountain where Jesus had told them to go. When they saw him, they worshiped him; *but some doubted* (Matt. 28:16–17). They were slow to learn.

Judas Iscariot and Simon the Zealot had accepted Jesus' call to become disciples to further their own political purposes. But the self-centeredness of the disciples went far deeper. As Jesus and the Twelve made their way to Jerusalem, Jesus focused His thoughts on the cross. Peter, however, was thinking about all the sacrifices they had made and what little it had gained them: "We have left everything to follow you! What then will there be for us?" (Matt. 19:27). Self-centered. Even more pointed was the selfish request of James and John. Just look at the context:

The Disciples Were Self-centered

> They were on their way up to Jerusalem, with Jesus leading the way, and the disciples were astonished, while those who followed were afraid. Again he took the Twelve aside and told them what was going to happen to him.
>
> "We are going up to Jerusalem," he said, "and the Son of Man will be betrayed to the chief priests and teachers of the law. They will condemn him to death and will hand him over to the Gentiles, who will mock him and spit on him, flog him and kill him. Three days later he will rise."'
>
> Then James and John, the sons of Zebedee, came to him. *"Teacher," they said, "we want you to do for us whatever we ask."*
>
> "What do you want me to do for you?" he asked.
>
> They replied, *"Let one of us sit at your right and the other at your left in your glory."*
>
> "You don't know what you are asking" Jesus said (Mark 10:32–38a, author's emphasis).

Jesus had just spoken of His own terrible death, but James and John were thinking more of their own positions of power.

At another time, Jesus told the disciples they were going to the other side of the Sea of Galilee (Mark 4:35). As they were making their way across the lake, a violent storm came up and nearly swamped the boat. What was their reaction? "Teacher, don't you care if we drown?" (Mark 4:38). Jesus' response clearly revealed their self-centeredness: 'Why are you so afraid? Do you still have no faith?' (Mark 4:40). He had told them they were going over to the other side. Drowning in a storm had not been part of His plan. While the instinct for survival is different from self-centeredness, the perspective of the disciples still reflected a lack of faith in what Jesus said.

Still another example of their self-centeredness occurs at the arrest of Jesus. We've already noted Peter's false bravado: "I will lay down my life for you" (John 13:37). And again, "Even if all fall away on account of you, I never will" (Matt. 26:33). Then Jesus told Peter he would disown Him three times before morning (v. 34). "'Even if I have to die with you, I will never disown you.' And all the other disciples said the same" (v. 35). But when the reality of Jesus' arrest arrived, "all the disciples deserted him and fled" (v. 56), and by morning, Peter had denied even knowing Jesus three times (vv. 69–75). The disciples cared for themselves first.

The Disciples Were Uneducated and Unprofessional

The center of higher learning in Jesus' day was Jerusalem, and many of the inhabitants of Judea were well educated in the Law. Galilee was a different matter. Galilee provided rich soil for farming, an abundance of hard workers for a vast array of trades and businesses, and a bountiful lake for fishing. Its beauty might lead to meditation and prayer, but it certainly did not evoke the morbid fanaticism of the faithful in Jerusalem. So, while Galilee was home to generous spirits, warm hearts, simple manners, and earnest piety, it was looked down upon by the rabbinic leaders in the South.[3] Edershiem reports it was a common saying: "If a person wishes to be rich, let him go north; if he wants to be wise, let him come south."[4]

Jesus began and built His ministry in Galilee (Luke 23:5) and chose men of the north to be His disciples. They were not learned men, but, being sick of the legalistic, domineering "righteousness" then in vogue, they hungered for the real thing. They demonstrated the rudiments of faith and devotion. They displayed a willingness to grow, to learn. Jesus saw great potential in these men.[5] That's why He could call unstable Simon "Petros, the rock," because He saw the "rock" that Simon would ultimately become.

The Disciples Were Apprentices, not mere Learners

The differences between north and south can also be seen in two words used for "learner." Coleman makes the distinction between *mathetas* (a craftsman's apprentice learning a skill) and *talmid* (an academic scholar learning by rote).[6] The disciples were *mathetas* learning a skill. Bruce underscores the idea of "mathetas" when he writes that Jesus "desired not only to have disciples, but to have about Him men whom He might train to make disciples of others." And again: "The careful, painstaking education of the disciples secured that the Teacher's influence on the world should be permanent; that His kingdom should be founded on the rock of deep and indestructible convictions in the minds of a few, not on the shifting sands of superficial evanescent impressions on the minds of the many."[7]

They were not trained, but they were trainable. They had not been taught, but they were teachable. Nothing more in learners should a teacher desire, and nothing more does a teacher need!

In summary, the disciples were rough hewn, imperfect, self-centered, and untrained when Jesus chose them. They were normal people, with all the problems and potential of people today. Yet from among these twelve came leaders who turned the entire known world upside down for the Lord. How can we teach so that our people can become *mathetas* and, in time, leaders and teachers of others? What can we glean from Jesus' words and actions that will help us develop our skills in the teaching ministry of the church? It is to the Teacher that we now turn our attention.

In both the Ten Commandments and the Sermon on the Mount, who we are in the Lord comes before what we do for the Lord. The best teaching flows not merely out of our mouths, but from our hearts. So before we look at the *methods* of Jesus, we need to learn something of the *Person* of Jesus.

I used to tell my students that Jesus was a *model* of what He taught, but what some understood by that missed my intention. Jesus did not "model His teaching" like a fashion model parading the latest fad. His lifestyle was not a put-on conceived to strengthen the words He spoke. Jesus simply lived what He taught. What He taught flowed out of Who He was. One day Jesus was praying. One of the disciples noticed something about Jesus' praying that intrigued him. So when Jesus had finished, the disciple asked to be taught on the subject (Luke 11:1–2). Educators call this kind of event a *teachable moment*. Creating a climate of teachable moments, particularly in a formal class setting, is difficult. Jesus wasted no time responding to the request of the disciple.

Jesus lived, and out of His life flowed teaching. His words and actions reinforced each other with an authority that amazed His hearers. "What we are" speaks more loudly than "what we say." Faith learning is more "caught from" than "taught by" a teacher. Some thirty years after Jesus had ascended to heaven, Peter wrote to pastors: "Be shepherds of God's flock that is under your care . . . not lording it over those entrusted to you, but being examples to the flock" (1 Pet. 5:2–3). Jesus was the example to Peter and to the Twelve and to all who would follow Him. If we are to pattern our

"In both the Ten Commandments and the Sermon on the Mount *who we are in the Lord comes before what we do for the Lord"*

THE CHARACTERISTICS OF JESUS AS TEACHER

Jesus Was What He taught

teaching after Jesus, we too must strive to be the proper kind of example.

Jesus Was Comfortable with People of All Kinds

Teachers must be able to establish rapport with learners if they are to be effective. Rapport building is a social skill which requires some degree of sensitivity to those you teach. The Scriptures reflect Jesus' amazing ability to be "at home" with a wide range of people—whether they were poor or wealthy; Jew, Gentile, or Roman; male or female. Let's look at just a few examples.

Jesus spoke earnestly and confidently with Nicodemus, a devout Jewish leader, and showed no anxiety as He taught a member of the ruling Sanhedrin (John 3).

He invited Himself to dinner at tax collector Zacchaeus' house, and demonstrated no discomfort being in the company of wealth (Luke 19). He chose another tax collector, Matthew, as one of His disciples (Matt. 9:9–12).

He conversed openly with a Samaritan woman who had come to draw water from a well and appeared to be unconcerned that, in the custom of His day, a respectable man did not talk with women in public, nor a respectable Jew to Samaritan "half-breeds." But Jesus broke social customs to draw this Samaritan woman to faith in Himself. And through her, He reached into her village (John 4:28–30).

Jesus healed the demon-possessed daughter of a heathen woman after He taught her Who He was (Matt. 15:22–28).[8] He did not reject Roman soldiers like His oppressed Jewish brothers. In fact He once commended a Roman centurion's faith above that of any in Israel (see Matt. 8:5–13).

The disciples rebuked parents for bringing their little children to Jesus, but the Lord welcomed them: "Let the little children come to me, and do not hinder them, for the kingdom of heaven belongs to such as these" (Matt. 19:14).

Besides these instances, Jesus surrounded Himself with people of all kinds: the sick as well as the healthy (Mark 1:34), the deaf as well as the hearing (Mark 7:32ff), the blind as well as the sighted (John 9:1ff), the lame as well as the able-bodied (Matt. 21:14) and the leprous as well as the clean (Matt. 8:3). He even healed the ear of Malchus, one of the high priest's servants, during His false arrest (Luke 22:51; John 18:10).

We naturally tend to stay with "our own kind." We like people like us. Discomfort increases as we deal with people much richer, or poorer, than ourselves. It isn't easy to deal with people of a different race, or language, or age bracket. To do so requires an extra degree of energy and commitment. But the teacher who can build bridges to all people will be the most effective.

Jesus was compassionate toward the needs of others, and was quick to help people in need. He cared more for His learners than for lessons. One day He was teaching on the subject of fasting. He was suddenly interrupted by Jairus, ruler of the synagogue, whose daughter had died. Jesus broke off His teaching session and went with him immediately (Matt. 9:18–19). On the way to the religious leader's home He was interrupted by a "woman who had been subject to bleeding for twelve years" (Matt. 9:20), making her ceremonially unclean (Lev. 15:19–27) and a social outcast among her people. Jesus gives no evidence of irritation at these interruptions. The Father is in control! Jesus stopped to help the lady. Then He continued on to Jairus' house and brought his daughter back to life. The interruptions of our routine are often the best opportunities for ministry.

Jesus Was Compassionate Toward His Learners

Jesus was moved with compassion as He considered the masses of people (Matt. 9:36; 14:14; 23:37). He did not condemn them for their lack of faith. Rather, He strengthened what little faith they had, and in so doing He fulfilled Isaiah's prophecy: "A bruised reed he will not break, and a smoldering wick he will not snuff out" (Isa. 42:3; Matt. 12:20).

Jesus protected the disciples from harm (John 17:12). He gave the disciples instructions before He sent them out (Matt. 10). Whether He used a strong rebuke (Matt. 16:23; Luke 24:25) or a gentle explanation (Matt. 16:21; Luke 24:27), His focus was on the disciples' welfare: the Son of Man did not come to be served, but to serve, and to give his life as a ransom for many" (Matt. 20:28).

"The Son of Man did not come to be served, but to serve, and to give his life as a ransom for many" (Matt. 20:28)

The many recorded healings of Jesus point to His compassion for the needs of people. He cleansed a leper (Matt. 8:2ff), healed Peter's mother-in-law (Matt. 8:14ff), healed a paralytic (Matt. 9:1ff), restored sight to two blind men (Matt. 9:27ff), and healed "every kind of disease and sickness. When he saw the crowds, he had compassion on them, because they were harassed and helpless, like sheep without a shepherd" (Matt. 9:35–36). He healed a man's hand on the Sabbath and showed through this act that mercy is always appropriate (Matt. 12:9ff). He healed an epileptic (Matt. 7:15) and restored the severed ear of a temple guard during His arrest (Luke 22:51). So much did Jesus do in meeting people's needs that if "every one of them were written down . . . even the whole world would not have room for the books that would be written" (John 21:25).

Again and again we find Jesus using His power and authority to serve the Father and meet people's needs. He did not exalt Himself with His authority, though He was tempted to do just that at both the beginning—the wilderness temptations—and the end ("Let him come down now from the cross, and we will believe him," Matt. 27:42) of His earthly ministry.

Jesus Had a Strong Self-Concept

Our society has gone overboard with the idea of self-esteem and positive self-concept. A recent research study showed that American high schoolers are significantly *more confident* in their math and science skills than are their Japanese counterparts. The only problem is that the Japanese high schoolers are significantly *more capable* in math and science than American students.[9] For thirty years we have worshipped "feel good" at the expense of "think right" and "do well." The result is more self-esteem problems than ever.

Still, a healthy self-concept is important. For the Christian, knowing Whose we are is an essential part of learning who we are. And knowing who we are in the Lord gives us the confidence we need to teach others. Let's look briefly at the evidence that Jesus had a healthy self-concept.

Jesus was a man on mission, and this gave Him power. He did what He did because He was sent by the Father (John 5:23). His work was what the Father had given Him to do (John 5:19–36). His work was a result of the Father working through Him (John 14:10). Jesus' self-concept was not based on the "me first" philosophy of our day. It was based on a "Father first" philosophy. He sought His Father's will and did it, not turning to the left or right. He was a man on mission—and it gave Him power to teach with authority.

Each of us has spiritual gifts to be used in Kingdom service. We have a unique yoke—His yoke—a mission to perform. When we find that mission, and accept it, we find rest and refreshment in the Lord, and learn from Him (Matt. 11:28–30). In short, we find our "self" as God created us to be, and this is far better than trying to make something of ourselves for the Lord! Find the Lord's place for you and give yourself to it.

Jesus was a man of dynamic humility. Nowhere in the Gospels do we find Jesus demanding worship from the disciples. We cannot find a hint of Jesus' fretting about a lack of recognition, or grumbling that those He healed weren't more grateful, or that the religious leaders didn't give Him the respect He deserved. Though He did not demand worship or honor, He did on at least one occasion acknowledge it when it was given. But look how He used it: "You call me 'Teacher' and 'Lord,' and rightly so, for that is what I am. Now that I, your Lord and Teacher, have washed your feet, you also should wash one another's feet. I have set you an example that you should do as I have done for you. I tell you the truth, no servant is greater than his master, nor is a messenger greater than the one who sent him. Now that you know these things, you will be blessed if you do them" (John 13:13–17).

Jesus came as the "Suffering Servant" (Isa. 53; Matt. 16:21). But His humility was not passive. He never played the victim, apologetically kicking the dirt because people—His own people—rejected Him. His was a dynamic humility, an energetic submission. Even when He stood before Pilate, the one man who, humanly speaking, could rescue Him from the cross, we see our Lord submissive and powerful: "You would have no power over me if it were not given to you from above" (John 19:11). Jesus had dynamic *humility*.

Further, Jesus had *dynamic* humility. That is, He was not self-abasing. Jesus did not put Himself down, except to exalt the Father (Luke 18:19). He never belittled His ministry. He never grinned with embarrassment when people praised Him. He displayed the dignity of authority. He did not reject worship when it was offered Him. When the rich young ruler fell on his knees before Him, Jesus did not stammer and stutter in embarrassment, trying to get the man back on his feet before anyone saw him. He simply dealt with his desire (eternal life) and his need (to be rid of his wealth) in order to follow Jesus (Mark 10:17–22). When Thomas saw Jesus after the resurrection and exclaimed, "My Lord and my God!" Jesus did nothing to curb Thomas' worship. He gave no indication Thomas' adoration was out of line (John 20:28–29).

Jesus did not degrade Himself or His ministry. Neither did He flaunt Himself or His powers. His dynamic humility was not the wimpy self-effacing "I'm sorry I didn't do better" kind of passive, put-down humility. It was not the arrogant self-promoting "Why can't you be as good as me" kind of dynamic. But His dynamic humility was a vigorous meekness, a vital submissiveness, an aggressive lowliness.

Jesus' calmness under attack shows His strong self-concept. Jesus healed two demon-possessed men[10] by casting the demons into a nearby herd of pigs. Those tending the pigs ran into town and told what had happened. The whole town went out to confront Jesus over their loss "because they were overcome with fear" (Luke 8:37) (fear of Jesus' power and anger over their loss). There is no more volatile mix of human emotions than fear and anger. They pleaded with Jesus to leave (Matt. 8:34). And how did Jesus react?

Now if I were in that situation, I would want to defend myself and my actions. I would want to explain to these villagers that I was the Son of God, and I had just restored two men to their right minds by casting out a legion of demons. I would want them to understand that what I had done had been for the best, really. But Jesus, apparently without a word of defense or explanation, "stepped into a boat, crossed over and came to his own town" (Matt. 9:1).

Jesus' patience with His disciples showed His self-concept. Insecure teachers easily lose patience with students because they see in their failure to learn a negative reflection on their own teaching ability. Secure teachers simply back up and try again until their learners master the subject. As we have seen, the disciples had many weaknesses. Yet Jesus never gave up on them. "None has been lost except the one doomed to destruction so that Scripture would be fulfilled" (John 17:12).

He demonstrated patience with their lack of faith in the storm: "Why are you so afraid? Do you still have no faith?" (Mark 4:40). He demonstrated patience at their lack of ability to heal the demon-possessed boy: [Why could you not heal him?] "Because you have so little faith" (Matt. 17:20). He demonstrated patience when they fell asleep in the garden: "Could you men not keep watch with me for one hour?" (Matt. 26:40). He never gave up on His disciples because they were a part of His mission: "I pray for . . . those you have given me, for they are yours" (John 17:9).

Jesus identified with the Father through prayer. At the beginning of the chapter, we underscored the dependence of Jesus on the Father for His work and teaching. The connection between Them was prayer. We find several specific references to Jesus' prayer life. He went out "very early in the morning, while it was still dark . . . to a solitary place, where he prayed" (Mark 1:35). On another occasion, Jesus "spent the night praying to God" (Luke 6:12). Luke tells us that Jesus prayed often, and in lonely places (5:16). The disciples noticed how prayer strengthened Jesus, and so asked Him to teach them how to pray (Luke 11:1). Later, Jesus reinforced the importance of prayer by telling His disciples they "should always pray and not give up" (Luke 18:1). Further, Jesus underscored the importance of *asking* the Father (Matt. 7:11; 18:19; Luke 11:13; John 14:13; 15:16; 16:23, 26).

Prayer—connection with the heavenly Father—was an essential part of Jesus' self-concept. And if He, the Second Person of the Trinity (Matt. 28:19), in Whom the fullness of the Godhead dwelt bodily (Col. 2:9), needed time alone in prayer, how much more do we?

But we have grown up in a society saturated with existential thinking. "I am who I make myself. The only true reality is the reality I choose for myself. I am important because I am me. Good is what is good to me. Beauty is what I choose it to be. I am my own god. I choose my own universe. I make my own rules." Such philosophy leaves no room for submission, or obedience, or sacrifice, or surrender to the Lord. No room for the absolutes of God or His Word, which says "See to it that no one takes you captive through hollow and deceptive philosophy, which depends on human tradition and the basic principles of this world rather than on Christ" (Col. 2:8).

Prayer is the connection. The Word is the means. The Spirit is the Power. Jesus is our Lord and Example. All combine to remake us after His image. And as you make this Holy Journey, you will find you have no problem with your self-concept, because Jesus declares that He came so that you "may have life, and have it to the full" (John 10:10).

One of the reasons Jesus' teaching was so special is that it focused on the real life needs of those He taught. Jesus knew His learners, and He used that knowledge to focus His teaching for maximum effectiveness in each situation.

Jesus' knowledge was both divine and human. Being divine, He could read the hearts and minds of the people around Him. When the Pharisees claimed Jesus' miracles were done by the prince of demons[11] (Matt. 12:24), Matthew tells us "Jesus knew their thoughts" (v. 25). When many people believed in Him because of the miracles, John writes, "Jesus would not entrust himself to them, for he knew all men. He did not need man's testimony about man for he knew what was in a man" (John 2:24–25). Later, when many of His followers began to desert Him, John tells us "Jesus had known from the beginning which of them would not believe and who would betray him" (John 6:64).

"Jesus' dynamic humility was a vigorous meekness, a vital submissiveness, an aggressive lowliness"

Jesus Knew His Learners

But Mark gives us the clearest picture of Jesus' ability to discern the thoughts of others. One day four men brought their paralytic friend to Jesus to be healed. They could not get inside the house, so they made an opening in the roof and let him down on his mat. "When Jesus saw their faith, he said to the paralytic, 'Son, your sins are forgiven.' Now some teachers of the law were sitting there, thinking to themselves, 'Why does this fellow talk like that? He's blaspheming! Who can forgive sins but God alone?' *Immediately Jesus knew in his spirit that this was what they were thinking in their hearts,* and he said to them, 'Why are you thinking these things?'" (Mark 2:5–8).

Jesus had the power to read thoughts and hearts, but it is interesting to me how much Jesus depended on His human knowledge of people. Much of what He knew He learned the same way you and I do—through observation, or conversation, or by asking questions. "What do you think, Simon?" (Matt. 17:25). To the Pharisees, "What do you think about the Christ? Whose Son is He?" (Matt. 22:42). To Pilate, "Is that your own idea . . . or did others talk to you about me?" (John 18:34).

"But whether Jesus used His divine or human knowledge, He *used* that knowledge in order to teach"

But look! Whether Jesus used His divine or human knowledge, He *used that knowledge in order to teach.* He knew the Samaritan woman's need for water and, on a deeper level, a satisfying marriage, and deeper still, salvation. So He taught her about Himself with water and husbands. Jesus understood the heathen woman's ignorance of the true Messiah, and so He taught her about Himself with children and dogs before granting her request. Nicodemus was a teacher of Israel (John 3:10); yet he did not understand the meaning of what he taught until Jesus instructed him. Jesus knew His learners and used that knowledge to mold and focus His teaching.

Jesus Was a Master of the Old Testament

While the scribes and Pharisees had embellished the Old Testament with their own corollaries and exceptions, Jesus displayed a fluent mastery of Scripture. For example, the Pharisees hated Jesus because He healed on the Sabbath (Matt. 12:9–14). They justified their hatred and indignation by reckoning Jesus' healing as "work," which was forbidden on the Sabbath (Exod. 20:8–11). Jesus pointed out their own hypocrisy and interpreted the Law in light of the whole Old Testament: "If any of you has a sheep and it falls into a pit on the Sabbath, will you not take hold of it and lift it out? How much more valuable is a man than a sheep! *Therefore it is lawful to do good on the Sabbath"* (Matt. 12:11–12, author's emphasis).

A Jewish rabbi once told me that it was common practice in Jesus' day to carry a rug when traveling on the Sabbath. Jewish Law limited travel on the Sabbath to about three-fifths of a mile from home (a "Sabbath Day's journey"). By carrying a rug from home, the traveler could walk three-fifths of a mile, put down the rug, sit down to establish his new "home" and then proceed to travel another three-fifths of a mile. And there was no limit on how often one could do this!

For the Pharisees, principles were more important than people, because they derived their own power from holding principles over people. Jesus explained it this way: "[The Pharisees] tie up heavy loads and put them on men's shoulders, but they themselves are not willing to lift a finger to move them" (Matt. 23:4). For Jesus, people were more important than arbitrary principles. The Jewish leaders had twisted the Old Testament to their own purposes of power and control. The "Sabbath rule" was one example of this. They would rather a man or woman go unhealed rather than violate their interpretation of Sabbath rest:

> Indignant because Jesus had healed on the Sabbath, the synagogue ruler said to the people, "There are six days for work. So come and be healed on those days, not on the Sabbath." The Lord answered him, "You hypocrites! Doesn't each of you on the Sabbath untie his ox or donkey from the stall and lead it out to give it water? Then should not this woman, a daughter of Abraham, whom Satan has kept bound for eighteen long years, be set free on the Sabbath day from what bound her?" When he said this, all his opponents were humiliated, but the people were delighted with all the wonderful things he was doing (Luke 13:14–7).

So which was primary in the Old Testament, principle or people, rules or relationship? Jesus spoke plainly when He said, "The Sabbath was made for man, not man for the Sabbath" (Mark 2:27). Even the Old Testament accuses the Pharisees: "Will the LORD be pleased with thousands of rams, with ten thousand rivers of oil? Shall I offer my firstborn for my transgression, the fruit of my body for the sin of my soul? He has showed you, O man, what is good. And what does the LORD require of you? *To act justly and to love mercy and to walk humbly with your God"* (Mic. 6:7–8).

When the Pharisees threw the adulterous woman at Jesus' feet, their intent was to uphold the Law and trap Jesus (John 8:5–6). The Law was clear. There was no shade of gray: "must be put to death" (Lev. 20:10). They cared nothing for the woman. Their intent was to destroy this One Who questioned their authority and power. Principle and power, not people.

But Jesus cared for the woman and led her away from her sin. He displayed the loving-kindness of Jehovah God of Israel. His challenge, "If any one of you is without sin, let him be the first to throw a stone at her" (John 8:7), refocused their attention on themselves and their own need. The oldest, and evidently the wisest, were the first to understand Jesus' meaning. They dropped their stones and left, followed by the younger men.

Jesus did this because He was Master of the heart of the Old Testament. In a fanatically religious nation, religion was the means to power. The scribes and Pharisees were trapped, as it were, by their own egotistical need for power. The Word of God was merely another tool to be used to maintain control. But for Jesus, the Old Testament was God's Word, the revelation of His Father. The entire Law and all of the Prophets could be summarized in two brief statements of relationship: "Love the Lord your God . . . and love your neighbor as yourself" (Matt 22:37–40). These were not New Testament teachings. Jesus was quoting the Old Testament: "Love the LORD your God with all your heart and with all your soul and with all your strength" (Deut. 6:5). "Do not seek revenge or bear a grudge against one of your people, but love your neighbor as yourself. I am the LORD" (Lev. 19:18).

Jesus went beyond knowledge of the Scripture. He had analyzed its teachings and synthesized the central thrust of the Father's perfect loving-kindness. But He went beyond understanding. He expanded the Old Testament in His "you have heard it said . . . but I say unto you" teachings (Matt. 5:21, 27, 33, 38, 43).

Have you noticed the balance in Jesus' teaching? He was Master of the Scripture, and yet He focused that mastery on *teaching people* where they were. *People* were His focus. *Scripture* was His means. As He applied Old Testament Scripture to real problems in His learners, He provided solutions uniquely suited to each one. The Eternal Word meeting today's personal need: the result is changed lives.[12]

JESUS' METHODS OF TEACHING

Jesus Established Relationship with His Learners

Now that we have an idea of Who Jesus was, what did He do as He taught? What methods did He use? What were His primary emphases in teaching? We will look at ten such areas.

Teaching from mouth to ear is very different from teaching heart to heart. If "getting the lesson across" is the main goal, there is little need for relationship between teacher and student. But if transforming students toward Christlikeness is your goal, a warm positive relationship is essential.

Jesus "appointed twelve, to be with him" (Mark 3:14, RSV). Bruce indicates that their selection passed through three stages. In the first stage, the Twelve were simply believers in Him as the Christ and occasionally accompanied Him at their convenience. The second stage involved leaving their secular occupations and traveling with Him. The third stage began when they were chosen by the Lord and formed into a select band, to be trained for the great work of apostles.[13]

They lived together and ate together. They witnessed the miracles of Jesus together. They suffered rejection together. All the while, Jesus loved them, taught them, protected them.

Like coals in a fire, their mutual support and service strengthened them. Pull a coal from the fire, and it soon cools down—Peter's denials, Thomas' doubt, the Twelve scattering at Jesus' arrest—but Jesus fanned the individual sparks of the Twelve into a Family of Fire, and within that context, He taught them.

Jesus stimulated interest with dramatic illustrations and exaggeration. His illustrations included an unmerciful servant (Matt. 18:23ff), equal wages for unequal work (Matt. 20:1ff), murdering tenants (Matt. 21:33ff), undeserving wedding guests (Matt. 22:1ff), unprepared virgins (Matt. 25:1ff), wise and foolish investors (Matt. 25:14ff), wise and foolish builders (Luke 6:46ff), a Good Samaritan (Luke 10:30ff), a rich fool (Luke 12:16ff), a lost sheep and coin and son (Luke 15:3ff), a shrewd manager (Luke 16:1ff), a rich man in hell (Luke 16:19ff), and the condemned Pharisee and forgiven tax collector (Luke 18:9ff). Such stories seized the hearts of Jesus' listeners because they came directly out of their own frustrations and disappointments.

Jesus Stimulated and Maintained Interest

Jesus also used exaggeration in His teaching. If your hand or foot causes you to sin, "cut it off" (Mark 9:43, 45). If your eye causes you to sin, then "pluck it out" (Mark 9:47). The only way to be Jesus' disciple is to "hate [your] father and mother, [your] wife and children, [your] brothers and sisters—yes, even [your] own life" (Luke 14:26). Illustrations and exaggerations helped to stimulate interest.

"Jesus' stories seized His listeners because they came from their own disappointments"

But Jesus did more than stimulate interest—He also maintained it. He asked questions. He focused His teaching from the perspective of His learners. He used parables with the masses, but waited until He was alone with His disciples to explain them (Matt. 13:10–18;

Mark 5:33–34). Those who truly hungered for righteousness would follow and learn and grow. Those who were merely curious would fall by the wayside.

Jesus Taught
by Example

The first point under section 3 was "Jesus Was What He Taught." There the focus was on His Person. Here the focus is on His method. Jesus inspired His disciples to imitate Him. Pray as I pray. Love as I love you. Serve as I serve. Take up your cross as I take up mine. Care for the sheep as I care for the sheep. Finish your course as I finish mine.

The best teachers are living case studies of their subject matter. Thirty years after Jesus returned to the Father, Peter wrote to young pastors, "Be shepherds of God's flock that is under your care, serving as overseers . . . not lording it over those entrusted to you, but being *examples to the flock*" (1 Pet. 5:2–3, author's emphasis). Bible study, whether it be in church or at a college or seminary, should mold us into better examples of the Truth, not merely living libraries of it.

Jesus Taught People,
Not Lessons

Not once in Scripture do we find Jesus sitting down to teach and saying, "Our lesson for today is Leviticus, Scroll 3." His teaching flowed out of the needs of the people He taught. It flowed out of problem situations they presented. It flowed out of the real crises of life.

This is not to say that an organized curriculum is unnecessary. Curriculum writers provide enormous assistance to teachers in our churches. Well-designed materials target a wide range of issues relevant to growing in the Lord. But the emphasis in our classes must be the people in the chairs, not the lines in the lesson. God's Word is Truth. But it becomes Truth-that-Matters-to-Me as it intersects me where I live.

Jesus understood the balance of Scripture and needs, as we have already shown. Many teachers in our churches, both volunteer and ministerial, do not. The overriding goal in many classes is to "cover the lesson." In the name of "covering the lesson," questions are ignored, comments curtailed, personal experiences restricted. The teacher who says, "Mildred, I wish we could spend some time dealing with your question, but I have four more verses to cover" may finish the lesson, but he hasn't taught Mildred. Plan for interruptions and questions. Encourage discussion and openness. Teach people, not lessons.

The Pharisees had their content down. They memorized the five books of Moses. They mastered the myriad details of proper prayer, almsgiving, and fasting. Their religion was a superficial, technical, and external show of rote actions and memorized rules, a tedious rule book which led them to become "sanctimonious faultfinders."[14]

Jesus described the ethics of the kingdom as a "stream of life, having charity for its fountainhead; a morality of the heart."[15] Character focuses on the heart: mind, emotions, conduct, and will. The mind-focus is: "How do you comprehend this?" The emotional focus is: "How do you value this?" The conduct-focus is: "What will you do with this?" These questions form a trilogy, with the will in the center, of character-building teaching.[16]

For learners to grow in their character, they must have freedom to think and decide for themselves. Jesus understood this. His disciples freely chose to follow Him. The rich young ruler freely chose not to. Judas chose to betray Jesus. Thomas chose to doubt. Peter chose to deny the Lord. The disciples chose to run away when Jesus was arrested.

The Pharisees hated this freedom because their concern was how to control their followers. Look at this revealing story:

> Then some Pharisees and teachers of the law came to Jesus from Jerusalem and asked, "Why do your disciples break the tradition of the elders? They don't wash their hands before they eat!"
>
> Jesus replied, "And why do you break the command of God for the sake of your tradition? For God said, 'Honor your father and mother' and 'Anyone who curses his father or mother must be put to death.' But you say that if a man says to his father or mother, 'Whatever help you might otherwise have received from me is a gift devoted to God,' he is not to 'honor his father' with it. *Thus you nullify the word of God for the sake of your tradition.* You hypocrites! Isaiah was right when he prophesied about you: 'These people honor me with their lips, but their hearts are far from me. They worship me in vain; their teachings are but rules taught by men.'
>
> Jesus called the crowd to him and said, "Listen and understand. What goes into a man's mouth does not make him 'unclean,' but what comes out of his mouth, that is what makes him 'unclean'" (Matt. 15:1–11).

Or the time the disciples "harvested grain" on the Sabbath:

> At that time Jesus went through the grainfields on the Sabbath. His disciples were hungry and began to pick some heads of grain and eat them. When the Pharisees saw this, they said to him, "Look! Your disciples are doing what is unlawful on the Sabbath."
>
> He answered, "Haven't you read what David did when he and his companions were hungry? He entered the house of God, and he and his companions ate the consecrated bread—which was not lawful for them to do, but only for the priests. Or haven't you read in the Law that on the Sabbath the priests in

Jesus Emphasized Character More than Content

the temple desecrate the day and yet are innocent? I tell you that one greater than the temple is here. If you had known what these words mean, 'I desire mercy, not sacrifice,' you would not have condemned the innocent. For the Son of Man is Lord of the Sabbath" (Matt. 12:1–8).

The disciples did not follow the Pharisees' rules, and the Pharisees hated Jesus for it. For all their religious content, the Pharisees were whitewashed tombs "which look beautiful on the outside but on the inside are full of dead men's bones and everything unclean" (Matt. 23:27). Jesus was more interested in the disciples' "Kingdom *character*," which Bruce describes like this: "humble, retiring, devoted in singleness of heart to God . . . contentment, cheerfulness, and freedom from secular cares for its fruits; and finally, as reserved in its bearing towards the profane, yet averse to severity in judging, yea, to judging at all, leaving men to be judged by God."[17]

Jesus Focused on Ever Smaller Groups

"Large crowds from Galilee, the Decapolis, Jerusalem, Judea and the region across the Jordan followed [Jesus]" (Matt. 4:25). Throughout His ministry, Jesus taught the crowds (Matt. 5:1; 8:1; 9:36; 11:7; 12:46; 13:2; 13:34; 14:13; 15:30; 19:2; 20:29; 21:8; 23:1).

Out of the crowds He chose two specific groups of workers. He first chose the Twelve (Matt. 10:1ff), as we have seen, to be trained as apostles to carry on the work after He left. Later "the Lord appointed seventy-two others and sent them two by two ahead of him to every town and place where he was about to go" (Luke 10:1). The Twelve were chosen to be with Him, the Seventy-two to go before Him. Both groups were given power to drive out demons, but only the Twelve were given power to heal diseases (cf. Matt. 10:1 and Luke 10:1, 17).

Out of the Twelve, Jesus chose three for special attention: Peter, James, and John. These three men experienced things with Jesus that the other nine did not. These three witnessed the transfiguration of Jesus (Matt. 17) while the nine remained at the bottom of the mountain. These three accompanied Jesus into the home of Jairus when Jesus raised his daughter from the dead (Mark 5:37) while the nine stayed outside (Luke 8:51). When Jesus and the disciples went to Gethsemane, the nine stayed back while the three moved forward with Jesus into the garden (Mark 14:32–33). The result of their advanced training and personal attention was that they became, according to Paul, pillars in the early church (Gal. 2:9).

But of the three, Jesus paid the greatest attention to Simon. He gave Simon the new name of Peter [Petros, rock] (John 1:42). He healed Peter's mother-in-law (Matt. 8:14-15). He allowed Peter to try something miraculous and fail (Matt. 14:28–33). He recommissioned Peter after his denial of Jesus (John 21:15ff). Peter served his Lord faithfully until his death.

Dr. Howard Hendricks, noted Christian educator at Dallas Theological Seminary, once remarked to some of his former students that he was finished with "building great churches." He wanted to give the rest of his life to building great people. "Even if you build a church of 3,200 people, if none of them develops, 3,200 times 0 still equals 0. But 1 times 1 equals 1, and that is 100% better. The question you must ask is, "Whose life are you impacting?"[18] This approach to ministry is certainly in line with Jesus, Who poured Himself into ever-smaller groups.

Local church ministry is people-intensive. We can plan programs, but without people to lead those programs and staff the programs, and reach others to participate in the programs, our planning is vain. In the hustle-bustle of church ministry, it is easy to focus more on "getting the job done" than on those who are doing the job. In this kind of corporate atmosphere, learners are no more than the means by which we do ministry. It is a utilitarian view of people: "You are valuable so long as you can produce. Fail to meet organizational standards, and we'll replace you with someone more dedicated to the company." The bottom line to all this is that, in many churches, the people of God are being abused in the name of reaching strangers.

Jesus Recognized the Worth of His Learners

The disciples were not merely the *means* of Jesus' ministry. They were the *ends* of it. Jesus did not use (i.e., abuse) His disciples to reach the crowds. He pulled away from the crowds in order to teach them. They were not tools in the hands of a clever public relations man. They were beloved children. He poured His own heart into them, and after He left, they carried on His work.

"In many churches the people of God are being abused in the name of reaching strangers"

Many in our churches are hungry for ministers who care about them for who they are, and not merely for what they can do for the minister's own career. Before being challenged to reach "ten more next Sunday," they would like to know that we've noticed them, that we care for them, that we love them. Discipleship and evangelism go hand in hand (Matt. 28:19–20). Our flock is worthy of compassion, and we are called to lead in that way (1 Pet. 5:2).

The "quality vs. quantity" debate has long raged among church leaders. Those who emphasize "quality Bible study" in Sunday school may create classes that are self-sufficient, satisfied, and indifferent toward outsiders. Those who emphasize "quantity" through outreach efforts may create classes that are shallow, spiritually stagnant, and indifferent to each other. The Great Commission calls for both reaching (evangelism) and teaching (discipleship). But we have already seen Jesus' preference. Bruce's observation bears repeating: "The careful, painstaking education of the disciples secured that the Teacher's influence on the world should be permanent; that His kingdom should be founded on the rock of deep and indestructible convictions in the minds of a few, not on the shifting sands of superficial evanescent impressions on the minds of the many."[19]

A common question among ministers is "Howmanyjahave?" When we start a new Sunday school class, "Howmanyjahave?" When an early worship service is begun, "Howmanyjahave?" A new course in Discipleship Training begins, "Howmanyjahave?" Someone hears that a recent revival produced many baptisms, "Howmanyjahave?" It is pervasive, almost second nature, to ask that question. Every measure of spiritual vitality seems to be tied to how many people attended, not what happened in those people because they attended. *Jesus did not brag or exaggerate about the crowds of people who gathered around Him to be healed or fed or taught.* Attendance levels were not His concern; people were. Okay, I *know* that numbers are people. But when we are overly concerned about "ten more next Sunday," we don't really care about who those ten are—so long as we have ten. This is different from looking for Sally, and Tom, and Jane, and Stan. Put it in a business sense. Let's say my goal is to sell ten thousand hamburgers this month. *Do I care whether a particular customer gets a bad hamburger?* If I reason that I can still sell ten thousand with or without him, then my focus is *quantity.* If I reason that I want to make every customer satisfied with my food and service, then my focus is *quality.* Ask McDonald's—or for that matter, Ford or Honda—and they'll tell you the one who focuses on quality increases sales now, and increases sales for a long time to come. Reach people? Absolutely! One person at a time.

Later, *Jesus did not change His message when the crowds began to leave Him.* As He focused on life surrender and "yokes" and "crosses," people began to drift away. The rich young ruler walked away from Jesus, unwilling to pay the cost of discipleship. But Jesus did not change His style or His message. He did not evaluate the quality of what He was doing by the quantity of people who followed Him. He knew He was in the Father's will, and He was faithful.

One other story illustrates this quantity/quality issue. In the Temple were money boxes where the faithful deposited their tithes and offerings. The coins were deposited in metal cones, made in the shape of a trumpet. When a person dropped several coins into the opening, they clinked and clanked as they fell through the cone. This was called "sounding the trumpets." The Pharisees loved to deposit a bag of coins into the box, so that people within hearing would know they had made a large offering. Then one day. . . .

> Jesus sat down opposite the place where the offerings were put and watched the crowd putting their money into the temple treasury. Many rich people threw in large amounts. But a poor widow came and put in two very small copper coins, worth only a fraction of a penny. Calling his disciples to him, Jesus said, "I tell you the truth, this poor widow has put more into the treasury than all the others. They all gave out of their wealth; but she, out of her poverty, put in everything—all she had to live on (Mark 12:41–44).

It was the quality of the gift, not its quantity, that caught Jesus' eye.

Which is more important: what we know or what we do? Where do we put the emphasis in our teaching efforts: on what learners know or what they do?

Jesus defined the terms "wise" and "foolish," not on the basis of what one *knows*, but on the basis of what one *does*, with His words (Matt. 7:24, 26). When learners leave our classes, have we helped them *practice what they've learned* from God's Word? They have heard the words, but do they practice them? If not, then Jesus says we have sent them out as fools. When your congregation leaves the sanctuary after worship, they have heard the words, but do they practice them? If so, then according to Jesus we have sent them out as wise.

Therefore give specific attention to how you encourage learners to practice what you study: assignments done during the week, case studies in class, personal experiences related to the subject, mission projects. Putting the Word into practice is essential in developing biblical wisdom in our learners.

"It was the *quality* of the gift not its quantity that caught Jesus' eye"

Jesus Emphasized Action More Than Knowledge

Jesus Focused
on Structure
More than Detail

Because Jesus was a Master of the Old Testament, He taught its key themes. Jesus majored on Truth, the Pharisees on trivia. Jesus majored on love, the Pharisees on legalism. Jesus majored on justice, the Pharisees on judgment.

When you teach, say, the story of the Good Samaritan, are you more interested in covering every verse in the story, or helping your learners become Good Samaritans? Do you curtail questions from learners in order to complete your lecture? When there are five major truths in a given lesson, are you more inclined to cover all five equally, or would you rather choose the one that relates best to your class needs and focus on it?

But the central truth of Scripture is summed up in Jesus' own statement: "I have come that [you] may have life, and have it to the full" (John 10:10). The pinnacle of our teaching ministry is lifting high the Lord Jesus and letting Him draw all our learners to Himself. There is no greater reward in teaching than to see a life transformed by the love and power of the Lord. May God grant you many such rewards as you offer your teaching ministry to Him.

It is easy to get lost in the details of a particular study and miss the central truth God is conveying. My son is an active "Bible Driller" at our church. He has just passed the Associational Drill competition with flying colors—headed to the state competition. He knows his memory work! We were practicing his verses the other day. After he perfectly quoted an Old Testament verse, I asked him what it meant. "We don't have to know what the verses mean, Dad. We're just supposed to memorize them!" Great on details; weak on structure. So I explained the meaning of the verse. Take care not to lose your learners in a mass of detail, even if the detail is God's Word.

Jesus Stressed
Long-term Rather than
Immediate Results

We have already noted that Jesus consciously chose to pour His life into a select band of believers, who would then carry on His mission after He left. He did this in spite of the fact He could have drawn a crowd anywhere He went with His dramatic teaching and miraculous works. He made this choice because the in-depth training of the Twelve formed the foundation for the early Church, which then carried His Gospel around the world.

There is a sense, and I approach this point with some fear of being misunderstood, that Jesus' training of the Twelve was *preparation* for ministry. His words and explanations and parables formed the raw material out of which the disciples learned to be apostles. But even at the end of Jesus' ministry, as He prepared to return to the

Father, the disciples were ill-suited to take on the power of the Sanhedrin and the power of Rome. They had been trained, but they
lacked the power to carry out their mission. But Jesus promised them
that they *would* "receive power when the Holy Spirit comes on you;
and you will be my witnesses in Jerusalem, and in all Judea and Sa-
maria, and to the ends of the earth." (Acts 1:8).

And so, on the Day of Pentecost, the Holy Spirit filled the believers and empowered them to do all that Jesus had commanded them.
They had been prepared. Now they were transformed. And the Day
of Pentecost forever divided history into two eras: the first, in which
the Holy Spirit was imparted to God's chosen for specific purposes
and short time periods, and the second, in which the Holy Spirit
takes up permanent residence (Eph. 1:13) in the life of the believer
in Jesus (1 Cor. 12:3).

Jesus knew that He had to return to the Father so that He could
return, by the Spirit, to dwell in the hearts of all believers everywhere: "But I tell you the truth: It is for your good that I am going
away. Unless I go away, the Counselor will not come to you; but if
I go, I will send him to you" (John 16:7). But the work of the Counselor, the Holy Spirit, is to glorify Jesus, not Himself (John 16:14).
He does not speak on His own, but speaks only what He hears—presumably from Jesus (John 16:13). And in His earlier teaching on the
Holy Spirit, Jesus intimated that He Himself would be coming to
them (John 14:16, 18). Both Peter and Paul used the terms "Holy
Spirit" and "Spirit of Christ" interchangeably—so when Baptists say
that Jesus lives in our hearts, we reflect this dual meaning.

The point of this is that the teaching of Jesus provided the raw
material for the transformation that took place at Pentecost by the
Holy Spirit. The Spirit called to remembrance all that Jesus had
taught the disciples, and used that teaching to grow them into the
leaders of the early Church.

Paul writes to the Corinthians, "I planted the seed, Apollos wa-
tered it, but *God made it grow*. So neither he who plants nor he who
waters is anything, but only *God, who makes things grow* (1 Cor.
3:6–7, author's emphasis). We may teach or preach our hearts out,
week after week, and see little spiritual fruit resulting from our efforts. Then one Sunday, for no apparent reason, the Lord moves in
the hearts of several of the members, and a spiritual breakthrough
occurs. There is an insidious temptation *to do whatever works* in order to make the church grow. This is fleshly, worldly thinking. Ends

justify the means. Focusing on an aggregation more than the congregation. We do not make the church grow—God does.

Does this mean we simply wait for God to do whatever He's going to do? No. Paul continues, "The man who plants and the man who waters have one purpose, and *each will be rewarded according to his own labor"* (1 Cor. 3:8). There is work to be done. And what is that work? Swindohl writes in *Rise and Shine* that the minister's primary work is prayer and the Word of God. Praying and teaching the Word: *that* is our labor. And God grows His Church by His Spirit—in His time and in His way. *Lord, give us the heart and the mind to labor in accomplishing our essential tasks of praying and teaching, so that we might provide "spiritual nourishment so that the saints might take up the work of the ministry."*

THE CONTINUING WORK OF JESUS THROUGH THE HOLY SPIRIT

Jesus continues his work of teaching today in the Person of the Holy Spirit. As we noted above, Jesus said He was sending the Holy Spirit to His disciples (John 16:7), but that in a sense He, Jesus, would be coming to them (John 14:16,18). The Holy Spirit is the Divine Personal Presence of Jesus.

The great distinction between secular teaching and Christian teaching is the Holy Spirit's work of illumination.[20] We can convey religious concepts (cognitive), change attitudes and values (affective), and develop ministry skills (psychomotor) in our learners "in the flesh," but developing spiritual understanding and growing in Christ ultimately depends on the teaching of the Holy Spirit.

The Holy Spirit teaches us through God's Word, moving us beyond biblical facts and information to spiritual truth.[21] The Holy Spirit teaches us through human teachers, helping them understand spiritual truth, to understand our learners, to walk a Christlike life.[22] The Holy Spirit works through developmental processes and personal experiences of learners to convict, regenerate, indwell, comfort and issue gifts.[23] The Holy Spirit works through the community of faith, the Body of Christ, to provide an environment of spiritual growth.[24]

Lawrence Richards says there are two ways to distort the work of the Holy Spirit as Teacher. "The first is to discount it, and to see Christian growth as simply a natural process."[25] This takes educational psychology too seriously—believing that the principles of Erikson, Piaget, Bruner, Skinner, and Rogers are all we need to be effective teachers of spiritual truth. "The second is to make it a magical thing, demanding that God work against all natural process-es and intervene in spectacular ways."[26] This repudiates education-al psychology as a useful tool in Christian teaching. The truth is that learning the things of God is a cooperative effort between the human and divine. He created us to learn of Him and His ways. Educational psychology is an analysis of His design. He teaches us beyond the bounds of educational psychology as we give Him freedom:

> Let the word of Christ dwell in you richly
> as you teach and admonish one another in all wisdom,
> and as you sing psalms, hymns and spiritual songs
> with gratitiude in your hearts to God.
> And whatever you do, whether in word or deed,
> do it all in the name of the Lord Jesus,
> giving thanks to God the Father through him (Col. 3:16–17).

The twelve learners Jesus chose to be with Him were real human beings, with all the problems and potential of our learners today:

IN SUMMARY

- imperfect,
- slow to learn,
- self-centered,
- theologically uneducated and unprofessional, but . . .
- Teachable.

Jesus demonstrated that godly character is the basis for spiritual teaching. His characteristics include:

- He was what He taught,
- comfortable with people of all kinds,
- compassionate toward learners,
- possessed a strong Father-focused self-concept,
- Man on mission,
- dynamic humility,
- calmness under attack,
- patient with disciples,
- identified with the Father through prayer,
- knew His learners,
- Master of the Old Testament.

Jesus used effective teaching approaches to communicate the gospel clearly and forcefully. Jesus:

- established relationships with people,
- stimulated and maintained interest,
- taught by example,
- taught people, not lessons,
- focused on ever smaller groups,
- recognized the worth of His learners,
- emphasized character more than content,
- emphasized quality of effort over quantity of learners,
- emphasized action over knowledge,
- focused on structure more than detail,
- stressed long-term rather than immediate results.

Jesus chose teachable men to be His learners. These learners were not merely followers or members of His group. They were apprentices of the Master Craftsman. But they did not remain apprentices. They became teachers in their own right. They obeyed the command of the Risen Lord to go to the whole world and make other disciples, teaching them all the things Jesus commanded them to do (Matt. 28:19–20). Within a generation, they had turned the world upside down with their teaching, and the process continues today, around the world. May God bless you as you endeavor to teach as Jesus taught. Ask the Lord to help you. Learn from Him as you teach. It's a trip like no other!

DISCUSSION QUESTIONS

1. Think of at least three positive and three negative examples of Jesus' personal characteristics you've seen in teachers.
2. Think of at least three positive and three negative examples of Jesus' methods you've seen in teachers.
3. Identify which component of the Christian Teachers' Triad relates to each of the personal characteristics and methods of Jesus.
4. Consider your own approach to teaching in light of Jesus' example. List at least four changes you will make in your approach to teaching as a result of Jesus' example.

NOTES

Sidebar notes have been placed at the end of their respective chapter in this section.

CHAPTER ONE

1. For an in-depth study of the Model, see Yount's *The Disciplers' Handbook*, chapter 1: "The Disciplers' Model," or the Disciplers' Video Series training tapes.

2. George Mouly, *Psychology Applied to Teaching,* 3rd ed. (New York: Holt, Rinehart & Winston, 1973), 906.

CHAPTER TWO

1. *American Heritage Electronic Dictionary*, 3rd edition (WordStar International, Inc., 1993), s.v. "empiricism."

2. Ibid., s.v. "empirical."

3. Ibid., s.v. "hypocrisy."

CHAPTER THREE

1. Norman A. Sprinthall, Richard C. Sprinthall, and Sharon N. Oja, *Educational Psychology: A Developmental Approach*, 6th ed. (New York: McGraw-Hill, Inc., 1994), 141.

2. Ibid., 142

3. Ibid.

4. Robert F. Biehler and Jack Snowman, *Psychology Applied to Teaching,* 7th ed. (Boston: Houghton Mifflin Company, 1993), 42.

5. Don Hamachek, *Psychology in Teaching, Learning, and Growth,* 4th ed. (Boston: Allyn and Bacon, 1990), 44.

6. Erik H. Erikson, Joan M. Erikson, and Helen Q. Kivnick, *Vital Involvement in Old Age: The Experience of Old Age in Our Time* (New York: W. W. Norton and Company, 1986), 32.

7. Ibid., 32–33.

8. Myron H. Dembo, *Applying Educational Psychology*, 5th ed. (New York: Longman, 1994), 439.

9. Erikson used generic terms for age ranges: "play age," "school age," and the like. Writers differ on exact age ranges for these stages. "Birth to twenty-four months" is the consensus for stage one, but Hamachek gives the range as birth to 18 months. Stage two is generally given as "two's and three's," but Hamachek suggests "18 months to three years" (43). There are so many facets to the development of personality that one should be cautious in setting boundaries too precisely. See also notes 28 and 33.

10. Thomas L. Good and Jere E. Brophey, *Educational Psychology: A Realistic Approach*, 4th ed. (New York: Longman, 1990), 97.

11. Ibid.

12. Ibid.

13. Dembo, *Applying Education Psychology*, 439.

14. Paul Eggen and Don Kauchak, *Educational Psychology: Classroom Connections*, 2nd ed. (New York: Macmillan College Publishing Company, 1994), 73.

15. Good and Brophey, *Realistic Approach*, 98.

16. Eggen and Kauchak, *Classroom Connections*, 72.

17. Sprinthall and Oja, *Development Approach*, 157.

18. Good and Brophey, *Realistic Approach*, 98.

19. Eggen and Kauchak, *Classroom Connections*, 72.

20. Sprinthall and Oja, *Developmental Approach*, 157.

21. Good and Brophey, *Realistic Approach*, 98.

22. Eggen and Kauchak, *Classroom Connections*, 72.

23. Good and Brophey, *Realistic Approach*, 99.

24. Hamachek, *Psychology in Teaching*, 49.

25. Dembo, *Applying Educational Psychology*, 439.

26. Eggen and Kauchak, *Classroom Connections*, 72.

27. Interview with Dr. Marcia McQuitty, Assistant Professor of Childhood Education, Southwestern Baptist Theological Seminary, Fort Worth, Texas, May 25, 1994.

28. Good and Brophey, *Realistic Approach*, 99.

29. Eggen and Kauchak, *Classroom Connections*, 72.

30. Good and Brophey, *Realistic Approach*, 99.

31. Hamachek, *Psychology in Teaching*, 49.

32. Dembo, *Applying Educational Psychology*, 439.

33. The actual ages of Erikson's stages, beginning with "School Age," have undergone some revision through the years. Traditionally the Industry/Inferiority stage covers years 6 through 11. Sprinthall (155) and Eggen (72) extend the stage to 12.This shift toward older ages grows more pronounced in adolescence and adulthood, as we'll see.

34. Good and Brophey, *Realistic Approach*, 99.

35. Sprinthall and Oja, *Developmental Approach*, 155.

36. Ibid.

37. Hamachek, *Pschology in Teaching*, 49.

38. Dembo, *Applying Educational Pschology*, 439.

39. Traditionally the Identity/Role Confusion stage covers ages 12 through 18. Sprinthall extends this stage to 13 through the college years (157). One implication of this is that male teenagers are marrying (Stage 6) before their identity is resolved (Stage 5). This would certainly lead to unstable marriages and increased divorce rates.

40. Sprinthall and Oja, *Developmental Approach*, 157.

41. Eggen and Kauchak, *Classroom Connections*, 74.

42. Good and Brophey, *Realistic Approach*, 100.

43. Sprinthall and Oja, *Development Approach*, 157.

44. Eggen and Kauchak, *Classroom Approach*, 75

45. Ibid., 74

46. Sprinthall and Oja, *Development Approach*, 159.

47. James E. Marcia, "Development and Validation of Ego Identity Status," *Journal of Personality and Social Psychology*, 3(5), 1966, 551–58. "Identity in Adolescence," in J. Adelson, ed., *Handbook of Adolescent Psychology* (New York: Wiley, 1980). "Identity and Self-Development," in R. M. Lerner, A. C. Peterson and J. Brooks-Gunn, eds., *Encyclopedia of Adolescence* (New York: Garland Publishing, 1991).

48. Good and Brophey, *Realistic Approach*, 100.

49. Ibid., 102.

50. Hamachek, *Psychology in Teaching*, 49.

51. Dembo, *Applying Educational Psychology*, 439.

52. Ibid., 443.

53. Good and Brophey, *Realistic Approach*, 103.

54. Eggen and Kauchak, *Classroom Connections*, 75.

55. Ibid.

56. Good and Brophey, *Realistic Approach*, 103.

57. Dembo, *Applying Educational Psychology*, 439.

58. Ibid., 443.

59. Erik H. Erikson, *Identity and the Life Cycle* (New York: W. W. Norton and Company,1980), 103.

60. Robert E. Slavin, *Educational Psychology: Theory and Practice*, 4th ed. (Boston: Allyn and Bacon, 1994), 56.

61. Dembo, *Applying Educational Psychology*, 444.

62. Eggen and Kauchak, *Classroom Connections*, 76.

63. N. L. Gage and David C. Berliner, *Educational Psychology*, 3rd ed. (Boston: Houghton Mifflin Company, 1984), 169.

64. Eggen and Kauchak, *Classroom Connections*, 76.

65. Dembo, *Applying Educational Psychology*, 443.

66. Gage and Berliner, *Educatioal Psychology*, 170.

67. Dembo, *Applying Educational Psychology*, 443.

68. Erikson, *Identity*, 103.

69. Dembo, *Applying Educational Psychology*, 439.

70. Good and Brophey, *Realistic Approach*, 103.

71. Dembo, *Applying Educational Psychology*, 443.

72. Slavin, *Theory and Practice*, 56.

73. Gage and Berliner, *Educational Psychology*, 170.

74. Eggen and Kauchak, *Classroom Connections*, 76.

75. Erikson and Kivnick, *Vital Involvement*, 33.

76. Ibid., 41.

77. Ibid., 45.

78. Ibid., 34.

79. Ibid., 42.

80. Ibid.

81. Ibid., 41.

82. Ibid., 34.

83. Ibid., 48.

84. Ibid., 34.

85. Sprinthall and Oja, *Developmental Approach*, 150.

86. Erikson and Kivnick, *Vital Involvement*, 35.

87. Ibid., 43.

88. Ibid.

89. Ibid., 35.

90. Ibid., 49.

91. *The American Heritage Electronic Dictionary*, 3rd ed. (Boston: The Macmillan Company, 1992), s. v. "fanaticism."

92. Erikson and Kivnick, *Vital Involvement*, 43.

93. Ibid., 35.

94. Ibid., 43.

95. Ibid., 37.

96. Ibid., 50.

97. Ibid., 44.

98. Ibid., 37.

99. Ibid., 72.

100. Ibid., 288–89.

101. Ibid., 51.

102. Ibid., 37–38.

103. Biehler and Snowman, *Psychology Applied*, 54.

104. Sprinthall and Oja, *Developmental Approach*, 153.

105. Biehler and Snowman, *Pschology Applied*, 54.

106. Ibid.

107. Letter from Dr. Joan Havens, Columbia Biblical Seminary, Columbia, South Carolina, April 5, 1994.

108. Hamachek, *Psychology in Teaching*, 45.

109. Pamela R.Rothstein, *Educational Psychology* (New York: McGraw-Hill, 1990), 64.

110. Ibid.

111. Hamachek, 46.

112. Anita Woolfolk, *Educational Psychology*, 5th ed. (Boston: Allyn and Bacon, Inc., 1993), 68.

113. Erikson, *Identity*, 93.

114. Bonnidell Clouse, *Teaching for Moral Growth: A Guide for the Christian Community—Teachers, Parents and Pastors* (Wheaton, Ill.: Bridgeport Books, 1993), 121.

115. Woolfolk, *Educational Psychology*, 70.
116. Ibid., 73.
117. Ibid.

A. Material drawn from Biehler, 41–42, Woolfolk, 66, and John J. Gleason, *Growing Up to God* (Nashville: Abingdon Press, 1975), 13–15.

CHAPTER FOUR

1. Slavin, *Theory and Practice,* 31.
2. Sprinthall, Sprinthall and Oja, *Developmental Approach*, 97.
3. Sprinthall, Sprinthall and Oja, *Developmental Approach*, 98.
4. Ibid., 100. Also, Slavin, *Theory and Practice*, 31.
5. Barry J. Wadsworth, *Piaget's Theory of Cognitive and Affective Development*, 3rd ed. (New York: Longman, 1984), 9.
6. Don Hamachek, *Psychology in Teaching,* 148.
7. Ibid.
8. Wadsworth, *Piaget's Theory*, 10.
9. Woolfolk, *Educational Psychology*, 28.
10. Biehler and Snowman, *Psychology Applied*, 59.
11. Woolfolk, *Educational Psychology*, 28.
12. Glover notes that Piaget differentiated between a scheme (pl. schemes) and a schemata (pl. schema). The first refers to learned behaviors, such as tying a shoe lace. The second refers to factual knowledge, such as "Birds have wings." Most texts, however, use the term "scheme" to refer generally to the basic building block of the cognitive structure. John A. Glover and Roger H. Bruning, *Educational Psychology: Principles and Applications*, 3rd. ed. (Glenview, Ill.: Scott, Foresman/Little, Brown Higher Education, 1990), 115.
13. Biehler and Snowman, *Psychology Applied*, 59.
14. Woolfolk, *Educational Psychology*, 28.
15. Wadsworth, *Piaget's Theory*, 11.
16. Ibid., 13.
17. Woolfolk, *Educational Psychology*, 29.
18. Biehler and Snowman, *Psychology Applied*, 60.
19. Ibid., 59.
20. Eggen and Kauchak, *Classroom Connections*, 35.
21. Biehler and Snowman, *Psychology Applied*, 59.
22. Glover and Bruning, *Principles and Applications*, 115.
23. Biehler and Snowman, *Psychology Applied*, 59.
24. Glover and Bruning, *Principles and Applications*, 115.
25. Eggen and Kauchak, *Classroom Connections*, 35.
26. Gage and Berliner, *Educational Psychology*, 143.
27. Guy R. LeFrancois, *Psychology for Teaching*, 8th ed. (Belmont, Calif.: Wadsworth Publishing Company, 1994), 58.
28. Hamachek, *Psychology in Teaching*, 149.
29. Dembo, *Applying Educational Psychology*, 355.
30. Good and Brophey, *Realistic Approach*, 55, and Sprinthall, Sprinthall, and Oja, *Developmental Approach*, 118.
31. Woolfolk, *Educational Psychology*, 29.
32. Wadsworth, *Piaget's Theory*, 14.
33. Glover and Bruning, *Principles and Applications*, 116.
34. Biehler and Snowman, *Psychology Applied*, 59.

35. Gage and Berliner, *Educational Psychology*, 143.
36. Dembo, *Applying Educational Psychology*, 355.
37. Good and Brophey, *Realisitic Approach*, 55.
38. LeFrancois, *Psychology for Teaching*, 58.
39. Woolfolk, *Educational Psychology*, 29.
40. LeFrancois, *Psychology for Teaching*, 58.
41. Good and Brophey, *Realistic Approach*, 55.
42. Wadsworth, *Piaget's Theory*, 16.
43. Ibid., 17.
44. Good and Brophey, *Realistic Approach*, 55.
45. Biehler and Snowman, *Psychology Applied*, 60.
46. This last statement may shock you. But I become a Christian, not by intellectually understanding the teachings of Jesus, but when I give my life to Him. The Christian faith is not found in understanding a religious creed but by living in union with the Righteous Redeemer. Understanding the gospel is a good first step, but until I personally surrender to the Lord, I have only engaged in an academic exercise.
47. Woolfolk, *Educational Psychology*, 31.
48. Glover and Bruning, *Principles and Applications*, 120.
49. Biehler and Snowman, *Psychology Applied*, 63.
50. Glover and Bruning, *Principles and Applications*, 123.
51. Eggen and Kauchak, *Classroom Connection*, 46.
52. Woolfolk, *Educational Psychology*, 33.
53. Eggen and Kauchak, *Classroom Connections*, 46.
54. Biehler and Snowman, *Psychology Applied*, 65.
55. Glover, and Bruning, *Principles and Applications*, 120, and Eggen and Kauchak, *Classroom Connections*, 46.
56. Eggen and Kauchak, *Classroom Connections*, 45.
57. Biehler and Snowman, *Psychology Applied*, 65.
58. Eggen and Kauchak, *Classroom Connections*, 35.
59. Sprinthall, Sprinthall and Oja, *Developmental Approach*, 117.
60. Biehler and Snowman, *Psychology Applied*, 59.
61. Glover and Bruning, *Principles and Applications*, 117.
62. Ibid., 123.
63. Ibid., 120.
64. Ibid., 114.
65. Sprinthall, Sprinthall and Oja, *Development Approach*, 98.
66. Woolfolk, *Educational Psychology*, 30.
67. Ibid.
68. Wadsworth, *Piaget's Theory*, 9.
69. Ibid., 27.
70. Glover and Bruning, *Principles and Applications*, 114.
71. Sprinthall, Sprinthall and Oja, *Developmental Approach*, 105.
72. Eggen and Kauchak, *Classroom Connections*, 44.
73. Sprinthall, Sprinthall and Oja, *Developmental Approach*, 105–6.
74. Eggen and Kauchak, *Classroom Connections*, 44.
75. Sprinthall, Sprinthall and Oja, *Developmental Approach*, 106.
76. Ibid.
77. Sprinthall, Sprinthall and Oja, *Developmental Approach*, 110.
78. Glover Bruning, *Principles and Applications*, 122.
79. Eggen and Kauchak, *Classroom Connections*, 45.

80. Glover and Bruning, *Principles and Applications*, 122.
81. Ibid.
82. Sprinthall, Sprinthall and Oja, *Developmental Approach*, 107.
83. Eggen and Kauchak, *Classsroom Connections*, 45.
84. Sprinthall, Sprinthall and Oja, *Developmental Approach*, 110.
85. Eggen and Kauchak, *Classroom Connections*, 44.
86. Sprinthall, Sprinthall and Oja, *Developmental Approach*, 109.
87. Ibid.
88. Ibid.
89. Glover and Bruning, *Principles and Applications*, 122.
90. Sprinthall, Sprinthall and Oja, *Developmental Approach*, 107.
91. Ibid., 108.
92. Dembo, *Applying Educational Psychology*, 359.
93. Ibid., 360
94. Ibid.
95. Ibid., 361
96. Eggen and Kauchak, *Classroom Connections*, 45.
97. Sprinthall, Sprinthall and Oja, *Developmental Approach*, 109.
98. Glover and Bruning, *Principles and Applications*, 124.
99. Eggen and Kauchak, *Classroom Connections*, 48.
100. Sprinthall, Sprinthall and Oja, *Developmental Approach*, 109.
101. Ibid., 110
102. Dembo, *Applying Educational Psychology*, 361.
103. Eggen and Kauchak, *Classroom Connections*, 45.
104. Ibid., 49.
105. Glover and Bruning, *Principles and Applications*, 124.
106. Ibid., 125.
107. Dembo, *Applying Educational Psychology*, 361.
108. Ibid., 362.
109. Glover and Bruning, *Principles and Applications*, 125.
110. Eggen and Kauchak, *Classroom Connections*, 50.
111. LeFrancois, *Psychology for Teaching*, 68.
112. Eggen and Kauchak, *Classroom Connections*, 50.
113. LeFrancois, *Psychology for Teaching*, 68.
114. Dembo, *Applying Educational Psychology*, 362.
115. Woolfolk, *Educational Psychology*, 36.
116. Eggen and Kauchak, *Classroom Connections*, 50.
117. Glover and Bruning, *Principles and Applications*, 129.
118. Eggen and Kauchak, *Classroom Connections*, 50.
119. Glover and Bruning, *Principles and Applications*, 128.
120. Eggen and Kauchak, *Classroom Connections*, 50.
121. Ibid., 51.
122. Woolfolk, *Educational Psychology*, 40.
123. Sprinthall, Sprinthall and Oja, *Developmental Approach*, 113.
124. LeFrancois, *Psychology for Teaching*, 69.
125. Wadsworth, *Piaget's Theory*, 32.
126. See Biehler and Snowman, *Psychology Applied*, 70, Gage and Berliner, *Educational Psychology*, 144, and Dembo, *Applying Educational Psychology*, 364.
127. Biehler and Snowman, *Psychology Applied*, 70, and LeFrancois, *Psychology for Teaching*, 71.

128. Biehler and Snowman, 70.
129. Biehler and Snowman, *Psychology Applied*, 70, Dembo, *Applying Educational Psychology*, 364, and LeFrancois, *Psychology for Teaching*, 71.
130. T. H. Epstein, "Brain Growth and Cognitive Functioning," in *The Emerging Adolescent: Characteristics and Educational Implications*, (Columbus, Ohio: National Middle School Association, 1980), as cited in Biehler and Snowman, *Psychology Applied*, 70.
131. Constance Kamii, "Autonomy: The Aim of Education Envisoned by Piaget," *Phi Delta Kappan*, 65(6), 410–15 as cited in Biehler and Snowman, *Psychology Applied*, 70.
132. N. A. Sprinthall and R. C. Sprinthall, *Educational Psychology: A Developmental Approach*, 4th ed. (New York: Random House, 1987), as cited in Biehler and Snowman, *Psychology Applied*, 70.
133. Biehler and Snowman, *Psychology Applied*, 70.
134. Dembo, *Applying Educational Psychology*, 364.
135. Gage and Berliner, *Educational Psychology*, 144.
136. Ibid.
137. Ibid., 145.
138. LeFrancois, *Psychology for Teaching*, 72.
139. Dembo, *Applying Educational Psychology*, 366.
140. Ibid., 367.
141. Ibid., 366.
142. Good and Brophey, *Realistic Approach*, 63.
143. "People to People," William J. Reynolds (Nashville: Broadman Press, 1971), in *Baptist Hymnal* (Nashville: Convention Press, 1975), 308.
144. Glover and Bruning, *Principles and Applications*, 132.
145. Slavin, *Theory and Practice*, 46.
146. LeFrancois, *Psychology for Teaching*, 73.
147. Dembo, *Applying Educational Psychology* 365.
148. LeFrancois, *Psychology for Teaching*, 74.
149. Dembo, *Applying Educational Psychology*, 366.
150. Slavin, *Theory and Practice*, 45.
151. Woolfolk, *Educational Psychology*, 33.
152. Glover and Bruning, *Principles and Applications*, 131.
153. Dembo, *Applying Educational Psychology*, 367.
154. From *Piaget Rediscovered*, p. 5 as quoted in Herbert Ginsburg and Sylvia Opper, *Piaget's Theory of Intellectual Development: An Introduction* (Englewood Cliffs, N.J.: Prentice-Hall, Inc., 1969), 231–32.

A. Biehler and Snowman, *Psychology Applied*, 57.
B. Sprinthall, Sprinthall and Oja, *Developmental Approach*, 100.
C. Wadsworth, *Piaget's Theory*, 2.
D. Sprinthall, Sprinthall and Oja, *Developmental Approach*, 100.
E. Biehler and Snowman, *Psychology Applied*, 57.
F. Ibid.
G. Sprinthall, Sprinthall and Oja, *Developmental Approach*, 100.
H. Slavin, *Theory and Practice*, 31.
I. Biehler and Snowman, *Psychology Applied*, 57.
J. Beilue, 2.
K. Eggen and Kauchak, *Classroom Connections*, 225.

L. Sprinthall, Sprinthall and Oja, *Developmental Approach*, 101.

M. Ibid.

N. Hamachek, *Psychology in Teaching*, 147.

O. Butler, 12 and Hamachek, *Psychology in Teaching*, 147.

P. Sprinthall, Sprinthall and Oja, *Developmental Approach*, 99.

Q. Clouse, *Moral Growth*, 225.

R. Ibid.

S. Sprinthall, Sprinthall and Oja, *Developmental Approach*, 100.

T. Eggen and Kauchak, *Classroom Connections*, 34.

U. Slavin, *Theory and Practice*, 31.

V. Good and Brophey, *Realistic Approach*, 53.

W. Clouse, *Moral Growth*, 225.

X. Biehler and Snowman, *Psychology Applied*, 57.

CHAPTER FIVE

1. Eggen and Kauchak, *Classroom Connections*, 63.

2. Biehler and Snowman, *Psychology Applied*, 73.

3. Ibid.

4. Slavin, *Educational Psychology*, 58. Biehler says ages 4–7.

5. Biehler and Snowman, *Psychology Applied*, 73.

6. Slavin, *Educational Psychology*, 58.

7. Biehler and Snowman say ages 7–10, 73

8. Ibid.

9. Slavin, *Educational Psychology*, 59.

10. Biehler and Snowman say ages 11–12, 73.

11. Ibid.

12. Slavin, *Educational Psychology*, 59.

13. Eggen and Kauchak, *Classroom Connections*, 63.

14. Quoted from Jean Piaget, *The Moral Judgement of the Child*, (Glencoe, Ill.: Free Press, 1948), 118, in Biehler and Snowden, *Psychology Applied*, 74.

15. Hamachek, *Psychology in Teaching*, 170.

16. Ibid.

17. Slavin, *Educational Psychology*, 59.

18. Biehler and Snowman, *Psychology Applied*, 73.

19. Woolfolk, *Educational Psychology*, 79.

20. Biehler and Snowman, *Psychology Applied*, 74.

21. Woolfolk, *Educational Psychology*, 79.

22. LeFrancois, *Psychology for Teaching*, 42.

23. Slavin, *Educational Psychology*, 59.

24. Biehler and Snowman, *Psychology Applied* 73, Hamachek; *Psychology in Teaching*, 171.

25. Ibid., 78.

26. Woolfolk, *Educational Psychology*, 79.

27. Biehler and Snowman, *Psychology Applied*, 78.

28. Woolfolk, *Educational Psychology*, 79.

29. LeFrancois, *Psychology for Teaching*, 42.

30. Slavin, *Educational Psychology*, 61.

31. Eggen and Kauchak, *Classroom Connections*, 63; Slavin, *Educational Psychology*, 60; Biehler and Snowman, *Psychology Applied*, 74.

32. Quoted from Lawrence Kohlberg, "Stage and Sequence: The Cognitive-Developmental Approach to Social-ization," in D. A. Goslin, ed., *Handbook of Socialization Theory and Research* (Chicago: Rand McNally, 1969), 376 by Biehler and Snowman, *Psychology Applied*, 76.

33. Clouse, *Moral Growth*, 234.

34. Woolfolk, *Educational Psychology*, 80.

35. Slavin, *Educational Psychology*, 61.

36. LeFrancois, *Psychology for Teaching*, 43.

37. Biehler and Snowman, *Psychology Applied*, 77.

38. Slavin, *Educational Psychology*, 62.

39. Good and Brophey, *Realistic Approach*, 55, and Sprinthall, Sprinthall and Oja, *Development Approach*, 108.

40. LeFrancois, *Psychology for Teaching*, 43.

41. Glover and Bruning, *Principles and Applications*, 230.

42. Clouse, *Moral Growth*, 228.

43. Ibid., 230.

44. Ibid., 208.

45. Slavin, *Educational Psychology*, 62.

46. LeFrancois, *Psychology for Teaching*, 43.

47. Slavin, *Educational Psychology*, 62.

48. Eggen and Kauchak, *Classroom Connections*, 65.

49. Glover and Bruning, *Principles and Applications*, 230.

50. Clouse, *Moral Growth*, 228.

51. Sprinthall, Sprinthall, and Oja, *Developmental Approach*, 179.

52. LeFrancois, *Psychology for Teaching*, 43.

53. Eggen and Kauchak, *Classroom Connections*, 65.

54. Sprinthall, Sprinthall and Oja, *Developmental Approach*, 179.

55. Eggen and Kauchak, *Classroom Connections*, 65.

56. Biehler and Snowman, *Psychology Applied*, 77.

57. Glover and Bruning, *Principles and Applications*, 230.

58. Eggen and Kauchak, *Classroom Connections*, 65.

59. Good and Brophey, *Realistic Approach*, 108.

60. Sprinthall, Sprinthall and Oja, *Developmental Approach*, 179.

61. Dembo, *Applying Educational Psychology*, 217.

62. Clouse, *Moral Growth*, 237.

63. Ibid., 234.

64. Eggen and Kauchak, *Classroom Connections*, 64.

65. Clouse, *Moral Growth*, 234.

66. Eggen and Kauchak, *Classroom Connections*, 65.

67. Good and Brophey, *Realistic Approach*, 108.

68. Woolfolk, *Educational Psychology*, 80.

69. Slavin, *Educational Psychology*, 62.

70. LeFrancois, *Psychology for Teaching*, 43.

71. Biehler and Snowman, *Psychology Applied*, 77.

72. LeFrancois, *Psychology for Teaching*, 43.

73. Slavin, *Educational Psychology*, 62.

74. Eggen and Kauchak, *Classroom Connections*, 65.

75. Glover and Bruning, *Principles and Applications*, 230.

76. Biehler and Snowman, *Psychology Applied*, 77.

77. Clouse, *Moral Growth*, 229.

78. Ibid.

79. Ibid., 247

80. Dembo, *Applying Educational Psychology*, 217.

81. LeFrancois, *Psychology for Teaching*, 43.

82. Sprinthall, Sprinthall and Oja, *Developmental Approach*, 183.

83. Clouse, *Moral Growth,* 229.
84. Glover and Bruning, *Principles and Applications,* 231.
85. LeFrancois, *Psychology for Teaching,* 43.
86. Slavin, *Educational Psychology,* 62.
87. Eggen and Kauchak, *Classroom Connections,* 66.
88. Biehler and Snowman, *Psychology Applied,* 77.
89. Eggen and Kauchak, *Classroom Connections,* 66.
90. Ibid.
91. Ibid.
92. Clouse, *Moral Growth,* 247.
93. Slavin, *Educational Psychology,* 62.
94. Eggen and Kauchak, *Classroom Connections,* 65.
95. Clouse, *Moral Growth,* 234.
96. Slavin, *Educational Psychology,* 62.
97. Sprinthall, Sprinthall and Oja, *Developmental Approach,* 183.
98. LeFrancois, *Psychology for Teaching,* 43.
99. Slavin, *Educational Psychology,* 62.
100. Eggen and Kauchak, *Classroom Connections,* 66.
101. Clouse, *Moral Growth,* 234.
102. Glover and Bruning, *Principles and Applications,* 231.
103. Sprinthall, Sprinthall and Oja, *Developmental Approach,* 181.
104. LeFrancois, *Psychology for Teaching,* 43.
105. Biehler and Snowman, *Psychology Applied,* 77.
106. Eggen and Kauchak, *Classroom Connections,* 66.
107. Clouse, *Moral Growth,* 232.
108. Dembo, *Applying Educational Psychology,* 217.
109. Clouse, *Moral Growth,* 238.
110. Ibid., 232.
111. Biehler and Snowman, *Psychology Applied,* 78.
112. Sprinthall, Sprinthall and Oja, *Developmental Approach,* 183.
113. Biehler and Snowman, *Psychology Applied,* 78.
114. LeFrancois, *Psychology for Teaching,* 43.
115. Slavin, *Educational Psychology,* 62.
116. Sprinthall, Sprinthall and Oja, *Developmental Approach,* 184.
117. Hamachek, *Psychology in Teaching,* 172.
118. Glover and Bruning, *Principles and Applications,* 230.
119. Quoted from M. L. King, *Why We Can't Wait* (New York: Harper & Row, Publishers, 1963), 84–85 by Sprinthall, Sprinthall and Oja, *Developmental Approach,* 184.
120. Clouse, *Moral Growth,* 233.
121. Hamachek, *Psychology in Teaching,* 174; Biehler and Snowman, *Psychology Applied,* 78.
122. Ronald Duska and Mariellen Whelan, *Moral Development: A Guide to Piaget and Kohlberg* (New York: Paulist Press, 1975), 86-99.
123. Ibid., 86.
124. Ibid.
125. Ibid., 87.
126. Ibid., 88.
127. Ibid., 91.
128. Ibid., 99.
129. Woolfolk, *Educational Psychology,* 81; Eggen and Kauchak, *Classroom Connections,* 67.
130. LeFrancois, *Psychology for Teaching,* 45.
131. Woolfolk, *Educational Psychology,* 81.
132. Ibid., 82.
133. Ibid.
134. LeFrancois, *Psychology for Teaching,* 45.
135. Woolfolk, *Educational Psychology,* 82.
136. Good and Brophey, *Realistic Approach,* 111.
137. Clouse, *Moral Growth,* 248.
138. Carol Gilligan, *In a Different Voice: Psychological Theory and Women's Development* (Cambridge, Mass.: Harvard University Press, 1982).
139. Clouse, *Moral Growth,* 249.
140. Ibid., 250.
141. Ibid., 249.
142. Slavin, *Educational Psychology,* 65.
143. Glover and Bruning, *Principles and Applications,* 234.
144. Woolfolk, *Educational Psychology,* 83.
145. Glover and Bruning, *Principles and Applications,* 236.
146. Eggen and Kauchak, *Classroom Connections,* 67.
147. Ibid., 68.
148. Ibid., 67.
149. Ibid.
150. Biehler and Snowman, *Psychology Applied,* 85.
151. LeFrancois, *Psychology for Teaching,* 46.
152. Ibid., 45.
153. Biehler and Snowman, *Psychology Applied,* 85.
154. Ibid.
155. Eggen and Kauchak, *Classroom Connections,* 69.
156. Ibid.
157. Good and Brophey, *Realistic Approach,* 112.
158. Biehler and Snowman, *Psychology Applied,* 85.
159. Good and Brophey, *Realistic Approach,* 113.
160. Hamachek, *Psychology in Teaching,* 176.
161. LeFrancois, *Psychology for Teaching,* 47.
162. Ibid.
163. Ibid.
164. Clouse, *Moral Growth,* 233.
165. *QuickVerse Computer Concordance,* s.v."pedagogue." Gal. 3:24.
166. James Fowler, *Stages of Faith* (San Francisco: Harper & Row, Publishers, 1981), xiii.
167. Fowler, *Stages,* xiii.
168. James W. Fowler, *Becoming Adult, Becoming Christian* (San Francisco: Harper & Row, 1984), back fly-leaf.
169. Ibid., front fly-leaf.
170. Fowler, *Stages,* xii.
171. Charles M.Sell, *Transitions Through Adult Life* (Grand Rapids, Mich.: Zondervan Publishing Company, 1991), 104.
172. Fowler, *Becoming,* 52.
173. Fowler, *Stages,* 119.
174. Fowler, *Becoming,* 53.
175. Fowler, *Stages,* 121.
176. Ibid.
177. Fowler, *Stages,* 121.
178. Ibid.
179. Ibid.
180. Jack L. Seymour and Donald E. Miller, *Contemporary Approaches to Christian Education* (Nashville: Abingdon Press, 1982), 86.

181. Ibid., 54.
182. Ibid.
183. Fowler, *Stages*, 134.
184. Seymour and Miller, *Contemporary*, 86.
185. Fowler, *Stages*, 135.
186. Ibid., 56.
187. Sells, *Transitions*,105.
188. Fowler, *Stages*, 149.
189. Ibid., 150.
190. Seymour and Miller, *Contemporary*, 86.
191. Ibid., 59.
192. Sells, *Transitions*, 105.
193. Ibid., 60.
194. Ibid., 61.
195. Ibid., 62.
196. Fowler, *Stages*, 173.
197. Ibid., 60.
198. Fowler, *Stages*, 173.
199. Ibid.
200. Seymour and Miller, *Contemporary*, 87.
201. Fowler, *Stages*, 179.
202. Ibid.
203. Ibid., 62.
204. Ibid.
205. Fowler, *Stages*, 182.
206. Ibid., 182–83.
207. Ibid., 183.
208. Seymour and Miller, *Contemporary*, 87.
209. Ibid, 64.
210. Ibid., 65.
211. Ibid., 66.
212. Ibid., 67.
213. Ibid., 68.
214. Fowler, *Stages*, 198.
215. Seymour and Miller, *Contemporary*, 87.
216. Ibid., 69.
217. Ibid., 70.
218. James Fowler, "Perspectives on the Family from the Standpoint of Faith Development Theory," *The Perkins Journal*, vol. 33, no. 1 (fall 1979); 13–14, quoted in Fowler, *Stages*, 201.
219. Fowler, *Stages*, 201.
220. Sell, *Transitions*, 107.

A. Clouse, 243.
B. Sprinthall and Sprinthall, 182.
C. Lawrence Kohlberg, "My Personal Search for Universal Morality," *Moral Education Forum* 11:1 (1986), quoted in Clouse, 234.
D. Clouse, 235.
E. Ibid., 235.
F. Sprinthall and Sprinthall, 182.
G. Clouse, 235.
H. Sprinthall and Sprinthall, 182.
I. Dembo, 218.
J. Eggen and Kauchak, 63.
K. Hamacheck, 172.
L. Clouse, 235.

M. Sprinthall and Sprinthall, 182.
N. Clouse, 235.
O. Ibid.

CHAPTER SIX

1. LeFrancois, *Psychology for Teaching*, 354.
2. Good and Brophey, *A Realistic Aproach*, 55 and Sprinthall, Sprinthall and Oja, *Developmental Approach*, 142.
3. "Terminal" means that the indication of learning comes at the end of the session. "Indicator" refers to student actions which demonstrate learning at a given level.
4. LeFrancois, *Psychology for Teaching*, 355.
5. Good and Brophey, *A Realistic Approach*, 143.
6. Woolfolk, *Educational Psychology*, 437.
7. Ibid.
8. Woolfolk, *Educational Psychology*, 437.
9. Biehler and Snowman, *Psychology Applied to Teaching*, 298.
10. LeFrancois, *Psychology for Teaching*, 356.
11. Woolfolk, *Educational Psychology*, 438.
12. LeFrancois, *Psychology for Teaching*, 356.
13. Woolfolk, *Educational Psychology*, 438.
14. LeFrancois, *Psychology for Teaching*, 356.
15. Woolfolk, *Educational Psychology*, 440.
16. These dates refer to his first book, *Preparing Instructional Objectives*. Other books include *Measuring Instructional Intent*, *Goal Analysis*, *Analyzing Performance Problems*, *Developing Vocational Instruction*, and *Developing Attitude Toward Learning*.
17. Gronlund wrote *Stating Behavioral Objectives for Classroom Instruction* (1972), *Determining Accountability for Classroom Instruction* (1975), *Measurement and Evaluation in Teaching* (5th ed., 1985), and *How to Write and Use Instructional Objectives* (4th ed., 1991).
18. LeFrancois, *Psychology for Teaching*, 357.
19. Leroy Ford, Professor of Foundations of Education at Southwestern Seminary in Fort Worth, Texas, 1966–1984. He has had as great an influence on Christian educators' views of instructional objectives as any contemporary writer. Ford's classic text on instructional objectives is *Design for Teaching and Training: A Self-Study Guide to Lesson Planning*, (Nashville: Broadman Press, 1978). His most recent book is *A Curriculum Design Manual for Theological Education: A Learning Outcomes Focus* (Nashville: Broadman Press, 1991). This text gives detailed procedures to developing a theological curriculum using instructional objectives.
20. Woolfolk, *Educational Psychology*, 439.
21. Gage and Berliner, *Educational Psychology*, 44.
22. Biehler and Snowman, *Psychology Applied to Teaching*, 290.
23. Ibid., 291.
24. Good and Brophey, *A Realistic Aproach*, 143.
25. Sprinthall, Sprinthall and Oja, *Developmental Approach*, 356.
26. LeFrancois, *Psychology for Teaching*, 357.
27. Ibid.

28. Sprinthall, Sprinthall and Oja, *Developmental Approach*, 356.

29. Woolfolk, *Educational Psychology*, 439.

30. Leroy Ford, *A Curriculum Design Manual for Theological Education: A Learning Outcomes Focus* (Nashville: Broadman Press, 1991), 295.

31. Ibid., 296.

32. *Course Descriptions* (1993–95), 139–40.

33. Benjamin S. Bloom, ed., *Taxonomy of Educational Objectives* (New York: David McKay Company, Inc., 1956).

34. Dembo, *Applying Educational Psychology*, 380.

35. Woolfolk, *Educational Psychology*, 443.

36. LeFrancois, *Psychology for Teaching*, 359.

37. Sprinthall, Sprinthall and Oja, *Developmental Approach*, 357.

38. Woolfolk, *Educational Psychology*, 443.

39. Dembo, *Applying Educational Psychology*, 380.

40. Woolfolk, *Educational Psychology*, 443.

41. Sprinthall, Sprinthall and Oja, *Developmental Approach*, 357.

42. Woolfolk, *Educational Psychology*, 443.

43. Key points in a lecture by Dr. William Hendricks in his course "The Theology of Paul and John," spring 1974, Southwestern Seminary. Dr. Hendricks now teaches theology at Southern Baptist Theological Seminary.

44. Dembo, *Applying Educational Psychology*, 380.

45. Sprinthall, Sprinthall and Oja, *Developmental Approach*, 359.

46. David Krathwohl, ed., *Taxonomy of Educational Objectives: Handbook II: Affective Domain* (New York: David McKay Company, 1964), iv.

47. Biehler and Snowman, *Psychology Applied to Teaching*, 281.

48. Woolfolk, *Educational Psychology*, 444.

49. Biehler and Snowman, *Psychology Applied to Teaching*, 281.

50. Woolfolk, *Educational Psychology*, 444.

51. Biehler and Snowman, *Psychology Applied to Teaching*, 281.

52. Woolfolk, *Educational Psychology*, 444.

53. Biehler and Snowman, *Psychology Applied to Teaching*, 282.

54. "Church Training," now called "Discipleship Training," is a regular Southern Baptist program which focuses on Christian Life issues: history, doctrine, polity, Christian living.

55. Woolfolk, *Educational Psychology*, 444.

56. Biehler and Snowman, *Psychology Applied to Teaching*, 283.

57. Glover and Bruning, *Principles and Applications*, 366.

58. Ibid.

59. Ibid., 367

60. Dr. Budd Smith, Professor of Foundations of Education, Southwestern Seminary, personal conversation on domains of learning.

61. Elizabeth Simpson, *The Classification of Educational Objectives: Psychomotor Domain* (Urbana: University of Illinois Press, 1972).

62. Biehler and Snowman, *Psychology Applied to Teaching*, 283.

63. Ibid.

64. Ibid.

65. Ibid., 284.

66. Ibid.

67. Ibid.

68. Ibid.

69. "Understanding" is the goal for cognitive levels of learning from comprehension through evaluation.

70. Glover and Bruning, *Principles and Applications*, 367.

71. Woolfolk, *Educational Psychology*, 447.

72. Biehler and Snowman, *Psychology Applied to Teaching*, 300.

73. Good and Brophey, *A Realistic Aproach*, 145.

74. Ibid., 145–46.

CHAPTER SEVEN

1. Good and Brophey, *Realistic Approach*, 55, and Sprinthall, Sprinthall and Oja, *Developmental Approach*, 153.

2. Sprinthall, Sprinthall and Oja, *Developmental Approach*, 241.

3. D. C. Phillips and Jonas Soltis, *Perspectives on Learning* (New York: Teachers College Press, 1985), 13.

4. Clouse, *Moral Growth,* 167.

5. Phillips and Soltis, *Perspectives on Learning,* 13.

6. Sprinthall, Sprinthall and Oja, *Developmental Approach*, 241.

7. Phillips and Soltis, *Perspectives on Learning* 13.

8. Traditional behaviorists believe that the mind is irrelevant to understanding why people behave as they do. Sprinthall, Sprinthall and Oja, *Developmental Approach*, 232.

9. Sprinthall, Sprinthall and Oja, *Developmental Approach*, 212.

10. Dembo, *Applying Educational Psychology*, 41.

11. Slavin, *Theory and Practice*, 154.

12. Eggen and Kauchak, *Classroom Connections*, 257.

13. Woolfolk, *Educational Psychology*, 199.

14. Good and Brophey, *Realistic Approach*, 155.

15. Glover and Bruning, *Principles and Applications*, 270.

16. Slavin, *Theory and Practice*, 155.

17. Good and Brophey, *Realistic Approach*, 153.

18. LeFrancois, *Psychology for Teaching*, 87.

19. Good and Brophey, *Realistic Approach*, 154; Eggen and Kauchak, *Classroom Connections*, 261; Woolfolk, *Educational Psychology*, 200.

20. Good and Brophey, *Realistic Approach*, 154.

21. Eggen and Kauchak, *Classroom Connections*, 260.

22. Woolfolk, *Educational Psychology*, 200.

23. Eggen and Kauchak, *Classroom Connections*, 258.

24. Dembo, *Applying Educational Psychology*, 42.

25. Good and Brophey, *Realistic Approach*, 155.

26. LeFrancois, *Psychology for Teaching*, 88.

27. Dembo, *Applying Educational Psychology*, 42.

28. Good and Brophey, *Realistic Approach*, 156.

29. Ibid., 155.

30. Ibid., 156.

31. Dembo, *Applying Educational Psychology*, 42.

32. Ibid.
33. Good and Brophey, *Realistic Approach*, 156.
34. LeFrancois, *Psychology for Teaching*, 91.
35. Dembo, *Applying Educational Psychology*, 42.
36. Good and Brophey, *Realistic Approach*, 156.
37. Slavin, *Theory and Practice*, 156.
38. LeFrancois, *Psychology for Teaching*, 91.
39. Good and Brophey, *Realistic Approach*, 156.
40. Sprinthall, Sprinthall and Oja, *Developmental Approach*, 215.
41. Dembo, *Applying Educational Psychology*, 44.
42. Good and Brophey, *Realistic Approach*, 157.
43. Sprinthall, Sprinthall and Oja, *Developmental Approach*, 215.
44. Ibid.
45. Eggen and Kauchak, *Classroom Connections*, 262.
46. LeFrancois, *Psychology for Teaching*, 91.
47. Dembo, *Applying Educational Psychology*, 44.
48. Woolfolk, *Educational Psychology*, 198. The term "S-R bond" was actually coined by E. L. Thorndike. LeFrancois, *Psychology for Teaching*, 90.
49. LeFrancois, *Psychology for Teaching*, 90.
50. Sprinthall, Sprinthall and Oja, *Developmental Approach*, 215.
51. Ibid.
52. Ibid.
53. Woolfolk, *Educational Psychology*, 202.
54. Eggen and Kauchak, *Classroom Connections*, 262.
55. Sprinthall, Sprinthall and Oja, *Developmental Approach*, 232.
56. Eggen and Kauchak, *Classroom Connections*, 262.
57. Woolfolk, *Educational Psychology*, 202.
58. Eggen and Kauchak, *Classroom Connections*, 262.
59. Woolfolk, *Educational Psychology*, 201.
60. LeFrancois, *Psychology for Teaching*, 92.
61. Woolfolk, *Educational Psychology*, 201.
62. Hamachek, *Psychology in Teaching*, 231.
63. Woolfolk, *Educational Psychology*, 202.
64. LeFrancois, *Psychology for Teaching*, 94.
65. Eggen and Kauchak, *Classroom Connections*, 262.
66. Glover and Bruning, *Principles and Applications*, 275.
67. Woolfolk, *Educational Psychology*, 203.
68. Ibid.
69. Eggen and Kauchak, *Classroom Connections*, 262.
70. Slavin, *Theory and Practice*, 158, and Woolfolk, *Educational Psychology*, 203.
71. LeFrancois, *Psychology for Teaching*, 94.
72. Slavin, *Theory and Practice*, 158.
73. Woolfolk, *Educational Psychology*, 203.
74. Dembo, *Applying Educational Psychology*, 51, and Slavin, *Theory and Practice*, 158.
75. LeFrancois, *Psychology for Teaching*, 97.
76. Skinner believed the word "reward" carried subjective undertones which he rejected. He wrote in 1986, "We reward people, but reinforce behavior." Dembo, *Applying Educational Psychology*, 44.
77. Woolfolk, *Educational Psychology*, 204.
78. Slavin, *Theory and Practice*, 159.
79. Hamachek, *Psychology in Teaching*, 234, and LeFrancois, *Psychology for Teaching*, 97.

80. Woolfolk, *Educational Psychology*, 205.
81. Dembo, *Applying Educational Psychology*, 51.
82. Woolfolk, *Educational Psychology*, 205.
83. Dembo, *Applying Educational Psychology*, 51.
84. LeFrancois, *Psychology for Teaching*, 97.
85. Eggen and Kauchak, *Classroom Connections*, 269.
86. LeFrancois, *Psychology for Teaching*, 97.
87. Woolfolk, *Educational Psychology*, 205.
88. Eggen and Kauchak, *Classroom Connections*, 274.
89. Woolfolk, *Educational Psychology*, 205.
90. Eggen and Kauchak, *Classroom Connections*, 274.
91. Woolfolk, *Educational Psychology*, 205.
92. Ibid.
93. Eggen and Kauchak, *Classroom Connections*, 276.
94. Ibid.
95. Woolfolk, *Educational Psychology*, 206.
96. Eggen and Kauchak, *Classroom Connections*, 276.
97. Slavin, *Theory and Practice*, 167.
98. Woolfolk, *Educational Psychology*, 205.
99. Ibid., 206.
100. Slavin, *Theory and Practice*, 167.
101. Eggen and Kauchak, *Classroom Connections*, 276.
102. Woolfolk, *Educational Psychology*, 206.
103. Ibid., 207.
104. Slavin, *Theory and Practice*, 167.
105. Woolfolk, *Educational Psychology*, 207.
106. Glover and Bruning, *Principles and Applications*, 283.
107. Eggen and Kauchak, *Classroom Connections*, 278.
108. Sprinthall, Sprinthall and Oja, *Developmental Approach*, 234.
109. Dembo, *Applying Educational Psychology*, 54.
110. Eggen and Kauchak, *Classroom Connections*, 271.
111. Sprinthall, Sprinthall and Oja, *Developmental Approach*, 235.
112. Eggen and Kauchak, *Classroom Connections*, 271.
113. Slavin, *Theory and Practice*, 172.
114. Eggen and Kauchak, *Classroom Connections*, 271.
115. Sprinthall, Sprinthall and Oja, *Developmental Approach*, 235.
116. Eggen and Kauchak, *Classroom Connections*, 271.
117. Woolfolk, *Educational Psychology*, 201.
118. Dembo, *Applying Educational Psychology*, 46.
119. Slavin, *Theory and Practice*, 171.
120. Woolfolk, *Educational Psychology*, 209.
121. Ibid.
122. Ibid.
123. Ibid.
124. Dembo, *Applying Educational Psychology*, 56.
125. Woolfolk, *Educational Psychology*, 211.
126. Eggen and Kauchak, *Classroom Connections*, 272.
127. Woolfolk, *Educational Psychology*, 211.
128. Eggen and Kauchak, *Classroom Connections*, 272.
129. Woolfolk, *Educational Psychology*, 212.
130. Glover and Bruning, *Principles and Applications*, 279.
131. Biehler and Snowman, *Psychology Applied*, 341.
132. Hamachek, *Psychology in Teaching*, 236.
133. Glover and Bruning, *Principles and Applications*, 279.
134. Biehler and Snowman, *Psychology Applied*, 337.
135. Hamachek, *Psychology in Teaching*, 239.

136. Richard Hamilton and Elizabeth Ghatala, *Learning and Instruction* (New York: McGraw Hill, Inc, 1994), 61.
137. Biehler and Snowman, *Psychology Applied,* 336.
138. Hamilton and Ghatala, *Learning and Instruction,* 61.
139. Hamachek, *Psychology in Teaching,* 240.
140. Hamilton and Ghatala, *Learning and Instruction,* 62.
141. Hamachek, *Psychology in Teaching,* 240.
142. Ibid., 241.
143. Slavin, *Theory and Practice*, 336.
144. Ibid.
145. LeFrancois, *Psychology for Teaching*, 333.
146. Slavin, *Theory and Practice*, 337.
147. LeFrancois, *Psychology for Teaching*, 334.
148. Biehler and Snowman, *Psychology Applied,* 338.
149. Slavin, *Theory and Practice*, 339.
150. LeFrancois, *Psychology for Teaching*, 332.
151. Klaus Issler and Ronald Habermas, *How We Learn: A Christian Teacher's Guide to Educational Psychology* (Grand Rapids, Mich.: Baker Books, 1994), 209.
152. Sprinthall, Sprinthall and Oja, *Developmental Approach*, 239, quoting B. R. Hergenbahn, *An Introduction to Learning Theories,* 2nd ed. (Englewood Cliffs, N.J.: Prentice-Hall, 1988), 84.
153. Phillips and Soltis, *Perspectives on Learning,* 29.
154. Ibid.
155. Phillips and Soltis, *Perspectives on Learning,* 30.
156. Ibid., 31.
157. Sprinthall, Sprinthall and Oja, *Developmental Approach*, 242.
158. Gage and Berliner, *Educational Psychology*, 295.
159. Gage and Berliner, *Educational Psychology*, 296.
160. Ibid., 297.
161. Woolfolk, *Educational Psychology*, 216.
162. Ibid., 217.
163. Ibid., 216.
164. Ibid.
165. Eggen and Kauchak, *Classroom Connections*, 281.
166. Woolfolk, *Educational Psychology*, 216.
167. Eggen and Kauchak, *Classroom Connections*, 281.
168. Sprinthall, Sprinthall and Oja, *Developmental Approach*, 235.
169. Eggen and Kauchak, *Classroom Connections*, 280.
170. Woolfolk, *Educational Psychology*, 217.
171. Eggen and Kauchak, *Classroom Connections*, 280.
172. Woolfolk, *Educational Psychology*, 217.
173. Ibid.
174. Ibid., 220.
175. Good and Brophey, *Realistic Approach*, 166.
176. Woolfolk, *Educational Psychology*, 220.
177. Ibid.
178. Dembo, *Applying Educational Psychology*, 57.
179. Sprinthall, Sprinthall and Oja, *Developmental Approach*, 259.
180. Eggen and Kauchak, *Classroom Connections*, 282.
181. Good and Brophey, *Realistic Approach*, 166.
182. Biehler and Snowman, *Psychology Applied,* 346.
183. Albert Bandura. *Social Learning Theory* (Englewood Cliffs, N.J.: Prentice-Hall, 1977).
184. Biehler and Snowman, *Psychology Applied,* 346.
185. Woolfolk, *Educational Psychology*, 221.
186. Eggen and Kauchak, *Classroom Connections*, 284.
187. Ibid., and Dembo, *Applying Educational Psychology,* 57.
188. Ibid.
189. Ibid., 57.
190. Woolfolk, *Educational Psychology*, 220.
191. Biehler and Snowman, *Psychology Applied,* 349.
192. Ibid., 348.
193. Eggen and Kauchak, *Classroom Connections*, 286.
194. Slavin, *Theory and Practice*, 174.
195. Biehler and Snowman, *Psychology Applied,* 348.
196. Eggen and Kauchak, *Classroom Connections*, 285.
197. Biehler and Snowman, *Psychology Applied,* 348.
198. Ibid.
199. Sprinthall, Sprinthall and Oja, *Developmental Approach*, 259.
200. Eggen and Kauchak, *Classroom Connections*, 286.
201. Slavin, *Theory and Practice*, 174.
202. Eggen and Kauchak, *Classroom Connections*, 286.
203. Good and Brophey, *Realistic Approach*, 168.
204. Gage and Berliner, *Realistic Approach*, 335.
205. Biehler and Snowman, *Psychology Applied,* 348.
206. Woolfolk, *Educational Psychology*, 221.
207. Biehler and Snowman, *Psychology Applied,* 348.
208. Sprinthall, Sprinthall and Oja, *Developmental Approach*, 259.
209. Woolfolk, *Educational Psychology*, 222.
210. Bandura used the term "reproduction" (Eggen and Kauchak, *Classroom Connections*, 288) to refer to this stage, but most recent texts use the term "production."
211. Eggen and Kauchak, *Classroom Connections*, 288.
212. Woolfolk, *Educational Psychology*, 222.
213. Many recent texts call this fourth stage "motivation" rather than Bandura's reinforcement (Eggen and Kauchak, *Classroom Connections*, 289; LeFrancois, *Psychology for Teaching*, 114; Biehler and Snowman, *Psychology Applied,* 348; Gage and Berliner, *Realistic Approach*, 335; Dembo, *Applying Educational Psychology*, 59; Slavin, *Theory and Practice*, 175).
214. Woolfolk, *Educational Psychology*, 222.
215. Biehler and Snowman, *Psychology Applied,* 349.
216. Woolfolk, *Educational Psychology*, 222.
217. Good and Brophey, *Psychology Applied,* 166.
218. Dembo, *Applying Educational Psychology*, 61.
219. Eggen and Kauchak, *Classroom Connections*, 289.
220. Dembo, *Applying Educational Psychology*, 60.
221. Woolfolk, *Educational Psychology*, 222.
222. Eggen and Kauchak, *Classroom Connections*, 289.
223. Slavin, *Theory and Practice*, 174.
224. Skinner was adamant in his defense of traditional behaviorism to the end of his life. Speaking to the American Psychological Association just days before his death, he said, "Cognitive science . . . is an effort to reinstate that inner initiating-originating-creative self or mind which, in scientific analysis, simply does not exist. . . . I think it is time for psychology as a profession and as a science to realize that the science which will be most helpful is not cognitive science searching for the inner mind or self, but selection by consequences represented by behavioral analysis." Quoted by Sprinthall and Sprinthall, 231.

225. Good and Brophey, *Psychology Applied,* 166.
226. Biehler and Snowman, *Psychology Applied,* 347.
227. Ibid.
228. Ibid. LeFrancois combines inhibition and disinhibition into the "inhibitory-disinhibitory effect" (Lefrancois, *Psychology for Teaching,* 109).
229. Woolfolk, *Educational Psychology,* 223.
230. Glover and Bruning, *Principles and Applications,* 313.
231. Woolfolk, *Educational Psychology,* 223.

A. Sprinthall and Sprinthall, 230.
B. Clouse. 156.
C. Sprinthall and Sprinthall, 230.
D. Clouse. 156.
E. Sprinthall and Sprinthall, 230.
F. Clouse. 156.
G. Sprinthall and Sprinthall, 231.
H. Ibid.

CHAPTER EIGHT

1. Eggen and Kauchak, *Classroom Connections,* 305.
2. Biehler and Snowman, *Psychology Applied,* 378.
3. Clouse, *Moral Growth,* 223.
4. Sprinthall, Sprinthall, and Oja, *Developmental Approach,* 213.
5. Slavin, *Theory and Practice,* 188.
6. Sprinthall, Sprinthall, and Oja, *Developmental Approach,* 220.
7. Slavin, *Theory and Practice,* 188.
8. Sprinthall, Sprinthall, and Oja, *Developmental Approach,* 245.
9. Slavin, *Theory and Practice,* 225.
10. Sprinthall, Sprinthall, and Oja, *Developmental Approach,* 213.
11. Morris L. Bigge, *Learning Theories for Teachers,* 3rd ed. (New York: Harper & Row, 1976), 61.
12. Sprinthall, Sprinthall, and Oja, *Developmental Approach,* 220.
13. Ibid.
14. Sprinthall, Sprinthall, and Oja, *Developmental Approach,* 218.
15. Slavin, *Theory and Practice,* 188.
16. Charles E. Skinner, Ira Morris Gast, and Hartley Clay Skinner, *Readings in Educational Psychology* (New York: Appleton & Cook, 1958), 407.
17. Sprinthall, Sprinthall, and Oja, *Developmental Approach,* 219.
18. Ibid., 221.
19. Ernest R. Hilgard and Richard C. Atkinson, *Introduction to Psychology,* 4th ed. (New York: Harcourt, Brace and World, 1967), 227.
20. Ralph Garry and Howard L. Kingsley, *The Nature and Conditions of Learning,* 3rd ed. (Englewood Cliffs, N.J.: Prentice-Hall, 1970), 112.
21. Hilgard and Atkinson, *Introduction to Psychology,* 225.
22. Ibid.
23. Ibid.

24. Ibid.
25. Sprinthall, Sprinthall, and Oja, *Developmental Approach,* 220.
26. Hilgard and Atkinson, *Introduction to Psychology,* 178.
27. Sprinthall, Sprinthall, and Oja, *Developmental Approach,* 220.
28. Hilgard and Atkinson, *Introduction to Psychology,* 178.
29. Sprinthall, Sprinthall, and Oja, *Developmental Approach,* 220.
30. Stephen S. Sargent, *The Basic Teachings: The Greatest Psychologists* (New York: Barnes & Noble, 1957), 150.
31. Hilgard and Atkinson, *Introduction to Psychology,* 178.
32. Sprinthall, Sprinthall, and Oja, *Developmental Approach,* 221.
33. Morris L. Bigge, *Psychological Foundations of Education,* 2nd ed. (New York: Harper & Row, 1968), 342.
34. Ibid., 342.
35. Garry and Kingsley, *Nature,* 112.
36. Hilgard and Atkinson, *Introduction to Psychology,* 273.
37. Sprinthall, Sprinthall, and Oja, *Developmental Approach,* 245.
38. Ibid., 243.
39. LeFrancois, *Psychology for Teaching,* 158.
40. Sprinthall, Sprinthall, and Oja, *Developmental Approach,* 243.
41. Biehler and Snowman, *Psychology Applied,* 427.
42. Sprinthall, Sprinthall, and Oja, *Developmental Approach,* 247.
43. Biehler and Snowman, *Psychology Applied,* 427.
44. Ibid.
45. Ibid.
46. Slavin, *Theory and Practice,* 249.
47. Sprinthall, Sprinthall, and Oja, *Developmental Approach,* 249.
48. Ibid., 224.
49. Ibid., 249.
50. Ibid., 245.
51. Biehler and Snowman, *Psychology Applied,* 426.
52. Woolfolk, *Educational Psychology,* 319.
53. Sprinthall, Sprinthall, and Oja, *Developmental Approach,* 247.
54. Ibid., 243.
55. Ibid., 247.
56. Ibid., 248.
57. Ibid., 243.
58. Ibid., 244.
59. B. F. Skinner, *The Technology of Teaching* (New York: Appleton-Century-Crofts, 1968), 110.
60. Robert F. Biehler, *Psychology Applied to Teaching,* 3rd ed. (Boston: Houghton Mifflin Co., 1978), 355ff.
61. LeFrancois, *Psychology for Teaching,* 160.
62. Slavin, *Theory and Practice,* 230.
63. LeFrancois, *Psychology for Teaching,* 160.
64. Some writers use the term "guided discovery." Dembo, *Applying Educational Psychology,* 270.

65. Jerome Bruner, *Toward a Theory of Instruction* (New York: Norton, 1966), 72.
66. Slavin, *Theory and Practice*, 225.
67. Ibid., 227.
68. Ibid., 228.
69. Slavin, *Theory and Practice*, 229.
70. Ibid.
71. Ibid.
72. Ibid., 229.
73. Ibid., 230.
74. Ibid.
75. Ibid.
76. Ibid.
77. Ibid.

A. Sprinthall, Sprinthall and Oja, *Developmental Approach,* 244.
B. Glen Snelbecker, *Learning Theory: Institutional Theory and Psychological Design* (New York: McGraw-Hill, 1974), 411.
C. Sprinthall, Sprinthall and Oja, *Developmental Approach,* 244.
D. Ibid., 245.
E. Biehler and Snowman, *Psychology Applied,* 425.
F. Leon Marsh, *Educational Psychology for Christian Education* (Fort Worth, Tex.: Southwestern Baptist Theological Seminary, 1982), 186.
G. Daniel Smith, *Educational Psychology and Its Classroom Applications* (Boston: Allyn and Bacon, 1975), 43.
H. Biehler and Snowman, *Psychology Applied,* 425.
I. Sprinthall, Sprinthall and Oja, *Developmental Approach,* 245.
J. Ibid.

CHAPTER NINE

1. Sprinthall, Sprinthall, and Oja, *Developmental Approach*, 285.
2. Ibid.
3. Biehler and Snowman, *Psychology Applied,* 378.
4. Ibid.
5. Sprinthall, Sprinthall, and Oja, *Developmental Approach*, 286.
6. Biehler and Snowman, *Psychology Applied,* 379.
7. Ibid.
8. Sprinthall, Sprinthall, and Oja, *Developmental Approach*, 288.
9. Biehler and Snowman, *Psychology Applied,* 379.
10. Eggen and Kauchak, *Classroom Connections*, 306.
11. Ibid.
12. Hamachek, *Psychology in Teaching,* 192.
13. Sprinthall, Sprinthall, and Oja, *Developmental Approach*, 287.
14. Slavin, *Theory and Practice*, 188.
15. Sprinthall, Sprinthall, and Oja, *Developmental Approach*, 288.
16. Hamachek, *Psychology in Teaching,* 194.

17. F. Smith, *Comprehension and Learning: A Conceptual Framework for Teachers* (New York: Holt, Rinehart and Winston, 1975). Quoted by Hamachek, *Psychology in Teaching,* 194.
18. Hamachek, *Psychology in Teaching,* 195.
19. Biehler and Snowman, *Psychology Applied,* 384.
20. Sprinthall, Sprinthall, and Oja, *Developmental Approach*, 288.
21. Hamachek, *Psychology in Teaching,* 195.
22. Eggen and Kauchak, *Classroom Connections*, 310.
23. Ibid., 311.
24. Sprinthall, Sprinthall, and Oja, *Developmental Approach*, 288.
25. Eggen and Kauchak, *Classroom Connections*, 311.
26. Sprinthall, Sprinthall, and Oja, *Developmental Approach*, 288.
27. Eggen and Kauchak, *Classroom Connections*, 312.
28. Hamachek, *Psychology in Teaching,* 197.
29. Eggen and Kauchak, *Classroom Connections*, 312.
30. Sprinthall, Sprinthall, and Oja, *Developmental Approach*, 289.
31. Eggen and Kauchak, *Classroom Connections*, 312.
32. Biehler and Snowman, *Psychology Applied,* 387.
33. Ibid.
34. Slavin, *Theory and Practice*, 193.
35. Ibid.
36. Dembo, *Educational Psychology*, 95.
37. Ibid.
38. Eggen and Kauchak, *Classroom Connections*, 313.
39. Hamachek, *Psychology in Teaching,* 198.
40. Eggen and Kauchak, *Classroom Connections*, 314.
41. Hamachek, *Psychology in Teaching,* 199.
42. Slavin, *Theory and Practice*, 193.
43. Eggen and Kauchak, *Classroom Connections*, 317.
44. Slavin, *Theory and Practice*, 216.
45. Biehler and Snowman, *Psychology Applied,* 388.
46. Slavin, *Theory and Practice*, 191.
47. Biehler and Snowman, *Psychology Applied,* 382.
48. Eggen and Kauchak, *Classroom Connections*, 308.
49. Biehler and Snowman, *Psychology Applied,* 382.
50. Ibid., 383.
51. Ibid.
52. Slavin, *Theory and Practice*, 188.
53. Eggen and Kauchak, *Classroom Connections*, 323.
54. Biehler and Snowman, *Psychology Applied,* 382.
55. Eggen and Kauchak, *Classroom Connections*, 322.
56. Biehler and Snowman, *Psychology Applied,* 384.
57. Eggen and Kauchak, *Classroom Connections*, 322.
58. Ibid., 312.
59. Ibid.
60. Sprinthall, Sprinthall, and Oja, *Developmental Approach*, 288.
61. Ibid., 290.
62. Biehler and Snowman, *Psychology Applied,* 384.
63. Ibid.
64. Eggen and Kauchak, *Classroom Connections*, 326.
65. Slavin, *Theory and Practice*, 191.

66. Biehler and Snowman, *Psychology Applied,* 384. "Some suggest that every experience a person has, especially when emotions are involved, leaves a permanent memory trace on the brain." Sprinthall, Sprinthall, and Oja, *Developmental Approach,* 292. This is "incidental" or "automatic" learning, discussed earlier in the chapter.

67. Eggen and Kauchak, *Classroom Connections,* 326.

68. Remember that these descriptions apply to intentional learning. Automatic processing occurs whether we engage in these processes or not.

69. Eggen and Kauchak, *Classroom Connections,* 327.

70. Sprinthall, Sprinthall, and Oja, *Developmental Approach,* 290.

71. Eggen and Kauchak, *Classroom Connections,* 329.

72. Ibid.

73. Ibid., 330.

74. Ibid., 331.

75. See the "Key Terms in Learning Theories" at the end of chapters 7, 8, or 10 examples of a matrix.

76. Eggen and Kauchak, *Classroom Connections,* 333.

77. Sprinthall, Sprinthall, and Oja, *Developmental Approach,* 290.

78. Ibid.

79. Eggen and Kauchak, *Classroom Connections,* 334.

80. Biehler and Snowman, *Psychology Applied,* 384.

81. Eggen and Kauchak, *Classroom Connections,* 336.

82. Biehler and Snowman, *Psychology Applied,* 394.

83. Gage and Berliner, *Educational Psychology,* 223.

84. Dembo, *Educational Psychology,* 108.

85. Biehler and Snowman, *Psychology Applied,* 396.

86. Ibid., 395, and Slavin, *Theory and Practice,* 209.

87. Dembo, *Educational Psychology,* 108.

88. Biehler and Snowman, *Psychology Applied,* 395.

89. Eggen and Kauchak, *Classroom Connections,* 338.

90. Dembo, *Educational Psychology,* 108.

91. Biehler and Snowman, *Psychology Applied,* 395.

92. Gage and Berliner, *Educational Psychology,* 223.

93. Ibid., 224.

94. Biehler and Snowman, 397.

95. Dembo, *Educational Psychology,* 109.

96. Biehler and Snowman, *Psychology Applied,* 397.

97. Ibid.

98. Ibid., 398.

99. Eggen and Kauchak, *Classroom Connections,* 339.

100. Slavin, *Theory and Practice,* 200.

101. Sprinthall, Sprinthall, and Oja, *Developmental Approach,* 299.

102. Dembo, *Educational Psychology,* 95.

103. Eggen and Kauchak, *Classroom Connections,* 339.

104. Ibid., 307.

105. Biehler and Snowman, *Psychology Applied,* 390.

106. Ibid.

107. Eggen and Kauchak, *Classroom Connections,* 347.

108. Ibid., 349.

109. Ibid., 350.

110. Biehler and Snowman, *Psychology Applied,* 390.

111. Ibid., 406.

112. Eggen and Kauchak, *Classroom Connections,* 342.

113. Dembo, *Educational Psychology,* 99.

114. Eggen and Kauchak, *Classroom Connections,* 342.

115. Biehler and Snowman, *Psychology Applied,* 410.

116. Dembo, *Educational Psychology,* 123.

117. Slavin, *Theory and Practice,* 237.

118. Dembo, *Educational Psychology,* 123.

119. Ibid., 112.

120. Ibid., 123.

121. Glover and Bruning, *Principles and Applications,* 135.

122. Ibid.

123. Eggen and Kauchak, *Classroom Connections,* 342.

124. Biehler and Snowman, *Psychology Applied,* 407.

125. Dembo, *Educational Psychology,* 122.

126. Ibid., 123.

127. Eggen and Kauchak, *Classroom Connections,* 343.

128. Dembo, *Educational Psychology,* 122

129. Eggen and Kauchak, *Classroom Connections,* 343.

130. Biehler and Snowman, *Psychology Applied,* 412.

131. Eggen and Kauchak, *Classroom Connections,* 343.

132. Biehler and Snowman, *Psychology Applied,* 411.

133. Slavin, *Theory and Practice,* 239.

134. Eggen and Kauchak, *Classroom Connections,* 343.

135. Biehler and Snowman, *Psychology Applied,* 383.

136. Dembo, *Educational Psychology,* 122.

137. Biehler and Snowman, *Psychology Applied,* 394.

138. Ibid., 408.

139. Biehler and Snowman, *Psychology Applied,* 414.

140. Dembo, *Educational Psychology,* 123.

141. Biehler and Snowman, *Psychology Applied,* 398.

142. Ibid., 399.

143. Ibid., 414.

144. Ibid., 399.

145. Ibid., 414.

146. Dembo, *Educational Psychology,* 110.

CHAPTER TEN

1. *The American Heritage [Electronic] Dictionary,* 3rd ed. (Wordstar International, 1993), s.v. "humanism."

2. Ibid., s.v. "Humanism."

3. Ibid., s.v. "secular."

4. "Essence" refers to the intrinsic or indispensable properties that characterize or identify something. "Existence" refers to the fact or state of being. In traditional philosophies, essence precedes existence. The nature or design of mankind precedes the actual existence of individuals. Existentialism reverses this order and states that individuals are first born, and then defined by the choices they make. First, existence; then, essence. A fundamental principle of Existentialism is "freedom of the individual from societal restraints." Daniel Smith, *Educational Psychology and Its Classroom Applications,* (Boston: Allyn and Bacon, 1975). 187.

5. *The Joyful Wisdom* (1882) quoted in Colin Brown, *Philosophy and the Christian Faith* (Downers Grove, Ill.: Inter-Varsity Press, 1968), 139.

6. From *Existentialism and Humanism* (1946), quoted in Colin Brown, *Philosophy and the Christian Faith* (Downers Grove, Ill.: InterVarsity Press, 1968), 183.

7. Ibid.

8. John Herman Randall, "What Is the Temper of Humanism?" *The Humanist* (Nov/Dec 1970): 34, quoted in Van Cleve Morris and Young Pai, *Philosophy and the American School* (Boston: Houghton Mifflin Company, 1976), 391.

9. John S. Brubacher, *Modern Philosophies of Education* (New York: McGraw-Hill Book Company, Inc., 1950), 279ff.

10. Paul A. Keniel, *Philosophy of Christian School Education* (Whittier, Calif.: Association of Christian Schools International, 1971), 156.

11. Some may object to the term "Christian humanism" as an oxymoron. But Keniel makes the point that the Reformation did place emphasis on the worth of the individual. This was not a result of man's innate goodness, as in the Southern European Renaissance, but from Scripture and the creation of man. Keniel himself does not use the term "Christian humanism," but many of the reforms in education—pleasant methods, trained teachers, and attractive classrooms—focus on the learner.

12. Keniel, *Philosophy,* 158.

13. Purely humanistic theorists like Maslow, Rogers, and Combs certainly have this view. It is interesting that Skinner believed himself to be a humanist. He was a signatory to the (secular) Humanistic Manifesto I and II, the blueprint for (secular) humanistic doctrine. Skinner saw programmed instruction as "humanistic" because it provided a pleasant learning environment that minimized failure and maximized reinforcement. In fact, many of the theorists we've discussed signed the Humanistic Manifesto documents, including Jerome Bruner and Abraham Maslow. This is why I made the distinction early in the text between understanding and using appropriate principles from these theorists without "believing" in them or their philosophical underpinnings.

14. Woolfolk, *Educational Psychology*, 338.

15. Dembo, *Applying Educational Psychology*, 202.

16. LeFrancois, *Psychology for Teaching*, 240.

17. Dembo, *Applying Educational Psychology*, 201.

18. Woolfolk, *Educational Psychology*, 339.

19. Eggen and Kauchak, *Classroom Connections*, 432.

20. Eggen and Kauchak, *Classroom Connections*, 439; Glover and Bruning, *Principles and Applications,* 246.

21. Glover and Bruning, *Principles and Applications,* 252.

22. Carl Rogers, "Freedom to Learn" [extracts] in Noel Entwistle, ed., *New Directions in Educational Psychology: 1. Learning and Teaching* (London: Falmer Press, 1985), 121.

23. LeFrancois, *Psychology for Teaching*, 241.

24. Biehler and Snowman, *Psychology Applied,* 475.

25. Dembo, *Applying Educational Psychology*, 209–10.

26. LeFrancois, *Psychology for Teaching*, 246.

27. Ibid., 247.

28. Ibid., 244.

29. Dembo, *Applying Educational Psychology*, 207–8.

30. Carl Rogers, *A Personal Approach to Teaching: Beliefs that Make a Difference* (Boston: Allyn & Bacon, 1982), 135.

31. Biehler and Snowman, *Psychology Applied,* 476.

32. Dembo, *Applying Educational Psychology*, 203.

33. Good and Brophey, *Realistic Approach*, 471, and Dembo, *Applying Educational Psychology*, 227.

34. Biehler and Snowman, *Psychology Applied,* 476–79.

35. Slavin, *Theory and Practice*, 296.

36. LeFrancois, *Psychology for Teaching*, 250.

37. Slavin, *Theory and Practice*, 298.

38. Eggen and Kauchak, *Classroom Connections*, 433.

39. LeFrancois, *Psychology for Teaching*, 250.

40. Slavin, *Theory and Practice*, 297.

41. Ibid.

42. Eggen and Kauchak, *Classroom Connections*, 433.

43. Slavin, *Theory and Practice*, 298.

44. Dembo, *Applying Educational Psychology*, 225; Smith, *Classroom Applications*, 201; and LeFrancois, *Psychology for Teaching*, 251.

45. LeFrancois, *Psychology for Teaching*, 251.

46. Dembo, *Applying Educational Psychology*, 227, and Good and Brophy, *Realistic Approach*, 471.

47. Slavin, *Theory and Practice*, 298.

48. LeFrancois, *Psychology for Teaching*, 252.

49. Ibid., 252.

50. Ibid., 253–54.

51. Quotes based on material in Biehler and Snowman, 485.

52. Tim LaHaye, *The Battle for the Mind* (Old Tappen, N.J.: Fleming H. Revell, 1980), (Introduction) as quoted in Clouse, *Moral Growth*, 326.

53. Clouse, *Teaching for Moral Growth,* 325–27.

54. Jerry Adler, et al, "Hey, I'm Terrific: The Curse of Self-Esteem," *Newsweek* (February 17, 1992): 46–51.

55. Of the nearly thirty recent educational psychology texts I have in my library, only seven devote chapters to humanistic learning. Only two of these seven discuss humanistic approaches under "learning theory." The remainder discuss these principles under motivation.

56. *The American Heritage Dictionary*, s.v. "humanism."

A. Clouse, *Moral Growth*, 300.

B. Sprinthall, Sprinthall and Oja, *Developmental Approach*, 340.

C. Clouse, *Moral Growth*, 300.

D. Ibid., 300-301.

E. Sprinthall, Sprinthall and Oja, *Developmental Approach*, 340.

F. Clouse, *Moral Growth*, 301.

G. Sprinthall, Sprinthall and Oja, *Developmental Approach*, 340.

H. Clouse, *Moral Growth*, 301.

I. Ibid.

J. Sprinthall, Sprinthall and Oja, *Developmental Approach*, 341.

K. Clouse, *Moral Growth*, 301.

L. Sprinthall, Sprinthall and Oja, *Developmental Approach*, 341.

M. Clouse, *Moral Growth*, 301.

CHAPTER TWELVE

1. Good and Brophey, *Realistic Approach*, 360.

2. Eggen and Kauchak, *Classroom Connections*, 427.

3. Hamilton and Ghatala, *Learning and Instruction,* 328.

4. Dembo, *Applying Educational Psychology*, 147.

5. Eggen and Kauchak, *Classroom Connections*, 427.

6. Ibid.

7. Hamilton and Ghatala, *Learning and Instruction,* 329.

8. Hamachek, *Psychology in Teaching,* 265.

9. Hamilton and Ghatala, *Learning and Instruction,* 329.

10. Hamachek, *Psychology in Teaching,* 265.

11. Ibid., 264.

12. Hamilton and Ghatala, *Learning and Instruction,* 329.

13. Hamachek, *Psychology in Teaching,* 267.

14. Ibid.

15. LeFrancois, *Psychology for Teaching*, 274.

16. Good and Brophey, *Realistic Approach*, 360.

17. Eggen and Kauchak, *Classroom Connections*, 428.

18. Hamilton and Ghatala, *Learning and Instruction,* 331.

19. Hamilton and Ghatala, *Learning and Instruction,* 328.

20. Eggen and Kauchak, *Classroom Connections*, 341.

21. Ibid., 431.

22. Ibid., 340.

23. Ibid., 341.

24. Ibid.

25. Ibid.

26. Ibid.

27. Hamilton and Ghatala, *Learning and Instruction,* 331.

28. Eggen and Kauchak, *Classroom Connections*, 436.

29. Hamachek, *Psychology in Teaching,* 272.

30. LeFrancois, *Psychology for Teaching*, 275.

31. Ibid.

32. Hamachek, *Psychology in Teaching,* 271, 274; W 377.

33. LeFrancois, *Psychology for Teaching*, 275.

34. Hamachek, *Psychology in Teaching,* 275, W 377.

35. LeFrancois, *Psychology for Teaching*, 275.

36. Ibid.

37. Hamachek, *Psychology in Teaching,* 271.

38. Ibid., 275, W 377.

39. Woolfolk, *Educational Psychology*, 220.

40. Good and Brophy, *Realistic Approach*, 166.

41. Woolfolk, *Educational Psychology*, 220.

42. Ibid., 222.

43. Biehler and Snowman, *Psychology Applied,* 349.

44. Woolfolk, *Educational Psychology*, 222.

45. Good and Brophy, *Realistic Approach*, 166.

46. Dembo, *Applying Educational Psychology*, 61.

47. Eggen and Kauchak, *Classroom Connections*, 289.

48. Dembo, *Applying Educational Psychology*, 60.

49. Woolfolk, *Educational Psychology*, 222.

50. Eggen and Kauchak, *Classroom Connections*, 289.

51. Slavin, *Theory and Practice*, 174.

52. Eggen and Kauchak, *Classroom Connections*, 436.

53. Woolfolk, *Educational Psychology*, 223.

54. Glover and Bruning, *Principles and Applications,* 313.

55. Woolfolk, *Educational Psychology*, 223.

56. Sprinthall, Sprinthall, and Oja, *Developmental Approach*, 259.

57. Eggen and Kauchak, *Classroom Connections*, 282.

58. Good and Brophy, *Realistic Approach*, 166.

59. Eggen and Kauchak, *Classroom Connections*, 286.

60. Slavin, *Theory and Practice*, 174.

61. Eggen and Kauchak, *Classroom Connections*, 286.

62. Good and Brophy, *Realistic Approach*, 168.

63. The Baptist Student Union is a Christian organization with chapters on college campuses around the country. BSU chapters provide spiritual support for college students through Bible studies and ministry opportunities.

64. Bandura postulated another approach to motivation called "self-efficacy." Self-efficacy is defined as the learner's perceptions of their ability to succeed on a certain task (Eggen and Kauchak, *Classroom Connections*, 434). The study of self-efficacy presents a new dimension to the subject of motivation and social learning theory, and is beyond the scope of this text. See Eggen and Kauchak, *Classroom Connections*, 434ff, Hamilton and Ghatala, *Learning and Instruction,* 332ff, and LeFrancois, *Psychology for Teaching*, 279ff.

65. LeFrancois, *Psychology for Teaching*, 274.

66. Good and Brophy, *Realistic Approach*, 360.

67. Wadsworth, *Piaget's Theory,* 11.

68. Biehler and Snowman, *Psychology Applied,* 60.

69. Woolfolk, *Educational Psychology*, 370.

70. Wadsworth, *Piaget's Theory,* 10.

71. Hamilton and Ghatala, *Learning and Instruction,* 337.

72. LeFrancois, *Psychology for Teaching*, 274.

73. Good and Brophy, *Realistic Approach*, 360.

74. Eggen and Kauchak, *Classroom Connections*, 433.

75. "Motivation and the Growth of Self," in *Perceiving, Behaving, and Becoming*, the Association for Supervision and Curriculum Development Yearbook (Washington, D.C.: National Education Association, 1962), 83–98.

76. Glover and Bruning, *Principles and Applications*, 246; Eggen and Kauchak, *Classroom Connections*, 439.

77. Eggen and Kauchak, *Classroom Connections*, 439.

78. LeFrancois, *Psychology for Teaching*, 276; Woolfolk, *Educational Psychology,* 349.

79. Glover and Bruning, *Principles and Applications*, 246.

80. Eggen and Kauchak, *Classroom Connections*, 439; LeFrancois, *Psychology for Teaching*, 276.

81. LeFrancois, *Psychology for Teaching*, 276.

82. Eggen and Kauchak, *Classroom Connections*, 439; Woolfolk, *Educational Psychology*, 349.

83. Eggen and Kauchak, *Classroom Connections*, 275.

84. Eggen and Kauchak, *Classroom Connections*, 439; LeFrancois, *Psychology for Teaching*, 275; and Woolfolk, *Educational Psychology*, 349.

85. Gage and Berliner, *Educational Psychology*, 383.

86. Ibid.

87. Glover and Bruning, *Principles and Applications*, 249.

88. LeFrancois, *Psychology for Teaching*, 275.

89. Glover and Bruning, *Principles and Applications*, 249; LeFrancois, *Psychology for Teaching*, 275; and Woolfolk, *Educational Psychology*, 349.

90. Ibid.

91. Clouse, *Moral Growth*, 304.

92. Gage and Berliner, *Educational Psychology*,

93. Eggen and Kauchak, *Classroom Connections*, 275.

94. Woolfolk, *Educational Psychology*, 349.

95. Gage and Berliner, *Educational Psychology*, 383.
96. Woolfolk, *Educational Psychology*, 349.
97. Eggen and Kauchak, *Classroom Connections*, 439.
98. Hamachek, *Psychology in Teaching,* 58.
99. Biehler and Snowman, *Psychology Applied,* 516.
100. Glover and Bruning, *Principles and Applications*, 249.
101. Abraham Maslow, *Motivation and Personality* (New York: Harper and Row, 1954), 92, as quoted in Slavin, *Theory and Practice,* 351.
102. Slavin, *Theory and Practice,* 351.
103. Clouse, *Moral Growth,* 305.
104. Glover and Bruning, *Principles and Applications*, 249.
105. The basic hierarchy consists of five levels. These are the four deficiency needs (survival, safety, belonging, and self-esteem) plus self-actualization. This organization is presented by Sprinthall, Sprinthall and Oja, *Developmental Approach,* 532, Good and Brophey, *Realistic Approach*, 364, Biehler and Snowman, *Psychology Applied,* 517, and Raymond Wlodkowski, *Motivation and Teaching: A Practical Guide* (Washington, D.C.: National Education Association, 1986), 60.
Biehler and Snowman add that levels 5 and 6 were later added to the hierarchy when Maslow discovered that self-actualized persons possessed those qualities. The majority of texts presented this expanded seven-level model. Dembo, *Applying Educational Psychology*, 205; Eggen and Kauchak, *Classroom Connections*, 440; Gage and Berliner, *Educational Psychology*, 383; LeFrancois, *Psychology for Teaching*, 277; Rothstein, "Motivation," 139; Slavin, *Theory and Practice*, 350; and Woolfolk, *Educational Psychology*, 349.
Two texts rearrange the upper levels. Glover (246) places self-actualization at level five after self-esteem (as in the basic model) and then adds knowledge and aesthetics at levels six and seven. Clouse swaps levels five and six, listing aesthetics before knowledge (304), but this may have simply been an offhand oversight in listing them together ["aesthetics and cognitive needs"].
Only one text included Maslow's eighth level (1968) of transcendence (Hamachek, *Psychology in Teaching,* 58).
106. Hamachek, *Psychology in Teaching,* 58.
107. Ibid., 57.
108. Eggen and Kauchak, *Classroom Connections*, 440.
109. Glover and Bruning, *Principles and Applications*, 262.
110. Eggen and Kauchak, *Classroom Connections*, 440.
111. Glover and Bruning, *Principles and Applications*, 262.
112. Ibid., 261, 250.
113. Ibid., 262.
114. Eggen and Kauchak, *Classroom Connections*, 436.
115. Ibid.
116. Hamilton and Ghatala, *Learning and Instruction,* 355.
117. Eggen and Kauchak, *Classroom Connections*, 436.
118. Ibid., 433.
119. Hamilton and Ghatala, *Learning and Instruction,* 338.
120. Woolfolk, *Educational Psychology*, 350.
121. Glover and Bruning, *Principles and Applications*, 257.
122. Ibid.
123. Ibid., 254.
124. Ibid., 257.

125. Woolfolk, *Educational Psychology*, 351.
126. Dembo, *Applying Educational Psychology*, 154.
127. Eggen and Kauchak, *Classroom Connections*, 444.
128. Some of Weiner's writings include "An Attributional Analysis of Achievement Motivation," *Journal of Personality and Social Psychology*, 15, (1970): 1–20. *An Attributional Theory of Motivation and Emotion* (New York: Springer-Verlag, 1985). "Understanding the Motivational Role of Affect: Lifespan Research from an Attributional Perspective," *Cognition and Emotion*, 4, 1989): 401–19. *Human Motivation: Metaphors, Theories and Research* (London: Sage Publications, 1992).
129. Dembo, *Applying Educational Psychology*, 154.
130. Weiner includes a third variable, called responsibility, which refers to the student's ability to control the cause of success or failure. The categories are "controllable" and "uncontrollable" (Woolfolk, *Educational Psychology*, 353). I have omitted this variable to simplify the discussion of attribution effects of stability and locus of control.
131. Dembo, *Applying Educational Psychology*, 155.
132. Biehler and Snowman, *Psychology Applied,* 522.
133. Ibid.
134. Biehler and Snowman, *Psychology Applied,* 522; Glover and Bruning, *Principles and Applications,* 259.
135. LeFrancois, *Psychology for Teaching*, 284.
136. Ibid., 285.
137. Woolfolk, *Educational Psychology*, 360.
138. Hamachek, *Psychology in Teaching,* 279.
139. Ibid., 280.
140. Woolfolk, *Educational Psychology*, 359.
141. Dr. Marsh used this text in his "ed psych" classes. His last edition was printed in 1982 in the seminary print shop.
142. Key ideas from Leon Marsh, *Educational Psychology for Christian Education* (Fort Worth: Southwestern Baptist Theological Seminary Print Shop, 1982), 261–64.

CHAPTER THIRTEEN

1. Smith, *Classroom Applications*, 155.
2. *American Heritage Dictionary*, s.v. "personality."
3. Hamachek, *Psychology in Teaching*, 398.
4. *American Heritage Dictionary*, s.v. "enthusiasm."
5. Hamachek, *Psychology in Teaching*, 399.
6. Ibid., 414.
7. Ibid., 417.
8. Ibid.
9. Ibid., 401.
10. Ibid., 417.
11. Ibid., 402.
12. *The Discipler's Handbook*, 28.
13. Ibid.
14. Hamachek, *Psychology in Teaching*, 398.
15. Ibid., 403.
16. Ibid.
17. Ibid., 404.
18. "Platform skill" refers to on-stage behaviors: presence, poise, calmness. Teachers with good platform skills appear unhurried, confident, in control—going somewhere impor-

tant. Teachers without platform skill appear to be distracted, anxious, confused—working hard but going nowhere.

19. Hamachek, *Psychology in Teaching*, 404, and Smith, *Classroom Applications*, 154.

20. Hamachek, *Psychology in Teaching*, 405.

21. Ibid., 406.

22. Ibid., 407.

23. Gage and Berliner, *Educational Psychology*, 628ff.

24. Ibid., 628.

25. Hamachek, *Psychology in Teaching*, 408.

26. Ibid.

27. Hamachek, *Psychology in Teaching*, 410, and Slavin, *Theory and Practice*, 373.

28. Hamachek, *Psychology in Teaching*, 410.

29. Slavin, *Theory and Practice*, 364.

30. Hamachek, *Psychology in Teaching*, 411, and Woolfolk, *Educational Psychology*, 403.

31. Hamachek, *Psychology in Teaching*, 413.

32. Gage and Berliner, *Educational Psychology*, 630.

33. Ibid., 629.

34. Raymond Wlodkowski, *Motivation and Teaching: A Practical Guide* (Washington, D.C.: National Education Association, 1986), 89–92.

35. Ibid., 90.

36. Ibid., 92.

37. Gage and Berliner, *Educational Psychology*, 632.

38. Ibid., 633.

39. Wlodkowski, *Motivation*, 98.

40. Craig Pearson, "Can You Keep Quiet for Three Seconds," *Learning: The Magazine for Creative Teachers*, vol. 1, number 6 (Palo Alto, Calif.: Education Today, February, 1980).

41. Gage and Berliner, *Educational Psychology*, 636.

42. Ibid., 637–38.

43. Ibid., 638.

44. Ibid., 641.

45. Ibid.

46. Ibid., 644.

47. *American Heritage Dictionary*, s.v. "compete."

48. Hamachek, *Psychology in Teaching*, 287.

49. Sprinthall, Sprinthall and Oja, *Developmental Approach*, 542.

50. Hamachek, *Psychology in Teaching*, 288.

51. Biehler and Snowman, *Psychology Applied*, 527.

52. Hamachek, *Psychology in Teaching*, 288.

53. *American Heritage Dictionary*, s.v. "cooperate".

54. Hamachek, *Psychology in Teaching*, 253–4.

55. Woolfolk, *Educational Psychology*, 376.

56. Dembo, *Applying Educational Psychology*, 171, and Hamachek, *Psychology in Teaching*, 293.

57. Dembo, *Applying Educational Psychology*, 172, Hamachek, *Psychology in Teaching*, 293.

58. Dembo, *Applying Educational Psychology*, 171, Hamachek, *Psychology in Teaching*, 293, and Woolfolk, *Educational Psychology*, 379.

59. Hamachek, *Psychology in Teaching*, 293, Dembo, *Applying Educational Psychology*, 171, Woolfolk, *Educational Psychology*, 378.

60. Dembo, *Applying Educational Psychology*, 171–72, and Sprinthall, Sprinthall and Oja, *Developmental Approach*, 543.

61. Hamachek, *Psychology in Teaching*, 293.

62. James W. Michaels, "Classroom Reward Structures and Academic Performance," *Review of Educational Research* (47, 1977): 87–98 as quoted in Biehler and Snowman, *Psychology Applied*, 524–55.

63. Hamachek, *Psychology in Teaching*, 419.

CHAPTER FOURTEEN

1. Slavin, *Theory and Practice*, 499.

2. Gage and Berliner, *Educational Psychology*, 730.

3. Slavin, *Theory and Practice*, 499.

4. Ibid.

5. Gage and Berliner, *Educational Psychology*, 731.

6. LeFrancois, *Psychology for Teaching*, 377.

7. Gage and Berliner, *Educational Psychology*, 731.

8. LeFrancois, *Psychology for Teaching*, 377, and Slavin, *Theory and Practice*, 499.

9. Gage and Berliner, *Educational Psychology*, 731.

10. Slavin, *Theory and Practice*, 498–99.

11. Smith, *Classroom Applications*, 488.

12. Eggen and Kauchak, *Classroom Connections*, 646.

13. Ibid.

14. Ibid., 647.

15. Dembo, *Applying Educational Psychology*, 575.

16. Eggen and Kauchak, *Classroom Connections*, 647.

17. Concurrent validity refers to how well a smaller, more convenient form of test matches the score of a longer, more complex test. With high concurrent validity, the smaller test may be used. Construct validity refers to how well a test measures a given construct, or complex concept, such as intelligence or spiritual maturity. Predictive validity refers to how well a test predicts future behavior, as in aptitude tests.

18. Slavin, *Theory and Practice*, 509.

19. Hamachek, *Psychology in Teaching*, 374.

20. Gage and Berliner, *Educational Psychology*, 709.

21. LeFrancois, *Psychology for Teaching*, 369.

22. Slavin, *Theory and Practice*, 509.

23. Jum C. Nunnally, *Educational Measurement and Evaluation* (New York: McGraw–Hill Book Company, 1972), 169.

24. David A. Payne, *The Assessment of Learning: Cognitive and Affective* (Lexington, Mass.: D. C. Heath and Co., 1974), 109.

25. Nunnally, *Measurement*, 160.

26. Payne, *Assessment*, 104.

27. Ibid.

28. Nunnally, *Measurement*, 163.

29. Hamachek, *Psychology in Teaching*, 374.

30. Nunnally, *Measurement*, 166.

31. Ibid., 160.

32. Dembo, *Applying Educational Psychology*, 581, and Biehler and Snowman, *Psychology Applied*, 582.

33. Payne, *Assessment*, 105.

34. Dembo, *Applying Educational Psychology*, 581.

35. Payne, *Assessment*, 105.

36. Woolfolk, *Educational Psychology*, 160; and Dembo, *Applying Educational Psychology*, 581.
37. Slavin, *Theory and Practice*, 512, and Payne, *Assessment*, 108.
38. Dembo, *Applying Educational Psychology*, 581, and Hamachek, *Psychology in Teaching*, 376.
39. Dembo, *Applying Educational Psychology*, 581; Nunnally, *Measurement*, 162; and Payne, *Assessment*, 106.
40. Dembo, *Applying Educational Psychology*, 581, and Payne, *Assessment*, 107.
41. Tom Kubiszyn and Gary Borish, *Educational Testing and Measurement: Classroom Application and Practice* (Glenview, Ill.: Scott, Foresman and Company, 1987), 73.
42. Dembo, *Applying Educational Psychology*, 581.
43. Hamachek, *Psychology in Teaching*, 376.
44. Dembo, *Applying Educational Psychology*, 581.
45. Payne, *Assessment*, 107.
46. Hamachek, *Psychology in Teaching*, 374, and Payne, *Assessment*, 108.
47. Payne, *Assessment*, 108.
48. Hamachek, *Psychology in Teaching*, 374.
49. Dembo, *Applying Educational Psychology*, 581.
50. Biehler and Snowman, *Psychology Applied*, 582; Payne, *Assessment*, 108; and Kubiszyn and Borish, *Testing*, 73.
51. Biehler and Snowman, *Psychology Applied*, 582; Payne, *Assessment*, 108; and Kubiszyn and Borish, *Testing*, 73.
52. Payne, *Assessment*, 106.
53. Not all authors agree with the 60–40 split. Biehler and Snowman (582) and Hamachek (377) both suggest an equal number of true and false items.
54. Kubiszyn and Borish, *Testing*, 77.
55. Slavin, *Theory and Practice*, 509.
56. Biehler and Snowman, *Psychology Applied*, 583.
57. Slavin, *Theory and Practice*, 510.
58. Biehler and Snowman, *Psychology Applied*, 584.
59. Dembo, *Applying Educational Psychology*, 579.
60. Glover and Bruning, *Principles and Applications*, 417; Nunnally, *Measurement*, 172; and Kubiszyn and Borish, *Testing*, 86–87.
61. Dembo, *Applying Educational Psychology*, 583.
62. Biehler and Snowman, *Psychology Applied*, 584.
63. Dembo, *Applying Educational Psychology*, 581.
64. Woolfolk, *Educational Psychology*, 547.
65. Biehler and Snowman, *Psychology Applied*, 584.
66. Payne, *Assessment*, 110.
67. Dembo, *Applying Educational Psychology*, 578; Payne, *Assessment*, 110; and Kubiszyn and Borish, *Testing*, 87.
68. Nunnally, *Measurement*, 172.
69. Hamachek, *Psychology in Teaching*, 374, and Payne, *Assessment*, 110.
70. Slavin, *Theory and Practice*, 510.
71. Ibid.
72. Kubiszyn and Borish, *Testing*, 87.
73. Nunnally, *Measurement*, 180, and Payne, *Assessment*, 112.
74. Biehler and Snowman, *Psychology Applied*, 584, and Nunnally, *Measurement*, 178, P112.
75. Dembo, *Applying Educational Psychology*, 579.

76. Biehler and Snowman, *Psychology Applied*, 584; Dembo, *Applying Educational Psychology*, 578; Hamachek, *Psychology in Teaching*, 375; Nunnally, *Measurement*, 174; and Payne, *Assessment*, 112.
77. Nunnally, *Measurement*, 174.
78. Kubiszyn and Borish, *Testing*, 87.
79. Nunnally, *Measurement*, 173; Payne, *Assessment*, 113; and Slavin, *Theory and Practice*, 512.
80. Hamachek, *Psychology in Teaching*, 374.
81. Dembo, *Applying Educational Psychology*, 579, and Nunnally, *Measurement*, 174.
82. Biehler and Snowman suggest listing the responses alphabetically (584).
83. Nunnally, *Measurement*, 176.
84. Ibid., 174.
85. Nunnally, *Measurement*, 174; Payne, *Assessment*, 113, and Kubiszyn and Borish, *Testing*, 87.
86. Slavin, *Theory and Practice*, 511.
87. Payne, *Assessment*, 116–26, and Kubiszyn and Borish, *Testing*, 84–87.
88. Hamachek, *Psychology in Teaching*, 378.
89. Nunnally, *Measurement*, 163.
90. Biehler and Snowman, *Psychology Applied*, 580.
91. Ibid., 581, and Hamachek, *Psychology in Teaching*, 378.
92. Ibid.
93. Nunnally, *Measurement*, 164.
94. Biehler and Snowman, *Psychology Applied*, 581, and Slavin, *Theory and Practice*, 513.
95. Hamachek, *Psychology in Teaching*, 378.
96. Biehler and Snowman, *Psychology Applied*, 581.
97. Payne, *Assessment*, 112.
98. Hamachek, *Psychology in Teaching*, 378.
99. Nunnally, *Measurement*, 164.
100. Dembo, *Applying Educational Psychology*, 581.
101. Payne, *Assessment*, 102.
102. Dembo, *Applying Educational Psychology*, 581.
103. Nunnally, *Measurement*, 164.
104. Dembo, *Applying Educational Psychology*, 581.
105. Nunnally, *Measurement*, 165.
106. Ibid.
107. Payne, *Assessment*, 104.
108. Dembo, *Applying Educational Psychology*, 581.
109. Biehler and Snowman, *Psychology Applied*, 581, and Nunnally, *Measurement*, 166.
110. Matching items can be made more complex by adding an additional column of related material, such as "authors," "books," and "major themes." But two-column matching questions are the most common.
111. Nunnally, *Measurement*, 167.
112. Biehler and Snowman, *Psychology Applied*, 582, Payne, *Assessment*, 128.
113. Biehler and Snowman, *Psychology Applied*, 582.
114. Ibid.
115. Nunnally, *Measurement*, 167.
116. Biehler and Snowman, *Psychology Applied*, 583.
117. Dembo, *Applying Educational Psychology*, 580, and Kubiszyn and Borish, *Testing*, 77.
118. Dembo, *Applying Educational Psychology*, 580.

119. Payne, *Assessment,* 129.

120. Nunnally, *Measurement,* 167.

121. Kubiszyn and Borish, *Testing,* 77.

122. Nunnally, *Measurement,* 167.

123. Ibid.

124. Biehler and Snowman, *Psychology Applied,* 583, and Kubiszyn and Borish, *Testing,* 74.

125. Payne, *Assessment,* 129.

126. Payne, *Assessment,* 129, and Kubiszyn and Borish, *Testing,* 74.

127. Dembo, *Applying Educational Psychology,* 580.

128. Kubiszyn and Borish, *Testing,* 75.

129. Ibid., 77.

130. Ibid., 103.

131. Ibid., 98.

132. Ibid., 103.

133. Ibid., 104.

134. Eggen and Kauchak, *Classroom Connections,* 661.

135. Dembo, *Applying Educational Psychology,* 582.

136. Kubiszyn and Borish, *Testing,* 105.

137. Dembo, *Applying Educational Psychology,* 582.

138. Biehler and Snowman, *Psychology Applied,* 586.

139. Kubiszyn and Borish, *Testing,* 106.

140. Nunnally, *Measurement,* 182.

141. Payne, *Assessment,* 143.

142. Biehler and Snowman, *Psychology Applied,* 587, and Kubiszyn and Borish, *Testing,* 106.

143. Nunnally, *Measurement,* 182.

144. Ibid., 184.

145. Kubiszyn and Borish, *Testing,* 106–12.

146. Dembo, *Applying Educational Psychology,* 584.

147. Slavin, *Theory and Practice,* 515.

148. Dembo, *Applying Educational Psychology,* 584.

149. Ibid., 585.

150. Biehler and Snowman, *Psychology Applied,* 587.

151. Biehler and Snowman, *Psychology Applied,* 592–94; Glover and Bruning, *Principles and Applications,* 421–23; Nunnally, *Measurement,* 186–196; Payne, *Assessment,* 274–76; and Kubiszyn and Borish, *Testing,* 122–30.

152. This is a tedious process, but well worth the effort when you review test results with students. Demonstrating that your test items are fair reduces the number and intensity of student complaints. But better than quelling student complaints is the fact that every item in your test is shown to be good! TestPRO, an MS-DOS program written by the author, eliminates the tedium of computing discrimination indices. Send $25.00 to Rick Yount, Box 22428, SWBTS, Fort Worth, Texas 76122 for your copy. Specify 5.25" or 3.5," DD or HD diskette type.

153. Slavin, *Theory and Practice,* 501.

154. Ibid.

155. Ibid.

156. Ibid.

157. Ibid.

158. Ibid.

159. Ibid, 502.

CHAPTER FIFTEEN

1. Sherwood Eddy, *Maker of Men* (New York: Harper & Brothers, 1941).

2. Alexander Balmain Bruce, *The Training of the Twelve* (4th. ed., New York: A.C. Armstrong & Sons, 1894; reprint, New Canaan, Conn.: Keats Publishing, 1979), 12. See also Alfred Edersheim, *The Life and Times of Jesus the Messiah,* vol. 1 (Grand Rapids, Mich.: Eerdmans Publishing Co., 1969), 348.

3. Edersheim, *Life,* 1:224–25.

4. Ibid., 223.

5. Bruce, *Training,* 5–8.

6. Lucien Coleman, *Why the Church Must Teach* (Broadman Press: Nashville, Tenn., 1984), 23.

7. Bruce, *Training,* 13.

8. The heathen woman entreats Jesus, "Lord, Son of David, have mercy on me!" Jesus' behavior appears rude: "Jesus did not answer a word" (Matt. 15:23). When she continued "Lord, help me!" (v. 25), His language sounds strangely harsh: "It is not right to take the children's bread and toss it to their dogs" (Matt. 15:26). Edersheim explains that the woman's approach to Jesus was "not as the Messiah of Israel but an Israelitish Messiah . . . this was exactly the error of the Jews which Jesus had encountered and combated, alike when He resisted the attempt to make Him King, in His reply to the Jerusalem Scribes, and in His Discourses at Capernaum. To have granted her the help she so entreated, would have been, as it were, to reverse the whole of His Teaching, and to make His works of healing merely works of power. . . . And so He first taught her, in such manner as she could understand—that which she needed to know, before she could approach Him in such a manner—the relation of the heathen to the Jewish world [dogs, children-RY] and of both to the Messiah, and then He gave her what she asked." (Edersheim, *Life,* 2:39).

9. Jerry Adler, et al, "Hey, I'm Terrific: The Curse of Self-Esteem," *Newsweek* (February 17, 1992): 46–51.

10. Mark and Luke record that Jesus healed one demon-possessed man (Mark 5:1; Luke 8:26). Edersheim explains this by saying, "From these tombs the demonized, who is specially singled out by Mark and Luke, as well as his less prominent companions, came forth to meet Jesus" (Edersheim, *Life,* 1:607).

11. Edersheim renders the name "Beelzebul" rather than "Beelzebub" which is a reference to Baalzebub, the "fly-god of 2 Kings 1:2". He translates "Beel" (Master) and "zibbul" (sacrificing to idols), so "Beelzebul" means the "lord or chief of idolatrous sacrificing" (Edersheim, *Life,* 1:648).

12. The Eternal Word and the needs of people are the two foundation stones in the Disciplers' Model. Chapter 1 of *The Disciplers' Handbook* discusses the practical problems in teaching associated with imbalance. Contact Dr. Yount concerning this text and the accompanying two video tape series.

13. Bruce, *Training,* 11–12.

14. Bruce, *Training,* 2.

15. Ibid., 43.

16. See chapter 11 for an in-depth discussion of this trilogy.

17. Bruce, *Training,* 43.

18. Student report on conference notes, Howard Hendricks, February 10, 1992. Dr. Hendricks is Professor of Christian Education at Dallas Theological Seminary in Dallas, Texas.

19. Bruce, *Training,* 13.

20. Comment by my teacher and mentor, Dr. Leon Marsh, in a letter received in March 1995.

21. Daryl Eldridge, "The Role of the Holy Spirit in Teaching," *The Teaching Ministry of the Church* (Nashville: Broadman Press, 1995), 62.

22. Ibid., 64.

23. Ibid., 66.

24. Ibid., 69.

25. Lawrence O. Richards, *A Theology of Christian Education* (Grand Rapids, Mich.: Zondervan, 1975), 323, quoted in Eldridge, "Role of the Holy Spirit in Teaching," 58.

26. Ibid.

NAME INDEX

A

Aristotle 35, 160
Atkinson, John 288
Ausebel, David 200, 242

B

Bandura, Albert 179, 271, 282
Bloom, Benjamin 140
Brown, George 238, 242
Bruner, Jerome 22, 196, 198, 201–202, 210, 218, 227, 237

C

Calvin, John 233
Combs, Arthur 235, 237–238, 242, 286
Crowder, N. A. 173

D

Dostoyevsky, Anton 233

E

Eddy, Sherwood 340
Eisner, E. W. 135–136
Erikson, Erik 22, 46–47, 51, 61, 122, 126, 279

F

Flavell, John 225

Ford, LeRoy 137, 139

Ford, LeRoy 137, 139
Fowler, James 122
Freud, Sigmund 46, 234

G

Gesell, Arnold 74
Gilligan, Carol 118
Gordon, Thomas 238
Gronlund, Norman 135–138

K

Kohlberg, Lawrence 103–109, 122, 124
Köhler, Wolfgang 194–195
Krathwohl, David 145

L

Lewin, Kurt 194–195
Locke, John 160, 179
Luther, Martin 233

M

Mach, Ernst 193
Mager, Robert 135–136
Marcia, James 52
Marsh, Leon 292
Maslow, Abraham 22, 235, 242, 286, 288
Murray, H. A. 288

SUBJECT INDEX

principled morality   112
proactive inhibition   224
procedural memory   214
production   182
program   173
    branching   173
    linear   173
programmed instruction   173
prompts   171, 177, 179
prophet   256
psychomotor domain   148
punishment   164, 168, 178
punishment/obedience   108
pure discovery   94
pure discovery learning   199–200
purpose   57

Q

questioning behaviors   303
questions   6, 8, 12, 97, 292, 303
    directing   304
    probing   305
    redirecting   305

R

random-access memory   211
reacting behaviors   305
reactions
    negative   306
    neutral   306
    positive   305
receiving   145, 234
reception learning   200, 218, 242
reciprocal determinism   180
recognition   211, 215–216
Reformation   233
rehearsal   211
reinforcement   165, 168, 174, 179
reinforcement schedules   168, 170, 177
reinforcer   165
relativism   128
relevance   237–238
reliability   319
removal punishment   168, 179
Renaissance   233
replication   31
repression   224
residual trace   215
responding   234
response   161–162
responsibility   300
retrieval   211

retrieving   225
retroactive inhibition   224
reversibility   82, 88, 124
reward   164, 166, 292
reward structures   310
rhymes   219
right pillar   12, 16, 22, 145, 244
ripple effect   185, 283
role confusion   65
role-playing activities   238
rote rehearsal   228
R-S association   165
R-S bonds   179

S

safety needs   286
schemes   75, 80, 179, 214
scholarship   300
secondary reinforcer   166
secular theories   1
secularism   233
selective observation and recall   32
self-absorption   67
self-actualization   286–287
self-attention   226
self-concept   348
self-esteem   287–288, 308
self-questioning   228
self-regulated learning.   238
self-regulation   271
self-reinforcement   183, 271, 282
semantic memory   214
sensitivity training   238
sensorimotor   90
sensorimotor stage   84–85
sensory registers   212, 215
seriation   89
set   149
shaping   280
short-term memory (STM)   213, 215, 218
signal giving   302
simulation games   238
Skinner box   165
social contract   112
social interaction   96
social learning theory   179, 185, 271, 282
specific determiners   321
specific motivation   279
spontaneous recovery   162
S-R bonds   164, 210
stages of faith   122
stimulus   161–162